Bangladesh's Economic and Social Progress

Munim Kumar Barai
Editor

Bangladesh's Economic and Social Progress

From a Basket Case to a Development Model

palgrave
macmillan

Editor
Munim Kumar Barai
College of International Management
Ritsumeikan Asia Pacific University
Beppu-shi, Oita, Japan

ISBN 978-981-15-1682-5 ISBN 978-981-15-1683-2 (eBook)
https://doi.org/10.1007/978-981-15-1683-2

This Palgrave Macmillan imprint is published by the registered company Springer Nature Singapore Pte Ltd.
The registered company address is: 152 Beach Road, #21-01/04 Gateway East, Singapore 189721, Singapore

Dedicated to
Mother Jogmaya and Father, the Late Narayan Chandra Barai
Wife Shashwati, Daughter Sharanya and Son Shambo
All the people of my home and village of Baropaika, Barisal, Bangladesh, who were the real inspiration to take up the case of success stories of Bangladesh

Preface and Acknowledgments

To be honest, no individual person inspired me to take up the challenge to write or edit a book on Bangladesh's evolution 'From a Basket Case to a Development Model' that would depict the economic and social progress the country has made in its arduous journey since 1971. My inspiration initially came from the experience of a month-long stay at my ancestral home in Barisal, Bangladesh, back in 2013. My month-long stay was after about thirty-four years of absence. Let me give you a bit of the background of this.

My father died in January 2013, and we decided to do all the religious rituals for him at his place of birth (my birthplace too). This decision was broadly influenced by his extreme desire to remain attached to his knowns, kith and keen (in fact all the villagers were so for him) in their good and bad days until the end of his life. Therefore, we thought that his soul might get more peace in heaven if his mortal remains were to rest at a place that he loved most. We did everything according to this, and for his departed soul we wanted to perform the last social and religious rite by inviting our relatives and near and dear ones for a meal that we call a *sraddha*. It was a big event by our standards, as more than 3000 people were invited to the ceremony. To organize such a program, I had to stay for a month there to arrange everything. During that month, I mixed with relatives, friends, and people, interacted with them, and could see and understand their surroundings. That opened my eyes, and I felt that something was revealing itself.

In the beginning, I found it difficult to get any able-bodied adult to help me with the preparations for the ceremony, as I wanted some of them to be around. During the daytime, almost all of them were busy and gone:

to the fields for *rabi* cropping, or to run their small shops, or to drive their vehicles for commercial transportation. And the children were gone to their schools. I remember that even I had to participate in two weekly NGO-monitored microcredit meetings for women entrepreneurs. However, I could feel the new economic vibrancy, a constant buzz, a desire to have food, shelter, education, drinking water, sanitary latrines, electricity, televisions, and even mobile phones. Some young village lads even trained me during that time how to take a selfie. I could see different kinds of tractors, tilling machines, and equipment for tilling lands, and manual or power threshers for separating paddy from the straw.

Gone are the days of cows plowing fields and men manually separating paddy by beating the crop by hand with a flail or by the trampling of animal hooves or by using their legs. As a result, women have more time to pursue their own choices. This was a total contrast, a completely different picture of things that dominated my memory for so long. My past vivid memory as a young boy who lived there thirty-five years ago could still see the long lines of men and women at daybreak going to other places for day-labor jobs, the children not very serious about going to school, no electricity, no sanitary latrines, and no television. Our family was then the proud owner of a three-band radio, but I had to go half a mile to our school to fetch tube-well water for drinking. Thus, gone are the days of scarcity of all sorts in most local households.

Then I was inspired and thought seriously to tell their progress stories to the world someday. More than six years have passed by since then as I waited for a moment when I finally could come forward with the initiative. This book has given me the chance to write or document those changes, though not with individual stories, but with a macro picture of the economic and social progress of the entire nation. I hope the effort will be well received by readers.

When I was struggling to develop and finally get going this broader picture of the success of Bangladesh, I found that the country has drawn the attention of many people, including development economists, because of its many economic and social success stories. However, most of these success stories have been discussed here and there on a fragmented and piecemeal basis. For example, various development agencies and NGOs engaged in development activities in Bangladesh have put forward their side of such stories of success. However, I realized that the academic world still lacks a book which presents most of these stories in one place so that interested parties and stakeholders will be able to better understand the paths that the economic and social progress of Bangladesh has taken so far.

The book has come to its present shape through some major challenges. At times I was on the verge of giving a second thought to the whole initiative. But once I could submit the proposal to Palgrave Macmillan in Singapore, an acceptance decision was given to me rather quickly. That helped me bring my act together to pursue the project to the end. So, I would like to thank the esteemed but anonymous reviewers who found the justification of the book proposal, its possible contribution to the literature, and its market potential acceptable. They reviewed the book proposal and recommended its publication. Without their positive reviews, this book may not have proceeded further with the present publishing house.

In ensuring the successful completion of the book, I received unqualified support from various friends and economists in many ways, and they deserve special mention. I start with Dr. Gour Gobinda Goswami, Treasurer, and Professor of Economics at the North-South University of Bangladesh, and Dr. Abdur Rob Khan, Professor and Dean of the School of Humanities and Social Sciences of the same university. They advised me on the content, the chronology of the chapters, and suggested a few authors for possible contributions. That truly helped me a lot to move forward with the book project.

As always, Prof. Arindam Banik, Director of the International Management Institute of Kolkata, offered me immensely valuable advice on the broader frame of the book for national and global readers. Special thanks are due to Dr. Md. Dulal Miah, Assistant Professor and Head, Department of Economics and Finance, University of Nizwa, Oman, for his timely support and contribution of a chapter, for bringing in a few more chapter contributors, and for reviewing two chapters as well as suggesting reviewers for other chapters. Dr. Miah's support for the book project has gone beyond any formal limit. At the same time, Prof. Rabi Narayan Kar, Principal of Shyam Lal College, Delhi University, India, who has been my friend since my days at Delhi University, came forward to assist me by reviewing some of the chapters. Dr. Swadhin Kumar Mondal, Assistant Professor, Department of Economics and Finance, University of Nizwa, Oman, and Dr. Kazi Mahmudur Rahman, Associate Professor at the University of Liberal Arts, Bangladesh helped the review process as well. My student Dr. Helal Uddin deserves special mention for his 'never saying no' spirit to assist me in this project.

I must take my hat off to the learned contributors who worked tirelessly in making their quality contributions to the book. Though the memory here is not totally full of roses, almost all of them tolerated from time to time the demands to incorporate changes in their chapters to make them more qualitative. Without their timely support, this work could not have been possible. I am also grateful to the Dean of my college, Prof. Toshitsugu Otake, for active encouragement and support in completing the book. Prof. Yasushi Suzuki and Prof. Abdullah Al Kafi Majumdar encouraged me from time to time. Prof. Malcom Cooper did an excellent job of proofreading some of the chapters.

On a personal level, I must recognize the time my family members had to sacrifice to keep me free from other obligations so that I could complete the project. They tolerated my absence and non-involvement in many of their important events. Finally, I would like to remember all the people of my home and village of Baropaika, Barisal, Bangladesh, who were the real inspiration for this book.

Beppu-shi, Oita, Japan — Munim Kumar Barai

Contents

Notes on the Editor and Contributors

Mohammad Zoynul Abedin is an associate professor at the Department of Finance and Banking, Hajee Mohammad Danesh Science and Technology University, Dinajpur, Bangladesh. Presently he is researching as a post-doctoral fellow at the School of Maritime Economics and Management, Dalian Maritime University, Dalian, China. He holds his PhD in Investment Theory from the Dalian University of Technology, Dalian. Abedin holds MBA and BBA degrees in Finance from the University of Chittagong, Chittagong, Bangladesh. Abedin's works have been widely published. More than thirty of his papers have been published in peer-reviewed local and international journals. His recent manuscripts have appeared on major indexing databases. Abedin's research interests include data science and business intelligence.

Nahid Afroz is a research associate at the Credit Rating Agency of Bangladesh (CRAB). She holds BBA and MBA degrees, both major in Finance, from the University of Chittagong, Bangladesh. Her research area focuses on Islamic finance, micro-finance, and development studies with a specific interest in Islamic securities (*Sukuk*), Islamic microfinance, and financial inclusion.

Mohammad Akhtaruzzaman is a career policy researcher with about twenty years of experience in central bank policy research. He became the Economic Adviser of Bangladesh Bank (BB) in June 2011. Before joining BB as a Deputy General Manager of the Research Department in 1999, Akhtaruzzaman was Associate Professor of Economics at Rajshahi University, where he taught economics for ten years. He completed his graduation and post-graduation in Economics from Jahangirnagar University. He received both MPhil and PhD degrees in Development and Trade Economics from Clermont-Ferrand University, France, in 1993 and 1997. He also worked as a post-doctoral visiting research fellow (VRF) at Tsukuba University, Japan, during 2002–04. Some of his research works/articles have been published in peer-reviewed international and national journals and the BB (PAU) Working Paper series. His current areas of research interest relate to monetary, fiscal, and trade policies. His responsibilities include contributing to the central bank's monetary policy formulation and management, as well as supervision and overall guidance for policy research and analysis to BB researchers. Akhtaruzzaman is a member of the following BB and Government policy-making committees: (i) Monetary Policy Committee; (ii) Investment Committee; (iii) Auction Committee for the management of BB's reserve money and money-market liquidity and public debt; (iv) National Working Group for Implementation, Monitoring, and Evaluation of Sixth Five Year Plan, Millennium Development Goals (MDGs) and Sustainable Development Goals (SDGs), Government of Bangladesh (GOB); and (v) Director, Board of Directors, Export Promotion Bureau (EPB) of Bangladesh.

Swapan Kumar Bala FCMA, is Professor of Accounting at the University of Dhaka and now on deputation to work as a Commissioner of Bangladesh Securities and Exchange Commission. Presently he is also a Board Member of the Bangladesh Institute of Capital Market; a Council Member of the Institute of Cost and Management Accountants of Bangladesh (ICMAB); and Member of a Government Committee to make specific recommendations for Bangladesh's long-term financing and capital market development. He also served the ICMAB as the editor of its journal. He has authored/co-authored eighty-five research articles/book chapters, nine research monographs, nine books, and one study manual. He publishes in the *International Journal of Disclosure and Governance* (Palgrave Macmillan), *VOLUNTAS: International Journal of Voluntary and Nonprofit Organizations* (Springer), *Managerial Auditing Journal*, *Indian Journal of Accounting* (India), *Journal of Accounting and Finance* (India), *AI & Society* (Springer-Verlag), and so on.

Prashanta Kumar Banerjee is Professor and Director, Research, Development, and Consultancy, at Bangladesh Institute of Bank

Management (BIBM). He served in King Faisal University in the Kingdom of Saudi Arabia (KSA) during 2009–11. He holds his PhD in Finance from the Punjab University, India, and later on, he did post-doctoral research as a Fulbright Scholar in the United States of America (USA). Banerjee has been awarded some prestigious academic and research awards and fellowships. They include, the i-Proclaim ARA-2017 Award as Distinguished Scientist (Awards for Publication Excellence by ABC Malaysia) and Bangladesh Education Leadership Awards 2017 by Asian Confederation of Business with CMO Asia. A good number of articles of Banerjee have been published in peer-reviewed US, European and Asian academic journals including *Empirical Economics*, *The Journal of Energy and Development*, *Southwest Business and Economics Journal*, *Journal of Developing Areas*, *Global Business and Finance Review*, *Finance India*, *Prajnan*, and so on. He works as an executive editor for a Journal named *Bank Parikrama* published by BIBM. Banerjee completed several consultancy works for International Finance Corporation (IFC) and has worked as the lead consultant for World Bank Group. Recently Banerjee completed a consultancy work titled Financial Sector Strengthening Project of Afghanistan with Da Afghanistan Bank (DAB), Central Bank of Afghanistan. His research interests are in banking, factoring, and Small and Medium Enterprises (SMEs) Financing, Corporate Finance and Economic Development, Environment, and Exchange Rate and Remittance.

Munim Kumar Barai is Professor of Finance at the Graduate School of Management, Ritsumeikan Asia Pacific University (APU), Japan. Earlier, he served at a number of universities in Bangladesh. Barai holds his Master's, MPhil, and PhD degrees from Delhi School of Economics, University of Delhi, India. He is a recipient of several international fellowships including ICCR Fellowship, UGC Junior and Senior Research Fellowship (India), Asian Scholarship Foundation (ASF) Fellowship and JSPS Grants-in-Aid (Japan). He was a Fulbright Scholar and completed post-doc research at the University of Pennsylvania, USA. Barai served as a visiting professor at the International Management Institute, Kolkata, India, in 2016–17. His present research interest includes banks and non-bank financial institutions, regional trade, microfinance, macroeconomic issues, and inclusive finance. He has published articles in *Contemporary South Asia*, *Transnational Corporation Review*, *Journal of Comparative Asian*

Development, *Asia Pacific World*, *Global Business Review*, *Finance India*, *Review of Integrative Business and Economics*, *Bangladesh Journal of Political Economy*, *Journal of Accounting Finance and Economics*, *Bank Parikrama* and so on. Barai is a joint editor of the book *Towards A Common Future: Understanding Growth, Sustainability in the Asia-Pacific Region* published by Palgrave Macmillan, Singapore. He has guest-edited recent issues of *South Asian Survey* and *Journal of Global Business Advancement.*

Liton Chakraborty is a PhD student (ABD) at the University of Waterloo, Canada. He started his career path in academia soon after completing his Master's in Economics and taught at three different universities in Bangladesh for seven years. After that, he left for the Uppsala University, Sweden, to study MSc in Business and Economics and finished with a distinction in the thesis. He obtained a second MA in Economics from the University of Waterloo. His research centers on social inequality analysis to environmental hazard exposure and economic valuation of preferences for risk and social vulnerability reduction measures across Canada. Most recently, he was awarded the 2019 'CRDCN Emerging Scholars' Grantees Designation. Chakraborty's ambition is to pursue a research-based academic career after PhD.

Ehsanul Huda Chowdhury is Assistant Professor of Marketing at the Department of Business Studies and Economics, University of Gävle, Sweden. His areas of research interest are supply chain management, international business management, marketing strategies, business network management, market orientation, and corporate social responsibility. His articles in the field of supply chain management, service marketing, brand management, consumer behavior, marketing communications, and corporate social responsibility have been published. He has fifteen years of teaching experience in universities in Sweden, Bangladesh, and the Philippines. He teaches courses of international business strategy, project management, strategic marketing, brand management, service marketing, and emerging markets at the graduate and undergraduate levels. He also supervises theses of graduate students. Presently, he is a member of the editorial board of two reputed international journals and reviewer of five reputed international journals.

Tamgid Ahmed Chowdhury holds his PhD in Economics from Macquarie University, Australia, and specialized in the fields of poverty and inequality. He is currently serving as an associate professor in the School of Business and Economics at North South University, Bangladesh. Chowdhury has several publications in the reputed international journals such as *Journal of Contemporary Asia*, *Journal of Non-profit and Public Sector Marketing*, *Journal of Asia-Pacific Business*, *European Journal of Development Research*, *Journal of Asia Business Studies*, *Oxford Development Studies*, *Journal of Socio-economics*, *Contemporary South Asia*, and *Journal of Economic and Social Policy*. Chowdhury has presented papers in several international conferences held in the USA, UK, Australia, Turkey, South Korea, Malaysia, and Thailand. He is the sole author of the book titled, *Relative Effectiveness of Alternative Microfinance-driven Poverty Alleviation Programs in Bangladesh*.

Ashit Baran Das is an experienced finance and accounts professional. He has developed commercial competencies and knowledge to lead and support major business decisions. Working at Bangladesh Rural Advancement Committee (BRAC), world's number one NGO, as the Head of Financial Planning and Management, he has been playing a key role in ensuring the best operational and financial decisions are being made while having a strong focus on strategic business planning support, cost optimization, historical performance analysis, and complex forecasting with his last two decades of experience, working at different business houses like Digicon Technologies Ltd, Pacific Bangladesh Telecom Limited, and Grameenphone Ltd. During this long tenure, he has furnished his leadership, analytical, operational, and decision-making knowledge efficiently and worked in diverse capacities in different functions. Das is contributing to the development sector with a zeal to explore and dedication. He holds his MBA from R.A. Poddar Institute of Management in India after completing post-graduation in Accounting from the University of Dhaka.

H. M. Jahirul Haque is the Vice Chancellor of the University of Liberal Arts Bangladesh (ULAB). Haque received his PhD degree in computer engineering from the Kharkov National University of Radio Electronics, Ukraine, in 2001 and Master's in Technical Sciences (Systems Engineering) from Cherkasy State Technological University, Ukraine, in 1995. In 2018, Haque researched at the University of Massachusetts Boston as a visiting Fulbright scholar. His current research interests are education, pedagogy, and leadership.

Rashedul Hasan is a senior lecturer in the Faculty of Business, Communication, and Law at INTI International University, Malaysia. Hasan holds his BBA (Accounting and Finance) and MBA (Finance) from American International University Bangladesh (AIUB) with summa cum laude distinction and PhD in Accounting from International Islamic University Malaysia (IIUM). His research interests include Islamic finance, voluntary disclosure, intellectual capital, sustainability, and corporate governance. Papers published by Hasan have appeared in *Thunderbird International Business Review*, *Islamic Quarterly*, *Journal of Economic Development and Cooperation*, *Journal of Islamic Economics, Banking and Finance*, *Journal of Islamic Economic Studies* and *International Journal of Public Sector Performance Management*. He has presented papers at several international conferences.

Md. Abdul Kayum a general manager of Bangladesh Bank, is working as a faculty member in Bangladesh Institute of Bank Management (BIBM), Dhaka. He obtained a Master's degree in Economics in 1990 and joined Bangladesh Bank as an assistant director in 1992 in the research department. He had worked there in various capacities until July 2017. In August 2017 he joined BIBM. He participated in a number of local and foreign training and seminars on various issues of the monetary and financial sector in the USA, the UK, India, Pakistan, Malaysia, and the Philippines. His paper on 'Examining the Interaction Between the Policy rate and Lending rate in Bangladesh' is published in the Bangladesh Bank website. Another article on 'Price and Income Elasticity of Imports in Bangladesh: ARDL Bounds Test Approach' has been published in the journal *Bank Parikrama*, BIBM.

Mausumi Mahapatro is Assistant Professor of Political Economy at Regis University, USA. With academic training in both economics and development studies, her research focuses on the causes and measurement of poverty, migration, and development from the lens of political economy. Mahapatro completed her Master's in Development Studies from the London School of Economics (LSE). As part of her PhD thesis at the School of Oriental and African Studies (SOAS) in the University of London, she conducted in-depth household surveys in selected regions of Bangladesh to inform some of her research findings on the nexus between land, migration, and welfare. Some of her papers have been published in peer-reviewed journals such as *Migration and*

Development and Economic and Political Weekly. She has also engaged directly in the development sector with organizations such as Action Aid International and the International Organization for Migration.

Dwijen Mallick has been working as a researcher at the Bangladesh Centre for Advanced Studies (BCAS), an independent research and policy institute in Dhaka. Trained in social sciences, he gathered wide-ranging experiences of designing and implementation of multidisciplinary research projects. Mallick has developed expertise in research and knowledge management in the three key areas: adaptation to climate change and resilience building; public policy review and institutional development; and rural development and livelihood proportion. He worked for several government ministries and departments, as well as working with development partners, academic institutions, NOGs, and INGOs. Mallick participated in several national, international, and regional scientific conferences, seminars, and workshops on sustainable development, economic growth and poverty alleviation, climate change adaptation, and DRR. He is leading the knowledge management publication unit of BCAS. He is the author of many book chapters, scientific papers, and journal articles published from home and aboard. He is also engaged in Research in Use (RiU) activities of BCAS to influence the national policies and practices of government and activities of the NGOs and communities. Most of his research work, knowledge management, and advocacy focus mainly on sustainable development and poverty alleviation, livelihood promotion, natural resource management, gender equity, adaptation to climate change, and resilience-building of the poor, women, and vulnerable communities.

Mohammad Dulal Miah is Assistant Professor and Head of the Department of Economics and Finance at the University of Nizwa, Oman. He holds his Master's degree (MBA) in Finance and PhD in Development Economics. Miah has coauthored three academic books published from Routledge and Palgrave and contributed more than thirty research papers to several peer-reviewed journals. He also has attended numerous international conferences as a speaker and facilitator. His research interest includes institutional economics, corporate governance, Islamic finance and banking, bank rent, comparative financial systems, and environmental finance. He serves as an editorial member of several journals.

Anis Pervez is a Cognition, Communication, and Cinema Researcher. He is a Senior Fellow at Bangladesh on Record, Dhaka, Bangladesh. Pervez is educated in media and communication, information and cognitive science, and sociology respectively from University of Dhaka, Indiana University Bloomington and Oslo University. Pervez has taught at different universities including Indiana University Bloomington and the University of Liberal Arts Bangladesh and also held a research position in various organizations in Bangladesh and Norway. He also has served development organizations of different kinds—NGOs, Think Tanks, and bilateral programs, which aided him to use his expertise in communication and knowledge management into development work. Pervez has published his research on communication, cinema, cognition, and development in several journals and books.

Atiq Rahman is a leading scientist and visionary thinker in South Asia. He has been honored with the highest UN Environment Award—the Champion of the Earth for the year 2008 in recognition of his outstanding and inspirational leadership at national, regional, and global levels in the fields of environment, natural resources management, and sustainable development. As Executive Director of Bangladesh Centre for Advanced Studies (BCAS), a leading think-tank in Asia on sustainable development, climate change negotiations, and activism by involving government, development agencies, and people. Research work of Rahman has primarily focused on the environment, sustainable development, and climate change science in the context of the reduction of human poverty and vulnerability. Rahman is an eloquent advocate on equity, justice, and good governance to protect the rights of the poor and developing countries in international climate change debates, negotiations, and global policy making. He has extensive publications on environment, natural resources, development, poverty, good governance, and climate change issues. He has designed, developed, and taught multidisciplinary postgraduate courses on sustainable development challenges and North-South Dialogue at Massachusetts Institute of Technology (MIT) and the Fletcher School of Law and Diplomacy, jointly managed by Harvard and Tufts Universities at Cambridge, Massachusetts, USA. Rahman is a lead author of the Intergovernmental Panel on Climate Change (IPCC), which won the Nobel Peace Prize in 2007. He played a leading role in UNCED, Rio, 1992, Intergovernmental Negotiations on

Climate Change (INC) sessions and all the Conferences of Parties and Climate Summits in Kyoto, 1997, leading to the Kyoto Protocol.

Kazi Mahmudur Rahman is an Associate Professor at the Center for Enterprise and Society, University of Liberal Arts Bangladesh (ULAB). He holds his PhD in International Relations from the University of Queensland (UQ), Brisbane, and MA in Development Studies from the International Institute of Social Studies (ISS), The Hague. Rahman is a Hansard/Chevening Research Scholar at the LSE, London. He was a senior research associate at the Centre for Policy Dialogue, Bangladesh, and visiting fellow at the BIGD, BRAC University. He has been involved in a three-year research project on 'Changes in the Governance of Garment Global Production Networks' funded by the Volkswagen Foundation. He carried out several research consultancies with the International Labour Organisation (ILO), Asian Development Bank (ADB), Department for International Development (DFID), United Nations Development Programme (UNDP), and UN-Women. His research covers various issues relating to labor markets: political economy of the ready-made garments industry, poverty, and inequality. He has published a number of book chapters, monographs, and peer-reviewed journal articles in various international and national fora.

Md. Masudur Rahman is Assistant Director of Bangladesh Bank—the Central Bank of Bangladesh. He worked as a research associate at the Centre for Policy Dialogue (CPD), a think-tank in Bangladesh. He holds a Master of Science in Economics from Jahangirnagar University, Dhaka, Bangladesh. Rahman worked on issues such as Bangladesh's graduation from LDC status, Sustainable Development Goals (SDGs), and green growth. His current research interests include monetary policy, macroeconomic management, and development economics.

Mohammad Monirul Islam Sarker is Deputy General Manager (DGM) at the Monetary Policy Department of the Bangladesh Bank. He holds an MS in Economics from North South University, Bangladesh, and a PhD in Economics from Jawaharlal Nehru University, India. Sarker has published research papers in *International Journal of Economics, Finance and Management Sciences*, *Thoughts on Banking and Finance*, *Journal of Economics and Behavioral Studies*, *Bank Parikrama*, and so on. Sarker has been working at Bangladesh Bank for more than twenty-one years and has developed avid interest and strength in the monetary policy of Bangladesh.

Helal Uddin has completed his PhD from Ritsumeikan Asia Pacific University (APU). Presently, he is working as a research assistant at the Research Office of APU. Uddin has published several research articles in peer-reviewed journals and attended various national and international conferences. His research interests are micro-credit and rural poverty, financial system, and Islamic microfinance. Previously, Uddin also served as an internal auditor at Moshihor Securities Ltd., a stockbroker of the Dhaka Stock Exchange, for three years.

S. M. Sohrab Uddin is a professor at the Department of Finance, University of Chittagong, Bangladesh. He obtained BBA and MBA from the University of Chittagong, and MBA and PhD from Ritsumeikan Asia Pacific University, Oita, Japan. His research area focuses on financial markets, institutions, and instruments with particular emphasis on banking sector development, including Islamic banking in developing countries. Uddin has published in various national and international peer-reviewed journals. He has co-edited the book *Finance for Sustainable Growth and Development* in 2018.

Abbreviations

ACC	Anti-Corruption Commission
ADAB	Association of Development Agencies of Bangladesh
ADB	Asian Development Bank
ADLI	Agricultural-demand-led-industrialization
ADP	Adolescent Development Program
ADP	Annual Development Plan
ADR	Advance-deposit ratio
AID	Artificially Intelligent Devices
AIIB	Asian Infrastructure Investment Bank
APA	Annual Performance Agreement
ATM	Automated teller machine
BACH	Bangladesh Automated Clearing House
BADC	Bangladesh Agricultural Development Corporation
BANBEIS	Bangladesh Bureau of Educational Information and Statistics
BBO	Bangladesh Bank Order
BBS	Bangladesh Bureau of Statistics
BCAS	Bangladesh Centre for Advanced Studies
BCCI	Bank of Credit and Commerce International
BDP	Bangladesh Delta Plan
BDT	Bangladeshi taka
BEFTN	Bangladesh Electronic Funds Transfer Network
BEP	BRAC Education Program
BGIIB	Bangladesh Government Islamic Investment Bond
BGMEA	Bangladesh Garment Manufacturers and Exporters Association
BGTB	Bangladesh Government Treasury Bonds
BMRE	Balancing, Modernization, Rehabilitation, and Expansion
BNCC	Bangladesh National Cadet Corps

BOESL	Bangladesh Overseas Employment Services Limited
BOP	Balance of payments
BRAC	Bangladesh Rural Advancement Committee
BRI	Belt and Road Initiative
BRICS	Brazil, Russia, India, China, and South Africa
BRRI	Bangladesh Rice Research Institute
BSB	Bangladesh Shilpa Bank
BSRS	Bangladesh Shilpa Rin Shangastha
BTRC	Bangladesh Telecommunication Regulatory Commission
BWDB	Bangladesh Water Development Board
CAGR	Compound annual growth rate
CAP	Corrective Action Plan
CBOs	Community-based organizations
CBRP	Commercial Bank Restructuring Project
CBSP	Central Bank Strengthening Project
CC	Control of Corruption
CCB	Capital conservation buffer
CCs	Community Clinics
CIB	Credit Information Bureau
CIO	Chief innovation officer
CRAR	Capital to risk-weighted assets ratio
CRR	Cash Reserve Ratio
CSR	Corporate social responsibility
DESCs	District e-Service Centers
DIFE	Department of Inspection for Factories and Establishments
DIS	Deposit Insurance Scheme
ECD	Early Childhood Development
ECOSOC	(United Nations) Economic and Social Council
EFA	Education for All
EOI	Export-oriented industrialization
EPZs	Export processing zones
ESCAP	Economic and Social Commission for Asia and the Pacific
EVI	Economic vulnerability index
FCBs	Foreign Commercial Banks
FCO	Foreign Contribution (Regulation) Ordinance 1982
FDI	Financial Development Index
FDI	Foreign direct investment
FDR	Foreign Donation (Voluntary Activity) Regulation Ordinance 1978
FI	Financial inclusion
FINAI	Financial Institutional Access Index
FLE	Financial Literacy and Education

FMA	Free Market Approach
FY	Fiscal Year
GATT	General Agreement of Tariff and Trade
GCR	Global Competitiveness Report
GDP	Gross domestic product
GE	Government effectiveness
GED	General Economic Division
GEP	General Education Project
GEP	Global Economic Prospect
GGGI	Global Gender Gap Index
GNI	Gross national income
GoB	Government of Bangladesh
GRS	Grievance Redress System
HCFS	Health Care Financing Strategy
HCI	Human Capital Index
HDI	Human Development Index
HEQEP	Higher Education Quality Enhancement Project
HIES	Household Income and Expenditure Survey
HRD	Human resource development
HRI	Human Resources Index
HtR	Hard-to-reach
ICT	Information and Communication Technology
IFEP	Integrated Non-formal Education Project
IMF	International Monetary Fund
IMR	Infant Mortality Rate
IO	Innovation officer
IPDC	Industrial Promotion and Development Company
ISI	Import-Substituting Industrialization
IT	Information Technology
KM	Keynesian Multiplier
KPSS	KwiaBDTowski-Philips-Schmidt-Shin
KSA	Kingdom of Saudi Arabia
LDC	Least developed country
LGIs	Local Government Institutes
LNOB	Leaving no one behind
MB	Mobile banking
MDGs	Millennium Development Goals
MEAs	Multilateral Environmental Agreements
MENA	Middle East and North Africa
MFA	Market-Friendly Approach
MFIs	Micro Finance Institutions
MFS	Mobile Financial Service

MoEWOE	Ministry of Expatriates' Welfare and Overseas Employment
MoF	Ministry of Finance
MNCs	Multinational corporations
MPC	Marginal propensity to consume
MPCR	Marginal propensity to consume of remittances
MPS	Marginal propensity to save
MPSR	Marginal propensity to save of remittances
MRA	Microcredit Regulatory Authority
MTBF	Medium-term budgetary framework
NBFIs	Non-bank Financial Institutions
NDC	Nationally determined contribution
NFA	No frills account
NFPE	Non-formal primary education
NGOAB	NGO Affairs Bureau
NGOs	Non-government organizations
NIEs	Newly industrialized economies
NIS	National Integrity Strategy
NPA	National Plan of Action
NPDs	Non-primary dealers
NPEA	New Political Economy Approach
NPL	Non-performing loan
NSDS	National Sustainable Development Strategy
NTPA	National Tripartite Plan of Action
ODA	Official development assistance
OOP	Out-of-pocket payments
ORT	Oral rehydration therapy
OS	Operating systems
PARC	Public Administration Reform Commission
PCA	Public choice approach
PCBs	Private Commercial Banks
PEA	Political economy approach
PEDP	Primary Education Development Program
PKSF	Palli Karma Sahayak Foundation
PMO	Prime Minister's Office
POs	Partner organizations
PPP	Purchasing power parity
PRC	People's Republic of China
PS&AV/T	Political Stability and Absence of Violence/Terrorism
PSDPCC	Private Sector Development Policy Coordination Committee
PSEs	Public sector enterprises
PwC	PricewaterhouseCoopers
QRPPs	Quick rental power plants

R&D	Research and development
RDRS	Rangpur Dinajpur Rural Service
RL	Rule of Law
RM	Remittance multiplier
RMG	Ready-made garments
ROA	Return on assets
ROE	Return on equity
RQ	Regulatory Quality
RTGS	Real-time gross settlement
RWA	Risk-weighted asset
SAARC	South Asian Association for Regional Cooperation
SAM	Social accounting matrix
SBI	State Bank of India
SDBs	Specialized Development Banks
SDGs	Sustainable Development Goals
SEDM	Solidary Economic Development Model
SEDP	Secondary Education Development Program
SLR	Sea level rise
SLR	Statutory liquidity ratio
SMEs	Small and Medium Enterprises
SOCBs	State-owned commercial banks
SPS	Service Process Simplification
SRA	Societies Registration Act of 1860
SSK	Shasthyo Suroksha Karmasuchi
SWR	Social Welfare Registration and Control Ordinance 1961
TCV	Time, cost, and visit
TFR	Total fertility rate
TI	Transparency International
UAE	United Arab Emirate
UDCs	Union Digital Centers
UGC	University Grant Commission
UISCs	Union Information and Service Centers
UK	United Kingdom
UN	United Nations
UNCSD	United Nations Conference on Sustainable Development
UNDESA	UN Department of Economic and Social Affairs
UNDP	United Nations Development Programme
UNHCR	United Nations High Commissioner for Refugees
UP	Utilization Permission
URL	Uniform Resource Locator
USA	United States of America
USD	US Dollar

V&A	Voice and Accountability
WDI	World Development Indicators
WEF	World Economic Forum
WHO	World Health Organization
WPC	Workers Participatory Committee

List of Figures

List of Tables

PART I

Introduction

CHAPTER 1

Introduction: Construction of a Development Model for Bangladesh

Munim Kumar Barai

Introduction

Let us begin with some recent socioeconomic statistics. In 2017, the life expectancy of the Bangladeshi population stood at 72.8 years, its population growth rate was 1.37 percent, literacy rate 72.3 percent, and infant mortality rate 24.0 per thousand live births. In 2018, the national poverty rate decreased further to 21.8 percent, while the extreme poverty rate also dropped to 11.3 percent (Table 1.2). On the economic front, Bangladesh achieved a 6 percent-plus growth for the first time in 2003–04 (6.27%). Then it broke the 6 percent growth trap in 2015. The pace of growth since then has been continuing to surpass each preceding year (7.28% in 2017 and 7.86% in 2018) (Table 1.1). According to the HSBC, Bangladesh is a US$300 billion economy now[1] and has been projected to reach US$700 billion in 2030. This will make Bangladesh the 26th largest economy in the world (from 42nd now): a 16 notch jump (Henry and Pomeroy 2018). The UN Department of Economic and Social Affairs (UN-DESA

M. K. Barai (✉)
Graduate School of Management, Ritsumeikan Asia Pacific University, Beppu, Japan
e-mail: baraimk@apu.ac.jp

M. K. Barai (ed.), *Bangladesh's Economic and Social Progress*,
https://doi.org/10.1007/978-981-15-1683-2_1

Table 1.1 Bangladesh—Some basic socioeconomic indicators, 1970–2018

Land Area: 130170 (sq. km), Population (2018)—161.4 million

Indicators/Factors	*1970*	*1971*	*1972*	*1980*	*1990*	*2000*	*2010*	*2016*	*2017*	*2018*
Birth rate, crude (per 1000 people)	47.8	47.5	47.1	43.6	35.4	27.6	21.2	19.0	18.6	
Death rate, crude (per 1000 people)	18.9	19.1	19.2	14.2	10.3	6.9	5.6	5.3	5.3	
Exports of goods and services (current US$ billion)	0.8	0.6	0.4	1.0	1.9	6.6	18.5	36.9	37.5	40.6
Imports of goods and services (current US$ billion)	1.12	0.94	0.86	3.24	4.13	9.06	25.11	47.17	50.61	64.24
External debt stocks (% of GNI)				20.9	38.1	28.3	21.6	16.6	18.1	
Foreign direct investment, net inflows (BoP, current US$ million)			0.09	8.51	3.24	280.4	1232.3	2332.7	2151.4	
GDP (current US$ billion)	9.0	8.8	6.3	18.1	31.6	53.4	115.3	221.4	249.7	274.0
GDP (constant 2010—US$ billion)	26.4	25.0	21.5	28.6	42.4	67.0	115.3	167.8	180.0	194.1
GDP growth (annual %)	5.62	−5.48	−13.97	0.82	5.62	5.29	5.57	7.11	7.28	7.86
GDP per capita (current US$)	140.0	133.6	94.4	227.8	306.3	418.1	781.2	1401.6	1564.0	1698.3
GDP per capita, PPP (current international $)					860.2	1346.7	2466.9	3696.8	3998.4	4364.0
Gross capital formation (% of GDP)	11.3	8.2	4.7	14.4	16.5	23.8	26.2	29.7	30.5	31.2
Government expenditure on education, total (% of GDP)				0.9	1.5	2.1		1.5		
Government expenditure on education, total (% of government expenditure)				5.3	11.2	20.5		11.4		
Grants, excluding technical cooperation (BoP, current US$ million)		0.02	199.7	1000.9	771.7	594.9	1095.4	944.9	45.7	
Labor force, total, million					34	46	57	63	67	68
Market capitalization of listed domestic companies (% of GDP)						4.1	36.1	31.8	34.5	28.2
Mobile cellular subscriptions (per 100 people)						0.2	44.6	83.4	91.7	

Source: World Bank (2019)

2018) reports: "Propelled by better health and education, lower vulnerability and an economic boom, Bangladesh looks likely to leave the LDC category by 2024."[2] The same UN body found Bangladesh exceeded the threshold level on the human assets index in 2016 (UN-DESA 2018).[3] So much so, that the World Economic Forum has recently assumed Bangladesh to be the next emerging tiger in Asia (WEF 2017). This economic and social progress picture of Bangladesh, to say the least, is impressive.

In fact, as a developing country, Bangladesh seems to have surpassed pundits' assessments and expectations on the way to achieving this development. That's why they are nowadays referring to Bangladesh as a development 'Surprise' (Asadullah et al. 2014) or 'Unexpected Success' or 'Bangladesh Paradox' (Hossain 2017), or even 'miracle' (Sawada et al. 2018). This is patently a contrast to the messy picture Bangladesh brought to our mind in previous years. The description of its worst—'a basket case'[4] (Smith and Keefer 2005) or a malevolent 'Test Case of Development' (Faaland and Parkinson 1976).

However, it may not be that surprising that the alternative 'not so friendly perception' arose when one looks at the whole realm of the functioning of Bangladesh as a sovereign economic, social, and political entity since its independence in 1971. By its geographic size, Bangladesh is a small country, but by population count, it is the eighth largest nation in the world or the largest least developed country (LDC). In the 1970s, Bangladesh looked like 'the poster-child for Malthusia' (Hossain 2017: 7), and "was ranked near the bottom of all economic and social indices" (Mahmud et al. 2018) as it had all the classic problems a developing country has—low income, low access to finance, high poverty, illiteracy, high birth rates with higher mortality, lack of hard and soft infrastructure, scarcity of health and hygiene facilities, lack of awareness, and so on. Politically, there was the assassination of the Father of the Nation Bangabandhu Sheikh Mujibur Rahman and the rule of authoritarian military regimes, to dysfunctional democracy and chaos. Therefore, it looks like a sheer paradox that Bangladesh has turned around to become the largest economy among the LDCs and is now projected to turn into the 26th largest of all by 2030, leaving behind the baggage described above.

So the question that puzzles the pundits is—how has this about-face taken place? Understandably, Bangladesh has just not grown organically in a void. According to Rahman (2018), "Both positive internal and external factors made this stunning transformation a reality." Though attempts have been made to identify and explain the factors behind the 'unexpected development' of Bangladesh, they have tried mostly on a piecemeal basis to include one or a few explaining variables. Hence, they do not present Bangladesh's development case inclusively. The broader objective of this book is to offer a systematic and empirically informed analysis of the development story of Bangladesh by its content, scope, and organization. This should help readers understand better where and how various development initiatives and arrangements produced better than expected results and what these effects are on the economic lives and social sphere. Indeed, the interactive dynamics of various development efforts together seem to have played a pivotal role in the overall development of Bangladesh, which on its part appears to have built a development structure from within. Those efforts somehow manifested to produce synergized outputs in various indicators of development. This has largely remained untold so far in a single framework. So, this book attempts to give an inclusive narrative of the 'development glory' of Bangladesh and a foundation for theorizing on its development, which is yet to dominate the academic and public discourse.

This chapter has some specific objectives as well. In the following section, we will first give a holistic view of the various competing economic development theories of different eras to equip ourselves with some background thoughts. This should help analyze the economic and social development of Bangladesh from a theoretical perspective. It is then followed by a descriptive picture of the progress Bangladesh has made in a number of economic and social sectors. To contextualize Bangladesh's development experience, the chapter then tries to analyze Bangladesh's development through the prism of theories to find their relevance to the understanding of the development of Bangladesh. The objective of this effort is to examine whether the development of Bangladesh can be analyzed from any existing theoretical perspectives or whether Bangladesh has followed a distinctive path to reach its present level of economic and social development. The author believes that there are some factors with positive externalities that may have influenced Bangladesh's progress, but their role so far has remained unexplained. Identifying and explaining their possible linkage to development has, therefore, been done in one section. The chapter ends with a brief glance at the other 12 chapters included in the book to explain Bangladesh's development.

Competing Theories of Economic Development

For perceptual ease, we need to have some views that define development in its economic and social contexts. According to Copestake (1999: 3), the term 'economic development' refers to long-term changes in systems of production and distribution of goods and services affecting human welfare. In contrast to 'economic growth,' it involves changes in the form as well as the scale of economic activity. On the other hand, the success of a society depends on the improvement and attainment of the well-being of social members so that they can reach their fullest potential. So, a country's economic and social development of its citizens is very much interlinked. In broader terms, therefore, development is, "The process of improving the quality of all human lives and capabilities by raising people's levels of living, self-esteem, and freedom" (Todaro and Smith 2015: 7). Thus, countries pursue both economic and social development goals to attain some specific objectives like economic growth, and a better quality of life for the people through access to basic facilities, poverty reduction, employment generation, human capital development, lowering social inequality and long-term sustainable development.

Nevertheless, it is not easy to explain the dynamics of growth and development of a country by a single theory, as many connected, and even independent factors may play a role in the development process. "There are, clearly, no sure-fire formulae for success; if there were, there would be more successes. Some strategies seem to work for a while, and then stall; some strategies seem to work in some countries, and not in others. Economic theory has evolved to account for the successes and failures" (Hoff and Stiglitz 2000: 389). But, explaining variations in long-term economic growth has remained the primary concern in all these theories (Copestake 1999). We are, however, making an effort to review briefly a number of thoughts that have evolved over time to deal with or identify various factors responsible for or work as prime movers of economic development. This should help put in context the exceptionality, if any, of the development of Bangladesh.

In the economic literature, we find a few approaches to classifying economic development theories. The common method is to discuss development theories in the order of their evolution as we see in Thirlwall (1999), Pieterse (2010), Dang and Sui Pheng (2015), and Todaro and Smith (2015). They offer a chronological exposure to these theories to ease the understanding of their contextual evolution. In contrast, Copestake

(1999: 2) reviews "theories of economic development according to whether economies are relatively open or closed to international trade, and actively managed by the state (*dirigiste*) or reliant upon private activity (*laissez-faire*)." An effort has also been made to classify the theories of development by synthesizing their main aspects: modernization, dependency, world-systems, and globalization (Reyes 2001).

We, however, have planned our discussion on theories of economic development based on the first approach. Following this, we have grouped the theories for discussion in the following order—Formative Stage or Classical Development Views, Neoclassical Theories on Development, and the Development of Contemporary Theories.

The Formative Stage of Development Views

Though thoughts on economic development of nations were in vogue from the initial stage of the emergence of economics as a separate discipline, development economics was established as a discipline within economics only in the 1950s (Dang and Sui Pheng 2015). Nonetheless, several classical economists such as Adam Smith, David Ricardo, Thomas Robert Malthus, and Karl Marx wrote extensively about the economic nature of the society and prosperity they lived in. They were, however, also concerned with understanding economic development in their own age of early industrialization (Copestake 1999). Some important views of that time are as follows:

Adam Smith and Capitalism

Through the publication of 'The Wealth of Nations' in 1776, Adam Smith heralded a new era of development ideas for enhancing a nation's wealth. His theory was premised on points of natural law, laissez-faire, private ownership of factors of production, division of labor, capital accumulation, agents of growth, and process of growth. He advocated the policy of laissez-faire in economic affairs and opined that natural laws are superior to the law of states. Taking farmers, producers, and businessmen as crucial agents of economic growth, Smith observed that the policy of laissez-faire allows the producers to produce the product, earn income, and save as much they can and like (Smith 1976). Adam Smith postulated that freedom of action brings out the best in an individual and increases society's wealth and progress, and he opposed any government intervention in industry and commerce (Economics Discussion 2019). He believed that it is safe to leave the economy to be propelled, regulated and controlled by the 'invisible hand,' that is, the forces of competition motivated by self-interest of private investors, which would maximize national output, promote public interests, reduce poverty by spurring economic development, and bring about the social and moral improvements of nations.

Although the 'invisible hand' doctrine has become the foundation for the working of the market economy or capitalism (Skousen 2007), on the downside, "freewheeling capitalism is often criticized for bringing wealth only to the rich, whereas the poor get poorer" (Dang and Sui Pheng 2015).

Karl Marx and Socialism

Marx's idea of socialism or state capitalism published in 'Capital' (Marx 1933),[5] influenced and revolutionized the thought process of economists and politicians at the beginning of the twentieth century. As opposed to Adam Smith, Marx showed that capitalists amass wealth through the exploitation of the surplus value created by their workers (proletariat). This leads to an increasing animosity between capitalists and workers (Marx 1933). This antagonism and the declining rate of profit due to competition in capitalism would pave the way for the destruction of capitalism and the emergence of socialism through revolution (Roemer 1988). So, Marx argued for state or social ownership of the means of production and said that coordination of economic activities should not be left to the market mechanism through prices. Instead, the state should plan and manage the economy of a nation to serve the interests of the masses.

But historical developments like the demolition of the Berlin Wall (1989), collapse of the former Soviet Union (1991), retrenchment of the socialist ideology from the whole of Eastern Europe, and the market-based economic orientation of China have raised questions about the applicability of the central planning paradigm of Marx over time and his model's ability to solve poverty and inequality in human society (Meier 2000).

The Malthusian Model of Population Growth

Though Malthus' theory is mostly seen as a population growth theory, it has relevance to the economic development of developing countries in particular. Malthus (1798) predicted that the population would outrun food supply leading to famine, conflicts over resources, and so on. This model assumed technological change was constant and increasing inputs could lead to diminishing returns. This led to the gloomy prediction that populations would grow faster than their capacity to feed themselves. "As a description of population-income interactions, the Malthusian model had a long period of success, covering most of human history in most of the world until the beginning of the industrial revolution" (Weil and Wilde 2010).

Though the technological revolution in various fields including agriculture has proved Malthus prediction of doom to be not that accurate, the "Malthusian channel by which a high level of population reduces income per capita is still relevant in poor developing countries that have large rural populations dependent on agriculture, as well as in countries that are heavily reliant on mineral or energy exports" (Weil and Wilde 2010). Malthus should be criticized because he under-predicted the capacity of technological improvements to increase food yields in particular, but not for the overall impact of over-population.

Classical Theories on Development

The establishment of 'classical development economics' during the 1950s is a useful reference point for the discussion of economic theories that have dominated the post–World War II literature on economic development. Indeed, there are four strands of thoughts that developed under classical views. We take them up here in a brief discussion.

Models of Linear-Stages-of-Growth

In the early years after World War II, two first-generation models on economic development came into prominence. They were Rostow's (1960) stages of growth model and the Harrod–Domar model. These theories viewed the process of development of countries as a series of successive stages of economic growth (Todaro and Smith 2015). These views assumed that the right quantity and mixture of saving, investment, and foreign aid were necessary to enable developing nations to proceed along an economic growth path. These models "focused on the utility of massive injections of capital to achieve rapid GDP growth rates" (Dang and Sui Pheng 2015: 16). In a sense, development thus became synonymous with rapid, aggregate economic growth (Todaro and Smith 2015: 119).

Rostow's Stages of Growth Model

Following the historical pattern of economic development of the developed countries, Walt Whitman Rostow penned his classic 'Stages of Economic Growth: A Non-Communist Manifesto' in 1960. He theorized development as a linear process from primitive to modern, and all countries have to pass through five stages to become developed: the traditional society, the preconditions for take-off, the take-off, the drive to maturity, and the age of high mass consumption. "The model asserted that all countries exist somewhere on this linear spectrum, and climb upward through each stage in the development process" (Jacobs 2019). As per this theory, the take-off stage is very decisive for developing countries, as they are expected to transit from an underdeveloped to a developed state through this phase. For such development, it is necessary to an increasing rate of investments to induce per capita growth (Dang and Sui Pheng 2015).

Harrod–Domar Model

Developed independently by Roy F. Harrod (1939) and Evsey Domar (1946), their model is considered to be a classical Keynesian model of economic growth. In development economics, the Harrod–Domar Model is used to explain an economy's growth rate in terms of the level of saving and productivity of capital. The model identifies three kinds of growth: warranted growth, actual growth, and the natural rate of growth and suggests that every country requires capital to generate investments. Moreover, the rate of saving needed for a nation can be determined if there is a target growth rate. According to the model, mobilization of foreign savings is required to meet any deficit in domestic savings.

Although these models established the vital role of investments, most closely correlated with the economic growth rate, they have been criticized for a number of weaknesses in their simplifying assumptions (Dang and Sui Pheng 2015). These are: the non-applicability of a single production function for all countries (Adelman 2000), the high nonlinearity of development process (Chenery 1960; Chenery and Syrquin 1975), the pursuance of distinct development paths (Morris and Adelman 1988), jumping stages, or becoming locked in one particular stage, or even regressing on many other complementary factors for a wide range of development projects (Todaro and Smith 2015) are some of them.

Structural Change Theories

Economic theorists in the 1960s and 1970s explored growth through structural shifts in the economy. It is a "mechanism by which underdeveloped economies transform their domestic economic structures from a heavy emphasis on traditional subsistence agriculture to a more modern, more urbanized, and more industrially diverse manufacturing and service economy" (Todaro and Smith 2015: 124). In this transformation process, the allocation of labor from the agricultural sector to the industrial sector is considered a critical source for economic growth. The 'two-sector surplus labor' theory of W. Arthur Lewis (1954) and the 'patterns of development' empirical analysis of Hollis B. Chenery (1960) and his coauthors (1968, 1975) are two well-known examples of the structural change theory.

The Lewis Two-Sector Surplus-Labor Theory

During most of the 1960s and early 1970s, the Lewis model became the general theory of development in surplus-labor developing nations. In the studies of the growth experience of China, the model has been widely used. Under this model, an underdeveloped economy consists of two sectors: a traditional, overpopulated, rural subsistence labor-surplus sector characterized by zero marginal labor productivity and a high-productivity modern, urban industrial sector where labor from the surplus sector is gradually transferred (Todaro and Smith 2015). However, the unlimited supply of labor from the traditional sector to the industrial sector will ensure continual subsistence wages for the transferred workers, generating re-investible excess profit for the modern sector. On the assumption that all profits would be reinvested, the modern sector continues to grow, creates further economic development, and furthers the labor transfer, making an output expansion chain. This process helps take place the structural transformation of a traditional subsistence economy to a more modern developed economy (Dang and Sui Pheng 2015).

Thus, both the Harrod–Domar and the Lewis models have a similar take on savings and investments as the driving forces of economic development, but they differ in the country context as the Lewis model is related to less developed countries. Also, Todaro and Smith (2015) argue that several of Lewis' assumptions such as those relating to rural surplus labor and the proportional rate of expansion in capital accumulation in the modern sector are not valid.

Structural Change and Patterns of Development

The most significant explanation of the structural change and patterns of development approach was provided by Chenery (1960), Chenery and Taylor (1968), Kuznets (1971) and Chenery and Syrquin (1975). Under Chenery's and coauthors' analysis, for economic growth, apart from savings and investments as argued in the Lewis theory, the steady accumulation of physical and human capital is also a necessary condition. Additionally, "a set of interrelated changes in the economic structure of a country are required for the transition from a traditional economic system to a modern one. These structural changes involve virtually all economic functions, including the transformation of production and changes in the composition of consumer demand, international trade, and resource use as well as changes in socioeconomic factors such as urbanization and the growth and distribution of a country's population" (Todaro and Smith 2015: 129).

But the structural change models have their limitations by becoming a misleading source of policy as the development emphasis on the industrial sector shifted and neglected the agriculture sector (World Bank 2000b), a vital sector of the developing economy. Similarly, the focus on human capital, that is, education and health (Meier 2000), especially in sub-Saharan Africa, has substantially improved the life expectancy and school enrolment rates but not economic growth since the early 1970s (World Bank 2000b). The hypothesis of the structural change models that the pattern was similar in all countries and was identifiable is now disputed as patterns of development can be different among countries due to a particular set of factors, including "a country's resource endowment and size, its government's policies and objectives, the availability of external capital and technology, and the international trade environment" (Todaro and Smith 2015: 130).

International Dependence Models

With their origins in developing countries, international dependence theories view obstacles to development as being primarily external in nature, rather than internal. Todaro and Smith (2015) identified the presence of three models, namely, the neocolonial dependence model, the false-paradigm model, and the dualistic-development model, within this stream of theories that views the underdevelopment of developing countries as being conditioned by the exploitative activities of developed countries and allies, the dualistic nature of developing economies, or their current patterns and lack of capital accumulation.

The advocates of the neocolonial dependence model advance the proposition that underdevelopment for developing countries is an externally induced phenomenon of the continuing exploitative economic, political, and cultural policies of former colonial rulers toward them. These theorists are flag bearers of Marxist thinking on the existence of unequal relationships between rich and poor countries and between groups within the domestic setup of developing countries. The presence of these types of relationships creates a center-periphery framework, wherein developing countries, representing the periphery, are caught up in a dependence and dominance relationship with the center represented by the developed economies and that this compromises development attempts of the poor countries (Oumar and Sama 2015). Multinational corporations (MNCs) and their capital have become vehicles to exploit this situation further and make developing countries more dependent on developed countries as they cannot expect sustained growth from that dependence. Thus, the theory espouses that developing countries should end dependence by breaking up their relationships with the developed world. Advocates of this stream of economic thought include Baran (1957), Sunkel (1966), Franck (1967), Rodney (1972), dos Santos (1973), Galeano (1973), Cardoso (1977), Wallerstein (1980), and others.

The false-paradigm model is a less radical international dependence approach to development. The model assigns faults in the development strategies of developing countries often prescribed by Western economists for their failure to develop. These strategies failed because they have been based on incorrect models of development, which emphasize much more on capital-output ratios, savings-investment ratios, and growth rates of GDP, thereby exposing them to the dynamism of developed economies at the expense of their own. The leading advocates of this school are Easterly (2001), Stiglitz (2002) and Rodrik (2008).

The Dualistic-Development Theory is based on the idea of a world of dual societies, of rich nations and poor nations and, in the developing countries, pockets of wealth within broad areas of poverty. This notion is implicit in structural change theories and explicit in international dependence theories (Todaro and Smith 2015). Advocates of dualistic-development model like Boeke (1953) and Higgins (1956) argue that there is a coexistence of disparities, which are even increasing, between different sets of conditions across the world. As per this theory, the dualistic conditions are chronic and more than a temporary phenomenon that can be easily rectified or eliminated by time. Moreover, the differences between the elements of superiority and inferiority are instead amplifying every year due to lack of the elements of superiority to pull up the elements of inferiority from their condition. Rather, the elements of superiority are seen to be continuous efforts to push down the elements of inferiority to a more advanced state of underdevelopment (Oumar and Sama 2015: 123).

Neoclassical Counter-Revolution Models

But the 1980s and 1990s saw the emergence of neoclassical counter-revolution economists who, through three approaches, namely the free market approach (FMA), the new political economy approach (PEA), and the market-friendly approach (MFA), countered the ideas of public ownership, planning, and regulation of economic activities by the state in the international dependence model. In this approach, neoclassical economists emphasized the critical role of free markets, open economies, and the privatization of inefficient public enterprises, and advocated the elimination of government-imposed distortions associated with protectionism, subsidies, and public ownership to stimulate growth. They argue that the state model has failed to bring economic development in developing countries because of excessive government control of the economy through wrong pricing policies, resource misallocation, corruption, and inefficiency in the socioeconomic environment, rather than from exploitative internal and external factors (Oumar and Sama 2015). The success stories of Singapore, Taiwan, and South Korea became case studies of these theories that argue that market fundamentalism is the key to economic development for developing countries. Scholars like Johnson (1971), Balassa (1971), Krueger (1978), Bhagwati (1978), Little (1982), Bauer (1984), and Lal (1985) have extensively discussed the FMA, PEA, and MFA in their works.

Solow's (1956) neoclassical development thought is also a part of the traditional neoclassical growth theory. The Solow neoclassical growth model expanded the Harrod–Domar formulation by adding a second factor, labor, and introducing a third independent variable, technology, which is provided exogenously, to the growth equation. Solow's model exhibited diminishing returns to labor and capital separately and constant returns to both factors jointly.

Solow (1956) stressed the importance of three factors of output growth of an economy: increases in labor quantity and quality (through population growth and education), increases in the stock of capital (through savings and investments), and technological improvements (labor-saving, capital saving, labor augmentation, capital augmentation) (Solow 1956; see also Dang and Sui Pheng 2015; Oumar and Sama 2015). With the same rate of technological progress, given that it is provided exogenously, economic growth rates would be expected to converge across countries. Developing countries can increase the rate of capital accumulation and return on investments if they can draw additional domestic and foreign investments by opening up national markets. As a result, developing countries tend to converge to higher per capita income levels (World Bank 2000b). However, these models explain that, in the short run, economies with higher rates of savings/investment (open/mid-income countries) grow faster (in the long run: growth is null) and tend to converge toward higher per capita income levels as opposed to economies with lower savings rates (closed/LDCs) (Oumar and Sama 2015).

Contemporary Development Theories

Ideas like the new growth theory, the coordination failure approach, and the big push model, and so on that emerged in the twenty-first century are labeled as contemporary models of economic development and underdevelopment. For successful development to take place, the new theories mainly argued that multiple stakeholders of the development process must have effective and efficient coordination, or that complementarities should exist among them (Oumar and Sama 2015).

The New Growth Theory

In the 1980s and 1990s, new growth theorists like Romer (1986), Lucas (1988), and Aghion and Howitt (1992) wanted to explain the poor performance of many less developed countries which followed neoclassical theories for their development endeavor. They considered the technological change to be an exogenous factor, in contrast to Solow's model, and found that technological change was neither equal nor exogenously transmitted in most developing countries (World Bank 2000b). This endogenous growth theory helps explain that the divergence in growth rates across economies is produced by the technological change to the production of knowledge. This approach emphasizes that it is the use of knowledge rather than labor and capital that brings increasing returns to economic growth. Higher rates of return, as expected in the Solow model for developing counties, get eroded due to lower complementary investment in human capital (education), infrastructure, or research and development (R&D). Investments in knowledge creation, in particular, can bring about sustained growth, as knowledge or innovation may require no additional cost for reuse or could create spillover benefits for other firms once it is obtained. In the new growth models, therefore, policy intervention and investment by governments in developing countries for human capital formation are critical as individuals may not have financial or other abilities to creating new knowledge for themselves. The encouragement of foreign private investments in knowledge-intensive industries such as computer software and telecommunications may form a complementary source in this regard (Meier 2000; Dang and Sui Pheng 2015). Nevertheless, the theory was criticized for treating the economy as a single firm and overlooking the importance of social and institutional structures (Skott and Auerbach 1995). Developing countries lack other factors like infrastructure, institutions, and capital and goods markets (Cornwall and Cornwall 1994), which may offer incentives to economic growth in developing countries. Policymakers should provide attention to these questions.

The Theory of Coordination Failure

In the 1990s, the theory of coordination failure became a leading economic-growth idea. At the core, this theory espouses the concept that the market may fail to achieve coordination among complementary activities. For example, when returns from one investment depend on the presence or extent of other investments in the market, then complementaries exist. "On the one hand, optimally, all investors as a whole are better off with all investments to be achieved at the same time. On the other hand, it would not make sense for an investor to take similar actions when he believes that others may not do the same as well. The market is said to have failed to coordinate investors' actions in this way" (Dang and Sui Pheng 2015: 20). This leads the market to an (equilibrium) outcome inferior to an optimally recourse-allocated market situation, and all agents would be better off. Consequently, underdevelopment equilibrium is possible (Hoff and Stiglitz 2000). Interestingly, Rosenstein-Rodan (1943) first raised coordination issues among complementary industries, and along with them economists like "Nurkse (1953) and Hirschman (1957) emphasized the role of the government to solve the problem. In order to reach an optimal level of coordination, the policy they recommended was a 'big push'—a public-led massive investment program—which can cause complementarities to take place in the rest of the economy" (Dang and Sui Pheng 2015: 21). In fact, the coordination failure economists advocated the role of the government strongly, particularly in the presence of multiple equilibria situations in the economy. In such market situations, the government, through selective intervention, can coordinate firms to move them into the domain of good equilibrium.

Though the theory of coordination failure has been criticized for an overemphasis on the role of government, the UNDP recommended that a 'big push' strategy by developing countries to break out of the poverty trap infrastructure is necessary (UNDP 2005).

Amartya Sen's Development Concept

Sen's concept of 'Development as Freedom' (1999) identifies development "as a process of expanding the real freedoms that people enjoy. Focusing on human freedoms contrasts with narrower views of development, such as identifying development with the growth of the gross national product, or with the rise in personal incomes, or with industrialization, or with technological advance, or with social modernization" (Sen 1999: 1). By focusing on increasing citizens' access and opportunities to the things they have reason to value, Sen challenged the mainstream concept of economic growth as a measurement of development (Evans 2002). By acknowledging the expansion of poor people's freedoms due to increases in their incomes, he contends that a rise in income alone "has at best uneven and at worst has detrimental impacts on the majority of a country's population, and radical redistributive measures are necessary for the poor to benefit from growth" (Selwyn 2011: 69). Even in the era of 'unprecedented opulence', Sen (1999) finds the presence of poverty, unfulfilled elementary needs, famines, the violation of political freedoms, and neglect of the agency of women. "Development consists of the removal of various types of unfreedoms that leave people with little choice and little opportunity of exercising their reasoned agency" (Sen 1999: xii). In his theory, Sen focuses on economic opportunities, political freedoms, social facilities, transparency guarantees, and protective security, the interconnected instrumental freedoms (Clifton 2013).

Sen's theory had a considerable influence on the establishment of a new paradigm in the early 2000s. His capability approach is viewed by most development practitioners as an invaluable analytical and philosophical foundation. However, it is argued that this base should not just be admired but built upon (Evans 2002). Selwyn argues that Sen's view of freedom in capitalist markets is myopic as the market is an institutionalized unfreedom. He asserts that Sen complies with Adam Smith's understanding of the market as an arena of choice and "does not propose radical, distributive, developmental policies and practices" (Selwyn 2011: 75).

The Millennium Development Goals and the Sustainable Development Goals

The globalization process has brought multiplier effects to economies in the form of unwanted migration, budgetary pressure to cover benefit programs for migrants and their children, and a persistent need for assistance in the domestic affairs of developing countries as a result of poor living conditions. These threaten the existence of the global order. To reverse the trend of events, middle-income countries advanced the Millennium Development Goals (MDGs) agenda that stressed eight universal values under the banner of the UNDP. The MDGs, however, gave the impression that the goals are concerned with the economic progress of all humanity (Oumar and Sama 2015). Nevertheless, the report named 'In Larger Freedom' indicated that the Millennium Development Goals of UNDP were guided by Sen's ideas (Annan 2005).

The MDGs proposed to achieve their agenda between 1990 and 2015. The primary agenda items of the MDGs focused on halving extreme poverty and hunger; creating full and productive employment and decent work for women and young people; giving children everywhere, boys and girls alike, at least a full course of primary education; eliminating gender disparity in all levels of education; and reducing child mortality rate by two-thirds. There were four other target goals on the agenda related to reducing maternal mortality and access to reproductive health; combating the incidence of HIV/AIDS, malaria, and other major diseases; ensuring environmental sustainability and sustainable access to safe drinking water and basic sanitation; developing a global partnership for trading and financial system with a commitment to good governance; and making available the benefits of information and communication technologies to LDCs (UNDP 2014). However, the record of successes in achieving these goals around the globe was mixed, and the targets were far from being achieved by LDCs at the end of the implementation period.

The MDGs have been replaced by a set of 17 sustainable development goals (SDGs) to transform the world by 2030. The goals are: GOAL 1: No Poverty, GOAL 2: Zero Hunger, GOAL 3: Good Health and Well-being, GOAL 4: Quality Education, GOAL 5: Gender Equality, GOAL 6: Clean Water and Sanitation, GOAL 7: Affordable and Clean Energy, GOAL 8: Decent Work and Economic Growth, GOAL 9: Industry,

Innovation, and Infrastructure, GOAL 10: Reduced Inequality, GOAL 11: Sustainable Cities and Communities, GOAL 12: Responsible Consumption and Production, GOAL 13: Climate Action, GOAL 14: Life Below Water, GOAL 15: Life on Land, GOAL 16: Peace and Justice Strong Institutions, and GOAL 17: Partnerships to achieve the Goal (UNDP 2019, https://www.un.org/sustainabledevelopment/sustainable-development-goals/).

Thus, the theories or models of economic development reviewed here have their strengths and weaknesses. All are significant, and all provide, in one way or the other, insights for our understanding of the dynamic process of economic development. But some theories are seemingly incompatible with others, and no single model can be proclaimed as universal and suitable for all situations because every developing country has different economic and social realities in spite of some commonalities among them.

A Picture of Economic and Social Progress of Bangladesh

Bangladesh started its journey as an independent nation in 1971 with all sorts of problems, a legacy of the more than two hundred years of colonial rule that culminated with the War of Independence. Ahsan (2018) summed up the post-liberation condition in the following way: "—in the wake of widespread devastation after nine months of the war, odds were stacked against Bangladesh. The war had destroyed thousands of roads, bridges, and culverts while Chittagong port—the lifeline to the world—lay blocked by mines and sunken ships. Ten million displaced individuals were returning from India, often to destroyed homes." With burnt schools, colleges, and marketplaces, no operative transport and distribution mechanisms, and a wholly shattered economy, Bangladesh was a true portrait of a bleak landscape. Soon it faced enormous new obstacles in terms of high population growth, mass poverty, famine, and the available resources to address these were direly insufficient. Nevertheless, Bangladesh mobilized its limited resources not only to overcome the 'bottomless basket' tag but also to advance impressively on its socioeconomic path. This section depicts the evolution of Bangladesh's economic and social development based on descriptive statistics, in some cases with comparative standpoints.

Table 1.1 has been prepared from the data in *World Development Indicators* (WDI) of the World Bank for some selected years between

1970 and 2018, to give a picture of the progress of Bangladesh. The year 1970 has been included in the table to identify some economic and social impacts during the year (and the year after the independence war). The progress Bangladesh has made since 1972 can be seen from the terminal figures of 2016, 2017, and 2018 included in the table. On the basis of these indicators and others, we will now proceed to discuss the economic and social progress Bangladesh has made.

Economic Growth

The economy forms the center of the success story of Bangladesh, considering the number of obstacles it faced to reach this stage. Table 1.1 includes five economic variables to show the state of gross domestic product (GDP), GDP growth rate, and per capita income position for Bangladesh. GDP has been presented in 'current US dollar' and 'constant 2010 US dollar' terms while 'per capita income' has been offered both in 'current international $' and 'Purchasing Power Parity' (PPP) values. In current price, Bangladesh has grown to become a US$274.0 billion economy in 2018 from a tiny US$8.8 billion in 1971, a 31.15-fold increase during this period. In terms of per capita income, the figures stood at $1698.3 in 2018 from $133.6 in 1971, a 12.7 times increase. In PPP terms, this stood at $4364 in 2018 from $860 in 1990, growing more than five-fold. What is interesting is that Bangladesh's "per capita income (in dollar terms) is now growing at nearly thrice the pace of income growth in India. —in 2016, Bangladesh's per capita income was up 40 percent in three years against 14 percent growth in India and 21 percent growth in Pakistan. At this rate, Bangladesh's per capita income would top India's by the year 2020" (Kant 2018).

As we have already pointed out, the inclusion of data for the economic and social indices for 1970 can give us an idea of the gravity of the economic and social problems Bangladesh experienced during the war of 1971. The severity of the war's impacts can be seen in the variables for which WDI data have been presented. All the indices for 1971 and 1972, be they GDP amount or growth rate, per capita income, import, export, gross capital formation, and so on, show a blanket deterioration from 1970. In 1971 and 1972, along with the drastic contraction of the economy, the birth rate also declined while the death rate went up.

Figure 1.1 depicts a further investigation of economic progress by including the GDP growth rate and GDP per capita at the current US$ for

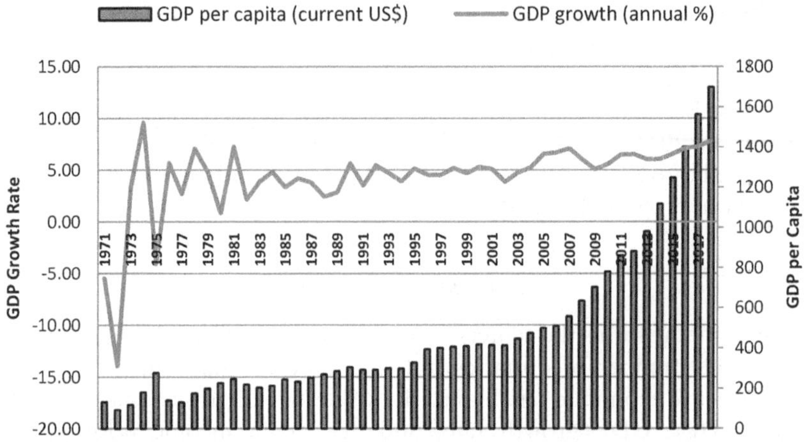

Fig. 1.1 GDP per capita and GDP growth rate, 1971–2018. (Source: World Bank 2019)

1971 to 2018. The growth story of Bangladesh can clearly be seen in the growth line. In the initial years of existence, the GDP growth rate of Bangladesh experienced massive turbulence due to the devastation of the war. For example, in 1971, the growth rate contracted by −5.5 percent, then further by −13.96 percent in 1972. However, the economy started to bounce back within a short time, as evident in the growth figure of 9.59 percent in 1974. But the aftermath of the Famine in 1974 is reflected in the contraction of the economy in 1975 by −4.09 percent. Interestingly, the economic growth figure of 9.59 percent in 1974, though it happened on the smaller GDP base of 1973, has so far remained the highest in the economic history of Bangladesh as the next highest rate of 7.8 percent was achieved only in 2018.

Structural Shift in GDP and Employment

Back in 1970, a year that was not disrupted economically, we find that the value-added of the primary sector (agriculture, forestry, and fishing) was 54.6 percent of GDP. However, in the 1970s, this sector saw the most significant structural reformation in terms of GDP contribution as its share came down to 32.8 percent in 1980. However, the pace of decline in the share was the lowest between 1980 and 1990, only 2.3 percent

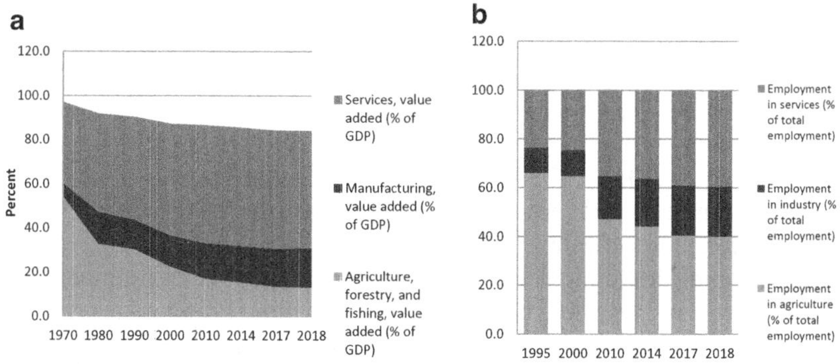

Fig. 1.2 (a) Sectoral contribution of GDP (%), 1970–2018; (b) sectoral share of employment, 1995–2018. (Source: World Bank 2019)

(from 32.8% to 30.5%), followed by 5.7 percent in the decade of the 2000s (from 22.7% to 17.0% between 2000 and 2010). The data for 2018 show further decline as the agriculture sector constituted 13.1 percent of GDP by this year (Fig. 1.2a).

The surprising change is the development of the service sector in Bangladesh economy. Since the 1970s, this sector has emerged as the largest contributor to GDP, replacing the agriculture sector, which was the single largest sector at the dawn of independent Bangladesh. With a 44.6 percent share in 1980, the service sector has gradually grown in subsequent decades and reached a peak in the 2000s. Since 2016, the share of this sector has been marginally declining—from 53.6 percent in 2014 to 53.5 percent in 2017, and then to 53.0 percent in 2018.

On the other hand, the manufacturing sector has generally remained the smallest contributor but has jumped to become the second largest sector recently. Its share rose from 5.8 percent to 16.1 percent between 1970 and 2010. But an expansion of industrial activities seems to have pushed its share up to surpass the agriculture sector in 2018; 17.3 percent versus 13.4 percent, respectively. The external demand for ready-made garments may have made a difference in this regard. Regardless of this, does the rise in the share of the manufacturing sector mark a new beginning of a structural shift in the economy of Bangladesh? As per the stages of economic growth, it seems to have taken a long time to happen, and was needed for the nation a long time ago.

By juxtaposing the shares of employment for agriculture, manufacturing, and service sectors against their GDP shares, we find an interesting picture. The available data for 1995 shows the sectoral shares of employment as 66.0 percent, 10.4 percent, and 23.6 percent for them, respectively. These employment distributions remained almost the same in 2000. Since then, however, a sizeable transformational shift had occurred by 2010 as the figures stood at 47.3 percent, 17.6 percent, and 35.1 percent, respectively. In 2018, the employment ratios changed further at 40.2 percent, 25.5 percent, and 39.4 percent, for the primary, secondary, and tertiary sectors, respectively.

Has Bangladesh followed Rostow's (1960) stages of development with the progress of time? Maybe, but after a long time. From an agricultural economy, the structural shift in terms of GDP contribution happened in the service sector within a short period of time, but the uneven development has not been able to address the fundamental economic problem—creating enough employment. The mass of people could have benefited more had an earlier push been given to build labor-intensive manufacturing industries rather than the service sector. Generally, the service sector is capital intensive and requires a smaller workforce, and that too has to be skilled and educated. So, the sectoral employment structure has remained highly disproportionate as the agriculture sector has continued to be the single largest employment source, though its share of GDP has declined to become the smallest among all sectors.

Poverty Reduction

Poverty in a society is the manifestation of many economic and non-economic underlying factors. For example, based on household consumption data, 82.9 percent of the population in Bangladesh lived below the poverty line in 1973–74 (Table 1.2), and the rate remained high in the 1970s, at about 71 percent of the population (Hossain 2014: 41). This very high incidence of poverty was seen as a consequence of the independence war, a very high inflation rate (about 40% annually), along with drought, flood, and famine in 1974, and political chaos during 1975–77 (Akash 2003: 129–132). Even in 1991–92, 58.8 percent of the population lived under the poverty line (Table 1.2). But since then, Bangladesh has scored a remarkable success in poverty reduction. "As recently as 2000, half of the country's population lived in poverty based on the national poverty line; by 2016, only 24.3 percent of Bangladeshis lived in poverty" (World Bank 2018a: 21). In fact, Bangladesh achieved the mark of reducing extreme poverty and hunger by 2013, the first target of the Millennium Development Goal (UNDP 2013: 64).

Table 1.2 Poverty trends in Bangladesh

Year	*Upper poverty line (% of the population)*			*Lower poverty line (% of the population)*		
	Rural	*Urban*	*National*	*Rural*	*Urban*	*National*
1973–74			82.9	–	–	–
1991–92	61.2	44.9	58.8	43.8	24.0	41.1
1995–96	54.5	27.8	50.1	39.5	13.7	35.2
2000	52.3	35.2	48.9	37.9	20.0	34.3
2005	43.8	28.4	40.0	28.6	14.6	25.1
2010	35.2	21.3	31.5	21.1	7.7	17.6
2016	26.4	18.9	24.3	19.8	10.8	12.9
2017	–	–	23.1[a]	–	–	12.1[a]
2018	–	–	21.8[a]	–	–	11.3[a]

Source: Compiled. Bangladesh Bureau of Statistics (BBS 2003, 2007, 2012 and 2018a) data from Bangladesh HIES 2000, 2005, 2010 and 2016 and GOB, General Economic Division, *vide* Kamal (2019: 102)
[a]Estimated

Table 1.2 also shows that the poverty situation and its reduction graph for Bangladesh nearly for the entire period of its existence. From the table, we can identify some of the features of the decline in poverty: First, the poverty reduction in Bangladesh was highest during the 2000–16 period as the national poverty level declined from 48.9 percent to 24.3 percent. Second, though both the rural and urban poverty rates have continued to decline, rural poverty has remained higher than urban poverty. Thirdly, between 2010 and 2016, the absolute poor in the urban areas increased, which went against the national trend.

Though Bangladesh may derive satisfaction from its success in poverty reduction, it still has one of the highest levels of poverty rate in South Asia as Fig. 1.3 highlights. Moreover, reports from World Bank indicate that poverty decline may have fallen into the 'law of diminishing marginal decline' trap, so the rate in decline is getting slower with the progress of time (World Bank 2018a).

Access to Finance and Financial Inclusion

In Bangladesh, the developmental impact of access to finance seems to have remained immense. Soon after independence, the number of people who had no or restricted access to formal sources of finance was deemed to be very high as 82.9 percent of the population lived below the poverty

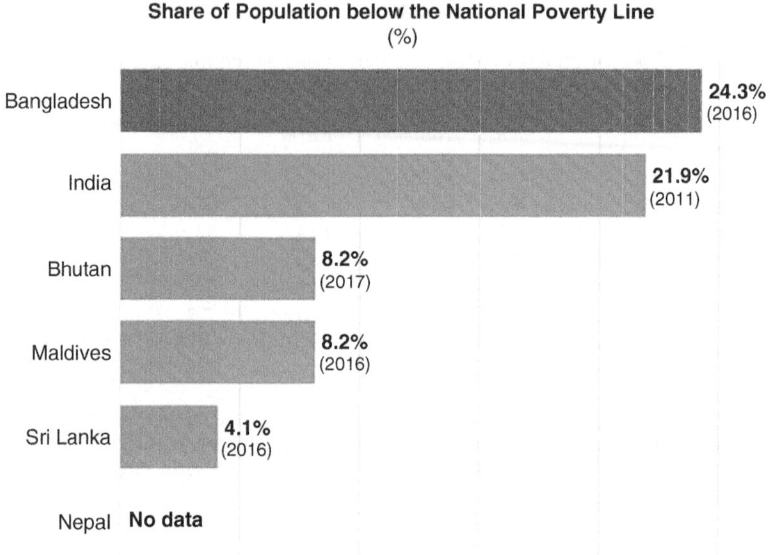

Fig. 1.3 Comparative poverty picture in South Asia. (Source: Asian Development Bank. *Basic statistics* 2019)

line in 1973–74 (Table 1.2). Understandably, a substantial portion of them was extremely poor. Giving them access to finance was an enormous challenge, and the introduction of microcredit with a model-based mechanism was a real innovation in the economic development context of Bangladesh at that point in time. This was done by Professor Md. Yunus, who began to lend small amounts of money to poor households under an action research project in 1976.[6] Since then, Bangladesh has come a long way to become a pioneering developing country to financially include the underprivileged in the society, particularly poor women through microfinance. The Microcredit Regulatory Authority (MRA) of Bangladesh estimates that a total of 25.11 million people or about 16 percent of the whole population of the country were the microcredit clients of around 670 Microfinance Institutions (MFIs) in June 2014 (MRA 2017).

However, financial inclusion (FI) in the broader sense means offering access to various financial products like credit, savings, payments, and the investments of different financial institutions. These financial instruments can be used for various consumption, income-generating, and investment-

Table 1.3 Households' access to financial market (%)

Area	*Any market (overall picture)*		*Formal market*		*Microfinance market*		*Informal market*	
	2010	*2014*	*2010*	*2014*	*2010*	*2014*	*2010*	*2014*
National	76.77	79.25	37.02	42.47	43.23	46.91	26.2	21.10
Rural	75.52	78.35	32.8	40.49	46.39	47.34	21.7	22.79
Urban	81.68	82.34	55.53	49.76	30.88	45.43	27.4	14.68
Non-poor	79.37	82.66	44.42	49.79	39.67	45.72	27.4	22.01
Poor	70.57	70.98	19.43	24.19	51.7	50.57	23.6	19.27

Source: Compiled. Data from Khalily et al. (2015)

related activities. As linkages, these activities should lead to the creation of long-term consumption demand, poverty reduction, income growth, employment, creation of social capital, and so on, affecting the development of a country.

Considering the socioeconomic context, Bangladesh seems to have achieved reasonable success in this area. Table 1.3 gives the level of households' access to the financial market or the FI position of Bangladesh for two years, namely, 2010 and 2014. As of 2014, about 80 percent of the households had access to financial markets—divided into formal, microfinance, and informal markets. Moreover, a 2014 study showed that around 40 percent of the adult population and 75 percent of households had access to financial services in Bangladesh (Khalily 2016: 11).

Interestingly, poor households in Bangladesh do not significantly differ from the rest as about 71 percent of them had access to financial markets against the national average of 80. Again, the rural and poor segments of the households dominated the microfinance market. The substantial presence of all sections of households in the informal market may not represent a healthy development, though. The proliferation of mobile banking in Bangladesh in recent years has added a new dimension in the overall digital FI, as in 2017, 14.48 percent of mobile phone users in Bangladesh have a mobile money account, presenting a lucrative opportunity for mass digital integration (BB 2018).

Rapid Urbanization

Urbanization is perceived to be the territorial response to structural changes in an economy. On its part, Bangladesh is seeing a process of adoption of the urban way of life through adaptation and large-scale migration of rural people to urban habitats. To substantiate this, in 1974, there were only 6.27 million people living in urban areas. The figure grew to over 39 million in 2011. The percentage of the population living in urban areas or the 'urbanization level' jumped from 8.78 percent to 27.66 percent during this period (Islam 2018). In between, the urban population grew to 19 percent by 1991, and 26 percent by 2005 (ADB 2012: 5). In an estimate of the World Bank (2012a), the average rate of urbanization in Bangladesh is 5 percent. According to Islam (2018), "the components of such rapid urban growth are: (i) A persistently high natural increase in the native urban population, (ii) The territorial extension of existing urban areas with the conversion of rural centers to urban ones, (iii) The re-definition of urban areas, and (iv) Rural to urban migration. Migration, of course, has been the most dominant component of urban population growth."

Like any other country in the world, this rapid urbanization in Bangladesh has vast economic significance. To substantiate, with a population share of about 28 percent, the contribution of the urban economy to GDP increased from 26 percent in 1973 to 42 percent in 1999. In 2012, the urban share of GDP became almost 50 percent, showing the rapid transformation of the economic structure of Bangladesh (ADB 2012). The developmental linkage of the urbanization of the economy lies with the construction of roads, the building of housing, education and health facilities, shopping malls, and other utilities. At the same time, cities attract domestic and international investment and bring jobs. In the whole process of urbanization, the structural shift in employment from primary to manufacturing and service sectors becomes an essential characteristic too. As we have seen, Bangladesh seems to be passing through this structural employment transformation, where the quick urbanization may have a role.

Success in Agriculture and Food Production

Historically, owing to the agrarian mode of social formation from ancient times, the agriculture sector has remained very important in the economy for the part of the world where Bangladesh is located. Even today, the sector has a substantial bearing on the economy of Bangladesh because, according to World Bank (2016), "More than 70 percent of Bangladesh's population and 77 percent of its workforce live in rural areas. Nearly half of all of Bangladesh's workers and two-thirds in rural areas are directly employed by agriculture, and about 87 percent of rural households rely on agriculture for at least part of their income." Moreover, due to its bitter experience of famine in 1974,[7] the issue of food sufficiency has remained very sensitive for Bangladesh.

With that background, "Bangladesh has made commendable progress over the past 40 years in achieving food security, despite frequent natural disasters and population growth (food grain production, for example, tripled between 1972 and 2014, from 9.8 to 34.4 million tons)" (World Bank 2016). Not only that, the agriculture sector has responded with a productivity growth supported by policy reforms in the 1980s, rapid irrigation expansion through groundwater pumps, better connectivity and linkages to packaging, processing, and widespread mechanization markets for farm products (and more efficient markets) through investment in roads, and technologization through the use of high-yielding plant varieties and fertilizer (Shahabuddin 2014). Table 1.4 lists some items of this transformation.

The reforms and investments have paid off in progress over the past 40 years in achieving food security, despite frequent natural disasters. Food grain production, for instance, tripled between 1972 and 2014, from 9.8 to 34.4 million tons (World Bank 2016). Table 1.5 shows that during 1990–2014, Bangladesh's agricultural sector registered an annual average

Table 1.4 Transformation of agriculture in Bangladesh (since the early 1970s)

Early 1970s (1972–73)	*Early 2010s (2012–13)*
Total food grain production: 10 million t	Total food grain production: 34 million t–35 million t
Average rice yield: 1 t/ha	Average rice yield: 3 t/ha
Less than 7% of net cultivated area is irrigated	More than 80% of net cultivated area is irrigated
Fertilizer use at 45 kg/ha (net sown area basis)	Fertilizer use at 530 kg/ha (net sown area basis)
Rainfed aus and aman = 78% of rice output	Irrigated boro = 57% of rice output
Total population: 71 million	Total population: 157 million
Food grain availability per capita: 410 g per day	Food grain availability per capita: 616–632 g per day

Source: Gautam and Rashid (2016)

Note: Aus is rice sown in March–April and harvested in the summer; aman is rice sown or transplanted in spring or summer and harvested in November–December; boro is rice grown in October–March dry season. g = grams; ha = hectare; kg = kilograms; t = tons (metric)

Table 1.5 Agriculture and population growth rates, 1990–2014 (%)

	1990–2014	*1990–99*	*2000–09*	*2000–04*	*2005–09*	*2010–14*
Agriculture, of which[a]:	3.7	2.3	4.2	2.7	5.0	3.2
Crops and horticulture	3.4	0.9	4.0	2.5	5.0	1.8
Animal farming	2.1	2.2	2.0	2.0	2.2	2.7
Forestry	4.5	3.3	5.0	4.9	5.3	5.3
Fishing	5.7	7.0	5.8	2.5	6.8	5.9
GDP[b]	5.2	4.5	5.6	4.5	6.1	6.1
Population[c]	1.6	2.1	1.3	1.5	1.1	1.2

Source: Gautam and Rashid (2016)
[a]Growth rates are trend growth rates for specific periods
[b]GDP data in constant FY 2005 prices from BBS
[c]Population growth rate from WDI (World Bank)

of 3.7 percent productivity growth, which was one of the fastest rates of growth in the world (second only to China). The average annual growth rate of 3.4 percent for crops and horticulture for the same period was much higher than the annual 1.6 percent population growth for the same period. Above all, "Bangladesh's rural economy, and specifically agriculture have been powerful drivers of poverty reduction in Bangladesh since 2000. Indeed, agriculture accounted for 90 percent of the reduction in poverty between 2005 and 2010" (World Bank 2016). Bangladesh has a target to be a food sufficient country by 2021.

Externalization of Bangladesh Economy

Bangladesh initiated the economic liberalization and globalization (L&G) process from the late 1970s and has continued to follow the neo-liberal path since then. As a member of the World Trade Organization (WTO) from the very first day of 1995, it has significantly reduced many tariff and non-tariff barriers to the movement of trade and investment. Its trade now is more than 38 percent of GDP (as of 2018, trade US$104.8/GDP US$274 billion (Table 1.1)); has a low tariff regime; allows a floating exchange rate, and so on. However, in the entire process of externalization of the economy, the success and hence importance of two factors in particular, namely exports of ready-made garments (RMG) and inflow of foreign remittances have become very significant. Indeed, the RMG has emerged to be the strategic sector for Bangladesh as it has been consistently contributing more than 80 percent export earnings since FY2013–14. This share has gone up to 84.21 percent in FY2018–19 as total earnings from RMG export stood at US$34.13 billion as against total exports of US$40.54 billion (Bangladesh Garments Manufacturers and Exporters Association 2019). In the meanwhile, Bangladesh has also emerged as the second-largest exporter of RMG in the world behind China (Fig. 1.4).

Likewise, remittances have emerged as a source of net inflow of foreign wealth in the economy of Bangladesh. Historically, petrodollars[8] induced massive investments in infrastructures in the Middle East countries in the 1970s, and rapid economic development of the newly industrialized economies (NIEs)[9] and Japan in the 1980s and 1990s created a high demand for cheap foreign labor in both the regions (Cruz 2005: 23). Fortunately, both these economic events created scope for short term employment opportunities for workers of labor-surplus Bangladesh. The World Bank's Migration and Remittances Data for 2017 estimated that Bangladesh has a total stock of 7.8 million migrants worldwide (World Bank 2018b), equivalent to about 4.9 percent of its total population, up from 5.38 million migrants in 2010 (World Bank 2012b: 58).

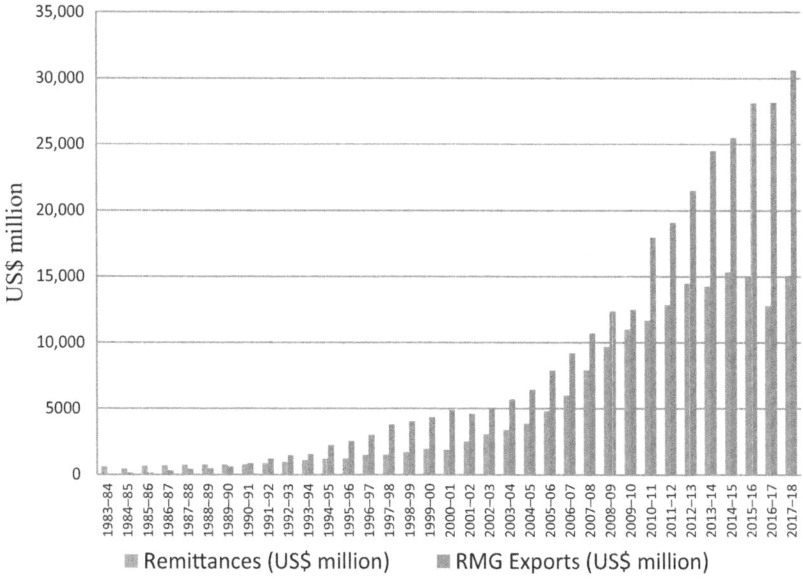

Fig. 1.4 Remittances inflow and RMG exports, 1983–84 to 2017–18. (Source: Constructed. Remittances data from MoF (2019), RMG export data from Bangladesh and BGMEA (2019), and trade information)

As a parallel development, the flow of inward remittances accelerated to become a regular and substantial source of wealth transfer to Bangladesh. However, remittances were trivial in size until 2000 and had little developmental relevance. But remittances now stand many folds to its foreign direct investment (FDI) and official development assistance (ODA) combined. According to the World Bank, the estimated remittances to Bangladesh have reached US$15.9 billion in 2018, making it the 8th largest remittance recipient country in the world (World Bank 2018b).

The economic and social developmental impacts of both these factors for Bangladesh are visible. For example, RMG-led investment and export has been playing a role in the transformation of entrepreneurial, economic, trade, and employment structures of the country. Due to labor-intensive and women employment friendly nature, the sector has been playing a role for the economic empowerment of women in the country as well. According to Rahman and Rahman (2016: 7), out of 4 million employees in the RMG sector, 3.2 million or 80 percent are women, contributing 11.26 percent of GDP. Similarly, getting overseas employment opportunities was a welcome relief for Bangladesh as its development strategies could not cope up with and accommodate the growing demand for employment from a fast-growing population. The consequent regular and high flows of remittances have upended the developmental significance of remittances, both in social and economic sectors, in the eyes of the policy strategists (Barai 2012).

Advances in Various Socioeconomic Indicators

Indeed, Bangladesh has remained a star performer in many social and economic indicators among the developing countries. In some areas, it has surpassed its neighbors in the recent past. The direct and indirect effects of these variables on development should not be overlooked in the context of our discussion. Figures 1.5a, b, c, and d have been drawn together to present the progress Bangladesh has made in the areas or population growth, life expectancy, adult literacy rate, and HD Index.

Though Bangladesh has remained a densely populated country and the overall number of people has remained a cause of concern, it has successfully lower the growth rate of population to a sustainable rate. As early as 2005, the population was still growing at 1.49 percent per year, which came down to 1.36 percent in 2009. Since 2013, the rate seems to have stabilized at 1.37 percent. But the underlying cause of concern remains, as the fertility rate of women in Bangladesh is still very high, 2.067 as of

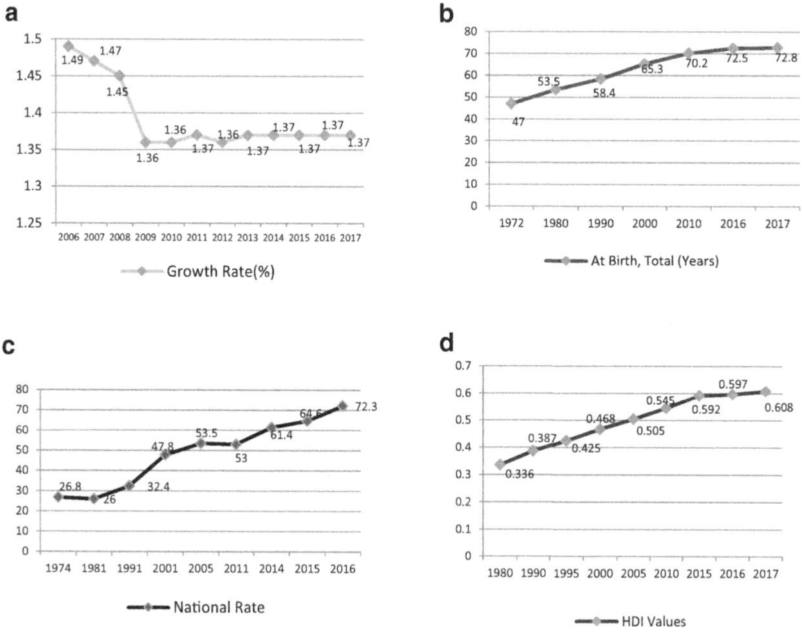

Fig. 1.5 (a) Population growth rate (%), (b) life expectancy at birth, (c) adult literacy rate, and (d) HD Index. (Sources: Constructed. Data sources are as follows—(a) Bangladesh Bureau of Statistics (BBS) and General Economic Division, GOB; *vide* Kamal (2019: 102), (b) World Bank (2019). World Development Indicator, (c) BBS (2001), Population Census of 1991 and 2001; BBS (2018b). Statistical Yearbook 2017, (d) UNDP (2018)

2019 (World Population Review 2019). Streatfield and Ahsan (2008) argued that if fertility rate declined through replacement rate to the level of Thailand (TFR or Total Fertility Rate around 1.8), the final population in Bangladesh could stop growing at 205–210 million, some 50–55 million lower than otherwise would be the case. Anyway, an increase in life expectancy at birth is another area where Bangladesh has achieved spectacular success. While in 1972, the life-span on average was only 47 years, this had risen to 72.8 years in 2017 (Fig. 1.5b). Also, though Bangladesh still has a lot of ground to cover in the field of literacy, it had reached an adult literacy rate of 72.3 percent (Fig. 1.5c) in 2016 from a low of 26.4 percent in 1974. The success here had started peaking since 2011, when 53 percent of adult male and female Bangladeshis were literate.

As we know, economic growth helps countries to improve their human development status in this way, but many studies have found two-way causal relations between growth and human development. That is, human development helps economies to grow and vice versa. In Bangladesh, human development indicators had improved even before a high economic growth was achieved. If female school enrolment is considered a proxy for human development, then Bangladesh's human development sharply improved from 1990 to 2017. Figure 1.5d shows Bangladesh's progress in the HDI indicator.[10] According to the UNDP's Human Development Indices and Indicators, the HDI value for 2017 was 0.608—which put the country in the medium human development category—giving it the rank of 136 among 189 countries in the world. Between 1990 and 2017, Bangladesh's HDI value increased from 0.387 to 0.608, an increase of 57.1 percent (UNDP 2018).

Empowerment of Women

Women make up about half of the population in Bangladesh, and much of the social change it has achieved may be attributed to the economic participation and empowerment of women in society. A supportive environment through various policy measures to ensure women's advancement to have control over their lives and role in society decision-making has helped the process. Both the government and NGOs played an important role in this regard. This is reflected by the efforts made in the 1990s to increase primary education, bring gender parity in secondary education through financial incentives to female students, and improve maternal mortality. Subsequently, the economic participation of women in the economy increased as 18.6 million women were working in 2016–17 up from 16.2 million in 2010 (Chaity 2018).

The resultant reduction in the gender gap for women in Bangladesh is very significant. The World Economic Forum that prepares the Global Gender Gap Index (GGGI) based on the four measures of economic participation, educational achievement, health and survival, and political empowerment, put Bangladesh in the top spot among the South Asian countries for the third consecutive year in 2018. Placed at 48th position in the global context, Bangladesh is well ahead of its neighbors Sri Lanka (100th), Nepal (105th), India (108th) and Pakistan (148th) (Table 1.6). Figure 1.6 shows how the gap in the adult literacy rate between male and female adults has declined over the years.

Table 1.6 Bangladesh in the Global Gender Gap Index, 2018

Country	*Global index*		*Economic participation and opportunity*		*Educational attainment*		*Health and survival*		*Political empowerment*	
	Rank	*Score (0–1)*	*Rank*	*Score (0–1)*	*Rank*	*Score (0–1)*	*Rank*	*Score (0–1)*	*Rank*	*Score (0–1)*
South Asia										
Bangladesh	48	0.721	133	0.441	116	0.950	117	0.969	5	0.526
Sri Lanka	100	0.676	125	0.549	90	0.988	1	0.980	65	0.188
Nepal	105	0.671	110	0.608	123	0.926	128	0.966	66	0.185
India	108	0.665	142	0.385	114	0.953	147	0.940	19	0.382
Pakistan	148	0.550	146	0.318	139	0.810	145	0.946	97	0.127
Other Asian countries										
Cambodia	93	0.683	45	0.719	119	0.938	75	0.975	108	0.102
China	103	0.673	86	0.653	111	0.958	149	0.915	78	0.164
Japan	110	0.662	117	0.595	65	0.994	41	0.979	125	0.081

Source: Compiled. Data from the WEF (2018: 10–11)

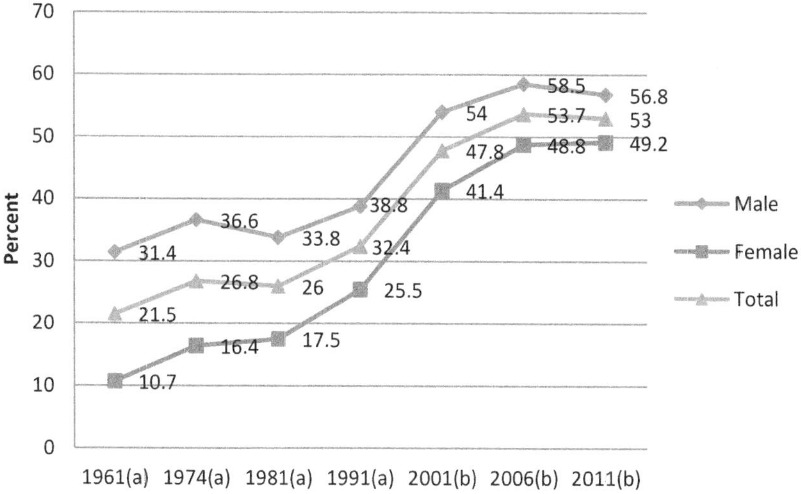

Fig. 1.6 Literacy rate persons for 15 years and over by sex, 1961–2011. (Source: (a) BBS (2001), Population Census 2001, (b) BBS (2018))

GO-NGOs Partnership

One of the signature elements of the present socioeconomic success of Bangladesh has been the working of government and non-government organizations (GO-NGOs) together. In fact, scholars tend to describe the Bangladesh development pattern as an 'NGO model'. Indeed, there was a surge of NGOs of different categories launching different programs after independence (Mohammad 2018). The NGO Affairs Bureau (NGOAB) gives an estimate that currently 2239 local and 255 foreign-registered NGOs are working in Bangladesh (NGOAB 2020). In addition to credit delivery, Bangladeshi NGO-MFIs are working tirelessly on overall social capacity development for rural population through relief and rehabilitation (such as *Swanirvor Bangladesh* and *Terre Des Hommes*), education (BRAC), health and family planning (Gono Shastho Kendra), microcredit (BRAC, ASA), empowerment and legal support (BELA), infrastructure development (DANIDA), sanitation and water supply (CARE), sustainable development programs (OXFAM), and research and communication (BRAC) (Bangladesh Bank 2018).

Understandably, Bangladesh's 'Development Surprise' comprises sustained economic growth; advancement in social indicators such as the reduction of population growth, improvement in food security through increased production of rice, reduction in crude death rate, and infant mortality rate; increase in literacy rate and attendance rate of children in primary schools; and elimination of gender disparity in secondary schools. And for the betterment of all these socioeconomic factors over the last four decades, NGOs have played a crucial role in supporting government initiatives. They also have collaborated with the corporate sector, civil society, and development partners in this regard. Despite the dwindling land base, falling fertility, the existence of a rural poverty cycle, and population growth pressure, Bangladesh also achieved many of the earlier MDGs. A strong presence of NGOs has helped the scaling up of programs through the spread of new ideas (Mahmud 2017), as an added quick-functionary organ of the country. Asadullah et al. (2014) suggest that these NGOs contributed to the development outcomes for which Bangladesh has been applauded by the international community. Undoubtedly, these achievements have resulted from a coordinated and cooperative approach involving the government, NGOs, and private organizations.

Explaining the Development Surprise of Bangladesh

How can we explain the 'Development Surprise' of Bangladesh? Has Bangladesh been following or complying with any or some of the existing theories to frame a development model of its own? Does the current literature identify all the development catalysts that explain the surprise success of Bangladesh? Are there more factors playing a role in this regard but are yet to come in the development discourse of Bangladesh? We make an attempt to address these questions in the following section.

Bangladesh's Development: Framing of a Model in Compliance with Existing Theories

In the section 'Competing Theories of Economic Development' of this chapter, we included most of the critical theories of development. This was followed by the section 'A Picture of Economic and Social Progress' that depicted key areas of economic and social progress Bangladesh made on its journey so far. With this background, we are now in a position to assess whether a single model and some of them can explain suitably the development progress of Bangladesh in its entirety. Table 1.7 makes an attempt in this regard.

So, by looking through the prism of development theories, we find the development path that Bangladesh has followed resembles not just one but many of them at the same time. In fact, not a single model can fully explain the development progress of Bangladesh in its entirety. This is because of the different economic and social realities, and peculiarities Bangladesh has in spite of some common features with the rest of the developing countries in the world. Moreover, of the theories themselves, some are seemingly compatible, while a few are irreconcilable with others. So explaining the development of Bangladesh in the frame of these theories could be difficult.

Indeed, like the country itself, the path Bangladesh followed for development changed over time. At its dawn as an independent nation, it embarked on the ideology of socialism by nationalizing manufacturing, financial, and public utilities. Then it deviated to the neoclassical counter-revolution model in the 1980s and 1990s. By the end of the 1990s, the relative importance of the state as a producer of goods declined to 20 percent of the total manufacturing output (World Bank 2000a). The pres-

Table 1.7 Development theories and their relevance to Bangladesh's progress

Competing theories of development		*Analyzing Bangladesh's development*
1. Formative stage or classical development views		
Capitalism	Free trade, private ownership of factors of production, and competition, freedom of action brings out the best in individuals which in turn increases society wealth (Smith 1976).	Since independence, Bangladesh was never a fully Capitalist economy.
Communism	Through exploitation, capitalists create surplus value, social or public ownership of property, and independence of foreign capital and goods (Marx 1933).	Soon after independence, Bangladesh nationalized banks and industries in 1972 as a first step to establish socialism, one of the four preambles of the first constitution.
The Malthusian model of population growth	Technological change is constant, but increasing inputs could lead to diminishing returns and a high level of the population reduces income per capita (Malthus 1798).	Initially, Bangladesh looked to be a classic case of the Malthus theory, having learned lessons and instituting strong population control measures. Was Malthus important? Seems to be so.
2. Neo/Classical theories on development		
The linear-stages-of-growth models	1. Rostow's Stages Growth Model (Rostow 1960) 2. Harrod–Domar Model (Harrod 1939; Domar 1946) (Development of countries is a process incorporating a series of successive stages of economic growth; savings and investments and foreign aid were necessary to enable developing nations to proceed along an economic growth path).	The government pursued policies to raise domestic savings for investment and capital formation, foreign aid through government and private (NGOs) routes were always welcome.
Structural change models	1. Lewis Two-Sector Surplus-Labor Theory (Lewis 1954) 2. Structural Change and Patterns of Development (Chenery 1960) (Transferring resources from low to high-productivity activities—from traditional/agricultural to modern/industrial sector, unlimited supply of labor at subsistence wage levels)	Like China, Bangladesh is another classic case of labor supply from the agricultural sector to the manufacturing sector, which is transforming the economic sectoral structure. The garment industry and urbanization have become the face of that change.

International dependence models	1. Neocolonial Dependence Model 2. False-paradigm model 3. Dualistic-Development Theory (Withdrawal from the international economy and pursuit of self-sufficiency or autarky to overcome the dependence)	From 1971 to 1975, due to colonial background and exploitation by the colonial masters this model seemed to fit the government's initiative to introduce 'Bakshal'[a] in 1974, a prelude to becoming a socialist country.
Neoclassical counter-revolution models	1. Free market approach (FMA), 2. New political economy approach (PEA)/Free Choice Approach (FCA) 3. Market-friendly approach (MFA) 4. Solow's (1956) neoclassical development thought/The traditional neoclassical growth theory (Liberalization, globalization, privatization, and stabilization, countering the international dependence models)	With the change of government, in the late 1970s and 1980s Bangladesh saw the sweeping economic changes through liberalization and globalization process, a political and economic counter-revolution. Industries and banks were divested, market forces were allowed to operate, and NGOs' participation was enshrined in the development paradigm.
3. Development of contemporary theories		
New growth theory	For a successful development to occur, there must be effective and efficient coordination of complementarities among the various stakeholders of the development process. The theory emphasizes that it is the use of knowledge rather than labor and capital that brings increasing returns to economic growth. Knowledge or innovation will lead to growth.	But over a period of time, especially under the Awami League Government, the political economy of Bangladesh seems to take shape where the government has more engaged in a more ***dirigiste*** development strategy, bringing the government at the center for development planning and execution.
Theory of coordination failure	Underdevelopment as a coordination failure among complementary activities and government intervention is needed to move the economy to a preferred equilibrium. The coordination failure economists highly advocated the role of the government, particularly in the presence of multiple equilibria circumstances in the economy.	But, at the same time, government intervention has been partial in setting the equilibrium process. Infrastructure for road transport and transport vehicle ownership shows that leaving spaces for the development stakeholders remains an integral part of the intervention strategy.

(*continued*)

Table 1.7 (continued)

Competing theories of development		*Analyzing Bangladesh's development*
Sen's theory of development	A process of expanding the real freedoms that people enjoy. This happens through focusing on increasing citizens' access and opportunities to the things they have reason to value.	Because of the socialistic orientation from the very beginning, endeavor to give citizens to various things they really value has remained a part of the development strategy of Bangladesh. Access to microfinance, increasing the social safety net, providing access to information, and so on are examples.
Millennium and sustainable development goal/ development goals	Though not a model but a goal-based approach to development for developing countries. A total of 15 Goals are there to achieve.	Bangladesh is a participatory country and appreciated very much for making impressive progress in areas like poverty reduction, gender equality, and empowerment of women.

Source: Author

[a]'Bangladesh Worker-Peasant's People's League' or BAKSAL was the political platform floated as the national party of Bangladesh by 'Father of the Nation' Sheikh Mujibur Rahman in February 1975. Bangladesh Awami League, Communist Party of Bangladesh, National Awami Party (Mozaffar) and Jatiyo League parties were merged together to form BAKSAL to place the Second Revolution in the country. All other political parties were banned in Bangladesh with the formation of BAKSAL. BAKSAL was, however, dissolved after the assassination of its founding father in August 1975

ence of the state marked a rapid decline in all manufacturing, financial, and service sectors in the subsequent years.

But with changes in time, passing the power button to different political parties, and developmental realities, it drifted further in its economic growth strategy from the theoretical line in the 2000s. At the moment, the management of the economic affairs looks quite close to both the New Classical Counter-Revolution Theory and the Theory of Coordination Failure, *albeit* these are two not-so-compatible models. The role of government in economic management has become paramount, though the ownership of the economic agents in the markets remains mostly with the private player. Say, for example, through a big push in infrastructure development, the government is trying to bring a preferred equilibrium in the transport and communication sector. This may be an initiative under the Theory of Coordination Failure, where the government's participation and approach are to coordinate and encourage complementarities among the various stakeholders for establishing equilibria in multiple situations. But, at the same time, users of the infrastructure projects for the business purpose mostly are from the private sector, compatible with the idea of the New Classical Counter-Revolution Theory.

Let us elaborate this further. For example, in the FY 2019–20 national budget, the transport and highway division alone has been allocated more than BDT 252 billion, or 12.41 percent, and the transport and communication sector overall received 26.1 percent of the total development budget (New Age 2019). The allocations for the transport sector could be understood by the fact that the ownership of all national and regional highways lies with the state. At the same time, vehicles, except the state-run BRTC buses, using the roads for transporting people are privately owned. While the ownership and operational responsibilities of the railway have remained solely with the state, air, road, and water transport systems are seeing the same patterns of ownerships distribution as for roads.

This opens further discussion on various stakeholders in the economy and a development linkage framework existing in the Bangladesh economy. In fact, we find the presence of four economic entities in the economy—the government itself, the private sector, NGOs, and households with ordinary citizens. Though international bodies, agencies, and governments may be parties to the development process of Bangladesh, we assume their views are reflected by the intentions and actions of one or more of the four entities we have already taken into consideration. So, from the point of the theory of growth and coordination failure,

Bangladesh seems to have moved to the direction of a 'Solidarity Development Model', where all the entities are intentionally and unintentionally working toward their self and national development goals. Interestingly, all the agents form both the supply and demand sides, at the same time.

In Fig. 1.7, we have drawn a network (Solidarity Economic Development Model or SEDM) linking all the agents to major development issues and

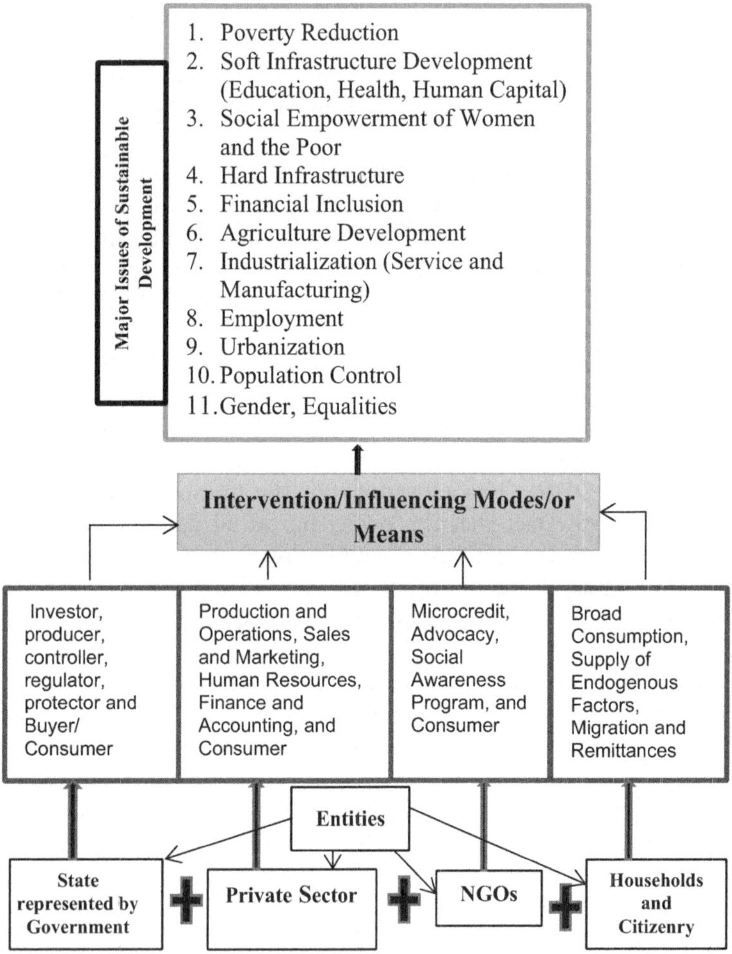

Fig. 1.7 Solidarity Economic Development Model (SEDM). (Source: Author)

are trying to prepare an inventory of the specific issues they respectively are connected with. Once again, it has to be noted that the linkages of entities with the primary issues are in the roles of both demand and supply agents:

(a) *The State Represented by the Government*: It is no surprise that the government is representative of both the people and the state at the same time and it is linked with all the 11 developmental issues we have listed here. These linkages or roles are established in the forms of the investor, producer, controller, regulator, and protector. The government is also the single largest buyer or consumer in the economy;
(b) *Private Sector*: The sector is primarily playing a role in the development of industries (manufacturing and services), employment, soft infrastructure development (education, health, and human capital), financial inclusion and agriculture development, indirectly the sector may be linked to some other issues, though. Again, various actions and roles are performed by the sector through production and operations, sales and marketing, human resources, finance and accounting, and finally, as a consumer.
(c) *Non-Government Organizations (NGOs)*: NGOs have gotten embedded in the entire development effort in Bangladesh in such a profound way that may not have any parallel in the world. Through their interventions of microcredit, advocacy, social-awareness program, and role as a unit of consumer, they have directly affected poverty reduction, social empowerment of women, gender and the poor, financial inclusion, education, health and hygiene, employment and population control. In fact, NGOs have impacted the economic and social lives of most of the people in Bangladesh.
(d) *Households and Citizenry*: Like the government, households and common people are parties to all the developmental activities that take place in the country in the capacity of buyers and/or sellers. But we can list some of the issues where they have predominant role linkages like poverty reduction, soft infrastructure development (education, health, and human capital), agriculture development, population control, and urbanization. The modes and means that have been used by them to be part of the development process are broad consumption, the supply of endogenous factors, migration, and remittances. Moreover, mass people have participated in

most of the development programs the government has initiated, except a few projects faced hostilities of the local residents and a section of the intelligentsia and political parties.[11]

Explaining the Factors Behind Social and Economic Success

In the previous section, though we have tried to see development efforts through the prism of development theories, we could not clearly identify the factors that have allowed for Bangladesh to reach a level of economic and social progress that is now more popularly described as a 'development surprise'. For Bangladesh, the progress in all areas is very impressive. In dealing with this issue, we have to keep in mind that though social development can synergize economic development and vice versa, they may not always go hand in hand. Say, for example, Kenya, which is almost at par with Bangladesh in HDI (Kenya 0.590 against Bangladesh's 0.608 in 2017) (UNDP 2018), could not match Bangladesh in terms of economic growth for about a decade. We have also pointed out earlier that emphasis on human capital creation, especially in sub-Saharan Africa has improved life expectancy and school enrolment rates substantially but not economic growth since the early 1970s (Meier 2000; World Bank 2000b). So, Bangladesh's human development and economic achievements may not be explained by the typical pathways to growth.

While dealing with pathways to human development, Sen (1999) argued that these could be 'income-mediated' and 'support-led'. While 'income-mediated' improvement in social indicators can be linked back to rapid- and broad-based economic growth (exemplified by Korea), 'support-led' development results from high public spending on welfare programs. South Korea and Sri Lanka are examples of those development approaches, respectively. Interestingly, Bangladesh does not fit either of these cases. Though the economic growth rate for Bangladesh rose significantly after 1990, it reached 6 percent only in 2003–04. At the same time, Bangladesh's "spending on education and healthcare (2.2 percent and 3.5 percent, respectively, of GDP in 2012) is below the average for low-income countries. Several other countries in South and Southeast Asia have grown at similar or higher rates than Bangladesh in the last 10 to 15 years, including India, Bhutan, Vietnam, Cambodia, and Laos. Yet, in comparison to these countries, Bangladesh's social development still stands out" (Al-Muti 2014). A look at Figs. 1.5a, b, c, and d can clarify this further.

In any case, to find the development pathways for Bangladesh, Asadullah et al. (2014) empirically investigated a number of possible variables, like trends in public expenditure for health, education; development of physical infrastructure, the construction of roads, bridges, and culverts; foreign aid, economic growth, public infrastructure, and so on. They observed relatively little emphasis on public spending for the soft and hard infrastructure in the 1980s, though that changed in the 1990s. However, their study found limited evidence in support of income-mediated and/or public expenditure (e.g., foreign aid, government spending)-led channels for social development in Bangladesh. But their study highlighted the simultaneous happening of several things to cause the development surprise. These include an inclusive development strategy in partnership with various non-government stakeholders, the NGOs in particular. They viewed this was instrumental to the social progress Bangladesh achieved. Reduction in fertility and child mortality, low-cost solutions for various socioeconomic problems, creation of social awareness, useful synergies between different social indicators, gender parity in schooling triggered by the introduction of demand-side incentive schemes, and so on played a role. Another set of "contextual factors such as history, demography, cultural heritage, and geography are likely to have shaped Bangladesh's development context. Putting women in the forefront, scale-up of innovations and resilience against natural disaster were also significant" (Asadullah et al. 2014: 151).

While going through the paper of Asadullah et al. (2014), the larger than life emphasis on the developmental role of NGOs seems to be interesting. This is not to mean that NGOs did not play an essential role in regard to the development of Bangladesh, but that should not overshadow the centrality of the role of successive governments in Bangladesh. We are of the view that the necessary first condition for the development of Bangladesh remains the government. As Hoff and Stiglitz (2000: 415) argue, "most of the 'success' cases of economic growth have involved heavy doses of government intervention. For instance, in the United States, the government has long played a role in financial market regulation (since 1863). The fact is that government is endowed with powers that the private sector does not have, and these powers are essential in addressing the public good/externality problems that are rife throughout the economy." The economic and social role of the Government of Bangladesh is fundamentally based on these powers. Mahmud (2017) takes into consideration this point while espousing his views on the pathways to human development in Bangladesh. His identified pathways are low-cost solutions and social mobilization, broad-based social and economic development, and government commitment.

Taking a political economy perspective, Hossain (2017) "argues that the key to Bangladesh's development success lies in understanding *why a strong political consensus emerged to pursue such a pro-poor development policy across governments and regimes*" (Tudor 2018). Hossain (2017) recognizes the critical role of the state "through its pursuit of a six-point plan: by creating sound macroeconomic policies; improving disaster management; making sound investments in public health and education; partnering with NGOs; supporting family planning; and encouraging labor migration" (Tudor 2018).

It should be noted that the exercise of finding and explaining the pathways to development in Bangladesh seems to have been done during the period up to the 2000s. Since then, the economy is on the verge of crossing the growth barrier of eight percent, the literacy rate has gone up, and life expectancy has increased further. So, by looking at the previous development path and the upsurge in economic and social indicators lately, one may have a feeling that there might be some other factors that may not have been investigated for their role in the development discussion of Bangladesh. In fact, their contribution may be significant in synergizing and compounding economic and social progress.

Role of Some Unexplained Factors

The incidence of overlooking the possible development role of some factors has promoted us to take them up in this section. Surprisingly, they seem to have remained unattended by development researchers so far. However, explaining Bangladesh's development without adequately assessing their role may fail to duly unravel the package of factors that may have synergized the development in an unseen and undetected way. We, however, caution the reader that further research needs to be done to examine and locate their exact contribution to the development process of Bangladesh.

Density of Population

In Bangladesh, both the number and the density of population are considered to drag on the overall development effort. To understand the gravity of the situation, let us look at a comparative picture of two countries, namely Bangladesh and Canada, on these grounds. As of 2017, Bangladesh, with a surface area of 147.6 thousand km^2, housed an estimated 164.7 million people (World Bank 2018a), giving a population density of 1115.62 people per square kilometer, while Canada, physically the second-largest country in the world, has an estimated population of 37.06 million (Statics of Canada 2018). That also means, despite being physically 67.5 times smaller than Canada, Bangladesh is 4.4 times bigger than it in population terms. In fact, Bangladesh is the tenth most densely populated country in the world. Thus, in the context of recent economic and social progress in Bangladesh, the question that comes to the fore is the role of population density in that progress.

Keeping the negative externalities of the larger size of the population in mind, we have to emphasize that it also means a larger labor force and a higher demand for domestic goods and services, which may push production activities upward. Indeed, there is a positive correlation between the denser population and the dissemination of technology and technological benefits from dissemination of information (Hakeem 2017). Similarly, believers in the benefits of higher population density think that it creates more scarcity and generates a stronger drive in humans to develop technology and to innovate. Boserup (1981) finds that population growth creates pressure on resources and stimulates resourceful people to innovate, especially in adversity. That may explain the linkage of higher density to greater innovation and a variety of technical skills.

The overcrowding in agriculture has associated short- and medium-run costs, but higher population density on agricultural land has a positive influence on infrastructural investment in transportation, communication, irrigation, markets, and so on (National Research Council 1986: 47–52). This might be happening in Bangladesh with the participation of the Government, private sector, and households.

Access to Production and Information Technology

The level of penetration of communication technology, particularly mobile phones and the internet, and production technology in agriculture could be pointers to the development analysts to find their influence in explaining the late surge in economic growth rate in Bangladesh. For instance, there were a total of 0.40 million users of mobile phones in 2004, but more than 157.5 million in January 2019. Most of the subscribers use private mobile phone companies' SIM cards (MoF 2019: 257). Again, there has been a quick rise in the total number of internet subscribers as well, to 91.4 million at the end of January 2019. Of the total internet subscribers, 85.6 million use mobile internet services (BTRC 2018).

A spillover effect of mobile users and their massive growth is the introduction of mobile banking (MB) in Bangladesh in 2011. MB offers the most popular tool for digital financial integration with little paperwork and almost no cost to open a mobile money account at nearby small agent outlets. Such accounts offer a number of services like cash out, cash payment, fund transfer, mobile recharge, bill payment, and balance inquiry facility with a low charge from a mobile phone. Due to the ease of operation and minimal financial literacy requirement, mobile banking has experienced an explosive growth of 2924.17 times in its six years of operation. In 2017, covering over 14.48 percent of mobile phone users with a mobile money account, more than 1875.64 million transactions were recorded in 481,081 mobile money outlets (Bangladesh Bank 2018). The developmental impact of such a digital financial innovation needs investigation.

The progress in agriculture production technology is another area where Bangladesh has excelled a lot. Uses of high-yielding varieties (HYV) of rice technology with corresponding support in the provision of modern inputs, such as chemical fertilizers, pesticides, institutional credit, product procurement, storage, improvement in the method and equipment for land tilling and irrigation, use of agricultural extension technology, diversification of cropping systems, and so on are considered to have played a role. But what is the role of communication technologies in the diffusion and access to modern knowledge and equipment of the farming communities? This could be quite important and significant.

Speed in Sharing Information at a Low/No Cost

In Bangladesh, some developments related to information and communication technology (ICT) are taking place simultaneously. While the number of communication gadgets used is increasing very rapidly, the cost of their uses is also declining fast at the same time, making the case of bidirectional causality. This has, however, affected two qualitative dimensions of the flow of information—speed and surface coverage. On the one hand, information—be it social, cultural, economic, or business in nature—is spreading in the communities very fast. Similarly, the coverage of the same information is getting bigger and bigger. Again, population density seems to have a role here. Klasen and Nestmann (2006) pointed out that there exists a concave relationship between population density and technological change and diffusion. The issue that has contextual importance here is—how far does this low cost or no cost speedy spread of information impact the economic, social, and behavioral response of the people that may have development connotations? We believe that this phenomenon is not without its negative externalities, but positive externalities with development leaning should be much higher in Bangladesh. The growth of a new net-based entrepreneurial class, online businesses, financial transactions, health services, education, and so on is much more real. The question of the digital divide may arise in society, but the trend cannot be overlooked.

The Role of Returnee Migrants

Though Bangladesh has a well-documented picture on the number of migrants leaving for overseas countries and the remittances they send back since 1977, it is almost a secret that no dependable figure is available for the returnee migrants in Bangladesh. By returnee migrants, we mean the people who came back to Bangladesh from their overseas employment base to settle in the home country.

As we can see, the World Bank's Migration and Remittances Data for 2017 estimated that Bangladesh has a total stock of 7.8 million migrants worldwide (World Bank 2018b), equivalent to about 4.9 percent of its total population, up from 5.38 million migrants in 2010 (World Bank 2012b: 58). This volume gives us the idea that the people who came back to live in Bangladesh continue to be substantial.

What is the developmental role of these returnee migrants in Bangladesh? For that matter, we have not come across any Bangladesh-related study that deals with the issue. Nonetheless, theoretically, temporary/return migration generates various gains. But non-randomness of return migration is the main challenge in assessing the impact. However, Wahba (2014) found that the tentative effects of returnee migrants are felt in the forms of investment and entrepreneurship, human capital, and norm and idea transfers. Evidently, all identified impacts are contributory components in the development process of a country.

Studies like Gubert and Nordman's (2011) for the Maghreb and Lindstrom's (1996) for Mexico showed that the evidence for many developing and emerging countries is that return migration has led to microenterprise development. Though Mayr and Peri (2009) saw the rise of education levels and skill upgradation of a migrant exporting country through return migration, findings on any wage premium have remained mixed (Wahba 2014). Spilimbergo (2009) and Batista and Pedro (2011) found positive impacts on political ideas and social norms from the returnee migrants in their home country. For Bangladesh, the returnee migrants from the Middle East countries in general, and Saudi Arabia in particular, may have brought a different kind of impact as well. That is that the religious and cultural relics they carry back from the host countries are now posing a challenge to the core values of their society.

'Big Push' Investment in Mega Projects

As of September 2019, Bangladesh is engaged in the construction of some of the biggest development projects in its independent history. It is also on the verge of launching a few more. Most of the projects are in the area of the energy and transportation sectors. We can list the names, and estimated costs of the 'mega projects' Bangladesh is undertaking in the following order: Padma Multipurpose Bridge (BDT 300 billion), Rooppur Nuclear Power Plant (BDT 1010 billion), Karnaphuli Tunnel (BDT 56 billion), Matarbari Power Plant (BDT 500 billion), Rampal Power Station (BDT 160 billion), Payra Power Plant (BDT 160 billion), Dhaka Metro Rail Project (BDT 220 billion), and Payra Deep Sea Port (BDT 1600 billion). Another notable project is the Bangabandhu Satellite-1 (BDT 20 billion) (Khan 2018). The combined costs of these projects stand at BDT 3866 billion. Of these projects, Bangladesh is fully funding the Padma Bridge, while foreign aid and loan from Japan, Russia, China, India, and different international development agencies have been arranged for all other projects.

Objectively, Bangladesh's investment drive in these mega projects seems to exemplify the 'Big Push' Theory of Rosenstein-Rodan (1943), but may not be applied in the true spirit of the theory. The theory argues that for economic development, instead of relying on the philosophy of economic gradualism, a big push may be applied to undo the initial inertia of the stagnant economy. On the supply side, the construction of social overhead capital may be the way for such a push. All the basic industries such as transport, power, communications, and other public utilities are included in social overhead capital. The theory argues their emergence will engage the demand side to grow, and overall, the economy to expand. The UNDP (2005) also recommended the 'big push' strategy in public administration, human capital, and key infrastructure to developing countries to break out of the poverty trap.

But Bangladesh seems to have initiated these projects when it was no longer in the state of poverty trap or inertia of the stagnant economy. It had been rather maintaining a robust economic growth of above six percent for more than a decade. Recently, it has climbed further in the growth rate ladder above seven percent, and optimists are hoping that this will go up to 10 percent in the near future. If that turns out to be accurate, will it have anything to do with the 'big push'? In other words, has the investment drive in the mega projects already started showing an impact on the economic growth rate of the country? This needs to be explored to examine the real reasons in the growth rate jump.

To end this story, Bangladesh is passing through a historical moment of transition, and expressions of developmental changes are reflected in economic and social activities. We can prepare a long list of factors that may be seen to have supported this progress. Some of these have played a big and crucial role in the attainment of this level of change. Others, in contrast, might have brought gains that are individually small but have compounded again and again across the economic and social life of the nation. This has created significant developmental synergy through complementarities to benefit Bangladesh.

Chapter Design

Overall, Bangladesh has achieved its present level of impressive economic and social transformation due to factors having both internal and external origins. Interestingly, the dissemination, augmentation, and regeneration of limited resources, knowledge, and technology have also played an important role in its progress. This book attempts to capture the success story of Bangladesh across various economic and social sectors. At the same time, it tries to identify the present and future development challenges based on which Bangladesh can develop some mechanisms to amend governance deficiencies. Moreover, the book attempts to identify some possible areas where Bangladesh's future growth may lie and suggests tentative policy measures to go into those areas.

All this has been done in five parts, consisting of a total of 13 chapters in this book. In doing so, the book has incorporated chapters from experts from different walks of life who are working across the globe. This resource pool includes academics, researchers, area specialists, and policymakers who have devoted time to discussing the significant issues which have largely contributed to the development progress of Bangladesh. Let us have a very brief look at the coverage of the parts and chapters of the book.

The very introductory part contains just one chapter. Chapter 1 gives an idea of the success story of Bangladesh and has attempted to shape a model of development—The Solidarity Economic Development Model. The chapter has also tried to identify some 'other factors' which may have to be factored in the development discourse to see whether they have played any role in the development of Bangladesh.

Part II includes three important chapters that look at the bigger boundary of development in Bangladesh. In that context, Chap. 2 examines a narrative of the development of Bangladesh in terms of poverty, growth, and social development. Chapter 3 depicts a picture of inclusiveness in the development process and then talks about how Bangladesh is pursuing a climate resilient form of development for its people. Chapter 4 examines Bangladesh's success in three vital variables of social development—education, healthcare, and life expectancy and then explores how these factors together have added value to the sustainable development effort of Bangladesh.

A number of contributors are convinced that access to finance has been an important trigger, if not the most vital one, of the present economic vibrancy of Bangladesh. Three chapters have been added in Part III to give a financial progress picture of Bangladesh and to investigate the role of this sector in fostering economic development. While Chap. 5 provides the financial sector development in Bangladesh since 1971 and tries to link economic development with the sector, Chap. 6 argues that access to finance has played an inclusive development role in Bangladesh. Chapter 7 evaluates the development dynamics of remittances in Bangladesh as a net surplus source of foreign exchange inflow.

Part IV also includes three chapters that deal with development in the economic sectors of Bangladesh. As we will see, two important economic sectors that have helped and have been helped by the development process in Bangladesh are the agriculture and RMG sectors. Chapter 8 takes up the case of agriculture development in Bangladesh. It argues that impacts of progress in the agriculture sector are multidimensional, the first being poverty reduction. The sector has also transformed the rural economy and has become a success story for Bangladesh. Chapter 9 depicts the role of the garments sector in transforming the economy and social sector of the country. In fact, in the context of Bangladesh, the RMG industry has turned out to be a sun rising industry—offering jobs, particularly to women, earning foreign currencies by exports and laying the foundation for the industrialization of the country. Chapter 10 sheds light on an industrial area that has the potential to become important due to changes in the industrial complexion of Bangladesh. Indeed, the light industry is an area where Bangladesh has enormous development potential and future employment avenues for its large population.

Two chapters have been added in Part V to bring out the 'governance and development' issue of Bangladesh. The literature on the development of Bangladesh seems to have refrained from assigning appropriate recognition to the government's role in the whole development process. Chapter 11 is devoted to listing the developmental activities governments were and are engaged in. The chapter also sheds light on how the officials are trying to develop an accountability mechanism to oversee that development works are appropriately implemented. Chapter 12 covers the role of another important player for the development of Bangladesh—the NGOs. The chapter on 'NGOs for Development' documents Bangladesh's development experience from the activities of NGOs. The development activities of BRAC have been showcased in this regard.

Part VI of the book contains the concluding Chap. 13. This chapter highlights that all may not be that well when it comes to the governance of development in Bangladesh. It explains the present governance deficit and challenges to sustaining Bangladesh's progress in the future. Then the chapter looks at the way forward for Bangladesh to continue on its successful development path and attain the future dream of becoming a developed country. In this discussion, the chapter identifies some possible areas where Bangladesh's future growth may lie and suggests tentative policy measures to go into those areas.

Notes

1. Due to various methods of calculation and sources, the figures for GDP and other economic data for Bangladesh may differ sometimes. So these figures have to be accepted in the context of the discussion each time.
2. The progress in the health and education sectors, the reduction of vulnerability of the people, and steady economic growth are the three parameters used by the UN for measuring the developmental status of a country.
3. Since the LDC category was initiated in 1971, only four countries have graduated to higher developing country status. They are Botswana in 1994, Cape Verde in 2007, the Maldives in 2011, and Samoa in 2014.

Bhutan, Kiribati, Sao Tome, and Principe and the Solomon Islands have also become eligible to exit the LDC group.

4. In a discussion with Alexis Johnson in December 1971, a US career foreign service officer and Under-Secretary of State for Political Affairs at that time, regarding the possibility of famine to occur in Bangladesh, Henry Kissinger termed Bangladesh to be "basket case" but not an American one (Smith and Keefer 2005: 666).
5. The original work (Das Capital) was published in 1867.
6. A Chittagong University team led by economics professor Muhammad Yunus began to lend small amounts of money to poor households in a few nearby villages under an action research project in 1976. "Borrowers were organized into small peer monitoring groups of four or five people (soon becoming single-sex groups, with a focus on women's groups) that met weekly with other groups to make loan repayments. Demand for credit grew rapidly, and repayment rates were good, so the project was able to secure loans for on-lending from the state-controlled Bangladesh Bank and other commercial banks" (Hulme and Moore 2006: 6).
7. Pre-partition Bengal also endured a famine in 1943 that killed more than three million people. So the same curse hit the people of this geographical location twice within 33 years.
8. Petrodollar is an outcome of the rise in oil prices because of the crisis in the 1970s due to the Arab-Israeli War and the subsequent oil-boom in the Middle East countries like the KSA, UAE, Kuwait, Iraq, Oman, and Iran.
9. South Korea, Singapore, Taiwan, Hong Kong, Malaysia, and Thailand are sometimes referred to as newly industrialized economies (NIEs) or Asian tiger economies. Now newly industrialized countries (NICs) are found all over the world.
10. The HDI is a summary measure for assessing long-term progress in three basic dimensions of human development: a long and healthy life, access to knowledge, and a decent standard of living. (Visit: http://hdr.undp.org/sites/all/themes/hdr_theme/country-notes/BGD.pdf).
11. For example, two projects, namely the Rampal power station (a proposed 1320-megawatt (MW) coal-fired power station at Rampal in Khulna division), and the Phulbari Coal Project, an open-pit coal mine project, in Dinajpur district faced protests against their implementation.

References

Adelman, I. (2000). Fallacies in development theory and their implications for policy. In G. M. Meier & J. E. Stiglitz (Eds.), *Frontiers of development economics: The future in perspective* (pp. 103–134). Washington, DC: World Bank/Oxford University Press.

Aghion, P., & Howitt, P. (1992). A model of growth through creative destruction. *Econometrica, 60*(2), 323–351.

Ahsan, A. (2018, December 17). The liberation war and Bangladesh's development. *The Daily Star*. Dhaka.

Akash, M. M. (2003). *Bangladesher Orthonitee* (The economy of Bangladesh). Dhaka: Bangladesh Open University.

Al-Muti, S. A. (2014, June 25). Bangladesh's development surprise: A model for developing countries. *INASIA*. The Asia Foundation.

Annan, K. (2005). In larger freedom: Decision time at the UN. *Foreign Affairs*. Retrieved March 26, 2019, from http://www.unis.unvienna.org/pdf/freedom_annan.pdf.

Asadullah, N. M., Savoia, A., & Mahmud, W. (2014). Paths to development: Is there a Bangladesh surprise? *World Development, 62*(C), 138–154.

Asian Development Bank (ADB). (2012, August). *The urban governance and infrastructure improvement project in Bangladesh*. Manila.

Asian Development Bank. (2019). Basic statistics 2019. Retrieved September 12, 2019, from https://www.adb.org/countries/bangladesh/poverty#targetText=In%20Bangladesh%2C%20the%20population%20living,2010%20to%2014.8%25%20in%202016.

Balassa, B. (1971). *The structure of protection in developing countries*. Baltimore: Johns Hopkins Press.

Bangladesh Bank (BB). (2018). *Annual report 2017–2018*. Retrieved June 15, 2019, from https://www.bb.org.bd/pub/publictn.php.

Bangladesh Bureau of Statistics (BBS). (2001). *Population census 2001*. Dhaka: BBS.

Bangladesh Bureau of Statistics. (2003). Household Income & Expenditure Survey, 2000. Dhaka: BBS.

Bangladesh Bureau of Statistics. (2007). Household Income & Expenditure Survey, 2005. Dhaka, BBS.

Bangladesh Bureau of Statistics. (2012). Household Income & Expenditure Survey, 2010. Dhaka: BBS.

Bangladesh Bureau of Statistics. (2018a). Household Income & Expenditure Survey, 2016. Dhaka: BBS.

Bangladesh Bureau of Statistics. (2018b). Statistical Yearbook 2017. Dhaka: BBS.

Bangladesh Garments Manufacturers and Exporters Association (BGMEA). (2019). Trade information. Retrieved September 2, 2019, from http://www.bgmea.com.bd/home/pages/TradeInformation.

Bangladesh Telecommunication Regulatory Commission (BTRC). (2018). License and statistics. Retrieved June 22, 2019, from http://www.btrc.gov.bd/telco/internet.

Bangladesh Telecommunication Regulatory Commission. (2019). Internet subscribers. Retrieved August 21, 2019, from http://www.btrc.gov.bd/content/internet-subscribers-bangladesh-january-2019.

Barai, M. K. (2012). Development dynamics of remittances in Bangladesh. *Sage Open, 2*, 1–12.

Baran, P. A. (1957). *The political economy of growth*. New York: Monthly Review Press.

Batista, C., & Pedro, C. (2011). Do migrants improve governance at home? Evidence from a voting experiment. *World Bank Economic Review, 25*(1), 77–104.

Bauer, P. T. (1984). *Reality and rhetoric: Studies in the economics of development*. London: Weidenfield & Nicolson.

Bhagwati, J. N. (1978). *Anatomy and consequences of exchange control regimes*. Cambridge: Ballinger Publishing Company.

Boeke, J. H. (1953). *Economics and economic policy of dual societies*. New York: International Secretariat, Institute of Pacific Relations.

Boserup, E. (1981). *Population and technological change: A study of long-term trends*. Chicago: University Of Chicago Press.

Cardoso, F. H. (1977). The consumption of dependency theory in the United States. *Latin American Research Review, 12*(3), 19–20.

Chaity, A. J. (2018, July 12). Women empowerment: Bangladesh sets example for the world. *The Dhaka Tribune*.

Chenery, H. B. (1960). Patterns of industrial growth. *The American Economic Review, 50*(4), 624–654.

Chenery, H. B., & Syrquin, M. (1975). *Patterns of development, 1950–1970*. London: Oxford University Press for the World Bank.

Chenery, H. B., & Taylor, L. (1968). Development patterns: Among countries and over time. *The Review of Economics and Statistics, 50*(4), 391–416.

Clifton, H. (2013). Discovering development. The dreams and the damage (Amartya Sen on development). Retrieved September 9, 2019, from https://developmenthannahclifton.wordpress.com/2013/04/03/amartya-sen-on-development/#targetText=Amartya%20Sen%20on%20Development,they%20have%20reason%20to%20value.

Copestake, J. (1999, August). *Theories of economic development*. UNESCO Encyclopedia of the Life Sciences. Retrieved September 2, 2019, from https://personal.utdallas.edu/~mjleaf/Copestakeunesco.html.

Cornwall, J., & Cornwall, W. (1994). Growth theory and economic structure. *Economica, 61*(242), 237–251.

Cruz, G. T. (2005). Migration in the Asian region: Retrospect and prospects. *World Mission, XVI*(3), 22–26.

Dang, G., & Sui Pheng, L. (2015). *Infrastructure investments in developing economies: The case of Vietnam*. Singapore: Springer.

Domar, E. (1946). Capital expansion, rate of growth, and employment. *Econometrica, 14*(2), 137–147. https://doi.org/10.2307/1905364

Dos Santos, T. (1973). The crisis of development theory and the problem of dependence in Latin America. In H. Bernstein (Ed.), *Underdevelopment and development: The third world today* (pp. 57–79). New York: Penguin Books.

Easterly, W. R. (2001). *The elusive quest for growth: Economists' adventures and misadventures in the tropics.* Cambridge: Massachusetts Institute of Technology Press.

Economics Discussion. (2019). Adam Smith theory of development in economics. Retrieved September 7, 2019, from http://www.economicsdiscussion.net/economics-2/adam-smith-theory-of-development-in-economics-main-features/4514

Evans, P. (2002). Collective capabilities, culture, and Amartya Sen's development as freedom. *Studies in Comparative International Development, 37*(2), 54–60.

Faaland, J., & Parkinson, J. R. (1976). *Bangladesh: The test case of development.* Boulder, CO: Westview Press.

Franck, A. G. (1967). *Capitalism and underdevelopment in Latin America.* New York: Monthly Review Press.

Galeano, E. (1973). *Open veins of Latin America.* New York: Monthly Review Press.

Gautam, M., & Rashid, F. (2016). *Dynamics of rural growth in Bangladesh: Sustaining poverty reduction: Directions in development.* Washington, DC: World Bank. https://doi.org/10.1596/978-1-4648-0876-0.

Government of Bangladesh (GOB). (2019, June). *The medium term budget framework 2019–20.* Dhaka: Finance Division, Ministry of Finance, Government of the People's Republic of Bangladesh.

Gubert, F., & Nordman, C. J. (2011). Return migration and small enterprise development in the Maghreb. In S. Plaza & D. Ratha (Eds.), *Diaspora for development in Africa* (pp. 103–126). Washington, DC: The World Bank.

Hakeem, M. A. (2017). *Effect of population density on the level of development.* MPRA Paper No. 82301. Retrieved September 11, 2019, from https://mpra.ub.uni-muenchen.de/82301/.

Harrod, R. F. (1939). An essay in dynamic theory. *The Economic Journal, 49*(193), 14–33.

Henry, J., & Pomeroy, J. (2018). *The world in 2030: Our long-term projections for 75 countries.* HSBC Global Research. Retrieved August 23, 2019, from https://enterprise.press/wp-content/uploads/2018/10/HSBC-The-World-in-2030-Report.pdf.

Higgins, B. (1956). *The dualistic theory of underdeveloped areas: Economic development and cultural change.* Chicago: The University of Chicago Press.

Hirschman, A. (1957). *The strategy of economic development.* New Haven: Yale University Press.

Hoff, K., & Stiglitz, J. E. (2000). Modern economic theory and development. In G. M. Meier & J. E. Stiglitz (Eds.), *Frontiers of development economics: The future in perspective* (pp. 389–485). Washington, DC: World Bank/Oxford

University Press. Retrieved from https://sites.hks.harvard.edu/cid/archive/events/cidneudc/papers/neudcstiglitz.pdf

Hossain, B. (2014). Poverty reduction during 1971–2013 periods: Success and its recent trends in Bangladesh. *Global Journal of Human-Social Science, 14*(5), Version 1.0, 38–47.

Hossain, N. (2017). *The aid lab: Understanding Bangladesh's unexpected success.* Oxford University Press.

Hulme, D., & Moore, K. (2006). *Why has microfinance been a policy success in Bangladesh (and beyond)?* GPRG-WPS-041. Retrieved August 30, 2019, from http://www.gprg.org.

Islam, N. (2018, October 24). Urbanisation in Bangladesh: Recent trends and challenges. *The Daily Sun.*

Jacobs, J. (2019, May 28). Rostow's stages of growth development model. Retrieved August 25, 2019, from https://www.thoughtco.com/rostows-stages-of-growth-development-model-1434564.

Johnson, H. (1971). A word to the third world: A western economist's frank advice. *Encounter, 37*, 3–10.

Kant, K. (2018, May 28). At current rates, Bangladesh could top India's per capita income by 2020. *Business Standard.* Retrieved September 1, 2019, from https://www.business-standard.com/article/economy-policy/bangladesh-pips-india-in-economic-growth-and-social-development-indicators-118052700710_1.html.

Khalily, M. A. B. (2016). *Financial inclusion, financial regulation, and education in Bangladesh.* ADBI Working Paper 621. Asian Development Bank Institute, Tokyo.

Khalily, M. A. B., Miah, P., Hasan, M., Akthar, N., & Muneer, F. (2015). Access to financial services—A demand side study, in institution of microfinance. *National convention on inclusive finance in Bangladesh*, Dhaka, pp. 27–52.

Khan, M. A. (2018, February 22). Mega projects and our hopes and concerns: Need for consensus and long-term planning. *The Daily Star.* Dhaka.

Klasen, S., & Nestmann, T. (2006). Population, population density and technological change. *Journal of Population Economics, 19*(3), 611–626.

Krueger, A. O. (1978). *Foreign trade attempts and economic development: Liberalization attempts and consequences.* Cambridge: Ballinger Publishing Company.

Kuznets, S. S. (1971). *Economic growth of nations: Total output and production structure.* Cambridge: Belknap Press of Harvard University Press.

Lal, D. (1985). *The poverty of 'development economics.* Cambridge: Harvard University Press.

Lewis, W. A. (1954). Economic development with unlimited supplies of labour. *The Manchester School, 22*(2), 139–191.

Lindstrom, D. P. (1996). Economic opportunity in Mexico and return migration from the United States. *Demography, 33*(3), 357–374.

Little, I. (1982). *Economic development: Theories, policies, and international relations*. New York: Basic Books.

Lucas, R. E. (1988). On the mechanics of economic development. *Journal of Monetary Economics, 22*(1), 3–42.

Mahmud, M., Otsuka, K., Sawada, Y., & Yamada, E. (2018). Development transformation in Bangladesh: An overview. In Y. Sawada, M. Mahmud, & N. Kitano (Eds.), *Economic and social development of Bangladesh: Miracle and challenges*. Singapore: Palgrave Macmillan.

Mahmud, W. (2017, August 16). Pathways to human development: Explaining the Bangladesh surprise. *VoxDev*. Retrieved September 12, 2019, from https://voxdev.org/topic/health-education/pathways-human-development-explaining-bangladesh-surprise.

Malthus, T. R. (1798). *An essay on the principle of population*. Library of Economics and Liberty, Ed. 6, Chapter II.

Marx, K. (1933). *Capital*. London: J. M. Dent.

Mayr, K., & Peri, G. (2009). Brain drain and brain return: Theory and application to Eastern–Western Europe. *B.E. Journal of Economic Analysis and Policy, 9*(1), 1–50.

Meier, G. M. (2000). The old generation of development economists and the new. In G. M. Meier & J. E. Stiglitz (Eds.), *Frontiers of development economics: The future in perspective* (pp. 13–50). Washington, DC: World Bank/Oxford University Press.

Microcredit Regulatory Authority (MRA). (2017). *Annual report 2017*. Dhaka: MRA.

Ministry of Finance (MoF). (2019). *Bangladesh economic review 2019*. Dhaka: Government of Bangladesh. Retrieved September 9, 2019, from https://mof.portal.gov.bd/site/page/28ba57f5-59ff-4426-970a-bf014242179e/Bangladesh-Economic-Review.

Mohammad, A. (2018). Rise of the corporate NGO in Bangladesh. *Economic and Political Weekly, 53*(39), 45–52.

Morris, C. T., & Adelman, I. (1988). *Comparative patterns of economic development, 1850–1914*. Baltimore: Johns Hopkins University Press.

National Research Council (NRC). (1986). *Population growth and economic development: Policy questions*. Washington, DC: National Academy Press.

New Age. (2019, June 14). Transport sector gets highest allocation. Retrieved September 12, 2019, from http://www.newagebd.net/article/75299/transport-sector-gets-highest-allocation.

NGO Affairs Bureau (NGOAB) of Bangladesh. (2020). List of NGOs. Retrieved January 29, 2020, from http://www.ngoab.gov.bd/site/page/54d2f83c-cd18-44af-8a52-202ec83f7582/-#.

Nurkse, R. (1953). *Problems of capital formation in underdeveloped countries*. Oxford: Basil Blackwell.
Oumar, S. B., & Sama, C. M. (2015). International dependency and the economic development of less advanced countries. *International Business Research, 8*(6), 117–134.
Pieterse, J. N. (2010). *Development theory: Deconstructions/reconstructions*. London: Sage Publications. https://doi.org/10.4135/9781446279083
Rahman, A. (2018, November 12). Bangladesh's graduation from LDC: A 'development surprise. *The Financial Express*. Retrieved September 4, 2019, from http://today.thefinancialexpress.com.bd/26th-anniversary-issue-1/a-development-surprise-1541934101.
Rahman, K. M. & Rahman, S. (2016). *International political economy and ready-made garments industry: The case of Bangladesh*. GSCG Project Working Paper. Retrieved August 2, 2019, from www.garmentgov.de.
Reyes, G. E. (2001). Four main theories of development: Modernization, dependency, world-system and globalization, *Nómadas. Critical Journal of Social and Juridical Sciences, 4*(2), 109–124.
Rodney, W. A. (1972). *How Europe underdeveloped Africa*. London: Bogle-L'Ouverture.
Rodrik, D. (2008). The real exchange rate and economic growth. *Brookings Papers on Economic Activity*, 2, 365–412. Retrieved September 8, 2019, from https://www.brookings.edu/wp-content/uploads/2008/09/2008b_bpea_rodrik.pdf.
Roemer, J. E. (1988). *Free to lose*. Cambridge, MA: Harvard University Press.
Romer, P. M. (1986). Increasing returns and long-run growth. *Journal of Political Economy, 94*(5), 1002–1037.
Rosenstein-Rodan, P. N. (1943). Problems of industrialization of Eastern and South-Eastern Europe. *The Economic Journal, 53*(210/211), 202–211.
Rostow, W. W. (1960). *The stages of economic growth: A non-communist manifesto*. Cambridge: Cambridge University Press.
Sawada, Y., Mahmud, M., & Kitano, N. (Eds.). (2018). *Economic and social development of Bangladesh: Miracle and challenges*. Singapore: Palgrave Macmillan.
Selwyn, B. (2011). Liberty limited? A sympathetic re-engagement with Amartya Sen's development as freedom. *Economic and Political Weekly, XLVI*(10), 68–76.
Sen, A. (1999). *Development as freedom*. Oxford: Oxford University Press.
Shahabuddin, Q. (2014). Bangladesh: Agriculture and food security policies. Background Paper for dynamics of rural growth in Bangladesh, agriculture global practice, World Bank, Washington, DC.
Skott, P., & Auerbach, P. (1995). Cumulative causation and the "new" theories of economic growth. *Journal of Post Keynesian Economics, 17*(3), 381–402.
Skousen, M. (2007). *The big three in economics: Adam Smith, Karl Marx and John Maynard Keynes*. New York: ME Sharpe Inc.

Smith, A. (1976). *An inquiry into the nature and causes of the wealth of nations.* Oxford: Clarendon Press.

Smith, L. J., & Keefer, E. C. (Eds.). (2005). *Foreign relations of the United States, 1969–1976, Volume XI, South Asia crisis, 1971.* Washington, DC: United States Government Printing Office.

Solow, R. M. (1956). A contribution to the theory of economic growth. *The Quarterly Journal of Economics, 70*(1), 56–94. https://doi.org/10.2307/1884513

Spilimbergo, A. (2009). Foreign students and democracy. *American Economic Review, 99*(1), 528–543.

Statics of Canada (StatCan). (2018). Retrieved from https://www.150.statcan.gc.ca/n1/en/type/data?MM=1

Stiglitz, J. E. (2002). *Globalization and its discontents.* New York: W.W. Norton & Company.

Streatfield, P. K., & Ahsan, K. Z. (2008). Population challenges for Bangladesh in the coming decades. *Journal of Health Population and Nutrition, 26*(3), 261–272.

Sunkel, O. (1966). The structural background of development problems in Latin America. *Deutschland: Weltwirtschaftliches Archiv, 97*(1), 22ff. Also in Nisbet, C. T. (Ed.). (1969). *Latin America: Problems in economic development* (pp. 3–39). New York: Free Press.

Thirlwall, A. P. (1999). *Growth and development with special reference to developing economies.* London: Macmillan Press Ltd.

Todaro, M. P., & Smith, S. C. (2015). *Economic development* (12th ed.). New York: Pearson.

Tudor, M. (2018, August). Understanding Bangladesh's unexpected development success. Retrieved September 12, 2019, from https://www.youthkiawaaz.com/2018/08/understanding-bangladeshs-unexpected-success/

UN Department of Economic and Social Affairs (UN-DESA). (2018). Leaving the LDC category: Booming Bangladesh prepares to Graduate, New York. Retrieved March 13, 2019, from https://www.un.org/development/desa/en/news/policy/leaving-the-ldcs-category-booming-bangladesh-prepares-to-graduate.html.

United Nations Development Programme (UNDP). (2005). *UN millennium project—Investing in development: A practical plan to achieve the millennium development goals.* London: Earthscan.

United Nations Development Programme. (2013). *Human Development Report 2013.* New York: United Nations.

United Nations Development Programme. (2014). *The millennium development goals: Eight goals for 2015.* New York: UNDP. Retrieved April 9, 2015, from http://www.undp.org/mdg/

United Nations Development Programme. (2018). Human development indices and indicators: 2018 statistical update. Retrieved August 29, 2019, from http://hdr.undp.org/sites/all/themes/hdr_theme/country-notes/BGD.pdf.

United Nations Development Programme. (2019). Retrieved September 3, 2019, from https://www.un.org/sustainabledevelopment/sustainable-development-goals/.

Wahba, J. (2014). Return migration and economic development. In R. E. B. Lucas (Ed.), *International handbook on migration and economic development* (pp. 327–349). Edward Elgar Publishing Ltd.

Wallerstein, I. M. (1980). *The modern world-system II: Mercantilism and the consolidation of the European world economy* (pp. 1600–1750). New York: Academic Press.

Weil, D. N., & Wilde, J. (2010). How relevant is Malthus for economic development today?, *American Economic Review*, 100(2), 378–382. Retrieved September 6, 2019, from https://www.ncbi.nlm.nih.gov/pmc/articles/PMC4112762/

World Bank. (2000a, March). Better governance for a better future–reforming public institutions in Bangladesh. Washington, DC.

World Bank. (2000b). *Entering the 21st century—World Development Report 1999/2000.* New York: Oxford University Press.

World Bank. (2012a, June). *Bangladesh development series.* Vol. 2. Dhaka.

World Bank. (2012b). *Migration and remittances factbook 2011.* Washington, DC: Migration and Remittances Unit, World Bank.

World Bank. (2016, October 9). Bangladesh: Growing the economy through advances in agriculture. Retrieved September 4, 2019, from https://www.worldbank.org/en/results/2016/0/07/bangladesh-growing-economy-through-advances-in-agriculture.

World Bank. (2018a, April). *Bangladesh development update—Building on resilience.* Dhaka.

World Bank. (2018b). Migration and remittances data. Retrieved December 27, 2018, from http://www.worldbank.org/en/topic/migrationremittancesdiasporaissues/brief/migration-remittances-data.

World Bank. (2019). World development indicators. Retrieved August 12, 2019, from https://databank.worldbank.org/source/world-development-indicators#.

World Economic Forum (WEF). (2017, April 11). There could be a new 'Asian Tiger'. Here's why. Retrieved August 14, 2019, from https://www.weforum.org/agenda/2017/04/bangladesh-could-be-a-new-asian-tiger-heres-why.

World Economic Forum. (2018). *The Global Gender Gap Report 2018.* Geneva.

World Population Review. (2019). Total fertility rate 2019. Retrieved September 29, 2019, from http://worldpopulationreview.com/countries/total-fertility-rate/

PART II

Drawing the Boundary of Bangladesh's Development

CHAPTER 2

Examining the Distinct Features of Bangladesh's Development: Interactions between Growth, Poverty, and Social Development

Mausumi Mahapatro

Introduction

In nearly half a century of its development narrative, Bangladesh has made considerable strides in reducing the incidence of poverty. Moreover, achievements in selected social development indicators are considered to be atypical when considering Bangladesh's level of income per capita. In this chapter, these trends and interactions are explored in order to situate where Bangladesh stands, as far as competing theories of development go. For instance, has Bangladesh pursued a dirigiste model of development, or

The author wishes to thank the reviewer for constructive suggestions and feedback on an earlier version of this chapter. Thanks must also be given to Ahmed Adib and Tahreen Zahra for data compilation.

M. Mahapatro (✉)
Regis University, Denver, CO, USA
e-mail: mahap807@regis.edu

M. K. Barai (ed.), *Bangladesh's Economic and Social Progress*,
https://doi.org/10.1007/978-981-15-1683-2_2

can it attribute its success to market-led forces and increased globalization? The classic state versus market dichotomy is used to discuss the possible origins of Bangladesh's development. Moreover, can Bangladesh be considered a developmental state in contradistinction to a predatory one? What is the role of institutions and geography in shaping Bangladesh's development outcomes? This chapter seeks to shed light on Bangladesh's distinct typology of development as it relates to the poverty-inequality-growth triangle, social development, and other key aspects.

Social Development: A Comparative Perspective

Bangladesh having outpaced some of the countries within South Asia with respect to selected social development indicators is well established in the literature (Drèze and Sen 2013; Asadullah et al. 2014). For instance, Bangladesh has successfully increased female school enrolment rates at the primary and secondary level and reduced infant mortality rates in line with the Millennium Goal Development (MDG) targets. The founder of BRAC, for instance, compared Bangladesh's achievements in health to that of the Meiji restoration in Japan (Abed 2013).

A natural point of comparison for Bangladesh is with the neighboring state of West Bengal in India. Studies that have compared these two regions have focused primarily on agrarian relations and concentration of landholdings.[1] A comparison along the lines of social development indicators has not been made; those studies that have exclusively focused on social development were limited to the aggregate, all India statistics. Table 2.1 provides a snapshot of selected indicators.

For selected aspects of social development, there is a staggering difference between Bangladesh and its immediate neighbors. For instance, only 4.6 percent of the rural population was practicing open defecation in Bangladesh compared to 40 percent in West Bengal in 2011–12. Labor force participation rates for women are also higher for Bangladesh. However, maternal mortality rates are close to double that of West Bengal. In the case of infant mortality, Bangladesh has made remarkable strides and has surpassed India as a whole with rates comparable to that of West Bengal.

The picture that emerges suggests that Bangladesh's achievements with social development are indeed significant though not comprehensive. The evidence does not point toward wholesale, across the board progress. It does suggest, however, that Bangladesh has entered into a development mode with continuous progress being made in critical areas of social

Table 2.1 Comparison of selected social development indicators

	Bangladesh		*West Bengal*[a]		*India*	
	2011/2012	*2016/2017*	*2011/2012*	*2016/2017*	*2011/2012*	*2016/2017*
Infant mortality rate (per 1000 live births)	33.2	26.9	31 (2013)	26[b]	40[a] 43.2 (WDI)	35.2 (2015)
Maternal mortality rate (per 100,000 live births)	210	–	113 (2013)	–	180	170 (2013)
Literacy rate (%)	47	72.8	72	–	70	–
Percent of population (rural) practicing open defecation	4.6	0.106 (2015)	40	–	62.7	55.6 (2015)
Labor force participation rate (female)	30.5	33.0	25	–	31[a] 24.4 (WDI)	23.8

Source: World Development Indicators (WDI)

[a]West Bengal indicators at a glance, June 2017, World Bank

[b]Taken from National Health Profile, 2018, Central Bureau of Health Intelligence, Government of India

Table 2.2 The Venezuelan reversal

Indicator	*2008*	*2011*	*2017*
Maternal mortality (MMR)	63.4	72.2	
Under 5 mortality	17	16.6	30.9
Neonatal mortality	9.9	10.3	19.8

Source: World Development Indicators

development. No reversal of development is found within the context of Bangladesh, although, for certain indicators such as total fertility rate and labor force participation rate for women, progress has stalled. This stands in stark contrast to Table 2.2, which demonstrates the case of a reversal of fortune in Venezuela as far as social development in recent years.

Breaking the Cycle of Circular Causation

It was Gunnar Myrdal along with Nicholas Kaldor who famously proposed the thesis of circular or cumulative causation: that low levels of income would mean less provisioning for health, nutrition, and education and that this, in turn, would lower productivity and perpetuate the vicious cycle of poverty.[2] The genesis of the human development index (HDI) can be considered a consequence of this weakening of causality between income variables and human development indicators. Though they are strongly correlated, countries' relative ranks do differ, even significantly so, when ranked on these different criteria.[3]

This is also relevant for Bangladesh, which has achieved much in the way of development despite having a low per capita income (Asadullah et al. 2014). However, whether this disconnect also holds true at a more disaggregated level needs further examination. In fact, when examining division-wide differences, it is found that the link between income and social development is, in fact, disconnected or at least weak. What has been labeled as the 'Sylhet paradox,'[4] for instance, provides a troubling picture. Though one of the richer divisions of Bangladesh, this region has some of the highest infant and under-5 mortality rates.

Tables 2.3 and 2.4 reveal this discrepancy, particularly in the context of Rangpur and Sylhet. Although Sylhet has the lowest incidence of rural poverty using the upper poverty line, it has the highest incidence of infant mortality in comparison to other districts. Rangpur, on the other hand, though being one of the poorest districts does much better in terms of child mortality and infant mortality. Though this is not found across the

Table 2.3 Division-wise ranking based on head count rate using upper poverty line

Division	*HCR, Rural*	*HCR, urban*	*Rank (rural)*	*Rank (urban)*
Barisal	25.7	30.4	4	6
Chittagong	19.4	15.9	3	2
Dhaka	19.2	12.5	2	1
Khulna	27.3	28.3	5	5
Mymensingh	32.9	32.0	7	7
Rajshahi	30.6	22.5	6	4
Rangpur	48.2	41.5	8	8
Sylhet	15.6	19.5	1	3

Source: Taken from BBS (2016)

Table 2.4 Division-wise ranking based on mortality rates

Division	*Infant mortality*	*Under-5 mortality*	*Rank (IMR)*	*Rank (Under 5)*
Barisal	26	35	1	1
Chittagong	36	50	4	4
Dhaka	35	41	3	3
Khulna	47	56	6	6
Mymensingh[a]	NA	NA	NA	NA
Rajshahi	38	43	5	4
Rangpur	34	39	2	2
Sylhet	55	67	7	7

Source: National Institute of Population Research and Training (NIPORT), Mitra and Associates, and ICF International (2016)

[a]Mymensingh division was created in 2015 and is hence not a part of the Demographic Health Surveys conducted in 2014

board for all districts, there are clear changes that occur to the ranks that districts hold when using income centric poverty measures versus health-related measures.

Firstly, the tables above attest to the uneven nature of development. Though Bangladesh is a small country, even within such a small space, regional disparities have surfaced as reflected in striking differences in poverty headcounts. Some of these disparities have been referred to as an East-West divide. When disaggregated further, a similar disjoint between district-level GDP figures and social development indicators are found. Rangpur, for instance, moves down by 24 spots when ranked based on IMR instead of per capita district GDP. Sylhet moves up by 16 spots when ranks are based on literacy rates. This is despite a moderate, statistically significant correlation between these variables (Table 2.5).

A double log regression with the following functional form was used:

$$\mathrm{Ln}\, Yi = \beta o + \beta k\, \mathrm{Ln}\left(Xik\right) + \mathrm{error},$$

was also used where *Yi* represents the log of under 5 or infant mortality rates for the *i*th district. This was regressed on the log of the following variables: district-level per capita GDP, length of paved road, per capita allocation of the annual development budget, literacy rates, and electricity coverage. The regression results (Table 2.6) demonstrate that infant mortality rates are in fact, significantly influenced by per capita district GDP. No other variables were statistically significant. However, in the case of under

Table 2.5 District-specific changes in rank based on economic and social development indicators

District	*Per capita GDP (2010/11) (1)*	*IMR (2010) (2)*	*Change in rank (3)*	*Literacy rate (2011) (4)*	*Change in rank (5)*
Bagerhat	4	11	−7	9	−5
Bandarban	53	16	37	63	−10
Barguna	7	25	−18	12	−5
Barisal	14	13	1	6	8
Bhola	17	20	−3	52	−35
Bogra	29	18	11	32.5	−3.5
Brahmanbaria	58	51	7	49	9
Chandpur	40	5	35	15	25
Chittagong	3	31	−28	10	−7
Chuadanga	32	10	22	48	−16
Comilla	63	57	6	19	44
Cox's Bazar	24	2	22	60	−36
Dhaka	1	26	−25	1	0
Dinajpur	28	36.5	−8.5	21	7
Faridpur	48	6	42	35	13
Feni	61	60	1	8	53
Gaibandha	54	54.5	−0.5	54	0
Gazipur	6	23	−17	4	2
Gopalgonj	41	46	−5	11	30
Hobigonj	59	28	31	58	1
Joypurhat	9	43	−34	13	−4
Jamalpur	35	40	−5	61	−26
Jessore	10	9	1	16	−6
Jhalakathi	47	44	3	2	45
Jhenaidah	31	58	−27	38	−7
Khagrachhari	64	62	2	46.5	17.5
Khulna	2	4	−2	7	−5
Kishoregonj	52	17	35	57	−5
Kurigram	26	47	−21	55	−29
Kushtia	27	35	−8	44.5	−17.5
Lakshmipur	45	42	3	32.5	12.5
Lalmonirhat	38	52	−14	46.5	−8.5
Madaripur	33	3	30	40	−7
Magura	25	12	13	28	−3
Manikgonj	23	64	−41	34	−11
Meherpur	21	21	0	44.5	−23.5
Maulavibazar	56	56	0	27	29
Munsigonj	50	48	2	17	33
Mymensingh	36	38	−2	51	−15

(*continued*)

Table 2.5 (continued)

District	*Per capita GDP (2010/11) (1)*	*IMR (2010) (2)*	*Change in rank (3)*	*Literacy rate (2011) (4)*	*Change in rank (5)*
Naogaon	22	45	−23	39	−17
Narail	15	8	7	5	10
Narayangonj	5	15	−10	14	−9
Narsingdi	18	36.5	−18.5	30.5	−12.5
Natore	13	1	12	30.5	−17.5
Nawabgonj	57	41	16	53	4
Netrokana	43	22	21	59	−16
Nilphamari	60	34	26	50	10
Noakhali	51	19	32	25	26
Pabna	11	39	−28	43	−32
Panchagar	46	50	−4	24	22
Patuakhali	12	29	−17	18	−6
Pirojpur	34	24	10	3	31
Rajshahi	8	33	−25	20	−12
Rajbari	37	53	−16	22	15
Rangamati	19	7	12	29	−10
Rangpur	39	63	−24	37	2
Shariatpur	49	30	19	41	8
Satkhira	16	59	−43	23	−7
Sirajgonj	55	61	−6	56	−1
Sherpur	30	27	3	62	−32
Sunamganj	62	49	13	64	−2
Sylhet	42	54.5	−12.5	26	16
Tangail	44	14	30	42	2
Thakurgaon	20	32	−12	36	−16

Source: Data taken from Khondker and Mahzab (2015). All subsequent analysis is based on this data

5 mortality rates, it is actually the rate of literacy that significantly influences this type of mortality, not district product. Although income or output cannot be ruled out as an important determinant of social development, the findings do suggest that there are other factors at play.

A similar result is also found at the household level. Using DHS data for Bangladesh, a binary logistic regression was run to test whether the probability of infant mortality and under-5 mortality is influenced by wealth quintiles.[5] The regression took the following form:

$$\log\text{it}(Pi): \log\left(\frac{p}{1-p}\right) = \beta\text{o} + \beta(Xqi) + \text{error},$$

Table 2.6 Determinants of district-wise infant and under-5 mortality rates ($n = 64$)

Variable (log)	*Standardized coefficient*	*VIF*[a]	*Standardized coefficient*	*VIF*
	Beta		*Beta*	
	(log) district Infant mortality rates		*(log) district Under 5 mortality rates*	
Per capita district GDP	−0.492*** (−3.557)	1.355	−0.026 (−0.204)	1.355
Literacy rate	0.248 (1.627)	1.649	−0.423** (−3.021)	1.649
Electricity coverage (2010)	−0.149 (−1.059)	1.413	−0.194 (−1.496)	1.413
Per capita ADB expenditure (2008/09)	0.000 (.000)	1.020	−0.111 (−1.008)	1.020
Length of paved road (2009)	0.149 (1.189)	1.109	0.053 (0.463)	1.109
	R square = 0.210		R square = 0.333	

Note: *t* statistic in parenthesis. *** $p < 0.001$, ** $p < 0.01$

[a]The VIF values suggest that there is no significant multicollinearity between the variables

where p = probability of infant or child mortality for the *i*th household, β = log odds based on membership within wealth quintile for each household.

What was found at the district level is also found at a more granular household level. In the case of infant mortality, odds ratios monotonically decline as households fall into higher wealth quintiles relative to that of the richest quintile. However, odds ratios in the case of under-5 mortality are actually higher for the less poor. This confirms earlier findings made by Brown et al. (2017) within the context of Africa about how poor people, as identified through anthropometric measures, may not be located entirely in the poorest households as measured through income or wealth (Table 2.7).

The key to this discussion is that there are visible disconnects between income (as measured through the incidence of poverty and per capita district GDP) and health-related indicators that, though not across the board, do warrant further attention. The disconnect appears in the aggregate if we consider Bangladesh's overall achievements in social development, but also at a more disaggregated, district-specific level. This is not to say that

Table 2.7 Probability of infant or under-5 mortality across wealth quintiles

Wealth quintile	*S.E (infant)*	*S.E. (under 5)*	*Wald (infant)*	*Wald (under 5)*	*Df*	*Odds Ratio*	
						Infant	*Under 5*
Poorest	0.066	0.141	109.372	19.712	1.000	2.00***	1.87***
Poorer	0.067	0.141	85.858	22.096	1.000	1.862***	1.937***
Middle	0.068	0.145	72.214	10.347	1.000	1.71***	1.596***
Richer	0.071	0.155	22.631	1.395	1.000	1.402***	1.201
Richest	Reference						

Source: Demographic health surveys (BDHS) dataset, 2014

$N = 43{,}136$, $***p < 0.001$

income does not matter. Sharp disparities in terms of infant mortality rates still exist when disaggregated across income (Osmani 2015). However, income is not the sole determinant of health outcomes, as the evidence suggests. At the household level, although wealth remains an important predictor of infant mortality, in the case of under-5 mortality, odds ratios are significantly high for less poor households.

The channels of causation that link income with health and more specifically, mortality rates appear to be weak in certain contexts. It appears as though the transmission mechanisms that link income with other wider aspects of development are, in some cases, getting blocked. The income-nutrition link, for instance, is one such channel where we see such a blockage: Bangladesh still has very high rates of child malnutrition despite lowering income-based poverty.

Significant Reduction in Poverty, But with Rising Inequality

Another key facet of Bangladesh's development is the progress it has made as far as reducing income/expenditure poverty though the pace of this reduction varied over the decades. The incidence of poverty declined from 56.5 percent in 1991/92 to 31.5 percent in 2010 (GED 2015). The pace of this reduction, in fact, was beyond the MDG targets that were set for the country, thus leading to the country meeting its MDG target of halving poverty well ahead of time. The extent of reduction in poverty in Bangladesh is similar (though not as dynamic) to what some of the East Asian countries were able to achieve as part of what constituted the well-known 'Asian miracle.' (Tables 2.8 and 2.9)

Table 2.8 Percentage distribution of income accruing to deciles

Decile	*2016*			*2010*		
	National	*Rural*	*Urban*	*National*	*Rural*	*Urban*
Decile 1	1.01	1.06	1.16	2.00	2.23	1.98
Decile 2	2.83	3.00	2.99	3.22	3.53	3.09
Decile 3	4.04	4.33	4.18	4.10	4.49	3.95
Decile 4	5.13	5.47	4.99	5.00	5.43	5.01
Decile 5	6.23	6.63	5.91	6.01	6.43	6.31
Decile 6	7.51	7.95	7.17	7.32	7.65	7.64
Decile 7	9.12	9.44	8.35	9.06	9.31	9.30
Decile 8	11.13	11.78	10.49	11.50	11.50	11.87
Decile 9	14.84	15.49	13.31	15.94	15.54	16.08
Decile 10	38.16	34.84	41.44	35.84	33.89	34.77
Top 5%	27.89	24.25	32.12	24.61	22.93	23.39
Gini	0.483	0.454	0.498	0.458	0.430	0.452

Source: HIES 2016

Nevertheless, and similar again to the East Asian experience,[6] income inequality has been rising, although there was some speculation that the income-inequality link may have reached the Kuznets turning point. Based on the HIES, the Gini coefficient measuring income inequality rose from 0.458 in the 2010 round to 0.483 in 2016. Though this seems like a marginal increase, if we consider only the tails of the distribution through alternate measures like the Kuznets or Palma ratios, the increase in inequality is far more pronounced. In 2010, the bottom 5 percent of the rural population received 0.88 percent of income, which went down to a mere 0.25 percent in 2016 according to the latest round of HIES. At the other end, the top five percent of rural households' share of income rose from 22.93 percent in 2010 to 24.25 percent in 2016.

Further analysis of the HIES 2016 shows changes in the share of income that are leading to higher inequality. Nevertheless, they do not represent transfers from the middle deciles to upper deciles. The bottom 40 percent of the population held 14.32 percent of total income in 2010; this dwindled to 13.01 percent in 2016. The fact that it is occurring within the context of a significant reduction in absolute poverty is also intriguing. It also casts doubt on whether Bangladesh has been able to induce a pattern of growth that is inclusive (Table 2.10).

Table 2.9 Incidence of poverty in Bangladesh using CBN method (% of population)

Indicator	*HIES 1995–96*			*HIES 2000*			*HIES 2005*			*HIES 2010*			*HIES 2016*		
	National	*Rural*	*Urban*	*National*	*Rural*	*Urban*	*National*	*Rural*	*Urban*	*National*	*Rural*	*Urban*	*National*	*Rural*	*Urban*
Upper poverty line	50.1	54.5	27.8	48.9	52.3	35.2	40.0	43.8	28.4	31.5	35.2	21.3	24.3	26.4	18.9
Lower poverty line	35.1	39.4	13.7	34.3	37.9	20.0	25.1	28.6	14.6	17.6	21.1	7.7	12.9	14.9	7.6

Source: HIES various rounds

Table 2.10 Typology of interactions between poverty and inequality[a]

Poverty and inequality both rising	*Poverty rising, inequality falling*
No country in the South Asia[b] region	Pakistan (1998–2001)
Poverty and inequality both falling	*Poverty falling, inequality rising*
Nepal (2003–10)	Bangladesh
Maldives	India
India (1987–2003)	Pakistan
Pakistan (2005–10)	Sri Lanka (2009–16)
Sri Lanka (1985–90; 2002–09))	Nepal (1995 to 2003)
Bhutan	Bhutan (2007–12)
Bangladesh (1988–91; 2000–10)	

Source: World Development Indicators

Note: Poverty is reported as rising in Afghanistan but no Gini index is reported

[a]The trends reflected in this typology are still contentious and prone to criticism. The Gini index has been argued to underestimate inequality and further to this end, countries can exhibit low-income inequality but still have very high inequality in wealth, land, or other variables

[b]South Asia consists of the following countries: Afghanistan, Bangladesh, Bhutan, India, Maldives, Nepal, Pakistan, Sri Lanka

The typology above reflects the overall ramifications of economic growth and structural change on poverty and the distribution of income within the context of South Asia. South Asia embodies a diverse range of contexts, including fragile states such as Afghanistan and moderate to high growth contexts such as Bangladesh and India. There is also the small island state of the Maldives, landlocked countries such as Nepal and Bhutan and countries with the experience of prolonged conflict like Sri Lanka and Nepal. What it reflects is a general consistency in the reduction of absolute poverty though with a few exceptions. There has been no recorded reversal in poverty reduction in Bangladesh since independence, though the pace of poverty reduction has varied. Bangladesh has faced its share of episodic events that could have reversed the gains it had made: the phaseout of the multi-fiber arrangement (MFA) in the early 2000s and the rice price hike a few years later are two such examples. The Asian financial crisis in the late 1990s did reverse many gains that were made in some of the 'Asian miracle' economies in fact (Knowles et al. 1999). However, Bangladesh's success lies in its consistency as far as its track record on poverty and social development goes.

However, evidence suggests that inequality has fluctuated far more. In Bangladesh, the first decade of the 2000s registered a decline in income inequality as measured through the Gini index. Since 2010, however, income inequality is on the rise again. Others, such as Osmani (2015), have also suggested an increase in income inequality over the same period. It is very little in the way of the literature on Bangladesh that suggests that income inequality consistently declined over as long as a decade.

Even if we were to take the Gini index as reported in the World Development Indicators at face value, it is intriguing that inequality does not decline during the 1990s, when the country transitions to multiparty democracy, but rather a decade later. Similarly, in the case of Sri Lanka, inequality is declining just up to the end of the civil war and then rises in the immediate aftermath of the conflict. This is in stark contrast to the Nepalese civil war, where rising inequality is a precursor to the conflict that ensues and continues to rise during the Maoist insurgency, but then falls thereafter. It just goes to show that the relationship between inequality and conflict is just as conflictual and complex as that of the nexus between growth, inequality, and poverty.

In India, inequality is found to be declining during the decade of the 1990s, when India began to open up its economy and engaged in economic reforms. Other studies have actually suggested that inequality rose during this period for India (Pal and Ghosh 2007). Thus, the inequality trends need to be interpreted with caution. However, the decline of poverty for many of the countries like Bangladesh is certainly a point of consensus.

Demographic Change Precedes Structural Change

A consistent decline in poverty and significant improvements in social development characterize Bangladesh's experience with development. One of the successes for Bangladesh was also a substantial reduction in the total fertility rate (TFR) very early on and well before any headway was made as far as poverty reduction or economic growth. This also occurred in the absence of structural change from agriculture toward industry at that time that would propel urbanization. Chenery's 'patterns of development' theory that suggests that structural change precedes demographic change or at least occurs simultaneously is not the case for Bangladesh.

At the time of fertility decline, agriculture still constituted the lion's share of production, with very little in the way of industrialization. Even within agriculture, even as late as the year 2000, employment share in agriculture stood at approximately 50 percent. The structure of employment would certainly influence fertility decisions more than structure of production. Either way, no significant change was occurring in either of these at the time of fertility decline. In a similar vein, this demographic change cannot be entirely attributed to significant changes in women's labor market participation or levels of education. These trends occurred much later. The fertility decline that did occur early on, in fact, runs counter to the microeconomic household theory of fertility, which ultimately argues that it is through changes in the demand for children with which TFR can be lowered. Those factors that shape the demand for children include changes in income, for instance, which can, in turn, lead to households substituting the quality of children over quantity. Again, there were no significant increases in per capita income at the time of fertility decline (Asadullah et al. 2014).

Despite the proliferation of family planning initiatives early on, it is unlikely that the mere supply of such initiatives can trigger such a lasting change in reproductive behavior. A more compelling reason is discussed in Adnan (1998), who argues that fertility decline may have occurred due to the disassociation of the household as a unit of production. Bangladesh's average landholding size is already small, with a mere 7.5 acres classified as a 'large' landholding size. As such, it is widely reported that households have to rely upon multiple sources of livelihoods as the surplus generated from a farm-based livelihood is inadequate. A decline in average landholding size, as well as growing landlessness, would mean that the demand for children as family farm labor may have become weaker despite the persistence of poverty. This can explain the rationale behind demanding fewer children despite being situated in agriculture.

Agricultural Revolution or Stagnation?

The incompleteness of structural change raises another critical question as it relates to agriculture. Bangladesh's agriculture is characterized by small and fragmented landholdings. Though this is also the case for other countries in the region, the average farm size in Bangladesh is considerably lower. The need to engage in multiple rural livelihoods, in addition to farming to maintain the household, is also widely discussed (Toufique and Turton 2003). Given such a scenario, it is surprising when considered that food grain production trebled between 1972 and 2014, according to the World Bank and others. It is true that the numbers, as far as how much food is being produced, are prone to methodological errors and can be contentious.[7] Moreover, food production, in a context where natural disasters are a common occurrence, is prone to sharp fluctuations, so much so that Bangladesh remains a net food importing country. However, if we take these numbers at face value, it is mysterious as to how smallholder farmers, who need to engage in multiple livelihoods for their survival, can achieve this feat of increasing production of food and most notably, rice.[8] The two contexts seem to be at odds with each other.

The proposition that land size is inversely linked with productivity is one explanation, but this body of empirical scholarship has been widely discredited. There is a minimal empirical basis within the context of Bangladesh to argue that small farms are more productive; in fact, it has been demonstrated that the medium size farms are more productive vis-à-vis other size categories. A capitalist transition in agriculture that could potentially boost production is also considered to be absent within the context of Bangladesh (Mahapatro and Ullah 2014).

The technology and agricultural intensification argument provide a more plausible explanation in comparison to land size. A combination of high yielding varieties of seeds, access to agricultural inputs, such as fertilizer, irrigation facilities, such as shallow tube wells, and multiple cropping cycles contributed to production increases (Hossain et al. 2007). But it is important to note that this process did not occur in a vacuum. Though privatization and liberalization took place within agricultural input markets as part of externally induced structural adjustment reforms, the state still played an active role in agriculture. Multiple organizations were directly involved in the task of raising agricultural production including the Bangladesh Agricultural Development Corporation (BADC), Bangladesh Water Development Board (BWDB) and Bangladesh Rice Research Institute (BRRI) amongst others. These state agencies still continue to play an important role even in current times, though the nature of their roles have changed due to economic reforms involving privatization and liberalization. As Djurfeldt and Jirström (2005) rightly contend, the Green Revolution in Bangladesh was a 'state driven, market mediated' process.

Unlike some of the Southeast Asian countries, comprehensive land reform initiatives did not take off in Bangladesh. Land ceiling legislation, arguably, was not fully effective and was bypassed mainly through various means. However, the state did play a strong role in agriculture through other means. The government machinery pulled away in some instances such as fertilizer distribution and paved the way for private sector involvement. Similarly, the state also gave space for private sector import of irrigation equipment (Hossain et al. 2007). Even within a backdrop of privatization and liberalization, the state, through agencies like BADC and others, still maintained a footing to influence the direction agriculture has taken. Policies such as diverting limited power away from urban dwellers to power irrigation pumps or at other times closing down urea fertilizer factories in the interests of conserving energy are examples of how the state maintains its influence and the competing interests of agriculture and industry.

Geography, Institutions, and Channels of Persistence

Bangladesh's geomorphology places the country in a unique position to test theories of the nexus between geography and development. It was Sachs (2003) who strongly contended that geography does indeed matter using the case of landlocked countries, tropical climates, and other countries with distinct geographical characteristics. He claimed that these exogenous factors could have a significant impact on a country's development prospects. Bangladesh, as a low-lying delta, is highly susceptible and has already borne witness to the harmful impacts of climate change. River erosion and floods are a regular occurrence. But more than this, as a riverine country with an active delta, the recurring formation of alluvial lands known as chars is a distinct geographic trait that has significant and complex implications through its effect on property rights, investments in social infrastructure, and overall economic activity.

What Acemoglu and Robinson (2013) discussed dating back to the time when geography did influence the types of colonial regimes that emerged is relevant in contemporary times for Bangladesh. The types of institutions, or the lack thereof, in these riverine islands, is a direct result of the constraints of geography. Images of schools going underwater give a sense of how institutions are contingent on topography, climate, and the workings of nature. These are also some of the areas where land grabs, conflict, and intense primitive accumulation occur within the ambit of vague and fluid property rights (Adnan 2013).

How underdevelopment remains chronic within localized contexts is an important area to explore within the context of Bangladesh. Dell (2010) explored these channels of persistence in the case of the Mita districts of Peru, dating back to a colonial forced labor regime that has had a lasting impact on poverty and welfare even in contemporary times.

Banerjee and Iyer (2005) did a similar study that demonstrated how land tenure arrangements dating back to the colonial era have continued to impact productivity in current times. We find a similar persistence of underdevelopment in the Northwestern districts of Bangladesh, which tend to have the highest incidence of poverty in comparison to other regions. The same famine districts in Northwestern Bangladesh that were affected the most during the 1974 Bangladesh famine still face the problems of recurring seasonal hunger, a phenomenon known as Monga. What is interesting is that some of the districts in this region, notably Rangpur, were at the center of the earliest known peasant revolts and uprisings that took place in colonial Bengal dating as far back as 1783, when peasants set fire to administrative offices protesting the system of extraction imposed by the East India Company (Wilson 2005). Close to two centuries later, the Tebhaga movement in 1946–47 also finds its roots in North Bengal (Das 2013). This was the movement that called for landlords to ensure a two-thirds share of output to the sharecroppers known as *bargadars*. This region, particularly the jute growing areas of Rangpur, also bore witness to a long history of expropriation, exacerbated by the Great Depression of the 1930s, during which time jute prices plummeted and left indebted farmers with no choice but to give up their lands (Chatterjee 1997). Wilson (2005) mentions excerpts from the Floud Commission report of 1940, which provides detailed accounts of land concentration in the hands of a few, depeasantization, and a higher concentration of sharecropping in certain districts in North Bengal.

There is a long and far-reaching historical precedence to the current state of underdevelopment in the Northwestern region of Bangladesh. For one, there is a history of prolonged conflict and peasant revolt. Despite this level of mobilization amongst peasant groups in the region, however, the outcome has been that of 'thwarted' agrarian transition. Any discussion of seasonal famine or extreme poverty in this region must encompass an understanding of the colonial origins of this underdevelopment.

Where Does Bangladesh's Current High Growth Political Economy Come From?

So, what is the distinct political economy that has made way for Bangladesh to achieve growth rates over 7 percent and catapulted the country into middle-income status? There are certain attributes of Bangladesh's political economy that are developmental and have been favorable to multiple stakeholders. In addition to the success in terms of economic growth, the extent of poverty reduction and achievements in social development have also been considerable since independence, as discussed earlier. Simultaneously, however, there are features in Bangladesh's political economy that are also predatory, given the scale of bank loan default, the consistent underutilization of the annual development budget, and widespread corruption, as widely reported in news reports and cited in the literature.

Where can we place Bangladesh in Evan's typology of developmental and predatory states? The embedded autonomy argument that Evans (1989) claims as being the key reason for South Korea's success as a developmental state, however, is not fully evidenced in the case of Bangladesh. Although the government provides numerous incentives for industry, and in particular the RMG sector, this has not translated into a structural change within the industry (McCartney 2017), nor has it resulted in a full-fledged structural change from agriculture to industry (Khan 2013). Moreover, the fact that Bangladesh improved drastically in terms of social development in selected areas means that neatly categorizing Bangladesh into either developmental or predatory would be hasty and presumptuous. In more recent times, given growth rates hovering at over 7 percent, it can be argued that a distinct political economy has come into being that has, in turn, supported moderate to high growth consistently. Unlike Kohli's explanation for South Korea's high growth rooted in its colonial ties with Japan, this could not be the case for Bangladesh considering that its moderate to high growth commenced nearly two decades after independence (Kohli 1994). In fact, the economic outcomes for Pakistan and Bangladesh as far as economic growth and even social development indicators are actually in divergence and not the other way around as was the case for South Korea and Japan. Easterly (2001) labeled Pakistan as a case of 'growth without development,' which has clearly not been the case for Bangladesh.

It was Wade (2004) who contended very early on that some of the Southeast Asian countries, like South Korea and Taiwan, developed rapidly not because of rapid trade liberalization but due to strong, developmental states that could as he called it 'govern the market.' So, for instance, Wade (2004) discusses the case of Taiwan and how public officials were involved in maintaining relationships with selected domestic firms and 'nudging' them into higher value-added markets (Wade, p. 108). The genesis of the RMG sector in Bangladesh came about in a similar fashion:

dialogues between Daewoo officials and a retired civil servant with the support of the government (Khan 2013).

Thus, it can be argued that Bangladesh, notwithstanding its strong predatory inclinations, at least as far as industrial policy and in particular the RMG sector, still maintained the bearings of a 'developmental' state. Unlike South Korea and Taiwan, however, the government could not move the industry toward higher value-added if we consider the state of the RMG sector today. Nor has the state been able to induce structural change within manufacturing. Despite emerging industries such as the pharmaceutical sector, the industrial scene is still dominated by RMG. Moreover, the type of vertical integration that occurred in South Korea, for instance, through industrial conglomerates like that of the chaebol, did not take place in Bangladesh. The RMG sector, in fact, has witnessed more horizontal associations through structures like the BGMEA. What the state and private sector nexus did achieve, however, was to maintain export markets and in turn, keep the export-led growth model afloat. A similar nexus between the state and the private sector was also discussed in the case of agriculture.

What is interesting about the Bangladesh case is that its state apparatus is one that directs the development and has the power to constrain, undermine, or facilitate broader development objectives, all within the confines of a relatively weak bureaucratic and administrative setting. It can be argued that Bangladesh is also a state that oscillates between neoliberal pressures of opening up markets and privatizing versus that of retaining its hold over the private sphere. The state's ideologies and how they are manifested in policies and interventions characterize a *swing state*; however, its overall power and influence over the private sphere is one that can be argued to be dirigiste.

Conclusion

The purpose of this chapter has been to discuss the distinct features of Bangladesh's development trajectory as it relates to specific aspects of change, including social development, demographic change, and poverty. These trends all clearly have shaped up to represent a success story, despite rampant rent-seeking and corruption, coupled with the vagaries of climate-induced change. Bangladesh has made considerable progress in the area of social development and has reduced poverty consistently, without any reversals in fortune thus far. What can we attribute this success to? For one, size does appear to matter. Bangladesh, being a small and relatively homogenous country in terms of culture, language, and religion, unlike neighboring India, can be considered to be an advantage in the spread of ideas and innovative practices. Also, Bangladesh's size may have also played a role in fertility decline. Small land size holdings and the fragmentation of these landholdings over time may have weakened the demand for children even in the absence of material changes in well-being or structural change from agriculture to industry.

This chapter has argued that the links between income and selected development indicators may be weaker in some instances. This is found at the national, district, and household levels. Although attention has been given to how Bangladesh has achieved far more in the broader arena of social development relative to its per capita income, whether this is also the case at the more disaggregated district level, has not been explored. At the district level, some districts are better off as far as certain aspects of social development relative to district-level output per capita are concerned, while others are worse off. It is also demonstrated that district-level output is a stronger determinant of infant mortality rates than it is for under-5 mortality rates. Along the same lines, at the household level, belonging to the lowest wealth quintile significantly raises the odds of an infant dying. For under-5 mortality, the poorer (not the poorest) are found to have the greatest probability of a child dying. Thus, at each level—national, district, and household—a consistent picture emerges. Indeed, income and output are powerful determinants of social development. However, the evidence suggests that wheels of causation that link income to development are not so clear cut.

The experience of Bangladesh also calls into question some of the key theories of development. Bangladesh does not fall so neatly under the premises and predictions of the microeconomic household theory of fertility. Fertility decline has occurred before any significant changes in per capita income or incidence of poverty. Similarly, the pattern of development in Bangladesh is unlike that of the 'patterns of development' scholars, such as Chenery, who suggested that the process of urbanization and structural change would induce changes in household size. Fertility decline, again, has preceded significant changes in structural change.

This chapter also gives a considerable amount of attention to the role of the state and lays out how, despite claims of poor governance, the government has been, to some extent, a developmental, or dirigiste, state. This is evident in many sectors, including industrial policy and agriculture.

In the context of governance challenges and despite the trend of privatization reforms, the public sector has remained a strong force in both envisioning development and in navigating the path toward such development. What is interesting is that the state has arguably retained this dirigiste feature despite the precedence of political instability.

For example, Bangladesh was the first least developed country (LDC) to use the dispute settlement mechanism of the World Trade Organization (WTO).[9] This is the same country that has continued with the construction of the Padma Multipurpose Bridge even after the much talked about the cancelation of aid from the World Bank on charges of corruption. In more recent times, it could be argued that the government may be crowding out private sector investment through the higher returns it has offered on national savings certificates relative to bank deposits. All of these indicate that the government is playing a purposive, dirigiste role in the planning and promoting of development.

Whether the state or the private sector is the more efficient route in promoting such development is not a topic for discussion in this chapter. Clearly, there are limits to what both the state and the private sector have been able to achieve. Structural change from agriculture to industry is still incomplete, and even now, a vast majority of the population is still situated within agriculture in some shape or form. Child malnutrition is still high, despite significant reductions in poverty. The unevenness of development across regions within the country is also apparent.

In sum, Bangladesh's distinct trajectory is that of consistency in development outcomes without significant reversals in fortune. Much of the scholarship on Bangladesh has focused on the determinants of growth and development, both from economic and political economy perspectives. More research is needed, however, on the persistence of underdevelopment in selected areas or indicators within Bangladesh and the long-term origins of this underdevelopment.

Notes

1. See Rogaly et al. (1999) and Chatterjee (1997).
2. See O' Hara (2008) for analysis of these early economists' insights.
3. See the annual Human Development Reports (HDR) for further evidence.
4. It has been referred to by this name by the Bangladesh office of Helen Keller International.
5. Wealth scores in the DHS were determined based on an asset index.

6. There is some contention with regard to what happened to income inequality during the course of the Asian miracle although the decline in poverty goes uncontested.
7. M.A. Taslim (2019) provides a compelling critique of food production statistics and casts doubt on the accuracy of these numbers.
8. The author's field surveys in Noakhali also indicate that households who purchase land tend to do so through other means such as remittances and not through the value of agricultural surplus alone.
9. More on this particular case can be found in the World Trade Organization website at www.wto.org.

References

Abed, F. H. (2013). Bangladesh's health revolution. *The Lancet, 382*(9910), 2048–2049.

Acemoglu, D., & Robinson, J. A. (2013). *Why nations fail: The origins of power, prosperity, and poverty.* Broadway Business.

Adnan, S. (1998). Fertility decline under absolute poverty: Paradoxical aspects of demographic change in Bangladesh. *Economic and Political Weekly, 33*, 1337–1348.

Adnan, S. (2013). Land grabs and primitive accumulation in deltaic Bangladesh: Interactions between neoliberal globalization, state interventions, power relations and peasant resistance. *The Journal of Peasant Studies, 40*(1), 87–128.

Asadullah, M. N., Savoia, A., & Mahmud, W. (2014). Paths to development: Is there a Bangladesh surprise? *World Development, 62*, 138–154.

Banerjee, A., & Iyer, L. (2005). History, institutions, and economic performance: The legacy of colonial land tenure systems in India. *American Economic Review, 95*(4), 1190–1213.

Bangladesh Bureau of Statistics (BBS). (2016). *Report of the Household Income and Expenditure Survey 2016.* Dhaka.

Brown, C., Ravallion, M., & Van de Walle, D. (2017). *Are poor individuals mainly found in poor households? Evidence using nutrition data for Africa.* The World Bank.

Chatterjee, P. (1997). *The present history of West Bengal: Essays in political criticism.* Delhi; NewYork: Oxford University Press.

Das, S. (2013, January). Marginal communities in peasant movement: The sharecroppers' struggle for "Tebhaga" in North Bengal (1946–47). In *Proceedings of the Indian History Congress* (Vol. 74, pp. 640–651). Indian History Congress.

Dell, M. (2010). The persistent effects of Peru's mining mita. *Econometrica, 78*(6), 1863–1903.

Djurfeldt, G., & Jirström, M. (2005). The puzzle of the policy shift—The early Green Revolution in India, Indonesia and the Philippines. In *The African food crisis: Lessons from the Asian Green Revolution* (pp. 43–63). Wallingford, UK: CABI Publishing.

Drèze, J., & Sen, A. (2013). *An uncertain glory: India and its contradictions.* Princeton University Press.

Easterly, W. (2001). *The political economy of growth without development: A case study of Pakistan.* Paper for the Analytical Narratives of Growth Project, Kennedy School of Government, Harvard University.

Evans, P. B. (December 1989). Predatory, developmental, and other apparatuses: A comparative political economy perspective on the third world state. In *Sociological forum* (Vol. 4, no. 4, pp. 561–587). Kluwer Academic Publishers-Plenum Publishers.

General Economics Division. (2015). *MDGs to sustainable development transforming our world: SDG agenda for global action (2015–2030).* Dhaka: Bangladesh Planning Commission.

Hossain, M., Lewis, D., Bose, M. L., & Chowdhury, A. (2007). Rice research, technological progress, and poverty: The Bangladesh case. In *Agricultural research, livelihoods, and poverty: Studies of economic and social impacts in six countries* (pp. 56–102). Johns Hopkins University Press.

Khan, M. (2013). Bangladesh: Economic growth in a vulnerable limited access order. In D. North, J. Wallis, S. Webb, & B. Weingast (Eds.), *In the shadow of violence: Politics, economics and the problems of development* (pp. 24–69). Cambridge: Cambridge University Press.

Khondker, B. H., & Mahjzab, M. M. (2015). *Lagging district development.* A background study paper for preparation of the 7th Five Year Plan.

Knowles, J., Pernia, E., & Racelis, M. (1999). Social consequences of the financial crisis in Asia. Asian Development Bank.

Kohli, A. (1994). Where do high growth political economies come from? The Japanese lineage of Korea's "developmental state". *World Development, 22*(9), 1269–1293.

Mahapatro, M., & Ullah, M. (2014). An impasse in capitalist transition. *Economic and Political Weekly, 49*(2), 46–55.

McCartney, M. (2017). Bangladesh 2000–2017. sustainable growth, technology and the irrelevance of productivity. *The Lahore Journal of Economics, 22*, 183–198.

National Institute of Population Research and Training (NIPORT), Mitra and Associates, and ICF International. (2016). *Bangladesh Demographic and Health Survey 2014.* Dhaka, Bangladesh and Rockville, MD: NIPORT, Mitra and Associates, and ICF International.

O'hara, P. A. (2008). Principle of circular and cumulative causation: Fusing Myrdalian and Kaldorian growth and development dynamics. *Journal of Economic Issues, 42*(2), 375–387.

Osmani, S. R. (2015). *The growth equity nexusin Bangladesh.* An analysis of recent experience paper presented for conference on 'Towards sustained eradication of extreme poverty in Bangladesh', April 8–9, 2015.

Pal, P., & Ghosh, J. (2007). *Inequality in India: A survey of recent trends.* Working Papers 45, Department of Economics and Social Affairs, United Nations.

Rogaly, B., Harriss-White, B., & Bose, S. (1999). *Sonar Bangla?: Agricultural growth and agrarian change in West Bengal and Bangladesh.* Thousand Oaks: Sage.

Sachs, J. D. (2003). *Institutions don't rule: Direct effects of geography on per capita income* (No. w9490). National Bureau of Economic Research.

Taslim, M. A. (2019). The myth of food self-sufficiency. *Financial Express*, July 6. Bangladesh.

Toufique, K.A., & Turton, C. (eds). (2003). *Hands not land: How livelihoods are changing in rural Bangladesh.* A paper jointly supported by the Bangladesh Institute of Development Studies and Department for International Development.

Wade, R. (2004). *Governing the market: Economic theory and the role of government in East Asian industrialization.* Princeton University Press.

Wilson, J. E. (2005). 'A thousand countries to go to': Peasants and rulers in late eighteenth-century Bengal. *Past & Present, 189*(1), 81–109.

CHAPTER 3

Inclusive Economic Growth and Climate-Resilient Development in Bangladesh

Dwijen Mallick and Atiq Rahman

Introduction

Bangladesh was born in 1971 with widespread poverty, an increasing population, huge unemployment, illiteracy, food insecurity, and social insecurity. Frequent floods, drought, and other natural disasters also hit the economy, society, and lives of people very badly. At that time, very few people could feel hope for the economic development and prosperity of the country (Faaland and Parkinson 1976). The nation also went through a tough time politically after the assassination of Bangabandhu Sheikh Mujibur Rahman, the Father of the Nation. But the country has turned around, particularly from the mid-1990s, and has made steady progress in economic growth and social development. Bangladesh has leapt forward using its ability for economic risk reduction, and the will to graduate from a Least Developed Country (LDC) to a Developing Country (DC) status soon. It will receive formal recognition of this change in 2024 from the United Nations Economic and Social Council (ECOSOC). This organization will consider three aspects of development—per capita Gross National

D. Mallick (✉) • A. Rahman
Bangladesh Centre for Advanced Studies (BCAS), Dhaka, Bangladesh
e-mail: dwijen.mallick@bcas.net; atiq.rahman@bcas.net

M. K. Barai (ed.), *Bangladesh's Economic and Social Progress*,
https://doi.org/10.1007/978-981-15-1683-2_3

Income (GNI), Human Resources Index (HRI), and Economic Vulnerability Index (EVI) for the assessment. Interestingly, Bangladesh has already met these three criteria for graduation set by ECOSOC (Nathalie 2018; Khatun 2019).

This has not, however, happened overnight. In the last two decades, the economy of Bangladesh has been growing at nearly 6 percent per year. Presently, the gross domestic product (GDP) growth is hovering around 7 percent. In the Financial Year (FY) 2017, supply-side growth was driven by services and industry, which accounted for 3.4 percent of the officially estimated growth of 7.3 percent (World Bank 2018).This rapid economic growth in recent decades based on progress in exports and imports, ready-made garments (RMGs) and diversification of industrial products and exports, banking services, internal and external remittance for families and the rural economy, and the growth of urban-based service sectors, particularly ICT in the form of mobile phone and digital services in recent years, is visible. Bangladesh has also achieved laudable progress in social development (poverty alleviation, education for children, life expectancy, women's empowerment, food production, health promotion, and disease management) in the recent years despite some political unrest and frequent natural disasters. The poverty level dropped to 24.3 percent in 2017. This has been coupled with an increase in life expectancy, per capita income and food intake, although nutrition remains a significant concern (BBS 2017). The country achieved most of the previous Millennium Development Goals (MDGs) in the past decade. The Bangladesh Development Update of 2018 has noted strong economic growth, driven by public and private investment and consumption, which may continue in the coming years if there is political and social stability. Overall, the economy is moving forward; growing at a higher pace is possible by Bangladesh's own historical as well as international standards.

The country has made excellent progress in slowing down population growth from 3 percent in the 1980s to 1.3 percent in 2015. The improvement of education and health services in the rural and urban areas and agricultural development leading to increased food production and food security have been impressive. Greater participation of women in the formal economy labor force through the RMG sector and SMEs has also contributed to rapid economic growth and poverty reduction. Investment in physical infrastructure development and communication networks by the government has also supported trade, business, economic growth, and social development. In the infrastructure area, the construction of the Bangabandhu Multiple Purpose Bridge on the mighty Jamuna River has connected the Northwestern region of Bangladesh to the national economy and contributed to GDP and poverty alleviation in that region. Further, the development of agriculture (with improved seeds, fertilizer, and irrigation facilities for the dry season), crop diversification, and agribusiness have contributed to food security and rural development. The manufacturing industry, trade and business, and the service sectors are also expanding in the country. The service sector alone contributes 54 percent of the employment in the urban economy in Bangladesh (BBS 2017).

At the same time, Bangladesh has been experiencing rapid urbanization since the late 1990s. Dhaka has been experiencing 7 percent growth in its population annually because of pull factors (employment and income, trade and business, education, better living, and cultural attainment) and push factors (natural disasters, competition, conflicts over productive resources in rural areas, and climate change impacts). It is to be noted with grave concern that climate change is displacing thousands of poor and marginal sections of people in different ecologically stressed areas like coastal zones, riverine *charlands* (sands bars in the rivers, which look like islands but are facing flood and erosion), and hills every year, who ultimately end up in city slums and live in inhuman conditions. About 40 percent of the people live in poor quality of housing in Dhaka city without adequate basic civic amenities like water supply, sanitation facilities, health services, gas, and electricity (BCAS 2018).Further, rapid urbanization and industrialization (textiles and garments, leather, pharmaceutical, ICT, etc.) are also creating many environmental, ecological problems (many of the wetlands around the cities have been captured by the powerful elites for trade, business, housing, and industrial purposes), traffic congestion, air and water pollution, and public health risks. The climate change impacts in the rural areas and cities in the form of floods and water logging, heat stress, cyclones, and salinity problems in the coastal cities and heavy rain-induced landslides in Chittagong and Cox's Bazar are affecting infrastructure, small and medium enterprises (SMEs), large industries, investment and economic activities, agriculture, food security and water supply, and the social lives of the common people. Hence, the huge challenge for the country is to pursue a climate-resilient and socially inclusive development path. The effect of SDGs meeting the targets may lead the country to the right trajectory of climate-resilient and socially inclusive development.

For clarification, climate resilience development can be generally defined as the capacity of a socio-ecological system to absorb stress and maintain its functions in the face of external stresses imposed upon it by climate change, and adapt, reorganize, and evolve into more desirable configurations that improve the sustainability of the system, leaving it better prepared for future climate change impacts. With the rising awareness of climate change impacts by both national and international bodies, building climate resilience has become a major goal for these institutions. The critical focus of climate resilience efforts is to address the vulnerability that the communities, states, and countries have encountered with regard to the environmental and social consequences of climate change. Currently, climate resilience efforts encompass social, economic, technological, and political strategies that are being implemented at all scales of society (Folke 2006; Nelson et al. 2007).

On the other hand, inclusive economic growth and social development are about improving the well-being of every individual in society so they can reach their full potential. Real social development requires investing in people and enhancing their human potentials. It also requires the removal of barriers so that all citizens, particularly the poor and marginal sections of the society, can journey toward their dreams of development and livelihood outcomes, wealth and well-being with confidence and dignity. The UN Sustainable Development Goals (SDGs), known as the global sustainable development agenda for 2030, have also charted inclusive social and economic development pathways with specific targets. Further, based on five principles (i.e., people, planet, prosperity, peace and justice, and partnership), the SDGs aim at socially inclusive development so that no one will be left behind (United Nations 2015). The discourse of inclusive social development was elaborated in the World Summit for Social Development in Copenhagen recently, where the linkages between economic, environmental, and social aspects of sustainable development were assessed in the light of the Rio+20 Conference of 2012. The Rio+20 United Nations Conference on Sustainable Development (UN CSD), held in June 2012, acknowledged the need to integrate the economic, social, and environmental aspects of sustainable development. It stressed that sustainable development must be "inclusive and people-centered, benefiting and involving all people, including youth and children" (UN General Assembly 2012).

As issues of the economic development in Bangladesh are discussed broadly in various other chapters of the book, this chapter mainly focuses on the climate-resilient development of Bangladesh, which has not received the importance it really deserves. However, this chapter is primarily built on desk-based review and consultations with experts on climate change and sustainable development. Limited scale primary and secondary data on climate change trends and impacts in Bangladesh have also been used in section "Inclusive Growth and Development in National Policies, Plans and Strategies" of the chapter.

Inclusive Growth and Development in National Policies, Plans, and Strategies

The Government of Bangladesh has prepared the Perspective Plan of Bangladesh (2010–21) based on the Bangladesh Vision 2021 to mark the 50th anniversary of independence. The Perspective Plan provides a road map for accelerated economic growth and lays down broad approaches for the eradication of poverty, inequality, and human deprivation. It is interesting to note that the national vision and goals are commensurate with the UN SDGs 2030 to achieve inclusive social development whereby basic needs of the population are ensured, basic rights respected, where everyone is adequately fed, clothed, and housed, and has access to health care (GED 2012). The specific strategies and the tasks of implementation will be articulated through two five-year plans. The Perspective Plan further emphasizes that Bangladesh is a nation endowed with enormous potential that is yet to be realized. The national goals and targets sound good, and the challenges are effective planning and adequate resource allocation and implementation as per targets.

In recognition of the long-term development challenges, the government, under the leadership of Prime Minister Sheikh Hasina, has adopted Vision 2021, with associated development targets for Bangladesh. Those targets, if achieved, will transform the socioeconomic condition of Bangladesh from a low-income economy to the first stage of a middle-income economy. Along with higher per capita incomes, Vision 2021 lays down a development scenario where citizens will have a higher standard of living, will be better educated, face better social justice, and have a more equitable socioeconomic environment. The sustainability of development will be ensured through better protection from climate change and natural disasters. The associated political environment will be based on democratic principles with emphasis on human rights, freedom of expression, rule of law, equality for citizens, irrespective of race, religion, and creed, and equality of opportunities. It is expected that the Bangladesh economy will be managed within the framework of a market economy with appropriate government intervention to correct market distortions to ensure equality of opportunities, and to ensure equity and social justice for all (GED 2012). However, there are concerns about growing inequality, which need to be recognized by the government, policymakers, and actors, including the private sector, who are the key players of economic growth and social development in the country.

Thus, the development priorities of the Perspective Plan are distilled from the vision statement formulated to take Bangladesh to where it ought to be in the year 2021, given its human potential and natural resource endowments. Those development priorities include ensuring broad-based growth and reducing poverty; ensuring effective governance and sound institutions, but creating a caring society, addressing globalization and regional cooperation, providing energy security for development and welfare, building a sound infrastructure and managing the urban challenges, mitigating the impacts of climate change, and promoting innovation in a knowledge-based society. For Bangladesh, the journey to a middle-income country and high HDI (Human Development Indicator) status thus requires sustained growth with equity and fairness. The technical framework designed to achieve growth and related dimensions of the macroeconomy shows that the economy needs to grow at a consistently high rate over the next eleven years for the vision to be realized.

Further, a prudent macroeconomic policy will be required to ensure internal and external stability, low inflation, and high economic growth. It is expected that acceleration of economic growth and reduction of poverty—two principal goals of the Perspective Plan—will come about through the dynamism and inter-linkages among the three broad sectors of the economy already mentioned: agriculture, industry, and services. A vibrant and highly productive agricultural sector is a prerequisite for the kind of growth acceleration envisaged in the Perspective Plan. The provision of food security is also a constitutional obligation. Hence, both the Perspective Plan and the 7th Five-Year Plan have attached the highest importance to food security and social safety of the poor, marginalized groups, women, and indigenous communities (GED 2012). The food production, availability, marketing, transporting and supply in the remote parts of the country (such as *haor* basins, coastal islands, riverine *char-lands*, and hilly areas) are very often obstructed by climate change and natural disasters. The latter is to be addressed promptly by the government and the private sector, which dominate the market in the critical times during and after a devastating flood and cyclone.

The 7th Five-Year Plan (2016–20) of the government of Bangladesh has prepared the strategic directions and policy framework for both macro- and microeconomic development with utmost emphasis on GDP growth, structural changes, employment generation for higher income, and socio-economic transformation toward inclusive social development. The recent five-year plan has also put the focus on reducing poverty and income inequity, gender equity and social protection through fiscal policy and annual development plans of the government of Bangladesh. The challenge for the 7th Five Year Plan (2016–20) is to build on the successes of the immediate past while taking further actions to address emerging challenges and the areas of shortfalls of the past.

The first year of the 7th Plan also coincided with the launch of the UN post-2015 Sustainable Development Goals. In the backdrop of these factors, the 7th Plan centers on three themes: GDP growth acceleration, employment generation, and rapid poverty reduction. The Plan has a broad-based strategy of inclusiveness to empower every citizen to participate fully and get benefit from the development process. A sustainable development pathway that is resilient to disaster and climate change has also been charted, with emphasis on sustainable use of natural resources, environmental conservation and managing the challenges of increasing urbanization due to both pull and push factors like climate change impacts and human displacement (GED 2015). More policy attention to be given for displaced people. Higher resource allocation is to be made for the climate hotspots to address climate change impacts as well as to reduce human displacement. Further, the localization of SDGs through bottom-up planning, local capacity building, and engagement of local actors, including the local government institutes (LGIs) will be crucially important for achieving the SDGs in Bangladesh.

The government of Bangladesh has also prepared a National Sustainable Development Strategy (NSDS) in the backdrop of the SDG 2030 preparation. The NSDS (2012) emphasized economic development with social equity and environmental conservation for ensuring the suitability of the development outcomes. The economic imperatives that are reflected in the NSDS include growth with equity through industrialization, employment generation, and rural infrastructure. The social imperatives are an improvement of health, education and human resources development, participation, and gender equity. The environmental considerations are sustainable management and conservation of forests, water, lands and biodiversity, energy efficiency, air and water pollution control; and meeting all their relevant international obligations. The government is implementing multilateral environmental agreements (MEAs), including the Paris Agreement on climate change through the Nationally Determined Contribution (NDC). The challenges will be to build the capacity of the ministries and departments to integrate adaptation and mitigation options of the Bangladesh NDC into their sectoral programs.

The government has further prepared a road map and country strategy to implement the SDGs and has aligned the key ministries, departments, and agencies with their role and responsibilities to achieve their targets in Bangladesh. The UNDP is providing technical support and guidance to the Planning Commission of the government for mainstreaming the SDGs targets in sectoral programs. Inter-agency coordination and broader partnership of government with NGOs, local actors, and private sector would be needed for effective implementation of the SDGs with the core principle of Leaving No One Behind (LNOB). Millions are lagging behind in Bangladesh, because of many social and institutional factors, geophysical conditions (remoteness, bad communications, and exposure to climate change impacts), and market monopoly and technology divide. The SDG implementation process must endeavor to reach first those who are furthest behind with the principles of social inclusion, effective participation, wider partnership, and capacity building of the actors and stakeholders for the people who are living in the Hard to Reach (HtR) areas. It is crucially important to know—who are left behind in Bangladesh in both rural and urban contexts; what are the causes and what should be the strategies for reaching the left behind? Ensuring LNOB would require urgent and immediate actions for the poor, women, marginal groups, climate migrants, indigenous communities, and disadvantaged groups of the society.

Climate Change Impacts on Development and Livelihoods of Common People

Climate change poses the greatest threat to human security and civilization today. It puts an enormous challenge for sustainable development of the world. The problem was and is mainly being created by the rich and industrialized countries, while the poor are the primary victims of climate change impacts. Many negative impacts of climate change are being felt locally, particularly in poor and developing countries. Climate change will increase global food insecurity, hunger, poverty, social conflicts, and migration to cities. The enormous, forceful and devastating cyclones *Sidr* and *Aila* that hit the coast of Bangladesh recently not only killed thousands of people but also devastated the lives and livelihoods of millions. The devastating cyclone *Nargis* generated in the Bay of Bengal spared the Bangladesh coast but severely hit the Myanmar coast in May 2008, killing more than one hundred thousand people and injuring millions. The occurrence of the major cyclones in such proximity is consistent with IPCC projections about extreme climatic events. The most recent cyclones (such as Mahsen in 2016), and the massive rain-induced landslides in 2017 caused immense loss and damage to lives and properties in the coastal regions including in the hilly districts of Bangladesh.

The recent frequent and prolonged floods and cyclones in Bangladesh, Australia, the USA, China, India, and Indonesia have destroyed the lives and livelihoods of millions. The most recent unusual cold wave and snowfall in Europe and North America are early signals of catastrophic changes in weather patterns and climate change. Increasing drought in Africa is causing crop failure and reduction of yields, which created food insecurity for millions. These have a close link with global warming and climate change. Thus the extreme climatic events across the world reconfirmed the IPCC assertion that it is the poor of developing countries who are the most vulnerable to the onslaught of climate change and its impacts. The poor are at the forefront of natural disasters and climate change impacts. They have the least capacity to address the devastating effects of these disasters on their lives, livelihood, and health.

However, while climate change is obstructing development efforts and is compounding the poverty situation in developing countries. Global food price hikes induced by biofuel production and trading has also created huge food crises in developing countries and also led to food riots in a few African countries. A recent report by the World Bank confirms that 70 percent of the recent food price hike in the global market was caused by biofuel production and trading. In this context, Prof. Amartya Sen says that the stomachs of the poor are competing with the fuel tanks of the rich nations. A recent UN report (2018) has confirmed that food insecurity, hunger, and poverty are rising globally with unruly climate change; over 821 million people are undernourished in the world in 2017 (The Daily Star, May 2018). Hence, the poor and marginal communities need greater support to feed themselves and maintain their livelihoods (Fig. 3.1). The Fig. 3.1 shows major climate hazards in Bangladesh.

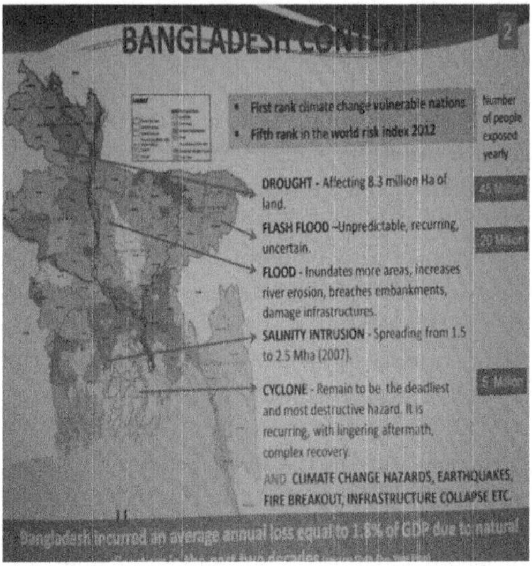

Fig. 3.1 Major climate hazards on the Bangladesh map. (Source: Quayyum 2015)

Bangladesh is already experiencing the adverse impacts of global warming and climate change. According to the world disaster risk index (2012), Bangladesh has been ranked first in climate change vulnerability and fifth as a disaster-impacted country in the world. It is affected by multiple climate disasters including floods and erosion, cyclones, sea-level rise (SLR), salinity and drought. Millions of people are affected by climate-induced natural disasters every year, which cause huge loss and damage to the economy, and is equivalent to 1.8 percent of the GDP of the country (Quayyum 2015). Besides the extreme events, the summers are becoming hotter, the monsoon is irregular, there is untimely rainfall and heavy rainfall over a short period, causing water logging and landslides. Crops are damaged due to flash floods and monsoon floods. Crop failure is also caused by increasing drought, prolonged cold spells, salinity intrusion along the coastal region. SLR and salinity put stress on freshwater leading to scarcity of potable water for drinking. The climate impacts are also evident in the forms of coastal erosion, riverbank erosion, deaths due to extreme heat and extreme cold, increasing mortality, morbidity, prevalence and outbreak of dengue, malaria, cholera, and diarrhea, and so on. Climate change impacts are already adding significant stress to physical infrastructure and environmental resources, human ability, and economic activities. The IPCC, in its assessment report-5, described the climatic

Table 3.1 Major climate change trend with physical and social impacts

Climate change trends and key physical impacts	*Major socio-economic impacts*
Temperature rise and heat waves Changes in rainfall patterns: untimely, inadequate and heavy rainfall Frequency and intensity of natural disasters • Floods and erosion • Cyclone and storm surges • Drought • Salinity, sea-level rise and • Water logging Changes in seasons (summer is becoming longer and hotter, winter is shrinking and monsoon is erratic) Water quality is affected by flood, drought, and salinity Severe impacts on mangrove forests, biodiversity, and coastal ecosystem	Water scarcity for irrigation, human consumption, domestic and industrial uses Loss of agricultural production, livelihoods, and food insecurity Diseases outbreaks (water borne and heat stress) and health risk Damages to infrastructures (roads and communications) and human habitats Human displacement and climate change induced migration Increasing urban poverty and conflicts over land and limited resources Loss and damage to industries, trade, and business, particularly SMEs

Sources: Constructed. Consultations with experts, 2018

anomalies and their impacts in Bangladesh. The current climate change trends and key impacts are presented in Table 3.1.

Climate Change and Development Linkages

The development has both positive and negative links with climate change. Industrialization and modernization, burning of fossil fuel, global trade and business, destruction of natural resources for industrial production and overconsumption particularly by the rich created the problem through GHG emissions and global warming. The current level of rapid climate change is the result of many anthropogenic factors and unequal development. On the other hand, climate variability and extreme events again affect natural resources base, ecosystems, human systems, social systems and the development process affecting poverty alleviation, food and water security and the livelihood of the billions in developing countries. The following diagram shows the complicated relationship between climate change and development as well as suggesting both mitigation and adaptation measures to protect socio-economic development (Rahman 2015) (Fig. 3.2).

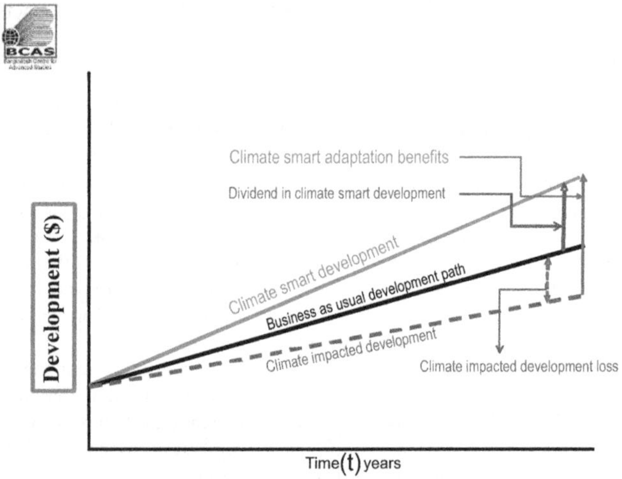

Fig. 3.2 Development over time in climate change scenario and adaption need

The Human Development Report of 2007–08 argues that the progress made in recent years in human development is being threatened by climate change (UNDP 2008). The signs can be already seen mainly amongst the poorest and most vulnerable populations and countries. The report warns about the loss of agricultural productivity leading to food insecurity and water stress and causing enormous health risks. Further, climate-induced natural calamities and climate inflicted bio-fuel issues affected the food production and food trade, which may result in a price hike for food grains in developing countries. Global wheat production has decreased sharply in the last few years because of increasing maize cultivation destined for biofuel production for the rich countries. The poor and marginal sections of populations are mainly the victims of this situation. It is acknowledged that climate variability and changes will affect agriculture and food security, water and human health, ecosystems, natural resources, and the livelihoods of ordinary people. The frequency, intensity and impact of climate change-induced natural disasters and possible sea-level rise may dislocate millions of people from the coastal districts of Bangladesh. Thus, they will increase rural to urban migration and social conflict over limited resources.

A recent study by BCAS (2018) in the Northwestern Region of Bangladesh has identified a range of climate change stresses and natural disasters in that region. The study covered 10 districts of the Rajshahi and Rangpur divisions and found that the major climate change-related disasters are: drought and heat stresses, flood and riverbank erosion, the drawdown of underground water, cold waves and fog, Nor'westers, thunderstorms, and pest attacks. The participants from all districts also reported erratic rainfall, hailstorms, and tornadoes as major climate disasters (Mallick et al. 2018). Please see the disasters matrix in Table 3.2, wherein disasters slightly differ across the sub-regions.

Villagers have consistently identified 10–12 climate disasters in their localities and have prioritized 5–7 disasters as the most devastating climate disasters considering their frequency and impacts on the lives and livelihoods of the people. In the Rajshahi and Naogaon districts, the communities have prioritized drought and heat stress as the number one climate disaster followed by drinking water scarcity, Nor'westers, falling groundwater levels, erratic rainfall, thunderstorms, and cold waves in winter. In the Dinajpur and Thakurgaon districts, cold waves and fog along with drought and heat stress were identified as the most harmful climate disasters in the study villages. They also identified Nor'westers, hailstorms, erratic rainfall, pest attacks, flood and other water crises as the major climatic disasters in their locality. In Rangpur region, the villagers have identified frequent floods and riverbank erosion as the most devastating natural

Table 3.2 Percentage distribution of responses regarding type of natural disasters

Type of hazards & disasters	*Rajshahi*	*Dinajpur*	*Rangpur*	*All*
Drought	100.0	97.7	19.8	68.1
Heat wave	99.2	99.2	37.3	77.4
Flood	2.4	83.8	100.0	65.7
River erosion	–	–	98.1	38.1
Draw down of ground water	98.4	96.2	27.2	70.0
Erratic rainfall	52.8	56.2	59.3	56.4
Cold wave	95.2	96.2	93.8	95.0
Thunder storm	16.8	43.8	55.6	40.3
Nor'wester	91.2	89.2	80.2	86.3
Water logging	25.6	2.3	2.5	9.4
Pest attack	57.6	84.6	75.9	73.1
Hail storm	37.6	0.8	9.3	15.1
Tornado	5.6	0.8	7.4	4.8
Others: Heavy rainfall	1.6	22.3	0.6	7.7

Sources: Field Survey by BCAS (2018)

disasters followed by a cold wave and fog, Nor'westers, drought and heat stress as well as sand storms and hail storms. Thus, drought, heat stress, cold waves, Nor'westers, drinking water scarcity, and pest attacks were found to be common in all the study villages.

The following sections briefly discuss the climate change impacts on key development sectors. The most impacted sectors in Bangladesh are agriculture and food security, water, fisheries and ecosystems, forest and biodiversity, economy and livelihoods, human health, and infrastructure and communication.

Agriculture and Food Security

Climate change poses a severe threat to agriculture, particularly in developing countries. Both climate variability (rise of temperature and changes in rainfall patterns) and the extreme climatic events like drought, flood, cyclone, and so on, affect agricultural productivity and food security. Over 60 percent of the people in Asia depend on agriculture for their employment, income, food, and livelihoods. Drought and climatic events have already decreased food production in recent years and degraded the food security situation there. There have also been increased pest attacks on tropical crops in the warmer climate, and this has also led to crop loss and food crises. Salinity intrusion and possible sea-level rise have already affected coastal agriculture and therefore, the livelihood of millions in Bangladesh (Mallick 2015).

Food price hikes in the global market also have a close link with biofuel production and the price of mineral oils. Considering the severity of the price problem, the former UN-Secretary General Mr. Ban Ki-moon urged the global community to take immediate and urgent actions to address it in a high-level meeting of the World Food Program (WFP) in Rome in May 2008. The technical sessions of this meeting discussed the vital links between climate change impacts, bio-fuel, and the global food crisis. The meeting suggested immediate- and long-term actions by various actors including government, development partners, research organization, and community organizations. The immediate actions would be food assistance for the most hungry and vulnerable communities while the long term efforts would be to support agricultural development with seeds and local innovation in input supplies to increase the resilience of the agricultural system in the context of climate variability and impacts.

Water and Ecosystems

The IPCC-AR5 report warned about the possible crisis and conflict over access and control of degraded water resources. The situation would be aggravated in warmer climates. Over 1.2 billion people lack access to safe water, and 2.5 billion do not have access to basic sanitation in the world (IPCC 2014).The Stockholm Environment Institute has estimated that by 2025, the proportion of the world's population living in countries of significant water stress will increase from approximately 34 percent (1995) to 63 percent. Global warming is exacerbating water stress by changing rainfall patterns, river flows, lake levels, and groundwater recharge patterns. In some places, water sources are becoming more depleted; other areas are being hit by floods. Globally, river basins and wetlands—where most of the world's populations live—are damaged and are less able to provide the conditions and processes that provide a water supply of adequate quality and quantity to ensure sustainable development and maintain vital ecosystems. Fisheries are becoming depleted and degraded. Freshwater resources are highly sensitive to weather and climate variability.

The rapid rise of temperature in the atmosphere and the consequent rapid changes in global climate will affect hydrological patterns at local and regional scales, which will, in turn, affect the availability of fresh water for agriculture, water for drinking and domestic uses. The climate model simulations available suggest that total flows of freshwater, the probabilities of extreme high and low flow conditions, seasonality, surface and groundwater interfaces, and water quality could all be significantly affected by climate change over the coming decades. Access to safe drinking water will be reduced in many regions resulting in human health problems, particularly in Africa and Asia (Reid et al. 2007).

Disease Outbreaks and Health Risks

Global warming will cause multiple impacts on human health and a wide range of vector-borne, water-borne, and respiratory diseases from the demonstrated links to warmer weather and climatic change. The most vulnerable people will be aged groups, children, and urban poor populations. Already some regions are suffering the consequences. For example, Bangladesh is already susceptible to outbreaks of climate-sensitive diseases. The incidences of malaria have dramatically increased in the last 30 years, and malaria is now a significant public health problem in the hilly districts of Bangladesh. Other diseases like diarrhea, skin diseases, asthma, hypertension, dengue fever, and dysentery are also increasing, especially during the summer and the monsoon period. Climatic factors, such as temperature, rainfall and salinity, are directly connected to incidences of diarrhea, skin diseases, malaria, dengue fever, and other illnesses. Climate change is also likely to affect the distribution, lifecycle, and population dynamics of the mosquitoes that spread dengue fever. Additional factors such as dehydration, malnutrition and heat stress, especially among children and the elderly, are closely linked to heat stress, water supply, sanitation, and low food consumption. All of these situations will be affected by global warming. Climate change will mean that there will be less clean water in a country where waterborne diseases are already responsible for 24 percent of all deaths (Reid et al. 2007).

Hurricanes, storms, and heavy rainfall have direct life-threatening impacts. Urban and coastal populations are particularly at risk from storm surges, flooding, and coastal erosion. Increased incidences of diseases also follow floods. Access to safe drinking water is compromised by drought and other factors, such as salinity in water supplies. The health of common people is further threatened when nutrition is undermined by the impact of weather extremes on farming. There has been a change in seasonal patterns: hot, long and dryer summers may increase the scarcity of water, which will cause various water-borne diseases in Bangladesh.

According to The New Climate Economy Report, "the poorest developing countries will be hit earliest and hardest by climate change, though they have contributed little to causing the problem" (Global Commission on the Economy and Climate 2014). The recent report of the IPCC has asserted that climate change will deepen poverty. The direct impacts of climate change include loss of life, destruction of asset bases, infrastructure and livelihoods of the poor from extreme climatic events. The livelihoods of the poor need to be protected and improved in the context of climate change risks and vulnerability. Resource support and alternative livelihoods are to be generated for the affected groups. The most vulnerable group may need social and economic rehabilitation. The policies and programs in a country should be devised in line with current and future risks.

Sea-Level Rise, Extreme Events, and Human Displacement

The possible sea-level rise will affect low-lying and coastal zones in Bangladesh. Millions of people would be displaced from their homes, occupations and livelihood, and many would be thrown into poverty again. The trend is already evident in the country. Bangladesh is experiencing a higher level of tidal inundation in the coastal districts. The country would be highly vulnerable to sea-level rise. The climate scientists viewed that the rate of sea-level rise would be faster than was predicted earlier. About a 45 cm sea-level rise will not only affect the vast coastal ecosystems, water tables and hamper agriculture and food production, but may also dislocate about 35 million people from 20 coastal districts by the year 2050 (Rahman 2015). This may create severe problems in rural livelihood, and regional and sectoral development as well as in sharing of scarce resources (land, water, forest, and fisheries) and thus it will enhance rural to urban migration and generate social conflicts in the near future. The emerging climate refugees will put enormous pressure on the Bangladeshi urban economy and infrastructure (housing and communication) as well as on essential services such as water supply, power, health and sanitation that are not within the affected zones.

International migration policies and programs are to be reformulated in the light of the influx of climate refugees, particularly from the climate hotspots in the country. Before people are forced to move, assistance should be provided with reasons to enable people to stay within their community and culture. Locational and regional scale rehabilitation and resettlement are to be advanced before the onset of sea-level rise to a greater extent.

Growing Vulnerability, Poverty, and Inequity

Bangladesh has to pay huge economic, social, and development costs due to climate change impacts and natural disasters. The global average annual cost of climate disasters has increased because of climate change-induced frequent and devastating floods, cyclonic storms, droughts, and heat waves. The economic loss and damage due to climate change have further increased substantially recently due to inadequate adaptation actions, particularly in the developing world, where climate change impacts are very high. A recent climate scenario by the UNEP suggests that tropical regions will be highly at risk of climate hazards, which will not only eat up the development gains but will threaten the future potential of development in the South Asian region including Bangladesh.

There is evidence in and around us that climate change undermines and will undermine most of the development gains already made by developing countries. Climate change will increase poverty and inequality in different climate zones in Bangladesh. Hence, enhancing resilience for climate risk reduction should be the central focus of the planning processes of Bangladesh. This was reflected in the report of the World Economic and Social Survey (2016). The report also says that 12 million poor people living in the coastal areas of Bangladesh are experiencing the severe negative impacts of climate change that affect their agriculture, food security, water, sanitation, health, employment, income, houses, communication, infrastructure, habitat, and livelihood. One of the top three reasons for failure in poverty alleviation globally is climate change. The report reiterates that the conditions of low-income people, who already face inequity, will worsen due to the impacts of climate change (UN-DESA 2016).

The impacts of climate change, degradation of natural resources and the ecosystem, and structural inequity are locked in a vicious cycle. Vulnerability and exposure to climate variability and extremes are closely linked to existing inequity and poverty. Restricted and differentiated access to physical, financial, and social capitals and unequal opportunity of access to government supports and services enhance vulnerability. Uneven access to health services, education, and employment (particularly of the poor, women, and communities living in hard-to-reach areas) and the perpetuation of discrimination under existing institutional and cultural norms create social conditions for greater vulnerability. These are being again aggravated by climate change, natural disasters, and other externalities like market shocks in Bangladesh. Further, the areas and habitats of the poor and marginal communities are exposed to climate hazards and they are highly sensitive to its impacts and shocks. Thus, the economic activities and livelihood of the poor living in both rural and urban areas (mainly in the slums and fringe areas) are severely affected by climate change and natural disasters, which will again deepen the poverty situation and inequity in the society.

An Agenda for Climate-Resilient and Inclusive Development in Bangladesh

The government, people, and other actors in Bangladesh are aware of the risk and vulnerability due to climate change that is affecting all the development and livelihood efforts in the country. People are coping with the adversity of climate change and taking measures for adaptation in agriculture, water, health, infrastructure, economy, and livelihood with limited resources, using their accumulated and increasing experiential knowledge. The government, NGOs, and development agencies are supporting community adaptation and sectoral adaptation as well as disaster risk-reduction activities. The government has prepared the National Adaptation Programs of Action (NAPA) and the Bangladesh Climate Change Strategy and Action Plan (BCCSAP), created Bangladesh Climate Change Trust Fund (BCCTF) and has developed the climate change fiscal framework. Over 400 projects of varying sizes are being implemented by the government departments, development agencies, and communities to address climate change in the areas of adaptation, mitigation, and disaster risk reduction in different climate affected zones (Mallick et al. 2018). However, these are inadequate compared to higher risks, vulnerability, and adaptation needs of the community and sectoral development. The adaptation and disaster responses are giving the basis for resilience-building resilience and contribute to the sustainable development of local communities and regeneration of ecosystems, where the poor and vulnerable communities are using their resources, indigenous knowledge, and social networks to confront many of the climate change impacts.

The Integration of the Paris Climate Agreement and SDG-13

The Paris Climate Agreement (2015) has provided a sound basis for climate actions by all member states of the United Nations. The Paris Climate Conference and its universal outcome have saved the multilateral negotiation and decision process. This offers a framework, principles, and a decision process. The conference has agreed on five-year pledge cycles for mitigation, adaptation, technology, and finance. A new mechanism for mitigation called the Nationally Determined Contribution (NDC) was agreed in Paris, although it was widely criticized as a nonbinding treaty. Paris has also agreed to create a fund of USD 100 billion per year from 2020 for adaptation and mitigation, although it is felt to be inadequate compared to the huge need for adaptation (Rahman 2015). The government of Bangladesh has prepared a road map for implementation of NDC, which has been already submitted to the United Nations Framework Convention on Climate Change (UNFCCC) secretariat. The NDC focuses on three key sectors: energy and power, transport, and industry. The country is committed to reducing 5 percent of GHG emissions in the three sectors voluntarily and 15 percent reduction by 2030 with financial support under the UNFCCC. The commitments of the Paris Agreement could be achieved through immediate and urgent actions in (i) integration of adaptation in national economic, social, and sectoral development policies and strategies included in the Five Year and Annual Development Plans; (ii) development and implementation of long-term mitigation strategy; (iii) allocation of finance; and (iv) monitoring and measuring the outcomes of climate actions.

The SDGs formulation process has rightly included the goal-13 for taking urgent climate action, which will again influence positive outcomes for all the other key goals. The country is committed to building adaptive capacity and resilience in social, human, and natural systems, as well as to undertake mitigation measures to stop rapid and dangerous climate change. Adaptation is the priority in Bangladesh because of a higher level of vulnerability. The government of Bangladesh has prioritized several adaptation measures in the National Adaptation Programs of Action (NAPA) and Bangladesh Climate Change Strategy and Action Plan (BCCSAP). Considering the growing needs and priority of adaptation to climate change, BCAS, with government and partners, is promoting a community-based adaptation (CBA) approach and practices in climate-affected zones in the country. BCAS and International Institute for Environment and Development (IIED) have organized a series of international conferences on CBA approaches and practices in the developing countries to share new knowledge and experiences on CBA as well as to promote collaboration among the governments, practitioners, scientists, and communities for mainstreaming adaptation in local and sectoral development (Rahman et al. 2012).

Ensuring Green Growth and Socially Inclusive Development

There have been good signs of an increasing young workforce (due to a positive demographic transition with about 40 percent youths), higher investment, and employment in key sectors such as Readymade garments (RMG), service sector and ICTs, agro-industries, and pharmaceuticals. The remittance from the migrant labor force has contributed to the recent economic growth and consumption. Transferring the population to improved human resources and enhancing productive employment in a politically stable situation can certainly lift Bangladesh to a rapid economic development path. But there are serious concerns about environmental degradation, climate change impacts on development potentials and increasing social inequity and disparity. The economic growth should be guided by sustainable development principles, where social and ecological objectives of development must take a central position in building a socially inclusive, environmentally sustainable, and democratically vibrant society. Good governance and environmental management must play a key role in charting out the future sustainable development path for Bangladesh. The country must pursue the path of green development and inclusive growth with distributive justice. Internalization, localization, and implementation of SDGs will help to continue that inclusive social development path where no one will be left behind and no one will suffer from a poverty of any dimension, or hunger, food insecurity, ill health, deprivation, and inequality.

The experiences in the west and industrialized countries suggest that the rapid economic growth with industrialization and urbanization will result in environmental degradation, increasing climate change, and social inequity. To avoid these ill-consequences, we must pursue economic growth with equity and justice, reduce environmental degradation and risks, which will promote green growth in the future. Most importantly, the economic growth and development path must ensure human well-being and peace in society. The growth and development path also must reduce carbon emission (which cause rapid changes in climate) and reduce pollution, enhance the use of renewable and energy efficiency, and prevent loss of biodiversity and ecosystems, which gives the basis for the livelihoods of millions in Bangladesh, particularly the poor, women, and marginal communities. Ecosystem services must be used for the well-being of the poor and marginalized communities.

Rebuilding Natural and Social Capital

The new development path must maintain, ensure and, where necessary, rebuild natural and social capitals as critical assets for economic development and livelihood for many. The sustained and equitable economic growth with investment in youth, employment generation, and job creation must also redirect attention and resources to poverty reduction and gender equity, while taking into account climate change through adaptation and mitigation.

The economic growth and productivity must not undermine the quality of life and ensure building resilience of the community, people, actors, institutions, and ecosystems to climate change. These would need a lot of investment by the government and the private sector, policy support, technology, and innovation at all levels from planning to implementation.

The key areas for intervention and innovation would be resources efficiency, technology transfer, resilient infrastructure, energy efficiency, climate and disaster risk management for key sectors, including agriculture and food system, water and nutrition, garments, particularly of the small and medium enterprises (SMEs), information technologies, and service sectors. These are to be supported by institutional integration and good governance.

Purposeful engagement of all actors from the government, development partners, NGOs, civil society, scientific communities to ordinary people, responsive private sectors, and resourceful, accountable government would lead us to a climate-resilient, socially equitable, and sustainable development. Translating the Paris Agreement, Sendai Framework on Disaster Risk Reduction (DRR), SDG, and Green Development principles will undoubtedly lead to socially inclusive and environmentally sustainable development.

Conclusions and Recommendations

Development is a multidimensional process, where the key objectives, including the social, economic, and environmental imperatives, are to be met through achieving socially inclusive, sustainable, and climate-resilient development. The achievement of one goal can influence the other positively. Further, good governance, freedom of choice to enhance the capacity of people (Sen 1998), democracy, and responsive institutions are the prerequisites for equitable, inclusive, and sustainable development. Appropriate and effective institutions at the national and local levels are required for better education and public awareness, human resources development, productive employment, health care, social safety net, and human well-being, particularly for the poor, women, and marginal communities. The government and actors are marching toward rapid economic growth and development, but growing inequality is a big concern in Bangladesh. This should be addressed immediately through policy reforms and practical measures.

The environmental, social, economic, and political implications of global warming are profound. It is evident that ecosystems—from mountain to ocean, from poles to tropics—are undergoing rapid change. Mitigating climate change, eradicating poverty, and promoting economic growth and political stability all demand the same solutions: we must kick the carbon habit to reduce our carbon footprint. We must reduce GHG and carbon emission urgently and immediately to save the planet and human civilization. The good news is that technologies already exist, or are under development, to make the consumption of carbon-based fuel cleaner and more efficient and to harness renewable energy from the Sun, wind, and waves. We all are parts of the solution. Conscious individuals, organizations, political authorities, and the private sector in the country and across the world must understand the problems and opportunities. They must undertake urgent and bold actions now for saving the mother earth.

The critical challenges are: (a) to stop climate change through urgent mitigation measures now and create effective implementation of post 2030 development agenda with commitments and greater participation of both developed and developing countries to halt dangerous climate change; (b) explore how to live in a warmer climate, which is now unavoidable; and (c) promote low carbon economy and curtail the extravagant lifestyles of the rich, who do the most harm through luxuries and overconsumption. The Agenda-21, UN-SDGs, and the Paris Climate Agreement under the UNFCCC give us the guiding principles toward a transformation and positive shift of economy, society, and the right types of development.

It is also strongly felt that for achieving sustained growth and inclusive development, both public and private investment to be enhanced in the country. The quality of investment to be ensured by improving planning and budgeting, as well as institutional strengthening and governance for monitoring and supervision (GED 2013). Further, Foreign Direct Investment (FDI) to be attracted by improving investment climate; and quality of education and Human Resources Development (HRD), which is to be upgraded for better employment, higher income and productivity, and quality of living. Export diversification as well as overseas employment with a more skilled and technical labor force to be pursued for sustained economic growth and inclusive development.

In addition, to build a resilient society, both sociopolitical and policy responses, as well as an ecological response to environmental conservation are needed. Science, innovation, and a technological response will be required to tackle climate change impacts and to build resilience in human, social, economy, and ecosystems to address climate change impacts and other externalities. Capacity building of all actors from grassroots to the national level is crucially important for planning and implementing the new approaches and activities toward a climate-resilient society.

Sustainable development is the key objective of every citizen of Bangladesh. We are at the threshold of a new integrative paradigm of development challenges and opportunities. Integrating the approaches of inclusive growth, confronting and building capacity for climate change adaptation, mitigation, and resource mobilization along with achieving transformative resilience to natural disasters and climate impacts will enable Bangladesh to enter this new phase of development and move rapidly toward sustainable development. Bangladesh's key actors, including the government, NGOs, CBOs, the private sector, and its communities, must decide on the key and urgent issues of appropriate institutionalization to succeed in this integrative paradigm of Sendai Framework on DRR, Paris Climate Agreement, and SDG frameworks for marching toward a sustainable future.

There are compelling arguments in favor of making the transition toward a climate-resilient and low-carbon economy and green development that presents a huge opportunity rather than a burden. Greening the global economy might cost as little as a few tenths of global GDP annually over the next 30 years, but it could be a driving force for innovation, new business, industries, and employment opportunities across the developed and developing worlds. Fighting climate change and poverty requires multiple, but combined and accelerated efforts by the governments, development agencies, relevant actors, and vulnerable communities. These may include both software and hardware as well as structural measures to raise awareness, build capacity, protect resource bases and the livelihood of the poor, and reduce the various risks and vulnerabilities of climate change. The key policy and institutional responses may include the following:

- Enhancing understanding and awareness about climate change impacts at local and social contexts.
- Developing urgent measures for stopping dangerous climate change by reducing GHG emissions and ensuring full implementation of the Paris Climate Agreement.
- Building the capacity of the poor and other stakeholders to reduce risk and vulnerability.
- Protecting the poor and their assets and livelihood from climate impacts.
- Advancing community adaptation to climate change.
- Improving DRR in the current and future threat of climate change.

- Ensuring sectoral adaptation and climate proofing of development efforts.
- Provisioning resource transfers and technological support for the poor and most vulnerable.
- Building greater resilience in natural, human, and social systems.
- Raising the voice of the poor, women, and marginal communities against climate injustice.

References

Bangladesh Bureau of Statistics. (2017). *Bangladesh statistics 2017.* Dhaka: Statistics and Information Division (SID), Ministry of Planning.

Bangladesh Center for Advanced Studies (BCAS). (2018). *Building resilience for sustainable and inclusive city: Dhaka a case study.* Paper presented at RISC workshop at the University of Leicester, UK.

Faaland, J. and Parkinson, J. R. (1976). *Bangladesh—The test case of development.* C. Hurst and the University of Michigan, USA.

Folke, C. (2006). Resilience: The emergence of a perspective for social-ecological systems analyses. *Global Environmental Change, 16*(3), 253–267. https://doi.org/10.1016/j.gloenvcha.2006.04.002

General Economic Division (GED). (2012). *Perspective plan of Bangladesh (2010–2021)—Making vision 2021 a reality.* Dhaka: Bangladesh Planning Commission, GoB.

General Economic Division. (2013). *National strategy for sustainable development.* Sher-e-Bangla Nagar, Dhaka: Planning Commission.

General Economic Division. (2015). *Seventh five year plan—FY 2016–FY 2020: Accelerating growth and empowering citizens.* Sher-e-Bangla Nagar, Dhaka: Planning Commission.

Global Commission on the Economy and Climate. (2014). *Better growth better economy: The new climate economy report.* Washington, DC.

IPCC. (2014). *Climate change: Impacts, adaptation and vulnerability.* Assessment Report-5, Working Group-II, WMO and UNEP.

Khatun, F. (2019, March 12). Looking beyond high growth in Bangladesh. *The Daily Star.* Dhaka.

Mallick, D. (2015). *Development challenges and poverty alleviation in the changing climate in Bangladesh.* Working Paper of BCAS. Dhaka.

Mallick, D., Karmaker, S., & Chowdhry, O. T. (2018). *Patterns and effects of climate change on food security and livelihoods in the Northwestern region of Bangladesh.* Dhaka: BCAS and NETZ Bangladesh.

Ministry of Environment and Forest. (2012). National Sustainable Development Strategy (NSDS) of Bangladesh. Segunbagicha, Dhaka.

Nathalie, R. (2018). *Bangladesh, UN consider expected LDC graduation in 2024.* IISD, SDG Knowledge Hub.

Nelson, D. R., Adger, W. N., & Brown, K. (2007). Adaptation to environmental change: Contributions of a resilience framework and resources. https://doi.org/10.1146/annurev.energy.32.051807.090348.

Quayyum, A. M. (2015). *Mainstreaming DRR and CCA across the sectors and actor.* Technical presentation in a workshop, organized by the CDMP-II, Ministry of Disaster Management and Relief, Bangladesh, Dhaka.

Rahman, A. (2015). Bangladesh vulnerability to climate change: Development and climate interface, Presentation in a Seminar of BCAS, Dhaka

Rahman, A., Rabbani, G., & Mallick, D. (2012). *Community based adaptation—Early learning from CBA conferences.* London: BCAS and IIED.

Reid, H., Simms, A., & Jahnson, V. (2007). *Up in smoke? Asia and the Pacific: The threat from climate change to human development and the environment.* London: IIED.

Sen, A. (1998). *Development as freedom.* New York: Oxford University Press.

The Daily Star. (2018, September 12). Hunger rising with unruly climate. Based on a UN Report, Dhaka.

The World Bank. (2018). *Bangladesh development update: Building on resilience.* Dhaka: The World Bank Office.

United Nations. (2012). Resolution adopted by the General Assembly, July 2012 on the Future We Want; 66th Session, New York.

United Nations. (2015). *Inclusive social development.* General Assembly, E/ESCWA/SDD/2015/2.

UN-DESA. (2016). *Climate change resilience—An opportunity for reducing inequalities.* World Economic and Social Survey, 2016. New York: United Nations.

UNDP. (2008). *Human Development Report 2007–2008.* New York: UN Plaza.

CHAPTER 4

Education, Health Care, and Life Expectancy in Bangladesh: Transcending Conventions

Anis Pervez and H. M. Jahirul Haque

Introduction

Conventional development models are struggling to explain the accomplishments Bangladesh has achieved in different sectors, of which education, health care, and life expectancy are vividly distinctive. For example, the average life expectancy of the people of Bangladesh has risen to 72.3 years in 2018, as compared to 72 years in 2017. It used to be only 49 years in the 1980s. This is coupled with the progressive growth of human capital as published by the World Bank Group's Human Capital Index (HCI) while a constant economic growth has become a mundane reality of Bangladesh since the 1990s. All these are accomplished when the country does not seem to have a proper context for development that the conventional development theories, such as modernization and dependency, would set as preconditions. The country has a large population, the 8th

A. Pervez (✉)
Bangladesh on Record, Dhaka, Bangladesh

H. M. J. Haque
University of Liberal Arts Bangladesh (ULAB), Dhaka, Bangladesh
e-mail: jahirul.haque@ulab.edu.bd

M. K. Barai (ed.), *Bangladesh's Economic and Social Progress*,
https://doi.org/10.1007/978-981-15-1683-2_4

largest in the world; housed in one of the smallest geographical territories, that is, 94th in the world; and prone to natural calamities. Also, Bangladesh is yet to establish good governance, as some findings report. Despite all these odds, improvement is progressively taking place. In education, the country has nearly established a ubiquitous primary education program. The health sector has thoroughly spread to the periphery. This is a triumph over underdevelopment that shatters the understanding of the way development has been explained so far, and it impedes comprehension of the feat Bangladesh has achieved.

Theoretically, from a conventional point of view, the causes of such accomplishments are puzzling (Asadullah et al. 2014). To answer this, one may need to transcend traditional thought on development and, instead, examine the process of development from a different perspective for a logical interpretation of such a seemingly indefinable scenario. This, as a knowledge and policy outcome, will contribute to redefining development thought that many nations, similar to Bangladesh, might find appropriate to adopt. This chapter analytically projects on the development that has taken place in education, health care, and life expectancy (EdheL) in Bangladesh, explaining what has caused this progress. Such analysis will aid in identifying a development model in the making.

EdheL and Human Capital: Development Redefined

The unprecedented development in Bangladesh—spreading over the economy to all other social sectors of which education and health are especially notable—is a "development paradox" (Sarker and Nawaz 2019; Hossain 2017) as the achievements transcend explanations of conventional development models. Regarding the growth of education and health services in spite of limited state resources in terms of budgetary allocation and the percentage of GDP expenditure in these sectors, the accomplishments are impressive. It is, therefore, a mystery to be unraveled through an examination through a different lens of the Bangladeshi context and its practices.

Opposing the development economists' findings that education does not necessarily have an economic return (Asadullah 2005, 2009), this chapter argues that education triggers human development necessary for improving consciousness leading to the accomplishment of other entitlements, including health. Complementing the government's attempt to spread education, non-state development organizations, that is, NGOs, have been working in the field under various programs—non-formal education, health education and so on—while also providing skill training, like vocational, health management, and finance and organization management, especially to those who receive microcredit for microenterprise (Zohir 2004). It is distinctive that the NGOs use an integrative model, where education is connected to health and both are again related to food security and nutrition, and further to income-generating activities. Thus, a full circle of human development is carried out by them, whereas in many other countries, the state organizations are expected to be responsible for them.

With the incremental growth of GDP, private sectors are coming onto the scene with investment in education and health. Even though such investment is city-centric, the private sector in education and health services are contributing to the quality development, which is likely to make an impact on the job market where the skilled worker is still a deficit.

Development literature independently shows education (Hossain 2004) and health (Ullah et al. 2006) as indicators of development, which the nations aim to accomplish. But dominant development studies—be it classical modernization theory (Lerner 1958), dependency theory, or economy-centric growth theory (Rostow 1960)—could not systematically establish how education and health in combination results in human capital development to upscale human cognitive competence and physiological fitness to maximize the use of material resources and non-material forces into shaping the world servicing community's need, let alone regenerate the resources in a sustainable way as knowledgeable and skillful people will live longer to sustain the reproduction of social goods.

We have developed the following model to unveil the triadic relationship between education, health, and life expectancy as they produce and reproduce social capital to ensure sustainable development (Fig. 4.1).

This model logically argues that education and health in combination affect life expectancy, which strengthens human capital required for appropriate use of available resources and constant regeneration of resources for further development. Such a triadic relationship, where individuals are educated and possess sound health to be able to actively live longer, makes citizens conscious about their entitlements, thus triggering further development.

According to this model, education provided knowledge and skills to improve cognitive competence for thoughtful pragmatic decision-making, which, aided by sound health—physical and mental—strengthen human capital for development. Therefore, in this chapter, instead of spelling out

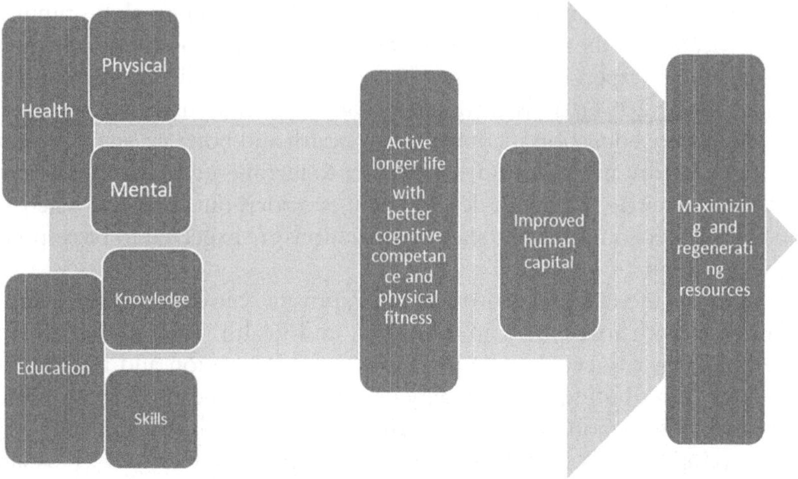

Fig. 4.1 Triadic relationship of health, education, and life expectancy toward development. (Source: Authors' construction)

a descriptive and suggestive scenario of the state of education and health in Bangladesh, we will present how development is practiced with notable success as a combined effort of state and non-state actors.

State of Education

Despite inadequate government expenditure on education as allocated in the national budget, which is much less than the world average, Bangladesh has achieved enormous success by ensuring universal primary education, dramatically improving the literacy rate and female enrolment at all levels of education, with a recent emphasis on employment-focused skills-based education (Rahman 2009). The government, in collaboration with NGOs and the private sector, is making fast progress to "ensure inclusive and equitable quality education and promote lifelong learning opportunities for all" as stated in the Sustainable Development Goal 4 by the United Nations (UN) (Fig. 4.2).

With the help of 150 thousand institutions and over a million teachers, the country provides education to 40 million students. According to the EFA 2015 National Review, primary and secondary level institutions comprise the lion's share of these statistics, with approximately 19 million and

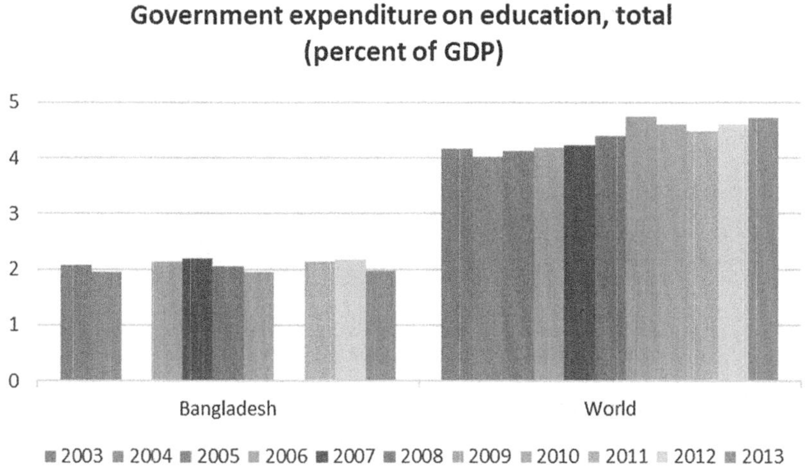

Fig. 4.2 GDP contribution in education: Bangladesh and the world. (Source: UNDP 2016)

12 million students, respectively. Basic education development in the country is guided by the Compulsory Primary Education Act 1990, Education for All (EFA) National Plan of Action (NPA) I and II, National Non-Formal Education Policy 2006, National Education Policy 2010, National Skills Development Policy 2011, Seventh Five-Year Plan (2016–20), and Perspective Plan 2011–21. Various initiatives concerning basic education such as Primary Education Development Program (PEDP) 1, PEDP2, and PEDP3 were implemented over the years.

The literacy rate in Bangladesh climbed remarkably over the previous decade to a high of 72.76 percent in 2016. This denotes a rise of 26.1 percent from 2007, when the literacy rate was an insignificant 46.66 percent. For the same period, the literacy rate for females has ascended from 43.74 percent to 69.90 percent, and for males from 49.83 percent to 75.62 percent (UNESCO 1917). The literacy rate for the age group between 15 to 24 years rose to 92.24 percent in 2016, up from 61.87 percent in 2007 (Khan 2018). The information additionally uncovered that the number of educated youth, both male and female, climbed drastically over the last decade. In 1971, at Bangladesh's emergence as an independent country, the literacy rate was 47 percent (Figs. 4.3 and 4.4).

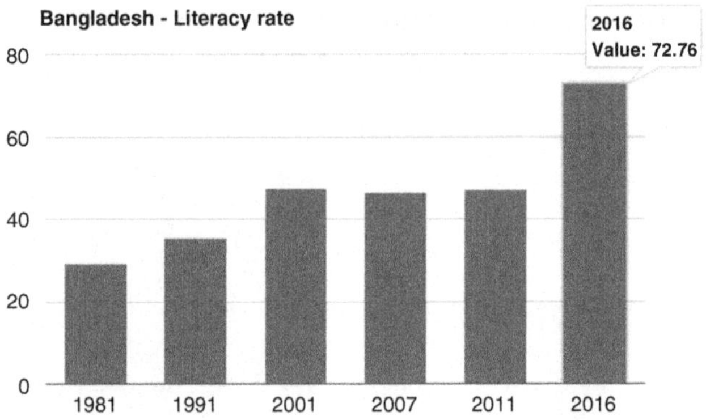

Fig. 4.3 Increase in literacy. (Source: UNESCO 2017)

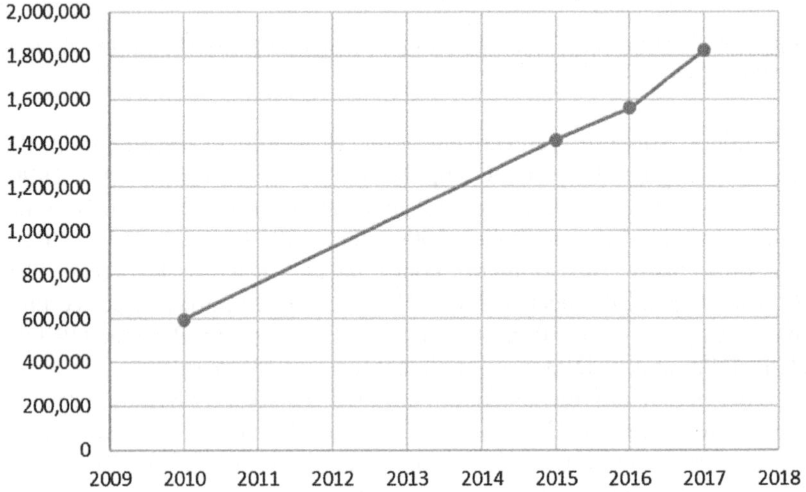

Fig. 4.4 Increase in girls' enrolment. (Source: Bangladesh Population and Housing Census (2011))

State Initiative

As data from BANBEIS (2018) indicates, since 2000, Bangladesh has shown significant advancement in quite a few areas in terms of educational accomplishments. These include:

1. Almost 100 percent access to primary education and almost 75 percent of children enrolled in the preprimary class
2. Around 66 percent of children in secondary schools
3. Increase in adult literacy rate from about 60 percent ten years ago to 73 percent
4. Zero-percent gender discrepancy in access to primary and secondary education
5. About 14 percent of secondary-level students (from 2 percent ten years ago) in the vocational track
6. Increased interest bolstered by extending stipend scheme and free textbooks
7. Improvement in student-teacher ratio, increase in teachers' wages, acceptance of student evaluation reforms, and improvement of school offices.

Table 4.1 lists some notable government initiatives.

To improve nationwide education, the government has launched the five-year Secondary Education Development Program (SEDP) at the cost of $17.2 billion. The SEDP will cover grades 6–12 annually, supporting more than 12 million students and 357,000 teachers from more than 20,300 general schools, 9400 madrasahs, and 1190 general schools with secondary school certificate (SSC) vocational stream programs. The purpose of the SEDP is to accomplish a progressively productive, impartial, comprehensive, and quality secondary education system for the twenty first century global citizens. Support includes waiving of tuition and examination fees and free books. There is also an allocation for student stipends in addition to teachers' and other stakeholders' training to upscale the quality of education.

The key elements of reforms are improved quality and relevance of curriculum; strengthened teacher quality; well-developed teaching-learning practices in Bangla, English, Mathematics, Science, and ICT; strengthened reading habits and skills among secondary-level students; enhanced classroom assessment; a better national learning and examinations structure; a more effective use of ICT for pedagogy; improved labor market relevance; increased equitable access and retention to secondary education; school infrastructure development; improved access and retention; enhanced cycle completion for girls and disadvantaged areas; strengthened governance, management, and planning; strengthened decentralized management; strengthened education management information system, monitoring, and evaluation; improved teacher management and

Table 4.1 A list of government policy and programs

Policy and program	*Description*
Sheikh Hasina National Youth Development Institute Act, 2018	• Made for the establishment of a central and modern standard institute for empowering potential youths through training and motivation. • To conduct research, higher education, training, and constructive activities for the youths in their overall development.
Higher Education Quality Enhancement Project (HEQEP)	• To improve the quality and significance of teaching and research conditions in higher education institutions through empowering both development and responsibility within universities and by upgrading the specialized and institutional limit of the higher education sector.
Seventh Five-Year National Development Plan (2016–20)	• To promote comprehensive improvement with unique consideration given to disadvantaged groups, women, children, and people with disabilities. • To grow the rate of higher education from 12 to 20 percent. • To enhance the standard and quality of university education and ensure quantitative expansion on desired lines without any compromise to quality. • To consolidate and strengthen existing universities. • To guarantee access to computer and Internet facilities. • To give top priority to science and technology, business administration, and teachers' training programs. • To legitimize enlistment among different disciplines. • To give more emphasis on research and training. • To initiate online education. • To further emphasize the development of libraries and laboratories. • To reinforce the University Grants Commission. • To establish the accreditation council. • To address gender discrimination in the education sectors. In higher education, only 40 percent of the enrolled students are female. The situation is worse at public and private universities, where just 26 percent of students are female. This arrangement consolidates procedures for elimination of gender discrepancy by giving special financial support to female students and bringing to light the importance of female training. • To modernize the Madrasa system. • To increase the number of educational facilities to meet the demand in the Madrasa sector. • To advance the vision of "Digital Bangladesh," ensuring more extensive access to ICT in Madrasas. ICT is to be consolidated in the teaching process of Madrasas. The government additionally endorsed multi-media classrooms at Madrasas.

(*continued*)

Table 4.1 (continued)

Policy and program	*Description*
National Education Policy, 2010	• To grow technical and vocational education to transform the enormous youth populace of Bangladesh into expert and talented human assets. This policy deems it essential to impart virtues, trustworthiness, patriotism, accountability, and social duty into young people as they acquire quality modern education and learning of contemporary science and technology. • To proficiently convey training to the students of the disadvantaged community and smaller ethnic groups, and the disabled students by catering to their special needs. • To develop fine arts and crafts education to address the issue of expanding chronic drug use among young people. Through development of structured intellectual activities, this training may be compelling enough to oppose this risk. • To introduce Scouts, Girl Guides, and Bangladesh National Cadet Corps BNCC to help adolescents and others develop into self-deferential, autonomous, honest, ethically stable, enterprising, mindful, self-aware productive members of the society and nation. • To help the students of colleges and universities secure effective, sound mentality and control through the activities under BNCC.

Source: BRAC (2018)

accountability; improved school management and accountability; strengthened sector planning, management, and coordination; and so on.

Non-State Contribution: NGOs

Non-state actors, particularly NGOs, are playing a significant role in implementing Sustainable Development Goal 4 (SDG4), that is, education, at the grassroots level by operating in remote regions. NGOs are largely concentrating on human development, that is, health, nutrition (Nisbett et al. 2017), and population (Guda et al. 2004); education (Hossain 2004; Blunch and Das 2015); water, sanitation, hygiene, skill development, environment, and climate change; both rural and urban development, agriculture, food security, migration, gender justice, and poverty eradication. The spirit of SDGs is "Leaving No One Behind" (LNOB). The NGOs are working mostly to address the left-behind groups like those living in geographically hard-to-reach (HtR) areas, deprived and underprivileged communities, and physically challenged population. Approximately a thousand NGOs in Bangladesh have different types of education and skill training programs, and they are actively involved in achieving the targets of SDG4. NGO programs are focused on both service delivery and advocacy. With a service delivery approach, NGOs are carrying out programs/projects to address the issues of dropouts and left-out children; inclusive education; early childhood development and care; girls' education; education services for geographically hard-to-reach areas; technical and vocational education; lifelong learning; adult education; multi-lingual education; tertiary and vocational education, and so on. According to the data, NGOs have already developed the following scenarios in the field:

- Delivered education services to 2.9 million learners (61.71 percent girls/female) through 79,573 learning centers/schools and continuing
- Operating 37,000 formal and non-formal centers/schools with 1.7 million learners (56.56 percent girls)
- Providing preprimary education support including Early Childhood Development (ECD) through 25,000 centers covering 700,000 learners
- Providing lifelong learning facilities through 20,000 community learning centers for 700,000 learners.

(Citizen's Platform for SDGs, Bangladesh, 2019)

BRAC, the largest NGO in the world, is a case in hand of how significantly NGOs in Bangladesh are contributing to educating the people in the country. Bangladesh has gained remarkable ground toward accomplishing Education for All (EFA). It has been adulated for its success in accomplishing gender equality at both primary and secondary school levels. Likewise, significant advancement has been made in the enrolment level. Nonetheless, it is assessed that 1.3 million primary school-age children still have no access to education. The rate of student dropouts from formal schools is likewise high, due to some degree of poverty as families are unable to afford the cost of education. Additionally, poor participation, a deficiency of trained teachers, and a high student-teacher ratio of 51:1 are undermining the quality of education and students' overall triumph. Hence, it is quite essential to advance educational reform just to execute ventures which supplement the formal education framework.

BRAC started the BRAC Education Program (BEP) in 1985 to address a portion of these difficulties.

BEP was at first propelled as BRAC Non-Formal Primary Education (NFPE) in 1985 and, in 2003, was renamed as BRAC Education Program (BEP). BEP completes its program exercises according to a five-year plan and is active in five major areas:

- One of the major programs of BRAC is non-formal primary education, through which poverty-stricken children receive quality primary education.
- The preprimary school program lays the foundation for primary school enrolment for children above 5 years of age across the country.
- Unguarded adolescents, especially girls, are trained in vocational skills, health awareness (including reproductive health), and leadership through the Adolescent Development Program (ADP) to improve the quality of their lives.
- The Multi-Purpose Community Learning Centers provide lifelong learning and IT facilities for all the people in a community and encourage their contributions toward promoting education.
- "The Mainstream Secondary Schools Support" initiative builds the abilities of rural secondary school teachers and helps to upgrade classroom pedagogy as well as the overall quality of education.

Under BEP, school premises are leased from the community, which also provides safe environments where children can play games or participate in co-curricular exercises. Besides, these communities cater to clean drinking water and proper sanitation. As indicated by the 2007 audit report, the yearly cost (January to December) of the program is BDT 3,322,331,606 (equivalent to USD 47,461,880 according to current exchange rates). The average expense per student is USD 23 per year. According to the 2015 audit report, the annual budget is BDT 4,389,896,386, which is approximately equivalent to USD 56,280,723. The present expense per student is USD 45 per year.

BRAC's educational ventures started in 1985 with 22 one-room schools. The programs secured three upazillas, served less than 700 children, and were managed by only five staff members. Today, BEP works on a national level. It accesses 470 of the 490 upazillas in every one of the 64 districts of Bangladesh. Also, the BRAC school models have been imitated on national and global levels. In Bangladesh, 714 smaller collaborating

NGOs are applying the BRAC non-formal school model to give basic primary education in remote territories. The BRAC school model has additionally been emulated in other nations, for instance, the likes of Afghanistan, Tanzania, Uganda, South Sudan, and Pakistan.

The following figures give a clear idea of BEP's impact:

- Throughout the country, almost 1.3 million children enroll in BRAC schools annually.
- To date, more than 11 million children have graduated from BRAC schools.
- Over 6 million children have finished the preprimary school level.
- The ADP serves more than 273,000 students, while the 2853 rural libraries in multi-purpose community learning centers (Gonokendras) and 9000 Kishori Kendras give members access to an array of reading materials. The community learning centers have 1.25 million members.
- 5.9 million students (approximately 61.4 percent of girls) have been transferred to a primary school after completing the preprimary course to date.
- 5.26 million graduates (roughly 65.3 percent young women) from primary school have been transferred to secondary schools to date.
- 78 percent of all students gain the expected skills upon completion of their courses.
- The overall dropout rate is a mere 6 percent.
- 88 percent of Gonokendras are self-funded.

Students are required to pass the Grade V examination set by the government. As indicated by BRAC's information, in 2015, 99.97 percent passed this examination, demonstrating that BRAC school students are on par with mainstream/formal primary school students. BRAC schools in this manner show that their students are taught indistinguishable abilities from government schools, even though they enlist and hold a greater extent of difficult-to-reach children, for instance, girls, who comprise 62 percent of the student body.

Several NGOs spread over the country are also running vocational training in addition to formal education. Areas of training include improved agriculture, para-veterinary, ICT skills, and so on. In this way, people in the periphery are developing sellable skills that ultimately contribute to the overall development of Bangladesh.

Non-State Contribution: Private Sectors

When state policy determined compulsory free primary education for all, with special emphasis on females to be educated to at least eighth grade, tertiary education flourished alongside. Continuous state initiatives and private sector involvement contributed to establishing more than a hundred universities, where, according to 2017 data from the University Grants Commission, the largest number of students were enrolled as illustrated in Fig. 4.5.

The total number of universities increased at the rate depicted in Fig. 4.6.

As seen in the chart above, it is distinctive that in this increase or expansion of tertiary education, the involvement of private sectors and their contribution is higher than the state. At present, 70.56 percent are private universities, and 29.13 percent are public universities.

The rise and expansion of private universities are phenomenal on many counts. For one, they accommodate students that the state universities cannot do due to limitations. Besides, private universities are market-oriented and, therefore, flexible. Moreover, private universities helped to diversify higher education and offered opportunities to the untapped population of Bangladesh. The contribution of the private sector to education complements the state efforts, and thus a countable workforce is being produced that any country will need to translate into economic growth. As a spillover effect, the employment sector is expanding, and, most remark-

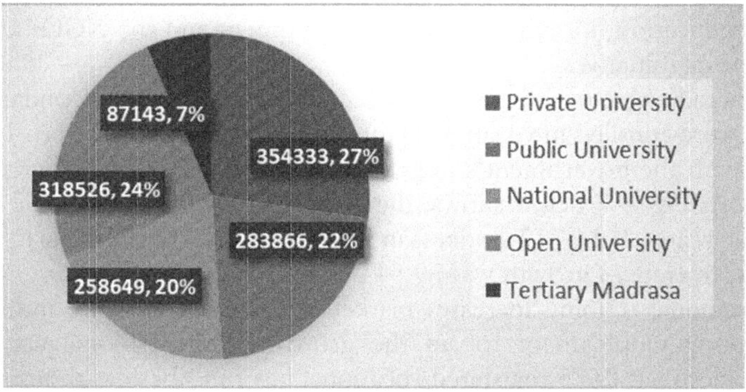

Fig. 4.5 Enrolment of students at tertiary level. (Source: Bangladesh University Grant Commission 2017)

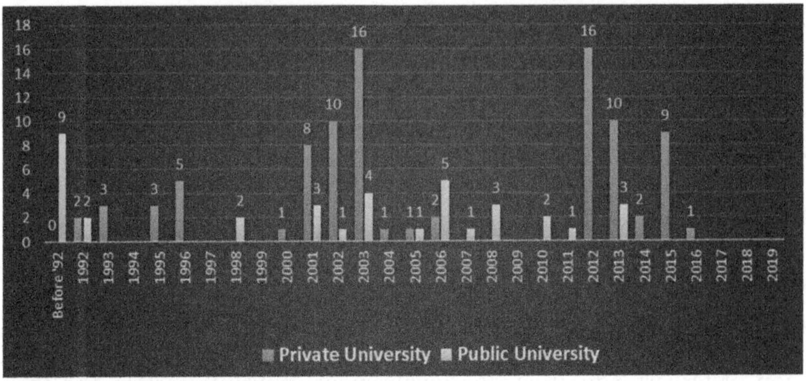

Fig. 4.6 Increase in number of universities. (Source: Bangladesh University Grant Commission 2017)

ably, a sizable number of youths have emerged as new entrepreneurs, which did not exist in the country even ten years ago.

Vocational Education: Using The Demographic Dividend

Bangladesh has a relatively young populace with 34 percent of the overall population aged 15 and below, and merely 5 percent aged 65 and above. At present, more than 65 percent of the population of Bangladesh is of working age, between 15 and 64. To exploit the full potential of this demographic dividend, the country needs to educate the youth in skills-based education, for which both the government and the NGOs are taking several initiatives.

A decade ago, only 2 percent of secondary and higher secondary students were enrolled in vocational education. This has increased to 16 percent, with the government's target being to increase it to 30 percent by 2030. As Fig. 4.7 below shows, the increase is significantly visible in the last five years—9,14,712 students in 2014 to 12,62,761 students in 2018, that is, the rate of growth was 59.54 percent.

Vocational training increases marketable skills in growing industries, generating employment to aid the growth of the national economy. Bangladesh has 8675 registered vocational institutes besides thousands of non-registered vocational schools run by the private sector and NGOs providing employment-focused skills in different trades. As the leading

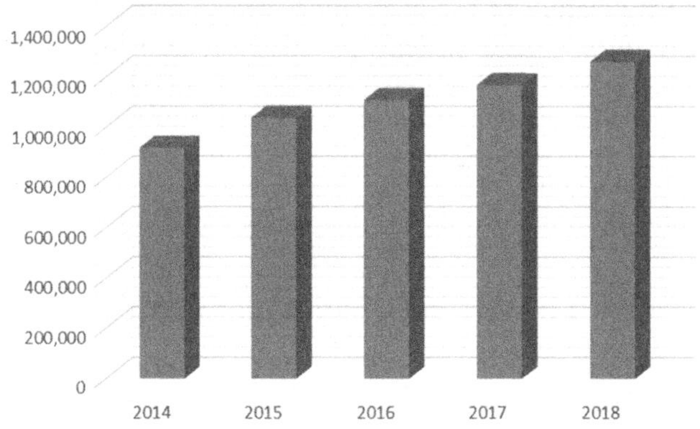

Fig. 4.7 Increase in higher secondary vocational education enrolment. (Source: Bangladesh Vocational Education Board 2018)

Bengali daily *Prothom Alo* reports on 2 June 2019, the government has decided to introduce one compulsory vocational course for all six graders in general schools and madrasas by 2012. Gradually, as it is planned, seventh and eighth graders will have a compulsory vocational course by 2022 and 2023, respectively.

Enhancing Quality

While education may be disseminated at every level, quality remains a concern. The government is now gradually addressing the issue and has already adopted a few programs like the Higher Education Quality Enhancement Project (HEQEP). Higher education is one of the significant stages of the education framework. The critical goals of advanced education are to provide new knowledge, investigate research opportunities on various social and development issues, foresee the requirements of the economy, and prepare profoundly skilled laborers. In such a context, higher education ought to be standard, and oriented toward welfare and sustainable development. In keeping with this goal, HEQEP plans to improve the quality and significance of teaching and research conditions in higher education foundations through empowering both innovation and accountability inside universities and by upgrading the technical and institutional limits of the higher education sector. Enhancing the quality of education is now at the forefront, but the country still has miles to go.

A complete picture of the magnitude of development in Bangladesh over the last quarter is not gained if the daunting activities launched and carried out successfully are not enumerated. This development was possible because of the timely state initiatives taken in collaboration with non-state actors. For a developing country, starting out with a very poor education system and coverage, the first act was to make education inclusive, and now it is time to enhance the quality.

Health Status in Bangladesh

Besides the devastation caused by the war in 1971 when an independent Bangladesh placed itself on the world map, the country inherited malnourished citizens in miserable health conditions, a high rate of child deaths, diarrhea, tuberculosis, and other tropical diseases. Life expectancy was only 47.52 years. Astonishingly, in the course of the last three decades, the nation has gained excellent ground in significant health pointers, such as a decrease in maternal mortality and under-five mortality, a decrease in total fertility, expanded inoculation inclusion, higher life expectancy at childbirth, and increased contraceptive use. This all happened despite very low public resources being allocated to this sector (Fig. 4.8).

Table 4.2 lists progress in some of the important health indicators.

Bangladesh has experienced a significant reduction in child mortality rate over the past decades, which helped the nation achieve the Millennium

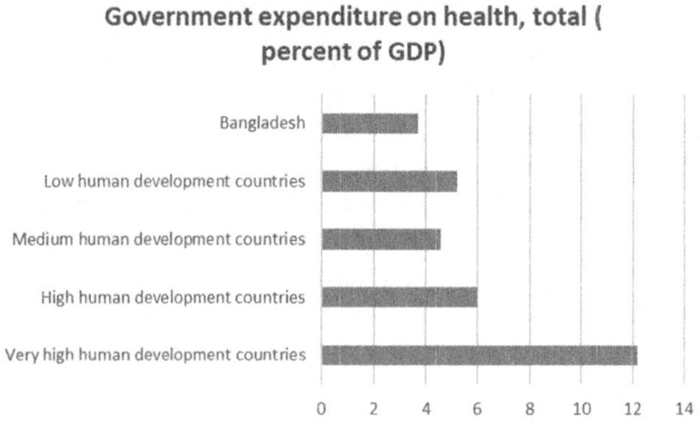

Fig. 4.8 GDP Contribution in health: Bangladesh and the world. (Source: UN Human Development Report 2016)

Table 4.2 Progress in some important health indicators, 2005–17

Indicators	*2005*	*2007*	*2011*	*2014*	*2017*
Life expectancy at birth	65.2	66.6	...	70.7	72
Crude birth rate per 1000	20.7	20.9	19.2	18.9	18.5
Crude death rate per 1000	5.8	6.2	5.5	5.2	5.1
Infant mortality rate per 1000 live births	50	43	35	30	24
Under-five mortality rate per 1000 live births	68	60	44	38	31
Maternal mortality ratio (MMR) per 100,000 live births	348	351	209	193	172

Source: SVRS (2010, 2017)

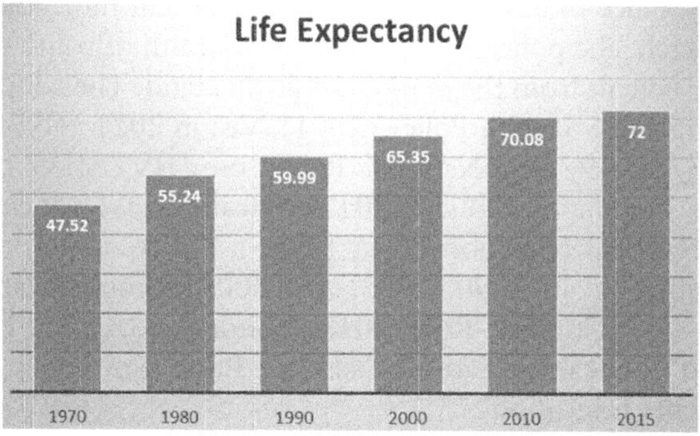

Fig. 4.9 Increase in life expectancy. (Source: Composite data from WHO's statistics for respective years)

Development Goal 4 (MDG 4) target. Progressive reduction of child mortality along with improved health service delivery by state and non-state endeavors are mirrored in the increasing life expectancy that now stands at 72 years (Fig. 4.9).

Government Initiatives

To accomplish universal health coverage, the government has built up the Health Care Financing Strategy (HCFS) 2012–32. The system plans to decrease out-of-pocket payments (OOP) from 64 percent in 2012 to 32 percent in 2032, and increase the health budget to 15 percent of the national budget by 2032 from the current allotment of below 5 percent.

In January 2016, a pilot venture titled Shasthyo Suroksha Karmashuchi (SSK) was started by the government to give well-being cards to one hundred thousand extremely poor family units who earned under USD 1.9 per day. Well-being cardholders and their relatives would receive free-of-cost medical services for 50 diseases.

To bring essential health care services to people's doorsteps, 10,723 community clinics (CCs) at a ratio of one CC for every 6000 people were set up during 1998–2001. In 2009, the CC activities were rejuvenated by the government. It has been reported that currently there are 13,500 CCs in the rural areas and another 4500 CCs will be set up soon.[1]

The government has adopted several policies to extend its existing health services. These policies aim to achieve an improved quality of life with the assurance of basic health care and sufficient nutrition for all citizens in general. The policies target improved health of youth in particular so that they benefit from the demographic dividend. The adopted policies include Bangladesh Health Policy (2011), Vision 2021 and 7th Five Year Plan (2015/15–19/20), National Policy on HIV/AIDS (late 1996), Bangladesh Population Policy (2012), Healthcare Financing Strategy 2012–32, National Nutrition Policy (2015), the Narcotics Control Act, 1990 (as amended in 2000, 2002, and 2004), Smoking and Tobacco Products Usage (Control) Rule, 2015, National Education Policy, 2010 (Health and Physical Education), National Education Policy 2010 (Fine Arts and Crafts Education).

Besides implementing the policies mentioned above, the government has increased the number of tertiary level health education institutions by establishing new medical colleges while allowing the private sector to operate some of these colleges. A total of 90 recognized medical colleges are in operation in Bangladesh, 36 of which are public and 54 private. Besides, there are six medical colleges that are run by the Bangladesh Armed Forces and, therefore, fall under the supervision of the Ministry of Defence.

The drug policy of Bangladesh is hailed by many as providing an extended policy and other necessary support for producing drugs. Bangladesh, for the last three decades, has been exporting medicines to both developing and developed countries. The latest drug policy of 2016 has brought allopathic, Ayurvedic, Unani, and homeopathic medicines under one umbrella. As indicated by the strategy, no one can purchase drugs without prescriptions from doctors, aside from 39 allopathic, 23 Ayurvedic, and 48 Unani medications. This is significant as the unregulated use of drugs, particularly antibiotics, is harmful to general well-being. The arrangement also accommodates the accessibility of compelling, safe, and standard medications, rational and safe use of medications, registration of medications, registration for importing medications, as well as manufacturing medications and their raw materials.

Non-State Contribution: NGOs

Non-state actors—NGOs and private sectors—are visibly active in the health sector of Bangladesh (Maruf 2013; Sarker 2015). They intervene where the state, with its constraints, cannot perform properly. NGOs are serving people in the villages, peripheries, and urban slums by giving them clinical health support while also producing para-veterinary workers from within the locality to sustainably provide primary health services to humans and animals.

It is NGOs, such as BRAC, that have popularized oral saline to combat diarrhea, cholera, and other similar diseases successfully. In 1980, BRAC conducted a campaign to get oral rehydration therapy adopted nationwide. The campaign's target group was mostly the illiterate populace and the outcome proved to be remarkably successful. The most recent public-health campaign to teach family planning, however, was not well received, since the messages the campaign needed to convey were complicated. A book published in Bangladesh, *A Simple Solution*, tells the story. The organization did not launch a mass-media campaign—only twenty percent of the population had a radio after all. It attacked the problem in a way that is routinely dismissed as impractical and inefficient: by going door to door, person to person, and just talking.

NGOs reach the periphery and the vulnerable with health services that the government, with its constraints, cannot. They provide two types of support—clinical and educational. NGOs offer primary health care services, such as vaccinations for humans and domestic animals. Most importantly, they train para-veterinary workers who are trained in primary level treatment, including midwifery. NGOs that are not concerned with health issues still play a large part in this sector with their awareness-building programs, as they make people aware of hygiene through behavior change communication. As preventive measures, they help the community build hygienic toilets, provide menstrual support to adolescent girls, and help them purify drinking water.

Private Sector Contribution

Private sector contributions can be categorized into two levels—producing medicines by establishing pharmaceuticals and building quality hospitals. Aided by the government's highly appreciated drug policy, Bangladesh produces surplus medicines which are exported to countries including Eastern Europe. Now state-of-the-art treatment is possible in the hospitals established by private effort. Private sector initiatives are also seen in spreading vocational and tertiary health education to produce doctors, nurses, and medical technicians.

As in the case of education, Bangladesh has made remarkable progress as a developing country, but the journey is far from over. Quality of health service is an essential need while rural health deliveries need to be modernized. Health policy 2016 is especially addressing this by chalking out several programs and activities.

Life Expectancy

The picture of life expectancy for Bangladesh is spectacular. In 2011, the average life expectancy of Bangladeshis was 69 years. According to the latest WHO data published in 2018, life expectancy in Bangladesh looks like this: for males, it is 71.1 years, for females, it is 74.4, and average life expectancy is 72.7 years, which gives Bangladesh a World Life Expectancy ranking of 97. The average life expectancy in Bangladesh surpassed South Asia's average, which is 69 (*The Dhaka Tribune* 2017) (Table 4.3).

The advancement of life expectancy over the last 25 years shows a parallel improvement in education, learning, and functional health as researched by *The Lancet* (2018). This only reconfirms the model above a

Table 4.3 Increase in life expectancy

	Male	*Female*	*All*	*M*	*F*	*All*
1960	41.0	39.9	40.5	136	153	144
1970	44.8	44.3	44.5	138	153	144
1980	48.9	48.7	48.8	142	152	147
1990	54.5	55.1	54.8	144	151	146
2000	64.9	65.6	65.3	103	124	118
2010	68.9	71.1	69.9	95	118	106
2016	71.1	74.4	72.7	86	109	97

Source: WHO (2018)

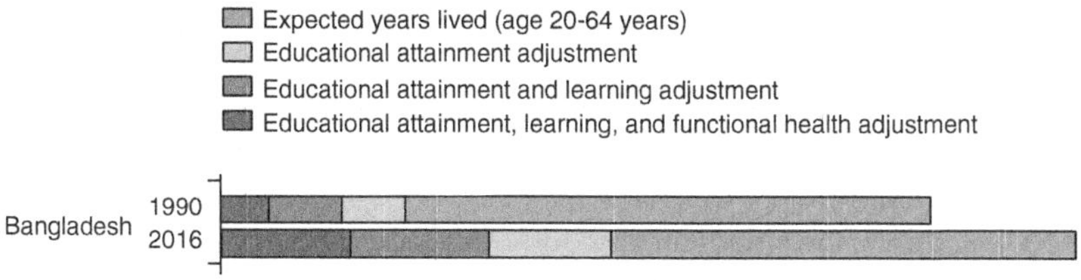

Fig. 4.10 Life expectancy and educational attainment, training and functional health. (Source: *The Lancet* 2018)

positive triadic relationship between education, health, and life expectancy (Fig. 4.10).

EdheL: A Collective Effort

A change has occurred—a paradigm shift one may say—in understanding development from a linear, mainly economic advancement, to a comprehensive perspective encompassing all aspects of human life. Organized knowledge about development has a history of less than a hundred years, starting with David Lerner's (1958) modernization theory of understanding the development of postcolonial traditional nations as a process of imitating western nations. W.W. Rostow (1960), in the same vein as stipulated in the modernization theory, emphasized solely on economic growth for a nation for poverty alleviation. He suggested the takeoff model of economic growth, arguing that economic modernization/development occurs in five basic stages of varying length: traditional society, prerequisites for takeoff, takeoff, drive to maturity, and high mass consumption. This view was debated, resulting in the emergence of contrasting views of development like the dependency theory. Gradually, development thought freed itself from the fallacy of viewing development merely as economic growth, acknowledging that non-economic and intangible aspects of human life also need to be addressed for proper development. The human development index (HDI), developed by Mahbubul Haq for the UNDP, is an institutional response to such changes that gradually led to a paradigm shift in development thought and practice on 27 September 2015 as 193 countries at the United Nations signed the "Transforming Our World: the 2030 Agenda for Sustainable Development," or the 2030 Agenda, in short.

To better people's lives and make the planet safe and sound for future generations, the 2030 Agenda addressed development on economic, social, and environmental dimensions, aiming to accomplish 17 integrated and indivisible sustainable development goals (SDGs), with 169 associated targets, by 2030.

Thus, a new development discourse has been ushered in that includes people from all walks of life from every nation-state spread over the globe. The object of the SDGs is to develop a world where no one is left behind from the benefit of development. To achieve such a world, the citizen, as an aggregate and an individual, needs to actively participate in actualizing SDGs.

An all-encompassing change meant to transform the world is an organic endeavor requiring multi-stakeholder collaboration—globally and nationally—in transforming the world. Therefore, inclusive participation is the core mantra of the 2030 Agenda. This was emphasized in the United Nations Development Group 2016 report (United Nations 2016) titled "The Sustainable Development Goals Are Coming to Life: Stories of Country Implementation and UN Support" that reads,

> Central to the quality and legitimacy of a society-wide agenda is the application of multi-stakeholder approaches to develop and implement policies. They encourage and facilitate partnerships between government and nationally and sub-nationally active stakeholder networks of civil society, universities, think tanks, the private sectors, and other development actors.

The multi-stakeholder approach works on two levels: horizontal and vertical. The parallel level denotes organizational structure that ties all the actors in a systemic way, while the vertical level emphasizes on deepening awareness among all the actors, which creates coherence between different levels and types of stakes. Vertical coordination is essential for localizing the 2030 Agenda by responding to the local needs and priorities aligned to a given society's organic strength and constraints. Non-state actors can especially coordinate at the vertical level as through them the community is best represented.

The catalyst to transform the world as envisioned in the SDGs is fortified human capital. Human capital is characterized as the aggregate levels of education, training, skills, and health in a population, affecting the rate at which technologies can be developed, adopted, and employed to increase productivity (Lim et al. 2018; Mitaj et al. 2016). It is recognized as the level of education and health in a population and is considered an essential determinant of economic growth. The World Bank has brought new attention to this topic through its recently introduced Human Capital Project. It has also called for measurement and annual reporting of human capital to track and motivate investments in health and education, thereby enhancing productivity.

From the discussions in the preceding sections, which highlight the advancements in the education and health sectors, it is evident that success was possible primarily due to the multi-stakeholder practice or collaboration between the government, NGOs, and private sectors (Fig. 4.11).

Both in education and the health sector, the government expenditure is painfully low in Bangladesh, far below the world average, let alone the UNESCO recommended a ratio of GDP. Besides, the country does not seem to have laudable good governance—which some consider as a prerequisite for development. In spite of all these and other constraints that a developing country is cursed with, Bangladesh has magically developed in both education and health primarily because of the state and non-state collaboration. Here one complements the other, and in many cases, one's

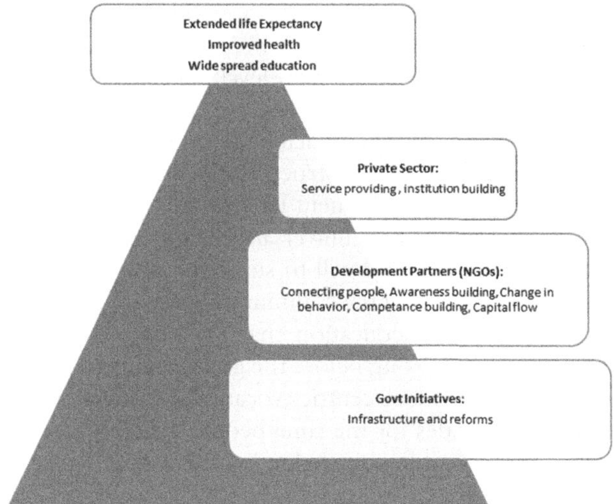

Fig. 4.11 Integrated effort of health, education, and life expectancy. (Source: Authors' construction)

shortcomings are overcome by the different stakeholders. An example is BRAC's widely recognized diffusion of oral saline. The government did not have the means to reach people from all walks of life to persuade them of the benefits of using oral saline to fight diarrhea. BRAC, by working with the community and having experience in behavior change communication, could do the job with much less effort.

The government, as the prime custodian of a country, works on the macro level—formulates policy, builds infrastructure, and delivers public goods and services. However, a macro-level intervention cannot always change human behavior, cultural practices, and individual attitudes. Neither can the government be an efficient entrepreneur. One needs macro- and micro-level involvement with communities to make them adopt the means and measures required for a given program by connecting to people on an intimate level to raise consciousness and motivation, thus reconfiguring their cognitive competence in adapting to any invention and adopting a lifestyle, breaking the traditional cultural practice generating human capital. It is an inherent attribute of NGOs to dip into the community's collective mind, which they have been doing as part of their motive of changing human behavior toward transforming the world to enhance well-being, or development, for all. The private sectors with their entrepreneurial zeal are better service providers and thus skilled in institution-building.

The government has adopted macro-level, that is, national, policies and programs in both education and the health sector in Bangladesh, as stated in the preceding sections. These policies and programs were implemented to the extent that governmental structures were able, but to work on a 360-degree horizon, the government needed NGOs.

The government's policy of universal primary education requires the community's preparedness and will to subscribe to the program. NGOs, having intimate knowledge of the community, were able to increase awareness of the advantages of education that rewards the community with enhanced human capital. Long before the government addressed the need of skills-based, employment-centric vocational education, NGOs ran training in different trades for the rural people. NGOs also ran, and continue to run, other valuable knowledge-broadening activities. They train people—men and women, young and elderly—in relevant areas that are important for their livelihood like fishing, cow-fattening, homestead gardening, a value-chain mechanism for small business development, that would not have been possible by the government alone.

Bangladesh still has resource scarcity, constraining a perfect primary health service delivery by the state mechanism, let alone developing health service infrastructure in the periphery. NGOs are ahead of the government in this area. They are making people aware of good hygiene to prevent diseases. In other words, they complement the government by supporting community health improvement. By offering training to the para-veterinary, NGOs are filling the gap of doctors for those who do not have a doctor in their vicinity or cannot afford treatment.

On the other hand, private sectors have established educational institutions from the primary to the tertiary level across the country that contribute to spreading education. In the last two decades, private funded modern hospitals were established, where one could receive state-of-the-art treatment for complex diseases, leading to lower mortality rates and contributing to higher life expectancy. Credit goes to the private sector for manufacturing surplus quality medicine supported by pragmatic state policies.

With a multi-stakeholder approach—a collaboration among government, NGOs, and private sectors—Bangladesh, over the last three decades, has performed a miracle in dispersing education and health service delivery across the country on a disaggregated level. As a result, a new Bangladesh is appearing with enhanced human capital with a higher life expectancy that is essential for development in all sectors. Such capital is primarily needed to maximize the benefit of the demographic dividend, which will make the country undergo a positive transformation. Transforming needs strategic thinking and effective leadership necessary to organize any development (Acemoglu and Johnson 2006). Sound health, both physical and mental, with a long productive life can produce a workforce to constantly develop the country and make citizens aware of their role in creating a just and fair society for all.

Conclusion

We have developed a model of a triadic relationship between education, health, and life expectancy. Some scholars have shown that education has a positive correlation with life expectancy. Education leads to a longer life for two reasons (Olshansky et al. 2012). First, education makes people aware of a hygienic and healthy life. And secondly, education brings returns in the form of material wealth, making a person able to take measures necessary for sound health.

Education, in its broader spectrum, goes beyond formal education provided by educational institutions. One gets in-school and off-school education. In-school or formal education is of primary importance, while off-school education in the form of socialization, collective dialogue, and training arranged by the civil society sharpens one's cognitive competence—one becomes aware of dos and don'ts, acquires marketable skills, becomes conscious of entitlements, and thus progressively becomes willing to actualize well-being for the self and others.

Bangladesh is a country constrained by many limitations, including inadequate public expenditure in the education and health sectors. Therefore, non-state actors—NGOs and the private sectors—are required to actively cooperate with the state agencies. It is important to recognize that NGOs, in their effort to educate the masses, especially those who are left behind, transcend the conventional understanding of formal education. By providing training on psychosocial support and disaster risk management that support the well-being and safety of children, life skills sessions that help youth and adolescents avoid threats and reduce their protection risks, technical training, and entrepreneurial start-up grants to help youth generate income for themselves and their families, NGOs are contributing to the development of a sustainable base in the society. They are equally active in the health sector, making people aware of a hygienic life, providing primary health service, and educating para-veterinaries.

The private sector is sufficiently supplying the country with pharmaceutical products while quickly bringing state-of-the-art health services to urban areas, primarily. Credit also goes to the private sectors for broadening tertiary education in the country.

The contribution of non-state actors was made possible by passable state policies. State policies promoted universal primary education with special emphasis on educating girls. Responding to the need of the market, the state is now implementing policies for providing more market-oriented skills-based education. In a concerted effort, the state and non-state actors are effectively contributing to developing human capital by expanding education and health services, leading to higher life expectancy. However, there are miles to go. It is time to deepen the service that has already been widened. Therefore, the priority in both education and health now is to improve quality and excellence.

Bangladesh is advancing fast, though, for many, it does not seem to have the preconditions fueling such a forward march. Some people call it a puzzle, and they strive to comprehend what the causes of such development are. As we have shown in this chapter, the answer to why improvements in education, the health sector, and life expectancy occurred lies in the concerted efforts of state and non-state collaboration.

A multi-stakeholder approach has the power of jumping over the puddle that conventional development scholars did not have the opportunity to experience. Bangladesh, once known as a "bottomless basket" is now metamorphosed to a model of development for most of the developing countries in the world battling various odds and thinking they do not even have a basket, while academics are now compelled to rethink their understanding of development. Collective effort to enhance human capital demystifies the success of education and health service delivery in Bangladesh.

Note

1. For details, please visit—http://www.theindependentbd.com/post/147427.

References

Acemoglu, D., & Johnson, S. (2006). *Disease and development: The effect of life expectancy on economic growth.* NBER Working Paper Series 12269, Cambridge, MA.

Asadullah, M. N. (2005). *Returns to education in Bangladesh.* QEF Working Paper Series 130.

Asadullah, M. N. (2009). *Returns to private and public education in Bangladesh and Pakistan: A comparative analysis.* QEF Working Paper Series 167.

Asadullah, M. N., Savoia, A., & Mahmud, W. (2014). Paths to development: Is there a Bangladesh surprise? *World Development, 62*, 138–154.

BANBEIS. (2018). Bangladesh Education Statistics. Dhaka.

Bangladesh Population and Housing Census. (2011). Bangladesh Bureau of Statistics. Dhaka, Bangladesh: Bangladesh Government.

Bangladesh University Grants Commission. (2017). *Annual report.* Dhaka.

Bangladesh Vocational Education Board. (2018). *Annual report.* Dhaka.

Blunch, N. H., & Das, M. B. (2015). Changing norms about gender inequality in education: Evidence from Bangladesh. *Demographic Research, 32*(6), 183–218.

BRAC. (2018). BRAC's youth policy tracking exercise (Draft).

Citizen's Platform for SDGs, Bangladesh. (2019). Citizen conclave: Four years of SDGs in Bangladesh. Dhaka.

Guda, D. R., Khandaker, I. U., Parveen, S. D., & Whitson, T. (2004). Bangladesh: NGO and public sector tuberculosis service delivery—Rapid assessment results. Bethesda, MD: Quality Assurance Project.

Hossain, N. (2004). *Access to education for the poor and girls: Educational achievements in Bangladesh*. Paper presented at the scaling up poverty reduction: A global learning process conference, Shanghai, May 25–27, 2004.

Hossain, N. (2017). *The aid lab: Understanding Bangladesh's unexpected success*. Oxford, UK: Oxford University Press.

Khan, A. (2018, July 16). Literacy and education, not the same. *The Asian Age*. Retrieved from https://dailyasianage.com/news/130740/literacy-and-education-not-the-same

Lerner, D. (1958). *The passing of traditional society: Modernizing the Middle East*. New York: Free Press.

Lim, S. S., Updike, R. L., Kaldjian, A. S., Barber, R. M., Cowling, K., York, H., … Murray, C. J. L. (2018). Measuring human capital: A systematic analysis of 195 countries and territories, 1990–2016. *The Lancet, 392*(10154), 1217–1234.

Maruf, M. H. (2013). *Health sector management of Bangladesh: An evaluation of BRAC's health program*. Dhaka: MAGD, BRAC University.

Mitaj, A., Muco, K., & Avdulaj, J. (2016). The role of human capital in the economic development and social welfare in Albania. *International Journal of Human Resource Studies, 6*(1), 63–72.

Nisbett, N., Davis, P., Yosef, S., & Akhtar, N. (2017, June). Bangladesh's story of change in nutrition: Strong improvements in basic and underlying determinants with an unfinished agenda for direct community level support. *Global Food Security, 13*, 21–29.

Olshansky, S., Antonucci, T., Berkman, T., & Binstock, R. (2012). Differences in life expectancy due to race and educational differences are widening, and many may not catch up. *Health Affairs, 31*(8). Retrieved from https://www.healthaffairs.org/doi/full/10.1377/hlthaff.2011.0746

Rahman, S. (2009). Farm productivity and efficiency in rural Bangladesh: The role of education revisited. *Applied Economics, 41*(1), 17–33.

Rostow, W. W. (1960). *The stages of economic growth: A non-communist manifesto*. Cambridge: Cambridge University Press.

Sarker, A. E., & Nawaz, F. (2019, June 6). Adverse political incentives and obstinate behavioural norms: A study of social safety nets in Bangladesh. *International Review of Administrative Sciences*, 1–18. https://doi.org/10.1177/0020852319829206

Sarker, V. K. (2015). *BRAC's innovation in health: A case study*. Dhaka: MAGD, BRAC University.

SVRS. (2010). Bangladesh Bureau of Statistics. Dhaka, Bangladesh: Bangladesh Government.

SVRS. (2017). Sample viral registration system. Bangladesh Bureau of Statistics.

The Dhaka Tribune. (2017, April 25). Life expectancy in Bangladesh higher than world average. Retrieved from https://www.dhakatribune.com/bangladesh/2017/04/25/average-life-expectancy-bang

Ullah, A. N. Z., Newell, J. N., Ahmed, J. U., Hyder, M. K., & Islam, A. (2006). Government-NGO collaboration: The case of tuberculosis control in Bangladesh. *Health Policy Plan, 21*(2), 43–55.

United Nations. (2016). The sustainable development goals (SDGs) are coming to life: Stories of country implementation and UN Support.

UNESCO. (1917). *Global Education Monitoring Report.* Paris.

WHO. (2018). Monitoring health for the SDGs: Stories of country implementation and UN Support. In *World Health Statistics 2017.* Rome: World Health Organization.

Zohir, S. (2004). NGO sector in Bangladesh: An overview. *Economic and Political Weekly, 39*(36), 4–10.

PART III

Finance and Development

CHAPTER 5

Financial Sector Development and Its Contribution to Economic Development of Bangladesh

Prashanta Kumar Banerjee, Md. Abdul Kayum, and Helal Uddin

Introduction

The economy of Bangladesh depends on banks, non-bank financial institutions, and financial markets. This becomes evident from the fact that in the fiscal year (FY) 2018, the amount of industrial term loans disbursed by banks and non-bank financial institutions stood at Bangladeshi Taka (BDT) 707.7 billion, and the amount of BDT

The views expressed here are the authors' own, and in no way reflect the same of the respective institutions they belong to.

P. K. Banerjee (✉) • M. A. Kayum
Bangladesh Institute of Bank Management, Dhaka, Bangladesh
e-mail: kayum@bibm.org.bd

H. Uddin
Ritsumeikan Asia Pacific University (APU), Beppu, Japan

M. K. Barai (ed.), *Bangladesh's Economic and Social Progress*,
https://doi.org/10.1007/978-981-15-1683-2_5

0.2 billion raised by new capital issues through private placements and public offerings in the capital market (BB 2018a).

In fact, the Dhaka branch of the then State Bank of Pakistan was converted into the Bangladesh Bank (BB), the central bank of the country, soon after the independence in 1971 and the banking system of Bangladesh started activities under its supervision. At the same time, all banks except foreign banks were nationalized by the government to provide financial services to the larger segment of people for equitable distribution of wealth, economic power, and opportunities (Abedin 1990). Accordingly, banking operations began in Bangladesh with six nationalized commercial banks, two state-owned specialized banks, and three foreign banks (Table 5.1).

In the 1980s, the banking industry made a noteworthy structural change with the establishment of banks under private ownership. Presently, all banks have to be registered under the Bank Company Act, 1991, and as of August 2019, a total of 58 scheduled banks are operating in Bangladesh. The break-up for them is as follows: 6 State-owned Commercial Banks (SOCBs), 40 Private Commercial Banks (PCBs), 9 Foreign Commercial Banks (FCBs), and 3 Specialized Development Banks (SDBs).[1] Again, 8 banks of the 40 PCBs practice Shari'ah-based Islamic banking. Several conventional banks with separate branches or windows are also involved in the Islamic banking practice. A few non-scheduled banks have been established for some specific objectives that are active in the financial system. Non-bank Financial Institutions (NBFIs)

Table 5.1 Six nationalized banks

Nationalized bank (After independence)	*Before independence*		
Sonali Bank	National Bank of Pakistan	Bank of Bhawalpur	Premier Bank Limited
Rupali Bank	Muslim Commercial Bank	Australasia Bank Limited	Standard Bank Limited
Agrani Bank	Commerce Bank Limited	Habib Bank Limited	
Janata Bank	United Bank Limited	Union Bank Limited	
Pubali Bank	Eastern Mercantile Bank Limited		
Uttara Bank	Eastern Banking Corporation		

Source: Authors

entered the financial system of Bangladesh in 1981 with the establishment of the Industrial Promotion and Development Company (IPDC) of Bangladesh Limited. Together, they are turning out to be prime movers of the economy.

Notably, over time, BB has got deeply engaged in the country's financial sector to pursue a social responsibility-oriented financial inclusion while maintaining and reinforcing macro-financial stability (Rahman 2016). As the share of the formal financial sector increases through greater financial inclusion, it yields a critical positive externality by making monetary policy transmission more effective.

On their part, commercial banks operating in the economy have contributed enthusiastically to the higher pace of credit expansion, expanding profitability and productivity, and an extensive focus on financial inclusion to make the banking industry more vibrant and stronger. According to BB (2018a), the total deposits with the banks in 2018 amounted to BDT 10,366.4 billion, whereas advances at the same period amounted to BDT 8470.2 billion. Micro Finance Institutions (MFIs), and off-branch financial services such as mobile banking and smart card, are also proving very effective in the financial inclusion initiative in Bangladesh. BB's green banking initiatives promoting environmentally responsible financing have also been embraced by the banking sector with warm enthusiasm.

NBFIs have also been performing instrumental roles in financial deepening. As of December 2017, 34 NBFIs with 225 branches are extending financial services across the country. Of the total 34 NBFIs, 3 are government owned, 19 privately owned local companies, and the remaining 12 are established under the joint venture agreement with foreign participants. But the expansion of NBFIs is moderate and mostly confined to a few city areas. The total amount of assets created by NBFIs was of BDT 870.3 billion as of June 2018, whereas NBFIs collected deposits of about BDT 480.1 billion at the end of the same period (BB 2018a).

A strong and sound financial sector is a pre-requisite for a country's economic prosperity and development. The financial sector development of Bangladesh disproves Henry Kissinger's assumption that Bangladesh is a 'bottomless basket'. Developing countries are facing a problem to identify the appropriate path to build their financial industry. Several researches have revealed the relationship between financial sector development and economic growth; still, no research has explained the development of the financial sector over time in the context of Bangladesh. To provide a detailed story of Bangladesh's financial sectors, this chapter has been organized in the following order. Section 'The Financial Sector of Bangladesh' describes the Bangladesh financial sector, banking, non-banking, and capital/Equity market. Section 'Evolutionary Changes in Bangladesh's Financial Sector' deals with the evolutionary reforms of the financial sector of the country. Section 'Current Status of the Banking Industry of Bangladesh' highlights the current status of Bangladesh's financial sector, Section 'Financial Sector Development and Economic Growth: Empirical Evidence' provides an empirical analysis of the linkage between financial sector development and economic growth. Section 'Conclusion' finally concludes the chapter.

The Financial Sector of Bangladesh

Historically, the President's Order of December 17, 1971 named the Bangladesh Bank Temporary Order, created the central bank of Bangladesh with effect from December 16, 1971, the day of Independence of the country. Later on, Bangladesh Bank was formally and permanently established through the enactment of President's Order No 127 promulgated on October 31, 1972, in the name of Bangladesh Bank Order 1972. However, the Bangladesh Bank Order (BBO) was amended in 2003, empowering Bangladesh Bank to regulate and supervise the banking sector more intensively and independently.

To constructively contribute to the economy, a Central Bank Strengthening Project (CBSP) was initiated in 2003, focusing on an effective regulatory and supervisory system for the banking sector, particularly for strengthening the legal framework, automation, and human resource development and capacity building of Bangladesh. Additionally, the Commercial Bank Restructuring Project (CBRP) was undertaken at the same time. Policy rates (Repo and Reverse Repo rates) have been introduced in 2003 for routinely liquidity management and avoiding excessive volatility in the money market. These modern monetary policy tools, along with other traditional ones, are now being effectively used for monetary management. Moreover, while keeping the provision for the central bank to intervene (sale/purchase) in the foreign exchange market to avoid excessive fluctuations, the floating exchange rate policy was introduced in May 2003 allowing banks/authorized dealers to determine the exchange rate on the demand-supply basis. Although the impact of introducing a floating exchange rate appears to have maintained stable foreign exchange reserves, and the exchange rate to be determined by the market mechanism, the fact goes in the opposite way. The exchange rate has been mostly stable on account of BB's prudential intervention (sale-purchase) in the foreign exchange market, and foreign exchange reserves have been allowed to move either way. Foreign exchange reserves stood at USD 32.94 billion at the end of FY 2018, gradually increasing from only USD 7.47 billion at the end of 2009.

Before the 1980s, there were no private banks in Bangladesh. Hence, Bangladesh Bank had to regulate and control only a few state-run banks and foreign commercial banks. At the beginning of the 1980s, private banks started to operate, and two banks, namely Pubali Bank and Uttara Bank, were denationalized. The number of banks, along with branches and non-bank financial institutions increased at a rapid rate. Whereas, banks provide short-term, middle-term, and long-term financing, and non-bank financial institutions are established basically for long-term financing. BB plays an active role in the development of banking and non-banking financial institutions in Bangladesh. Besides that, BB also continued its effort to develop a well-functioning financial market and maintaining its stability.

Bank Financial Institutions

As mentioned earlier, after independence, all the erstwhile East Pakistani and local commercial banks working in Bangladesh were nationalized in 1972. A total of 11 banks (reorganized) were operating in Bangladesh through 1169 branches as of December 31, 1971. In June 1975, a foreign commercial bank named 'State Bank of India (SBI)' was added to the banking industry of Bangladesh (BB 1973). The number of banks then stood at 12. The leading goals of the then banking policy were (a) to exercise state control over the financial assets, (b) to save an abandoned banking system from collapse, (c) to spread the coverage of the banking system to the rural areas for mobilizing financial resources, and (d) to provide easier access to bank financing to a broader constituency of borrowers drawn from a less privileged background (Moral 2012).

The government adopted a financial restraint framework based on the rigid central bank's regulations. The regulation primarily covered fixation of interest rate on deposits and credits, direction of credit to Public Sector Enterprises (PSEs), priority sectors, and expansion of bank branches. The system overwhelmingly increased bank branches, volume of deposits, and deployment of credits. The total number of bank branches and the number of rural branches increased to 4378 and 2851 (65.12 percent), respectively, as on June 30, 1981, compared to only 1169 and 453 (38 percent) in 1972. The volume of deposits amounted to BDT 5.24 billion and credit to BDT 4.27 billion at the end of June 1972(BB 1973). Meanwhile, some foreign banks like SBI, Bank of Credit and Commerce International (BCCI), and Bank Indosuez started their banking business in Bangladesh.

Non-banking Financial Institutions

NBFIs have been increasingly recognized as complementary to the banking system in Bangladesh. They comprise investment and finance companies, leasing companies, and so on. Though the primary business of NBFIs is lease financing, some of them are also diversifying into other lines of businesses like term lending, housing finance, merchant banking, equity financing, and venture capital financing. The NBFIs, numbering 34 as of June 2018, are regulated by the Financial Institutions Act, 1993 and the regulations made thereunder.

The minimum capital requirement of the NBFIs was raised to BDT 1.0 billion. Major sources of funds of NBFIs are capital, term deposit, credit facility from banks and other institutions like insurance, call money as well as bond and securitization, and high net worth individuals. NBFIs are allowed to collect funds from the call money market up to 15 percent of their total net assets. NBFIs cannot accept any such deposit as it is repayable on demand through check, draft, or order of the depositor. Therefore, they cannot offer account facilities like savings and current deposits, cash credits, overdrafts, and so on. They are still not covered under the Deposit Insurance Scheme by the Bangladesh Bank. Also, they are not allowed to deal with gold and foreign exchange. Nonetheless, they may obtain foreign currency loans from abroad subject to prior approval of Bangladesh Bank.

BB supervises NBFIs following a risk-based modern supervisory system. NBFIs are subject to the prudential guidelines/limits such as income recognition, asset classification, and provisioning norms, capital adequacy norms, single and group borrower limits, prudential limits on capital market exposures, classification and valuation norms for the investment portfolio, cash reserve ratio/and statutory liquidity ratio (CRR/SLR) requirements, accounting and disclosure norms, and supervisory reporting requirements issued by Bangladesh Bank.

Table 5.2 Structure of NBFIs

	2005	*2006*	*2007*	*2008*	*2009*	*2010*	*2016*	*2017*	*2018*[a]
No. of NBFIs	28	29	29	29	29	29	33	34	34
Government owned	1	1	1	1	1	1	3	3	3
Joint venture	7	8	8	8	8	8	11	12	12
Private	20	20	20	20	20	20	19	19	19
New branches	5	10	8	8	8	20	14	30	8
Total branches	54	64	72	80	88	108	224	254	262

Sources: BB (2011, 2018a)

[a]June end

IPDC, the maiden NBFI, was established in 1981. Since then, the number of NBFIs increased to 34 as of 2017. Among them, 3 are wholly government owned, 12 are joint ventures, and the remaining 19 are initiated by local private initiative. The number of branches of NBFIs increased to 262 as of June 30, 2018 (Table 5.2).

Financial Market

A financial market can be defined as a market place where financial instruments such as bonds, stocks, foreign exchange, and derivatives are exchanged. It may have both physical and non-physical locations. The development of Bangladesh's financial market is not achieved as expected. At present, the financial market of the country consists of the bond market and the Capital/Equity market. Even though some banking institutes are offering derivatives and currency swaps, there is no organized market for derivatives and currency or interest swaps in Bangladesh.

Bond Market

The bond market is considered as the best alternative investment source for the government and corporations. It is the easiest and fastest way to collect funds from the public market. The worldwide bond market stands at US$100 trillion, which is almost double of the world's total stock market (Ahmed 2018). Even though the bond market is flourishing worldwide, the current status of Bangladesh's bond market has not reached the level where it could have been (Table 5.3). The size of the Bangladesh government bond market, which is 8.06 percent of GDP, is very tiny compared to other selected Asian countries (Asian Development Bank 2019).

Table 5.3 Sizes of some Asian bond markets (percent of GDP) as of March, 2018

	China	*India*	*Malaysia*	*Bangladesh*
Government	49.1	15.85	51.36	7.86
Corporate	18.63	2.89	46.25	0.20
Total	67.74	18.74	97.62	8.06

Source: ADB (2019)

The largest government bond market as a percentage of GDP is experienced by Malaysia (51.36 percent), followed by China (49.10 percent), India (15.85 percent), and Bangladesh (7.86).

There are two types of bonds issued in the Bangladeshi bond market: government bonds and corporate bonds. Table 5.3 is indicative of the fact that the Bangladeshi bond market is small, and it is dominated by the government bonds, while corporate bonds constitute only a tiny portion of the whole market.

Government Bond Market

The government of Bangladesh issues two types of bonds: tradable and non-tradable bonds, and securities. The Non-tradable securities include National Savings Certificates, that is, Sanchaya Patras and Sanchaya bonds, which are only for retail investors. The tradable securities include Treasury bills, popularly known as T-bills, with a maturity of 91, 182, and 364 days and the Bangladesh Government Treasury Bonds (BGTB) with a maturity of 2, 5, 10, 15, and 20 years.

The government uses those bonds mainly to borrow money from the market/public. The government's borrowing through bond reached BDT 3469.52 billion, in FY 2016–17, which was BDT 178.33 billion during FY 2011–12. This indicates the growing dependency of the government on bond to finance in its budget deficit (Table 5.4).

The total outstanding government debt under T-bonds stood up to BDT 1291.23 billion at the end of June 2017, which was BDT 1277.26 billion at the end of June 2016 (Table 5.5). Among three types of tradable T-bills, 364 days T-bills constitute about half of the total instruments (48.32 percent) at the end of June 2016, although the proportion has decreased to 36.38 percent at the end of June 2017. In the case of T-bonds, 10-year T-bond has the highest concentration in the year 2016

Table 5.4 Government deficit financing through bond market

Year	*Non-tradable (BDT in Cr.)*	*Tradable (BDT in Cr.)*			*Grand total of outstanding amount (BDT in Cr.)*
	(NSD) (Amount and % of Total)	*T-Bills (Amount and % of Total)*	*T-Bonds (Amount and % of Total)*	*Total*	
2011–12	63,861.30 (35.81%)	29,426.21 (16.50%)	85,043.07 (47.69%)	114,469.28 (64.19%)	178,330.58 (100.00%)
2012–13	64,634.20 (36.09%)	29,426.21 (16.43%)	85,043.07 (47.48%)	114,469.28 (63.91%)	179,103.48 (100.00%)
2013–14	76,341.30 (34.74%)	40,783.18 (18.56%)	102,627.73 (46.70%)	143,410.91 (65.26%)	219,752.21 (100.00%)
2014–15	105,074.00 (41.73%)	31,429.47 (12.48%)	115,273.06 (45.78%)	146,702.53 (58.27%)	251,776.53 (100.00%)
2015–16	140,261.63 (47.58%)	26,800.00 (9.09%)	127,726.40 (43.33%)	154,526.40 (52.42%)	294,788.03 (100.00%)
2016–17	192,679.09 (55.53%)	25,150.00 (7.24%)	129,122.60 (37.23%)	154,272.60 (44.47%)	346,951.69 (100.00%)
Growth Rate	20.65%	−2.63%	7.35%	5.20%	11.98%

Source: BB (2018a)

(38.44 percent) and 2017 (38.61 percent) followed by 5-year T-bonds. However, 2-year T-bonds has the lowest share among all T-bonds.

Table 5.6 illustrates the investment pattern of government borrowing through bonds. The banking[2] sector acquired a significant share of the government bond investment and covers 80.22 percent of total stock holding (52.62 percent by PDs and 27.60 percent by NPDs) at the end of June 2017. The second-largest investor of government securities is life insurance companies (8.67 percent) followed by other long-term investors like pension funds (3.40 percent). BB holds about 3.27 percent of the stocks for its monetary operations. Corporate bodies, investment companies, foreign investors, individuals, and other investors hold the remaining securities.

Corporate Bond Market

The corporate bond market is almost non-existent in Bangladesh. The outstanding amount is only about 0.2 percent of GDP (ADB 2017).

Table 5.5 Composition of marketable government securities

Items		*End of June 2016*		*End of June 2017*	
		Amount (BDT in Cr.)	*(% of Total)*	*Amount (BDT in Cr.)*	*(% of Total)*
Treasury bills	91 days	8300	30.97	8000	31.81
	182 days	5550	20.71	8000	31.81
	364 days	12950	48.32	9150	36.38
	Total	*26800*	*100*	*25150*	*100*
Treasury bonds	2 years	9806	7.68	8950	6.93
	5 years	33170	25.97	31270	24.22
	10 years	49096.95	38.44	49849.17	38.61
	15 years	19166.25	15.00	20866.25	16.16
	20 years	16487.20	12.91	18187.20	14.08
	Total	*127726.4*	*100*	*129122.6*	*100*
Total		*154526.4*		*154272.6*	

Source: BB (2018a)

During 1988–2011, only 3 corporate bonds and 14 debentures were issued through public offerings. Many bonds and debentures were partially convertible to common stocks. The largest issue of the corporate bond was made first in 2007. It was a perpetual Islamic bond named 'IBBL Mudaraba Perpetual Bond' with a size of BDT 3.0 billion. Two more corporate bonds[3] are in the pipeline for raising capital (BSEC). Additionally, banks have issued a total of 57 subordinate bonds amounting to BDT 198.24 billion since 2009 to insert capital under Tier-II. It is imperative that both fixed and floating interest rates have been applied in issuing subordinate bonds.

Since 2004, BB started to issue the Bangladesh Government Islamic Investment Bond (BGIIB). Proceeds from selling bonds are invested in the Islamic Shari'ah-based banks/financial institutions for a maximum of 180 days. The profit rate of that investment is determined based on the short-term deposit rate (3 months and 6 months) of the banks.

Equity Market

Bangladesh's equity market is not broad or deep enough by the middle of FY 2019–20; there are around 3400 public limited companies of the country, only 10 percent are listed with stock exchanges (BB). A reasonable proportion of equity finance in a financial system is always positively

Table 5.6 Government bond market in Bangladesh: investors pattern of govt. debt securities

SI no.	*Category of owner*	*End of June 2016*		*End of June 2017*	
		Amount (BDT in Cr.)	*% of Total*	*Amount (BDT in Cr.)*	*% of Total*
1.	Bangladesh Bank (BB)	4,678.55	3.04	5,031.14	3.27
2.	Primary Dealers (PD)	81,018.68	52.72	80,869.92	52.62
3.	Non-primary Dealers (NPD)	43,871.96	28.55	42,407.06	27.60
4.	Non-bank Financial Institution (NBFI)	17.30	0.01	0.03	0.00
5	Amanat Bima Trust Tahbil	4,882.75	3.18	5,694.31	3.71
6	General Insurance Companies	142.99	0.09	136.22	0.09
7	Life Insurance Companies	12,336.95	8.03	13,329.12	8.67
8	Corporate Bodies	674.35	0.44	578.83	0.38
9.	Investment Companies	229.22	0.15	11.13	0.01
10	Provident/Pension/Trust/ Gratuity Fund	5,127.13	3.34	5,220.26	3.40
11	Mutual Fund	6.00	0.00	6.00	0.00
12	Foreign Investors	428.81	0.28	43.00	0.03
13	Individual	248.00	0.16	346.36	0.23
Total		*154526.4*	*100*	*154272.6*	*100*

Source: BB (2018a)

and significantly linked with the sustainable economic development of a country (Fig. 5.1).

The amount of market capitalization of Bangladesh capital market is BDT 7032.13 billion (Dhaka Stock Exchange BDT 3868.19 billion and Chittagong Stock Exchange BDT 3163.94 billion) as of August 25, 2019. There was a noticeable variation observed until 2004–05. Afterward, it demonstrated an upward trend. But since 2009–10, the upward trend curve of market capitalization has become steeper, maintaining a positive relationship with economic growth. However, the market capitalization seems to have stagnated of late.

The listed companies were successful in collecting BDT 10.20 billion in 2011–12, which increased to BDT 64.64 billion in 2013–14, but decreased hugely to BDT 3.68 billion in 2015–16 (Table 5.7). However, when these figures are put into relative terms, then they deduce a more aggravated picture. Say, for example, the highest percentage of Initial Public Offering

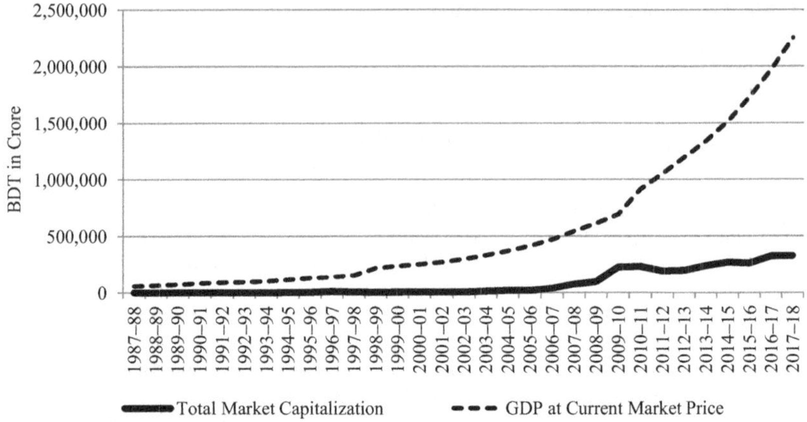

Fig. 5.1 GDP and market capitalization. (Source: Authors' calculation based on Bangladesh Bank, *Monthly Economic Trends*)

Table 5.7 Equity finance to economy, 2011–12 to 2014–15 (% of GDP)

Year	*IPO (Crore BDT.)*	*IPO to GDP*
2002–03	1351.17	0.04
2007–08	5613.00	0.10
2011–12	1020.59	1.12
2012–13	1246.02	1.20
2013–14	6464.42	0.48
2014–15	1407.39	0.09
2015–16	368.00	0.02
CAGR	−8.87	

Source: Authors' calculation based on BSEC annual reports, 2008–09, 2014–15 and 2017–18 issues

(IPO) to GDP was 1.20 in 2012–13, which came down to only 0.02 percent in 2015–16. Here, the policymakers should take note of the development and initiate policy measures to reverse the trend. Again, in terms of Compound Annual Growth Rate (CAGR) of IPO to GDP, the ratio of −8.87 percent looks further dismal, indicating a much lower than optimal use of the capital market. Therefore, it can be assumed that there is some room for further improvement.

Sector-wise IPOs elucidate that well-diversified industries are generating funds from the market (Table 5.8). Textile & Garments, Engineering,

Table 5.8 Equity finance through IPO: Industry-wise (BDT in Crore)

Name of the Industry	*2011–12*		*2012–13*		*2013–14*		*2014–15*		*2015–16*		*CAGR*
	BDT.	*%*	*BDT.*	*%*	*BDT.*	*%*	*BDT.*	*%*	*BDT.*	*%*	
Textile & Garments	262.75	26	316.227	25	441.24	7	534.48	38	286	85	1.71
Pharmaceuticals & Chemicals	0.00	0	329	26	5091.03	79	0	0	0	0	293.37
Engineering	90.00	9	134	11	459.5	7	80.46	6	0	0	−2.76
Food and Allied	40.00	4	65	5	47	1	290.26	21	0	0	64.13
Insurance	30.00	3	30	2	0	0	44.25	3	0	0	13.68
Cement	0.00	0	105.45	8	0	0	0	0	0	0	
Services & Real Estate	0	0		0	55.89	1	0	0	0	0	
Travel & Leisure	256.00	25	0	0	113	2	0	0	0	0	−33.56
Financial Institutions	47.65	5	160.06	13	0	0	0	0	0	0	83.29
Telecom	118.51	12	0	0	0	0	0	0	0	0	0.00
IT	41.95	4	0	0	0	0	0	0	12	4	
Paper & Printing	0.00	0	0	0	66.4	1	0	0	40	12	0.00
Power and Fuel	51.00	5	106.28	9	126.86	2	329.94	23	0	0	59.48
Miscellaneous	82.74	8	0	0	63.5	1	128	9	0	0	15.49
Total	1020.59	100	1246.02	100	6464.42	100	1407.39	100	338	100	−19.83

Source: Authors' calculation based on BSEC annual reports, 2015–16 and 2017–18 issues

Note: Percentage (%) mentioned in the table shows the percentage of total IPO

Food & Allied, and Power and Fuel sector almost regularly raised funds from 2011–12 to 2015–16. The pharmaceuticals and Chemicals industries also collected a substantial amount of funds in the year 2012–13 and 2013–14. In 2015–16, the major raiser of funds was the Textile and Garments industry followed by Paper & Printing and Information Technology (IT).

The experience of the equity market of Bangladesh in drawing Foreign Portfolio Investment (FPI) is mixed (Table 5.9). In some years, the flows of FPI are negative, meaning thereby that the outflow from the investment is more than inflow. However, the amount of FPI is positive for some other years. For example, the figure of FPI in 2017–18 is BDT 44,694 million. It needs to be noted that the inflow and outflow of FPI from an economy may depend on several internal and external factors. But more inflow figures plainly indicate the pulling or enticing factors in that economy. Bangladesh is expected to do better in the future with its robust economic growth along with financial stability and a stable political environment.

Table 5.9 Foreign Portfolio Investment

Year	*Foreign Portfolio Investment (in Crore BDT.)*
2001–02	−31.8
2002–03	5.6
2003–04	31.6
2004–05	0.3
2005–06	240.7
2006–07	727.7
2007–08	325.1
2008–09	−702.1
2009–10	−2029.5
2010–11	−6109.2
2011–12	4142.6
2012–13	742.9
2013–14	−3019.9
2014–15	−4157.5
2015–16	3977.3
2016–17	−1288.7
2017–18	4469.4

Source BB (2018b)

Evolutionary Changes in Bangladesh's Financial Sector

Immediately after the independence in 1971, the banking sector of Bangladesh was reorganized: local commercial banks were nationalized, downsizing to six. In addition, there were three foreign commercial and two state-owned specialized banks at that time. With these banks, the Bangladesh Bank started its journey to contribute to economic development. We know, real economic growth goes hand in hand with an increasing amount and diversity of activity of financial institutions, markets, and instruments. The financial structure mainly comprises two sets of elements, namely, financial instruments and financial institutions. In fact, the financial system's contribution to growth lies precisely in its ability to increase efficiency in financial deepening through the viable and effective financial market and financial instruments and profitable interaction with the progressive globalization. But, up to the mid-1980s, the banking sector was basically characterized by a 'financially repressed' regime scenario of low-interest rate, distortion in resource allocation, low rate of savings leading to financial disintermediation and the financial sector was being used to service the need of the government sector, and a few businesses houses with concomitant consequence of shallow financial system. The demand management aspect of macroeconomic variables was hardly taken care of. The loanable fund of the banks was disbursed mostly in publicly directed sectors without commercial consideration. The internal control system of commercial banks was very poor, the assets' quality of the banks was never evaluated on strict accounting principles; profitability and liquidity aspect of portfolio management was rarely discussed among the management personnel.

The widespread weakness in the money market was observed in the capital market also. Dhaka Stock Exchange, the only stock exchange of the country, was almost inoperative with a few enlisted companies. Bangladesh Shilpa Bank (BSB) and Bangladesh Shilpa Rin Shangastha (BSRS) were financing projects out of loans from the International Development Association (IDA) and Asian Development Bank (ADB) credit lines to projects. The cumulative effect of mismanagement in both money and capital market led to huge choke-up of non-performing loans for the financial sector, rising to about 42 percent of the total advances of the banking sector. Hence, the renovation of the financial sector was almost imperative. To find out the weaknesses of the banking sector, a National

Commission of Money, Banking, and Credit was constituted in 1984. The Commission submitted a report to the government in 1986, identifying the problem areas in the financial sector with specific recommendations to bring about structural, institutional, policy, and legal reforms.

Structural Reform

Ownership Reform Program of Banks

The government of Bangladesh undertook an ownership reform program in 1981–82. This phase of reform basically focused on the privatization of State-Owned Commercial Banks (SOCBs), and the entry of new private and foreign banks. As part of this program, the Arab-Bangladesh Bank, the first bank in the private sector of Bangladesh, was established in 1982. The number of banks increased to 16 in 1981–82. In the subsequent years, new private banks were opened, and two state-owned banks were denationalized. Now, 40 local private banks, including 8 Islamic Shari'ah-Compliant banks as of June 2018, are contributing to finance the economy. The share of private commercial banks in both deposit collection and assets disbursement of the banking sector has been remarkably increased to around 66 and 67 percent respectively (Table 5.10) of the total at the end of FY 2018 from 35 and 37 percent at the end of 2001.

Financial Inclusion Policy

Furthermore, various types of incentives like modest refinance schemes from Bangladesh Bank at subsidized rates and limited interest subsidies from government budget have been made available, wherever necessary, for promoting lending to marginal farmers, tenant farmers, sharecroppers, and Small and Medium Enterprises (SMEs). Almost all banks operating in Bangladesh, private or state-owned or local or foreign, have come forward enthusiastically in the financial inclusion initiative, moving toward new customer sections with new branches and innovative, cost-effective service delivery modes through local-based active MFIs, and off-branch mobile phone/smart card-based arrangements using agents in local communities. Furthermore, corporate socially responsible financing under financial inclusion drive and environment-friendly financing under BB's green banking initiatives have been lined up well with Bangladesh's banking sector.

Table 5.10 Status of the banking sector of Bangladesh (BDT in billion)

Types of banks	*As of June 2018*						*As of End 2001*					
	No. of banks	*Branches*	*Total assets*	*% share*	*Total deposits*	*% share*	*No. of banks*	*Branches*	*Total assets*	*% share*	*Total deposits*	*% share*
SOCBs	06	3721	3380	26	2701	27	04	3608	595	46	487	51
SBs	02	1407	318	2	273	3	05	1298	151	12	54	6
PCBs	40	4758	8758	67	6508	66	30	1331	446	35	349	37
FCBs	09	69	604	5	393	4	11	34	88	7	66	7
Total	57	9955	13059	100	9875	100	50	6271	1280	100	955	100

Source: BB (2011, 2018a)

Note: Minimal data inconsistency could be seen due to rounding

Deposit Insurance

The Deposit Insurance Scheme (DIS) was first introduced in Bangladesh in August 1984 to act as a safety net for the depositors. Bank Deposit Insurance Act 2000 is formulated, revising some points of Bank Deposit Insurance Ordinance, 1984. BB has adopted a system of risk-based deposit insurance premium rates applicable for all scheduled banks effective from January–June 2007. According to new instruction regarding premium rates, problem banks are required to pay 0.09 percent and private banks other than the problem banks and state-owned commercial banks are required to pay 0.07 percent, where the percent coverage of the deposits is taka one hundred thousand per depositor per bank. Furthermore, a draft law (The Deposit Protection Act, 2017) was prepared to replace the existing Bank Deposit Insurance Act 2000. The draft act had the provision to bring the NBFIs under the purview of the deposit insurance scheme to protect the interest of depositors.

Institutional Reforms

Liberalization of Interest Rate

Bangladesh Bank introduced a flexible market-oriented interest rate structure from January 1990. Interest rate bands were primarily prescribed for different categories of loans and advances and deposits, within which, banks were free to determine their respective rates. Lending rate bands were determined based on shadow lending rates, and deposit rate bands were determined, taking into consideration the expected rate of inflation and a positive real return for savers. Later on, interest rate bands were abolished excepting export, agriculture, and small and cottage industries. Banks have their discretion to charge differential rates of interest based on risks associated with borrowers and also on term loans based on the maturity period. As a result of the liberalization of interest rates, banks have been gradually competitive and their efficiency strengthened more than earlier.

Creation of Credit Information Bureau

To restore and strengthen the credit discipline and to provide adequate, reliable credit information among banks and non-bank financial institutions to facilitate loan sanctioning, a Credit Information Bureau (CIB) has been created in Bangladesh Bank in August 1992, and its operation started from 1993. Establishment of CIB in Bangladesh Bank is an important landmark in the banking sector reform process in the country, and as a data bank for bank credit, it is contributing significantly in quickening loan processing and decision-making in loan approvals. CIB also has a meaningful impact on bank regulation and supervision by the Central Bank in various ways, like approving new banks, and branches, sectoral credit planning, and so on. CIB has been providing online services since July 2011, which reduced the time and physical movement of banks and NBFIs in the submission of credit information and CIB report generation process.

New Loan—Classification Guideline

The commercial banks did not follow any norm to classify their bad and non-performing loans and did not keep provision for their poor-quality assets before the Financial Sector Reform Program (FSRP). Hence, there was a considerable provision shortfall and capital inadequacy of SOCBs. To address these fundamental problems in the banking sector, Bangladesh Bank introduced updated loan classification guidelines in 1989. Bangladesh Bank is continuously monitoring the bank's performance and improvement on the issue of provision and capital shortfall. Things have a positive direction due to strict regulation and close supervision. Now the loan classification criteria have been made more stringent, fulfilling the updated international standard regarding loan classification formulated by Bank for International Settlement.

Capital Adequacy Requirement

Before the introduction of FSRP, the banking sector did not bother to maintain the Minimum Capital Requirement. Although it was mandatory under section 13(2) of the Bank Companies Act, 1991 to provide 6 percent of total demand and time liabilities as capital, very few banks could fulfill the condition. Almost all the banks were undercapitalized, and because of provision shortfall and deteriorating condition of asset quality, further erosion of capital was faced by the banking sector. Hence, to safeguard depositors' interest and bring about a universally accepted status of our banking sector, risk-weighted capital adequacy requirement was introduced in January 1996, and it has been mandatory for the banks to maintain minimum capital to risk-weighted assets ratio (CRAR) at 8 percent since 1996. Later on, the ratio has been increased to 9 percent; and now it is 10 percent. Banks are strictly advised to maintain the adequacy element of capital, and Bangladesh Bank is continuously monitoring the status of commercial banks in this regard.

On-site and Off-site Supervision

Under FSRP, a major change has been made in the on-site and off-site inspection area of Bangladesh Bank. The evaluation of the performance of banks is now being made through 'CAMELS RATING'. Under the rating system, banking companies are assigned two sets of ratings—(i) performance rating, based on six individual ratings that address six crucial components of CAMELS like Capital Adequacy, Asset Quality, Management, Earnings, Liquidity, and Sensitivity to Market Risk; and (ii) overall composite rating based on a comprehensive assessment of the overall condition of the banking company. Each of these dimensions is to be rated on a numerical scale of 1 through 5 in ascending order of performance deficiency. Thus, '1' represents the best, '5' the worst level of operating performance. Any bank rated 4 or 5, that is, marginal or unsatisfactory under the composite CAMELS rating is generally identified as a problem bank. Large loan review cell and early warning systems have also been introduced in Bangladesh Bank as a part of prudential supervision. In addition, the accounting system, internal control, and compliance have been strengthened and updated by Bangladesh.

Current Account Convertible

All permissible transactions under the current account of Bangladesh, the balance of payments have been made convertible in May 1994 due to its importance and public demand-based necessity. Hence, foreign exchange transactions under the current account have been much easier for the international businessmen who contributed to the economic development of the country. The openness of the economy defined as total trade volume as a percentage of GDP increased amazingly from 19 in FY 1994 to 33 in FY 2018.

Floating Exchange Rate

As like interest rate, foreign exchange policy would also be used to be fixed by Bangladesh Bank, considering the underlying factors of the real effective exchange rate, foreign exchange reserves position, the balance of payments situation, and so on. Following FSRP, the foreign exchange rate has been liberalized, gradually moving from fixed to floating through setting flexible peg or crawling peg, official rate and open market rate, exchange rate band in the interim period. Finally, the floating exchange rate system was introduced in 2003, considering various macroeconomic fundamentals and adverse effects of a fixed exchange rate on foreign exchange reserves. Under the existing system of foreign exchange, banks are allowed to determine the exchange rate depending on the market forces while Bangladesh Bank can intervene in the market to avoid undue and excessive volatility.

Policy and Legal Reforms

(a) Banking Companies were guided under Bank Companies Ordinance, 1962 of erstwhile Pakistan, which was outdated in the changing environment of Bangladesh. Later on, Companies Act, 1991 was introduced, which provides Bangladesh Bank with a wide range of power to deal with banking sectors' monitoring, regulation, and supervision. The Act was amended later on in different years, updating various points in commensurate with the changed circumstances in the banks of Bangladesh. Also, Bangladesh Bank Order 1972 was amended in 2003, strengthening and empowering Bangladesh Bank as a central bank over the banking as well as the financial system of Bangladesh.

(b) The Financial Institutions Act, 1993, was formulated to deal with the affairs of Non-bank Financial Institutions (NBFIs). As per the provision of this Act, a cautious approach is taken to issue licenses to new NBFIs, and monitoring and supervision of the existing NBFIs are being made to ensure their sound operation.

(c) The Bankruptcy Act was enacted in 1997, and Bankruptcy Courts have been set up in the commercial areas of Dhaka and Chittagong and will be in operation within a month to deal with big delinquent defaulters. Adequate numbers of financial loan courts have also been created to deal exclusively with bank loan defaulters.

(d) Adaptation of Basel Accrued—The banks adopted Basel-I and II norms in 1996 and 2010, respectively, focusing on risk-based banking supervision. Finally, Basel-III has been introduced to strengthen the capital base of banks to promote a more resilient banking sector. The Basel-III regulation has been adopted in a phased manner starting from January 2015, with full implementation of capital ratios from the beginning of 2019. Now, scheduled banks in Bangladesh are required to maintain minimum capital of BDT 4 billion (BDT 5 billion by 2021) or Capital to Risk-Weighted Assets Ratio 10 percent, whichever is higher. In addition to minimum CRAR, Capital Conservation Buffer (CCB) of 2.5 percent of the total Risk-Weighted Asset (RWA) has been introduced, which is being maintained in the form of common equity tier 1 (CET-1). Besides the minimum requirement, all banks have a process for assessing overall capital adequacy about their risk profile and a strategy for maintaining capital at an adequate level.

(e) Furthermore, the Money Laundering Prevention Act, 2012, was introduced and amended in 2015. Similarly, the Anti-terrorism Act of 2009 was introduced and changed in 2013 to suit the latest financial sector scenario in the country.

All these structural, policy, and legal changes have been brought out in the financial sector of Bangladesh to make it more competitive, efficient, and sound, which are necessary and conducive for the economic development of the country.

Current Status of the Banking Industry of Bangladesh

The number of banks, branches, assets, and deposit liabilities increased; at the same time, contribution of private sector banks substantially improved, reversing the share of private sector banks in terms of both assets and liabilities (Table 5.10). While the state-owned banks were contributing a significant share of assets (58 percent) and liabilities (57 percent) in FY 2001, the private sector banks are now collecting deposits and providing loans and advances over 72 percent of the total.

The banking sector balance sheet size grew by 13.3 percent to BDT 14,014.9 billion at the end of FY 2018 compared to that of FY 2017 (BB 2018a). Figure 5.2 demonstrates that loans and advances, the largest segment of the asset items, constituted 65.4 percent of total assets in FY 2018, while it was 58.2 percent in FY 2014. On the other hand, assets share has been contracted from investment by 6.9 percentage points to 14.3 percent in FY 18 from 21.2 percent in FY 2014. Other shares remained more or less the same in both FYs, indicating the increase of the pre-determined income-earning share of assets in FY 2018.

Table 5.11 demonstrates the banking industry as a whole maintained capital requirement (above 10 percent) all over the years, FY 2009–18, except 2010. PCBs and FCBs are always maintaining CRAR above the

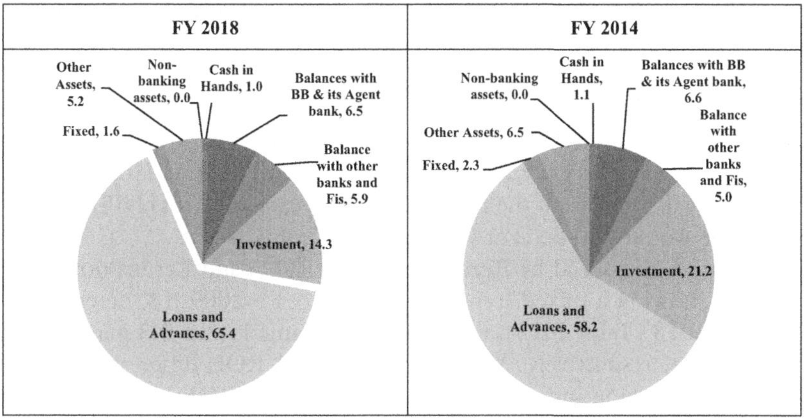

Fig. 5.2 Assets structure of banking sector in FY 2018 and FY 2014. (Source: Bangladesh Bank, *Financial Stability Assessment Reports*, April–June 2014, and 2018 issues)

Table 5.11 Capital to risk-weighted assets ratio by types of banks

Types of banks	*2009*	*2010*	*2011*	*2012*	*2013*	*2014*	*2015*	*2016*	*2017*	*2018*[a]
SOCBs	9.0	8.9	11.7	8.1	10.8	8.3	6.4	5.9	5.0	2.0
DFIs	0.4	−7.3	−4.5	−7.8	−9.7	−17.3	−32.0	−33.7	−35.5	−31.9
PCBs	12.1	10.1	11.5	11.4	12.6	12.5	12.4	12.4	12.5	12.2
FCBs	28.1	15.6	21.0	20.6	20.2	22.6	25.6	25.4	24.9	23.0
Total	11.6	9.3	11.4	10.5	11.5	11.3	10.8	10.8	10.8	10.0

Source: BB (2016, 2018a)

[a]End June

Table 5.12 Trends of gross NPL ratio by types of banks

Types of banks	*2009*	*2010*	*2011*	*2012*	*2013*	*2014*	*2015*	*2016*	*2017*	*2018*[a]
SOCBs	25.4	21.4	15.7	11.3	23.9	19.8	21.5	25.1	26.5	28.2
DFIs	25.5	25.9	24.2	24.6	26.8	26.8	23.2	26.0	23.4	21.7
PCBs	4.4	3.9	3.2	2.9	4.6	4.5	4.9	4.6	4.9	6.0
FCBs	1.9	2.3	3.0	3.0	3.5	5.5	7.8	9.6	7.0	6.7
Total	10.8	9.2	7.3	6.1	10.0	8.9	8.8	9.2	9.3	10.4

Source: BB (2016, 2018a)

[a]End June

stipulated rate. But SOCBs and development finance institutions (DFIs) altogether almost always failed to maintain CRAR over the years.

The asset quality of the banking industry in Bangladesh has deteriorated in FY 2018 as the ratio of gross Non-performing Loan (NPL) to the total loan outstanding stood at 10.4 in FY 2018. The underlying fact is that the NPL ratio is generally seen high at the end of June. Hopefully, the situation will improve in the future. In other years, the gross NPL rate was hovering around 9.0 percent (Table 5.12).

Earnings, measured by Return on Asset (ROA) and Return on Equity (ROE), showing a mixed trend over the years FY 2009–18, deteriorated in June 2018 (Table 5.13), recording an all-time low at 0.3 percent and 4.4 percent, respectively. Moreover, ROA and ROE differ significantly within the banking industry. Analyses of ROA and ROE by four types of banks reveal that both SOCBs and DFIS registered negative earnings, PCBs were able to bring a positive return, though less than earlier, while FCBs recorded more return.

The liquidity condition of the banking industry of Bangladesh remained almost always at a comfortable level over the years FY 2009–18. PCBs maintained liquidity ratio (liquidity components eligible for SLR to average total demand and time liabilities or ATDTL), which appeared to have decreased since 2015. A few banks of this group might have practiced aggressive lending, failing to maintain a balance between deposits and lending. Nevertheless, the overall situation of the banking industry remained comfortable to date. In addition, banks are instructed to bring down Advance-deposit Ratio (ADR) to a reasonable level on the back of some private banks' aggressive lending practices, setting by Bangladesh Bank at 83.5 percent for a traditional bank, and it has come down to around 76.7 percent in FY 2018 (Bangladesh Bank 2018a). Thus, the situation of asset-liability management has improved (Table 5.14).

Table 5.13 Trends of profitability ratio by types of banks (in percent)

Types of banks	*ROA*						*ROE*					
	2013	*2014*	*2015*	*2016*	*2017*	*2018*[a]	*2013*	*2014*	*2015*	*2016*	*2017*	*2018*[a]
SOCBs	0.6	−0.6	−0.04	−0.2	0.2	−0.7	10.9	−13.5	−1.5	−6.0	3.5	−12.3
DFIs	−0.4	−0.7	−1.2	−2.8	−0.6	−1.6	−5.8	−6.0	−5.8	−13.9	−3.1	−8.4
PCBs	1.0	1.0	1.0	1.0	0.9	0.6	9.8	10.3	10.6	11.1	12.0	8.2
FCBs	3.0	3.4	2.9	2.6	2.2	2.8	16.9	17.7	14.6	13.1	11.3	13.7
Total	0.9	0.6	0.8	0.7	0.7	0.3	11.1	8.1	10.5	9.4	10.6	4.4

Source: BB (2016, 2018a)

[a]End June

Table 5.14 Trends of liquidity ratio by types of banks (SLR) (in percent)

Types of banks	*2009*	*2010*	*2011*	*2012*	*2013*	*2014*	*2015*	*2016*	*2017*	*2018*[a]
SOCBs	25.1	27.2	31.3	29.2	44.3	42.0	41.4	40.0	30.4	31.7
DFIs	9.6	21.3	6.9	12.0	15.3	6.6	0.0	0.0	0.0	0.0
PCBs	18.2	21.5	23.5	26.3	28.0	28.2	19.7	17.8	14.8	14.9
FCBs	31.8	32.1	34.1	37.5	46.2	56.9	51.8	48.2	43.8	46.8
Total	20.6	23.0	25.4	27.1	32.5	32.7	26.5	24.9	19.9	20.3

Source: BB (2016, 2018a)

[a]End June

Financial Sector Development and Economic Growth: Empirical Evidence

In this stage, the chapter investigates the empirical relationship between financial sector development[4] and economic growth in Bangladesh. For studying the empirical relationship, log[5] of GDP at the current price (Ln *Y*), private sector credit given by banks (Ln BPSC), and market capitalization (Ln CAPI) are considered as indicators of economic growth, banking sector, and stock market development, respectively. Three possible regression models are estimated to know the relationship between economic growth and financial sector development.

The estimating regression models are specified as follows:

$$\mathrm{Ln}Y_t = \alpha + \beta_1 \mathrm{LnBPSC}_t + e_t \tag{5.1}$$

$$\mathrm{Ln}Y_t = \alpha + \psi_1 \mathrm{LnCAPI}_t + e_t \tag{5.2}$$

$$\mathrm{Ln}Y_t = \alpha + \beta_2 \mathrm{LnBPSC}_t + \beta_3 \mathrm{LnCAPI}_t + e_t \tag{5.3}$$

Annual stock data from 1974 through 2017 have been used when the econometric relationship is examined between economic growth and banks' credit to the private sector as data of both variables are available since 1974. However, data on market capitalization of Stock Exchanges are available only since 1988. To find out better results through using sufficient observations, quarterly data of market capitalization have been considered. However, in the absence of the availability of quarterly data of GDP in Bangladesh, GDP data has been converted into quarterly data by following Linear-match last method to match with the quarterly data of market capitalization. Then the econometric model between economic growth and stock market development has been run based on the converted data. Finally, in the case of finding a relationship between economic growth and both bank and stock markets, quarterly data have been considered for all three variables. As quarterly data for bank's credit to the private sector and market capitalization are available, we use only converted quarterly data for GDP for the estimation. Data are gleaned from various annual reports of Bangladesh Bank, and Economic Trends and Scheduled Banks Statistics published by the Bangladesh Bank.

In investigating time-series property, we have used ADF (Augmented Dicky–Fuller) and KPSS (KwiaBDTowski-Philips-Schmidt-Shin) tests for the unit root (nonstationarity), following Dickey and Fuller (1981), Kwiatkowski et al. (1992). In the event of nonstationarity of each variable, the co-integrating relationship among variables is studied by applying the Johansen-Juselius procedure (Johansen 1991; Johansen and Juselius 1990, 1992) to overcome the associated problem of spurious relationship and misleading inferences. In this procedure, all the variables must have the same order of integration. However, to address the issue of unequal order of integration, the Autoregressive Distributed Lag (ARDL) model or bounds-testing procedure, as suggested by Pesaran et al. (2001) has been applied.[6]

As shown in Column of 1 of Table 5.15, the coefficient of the error-correction term (ECM_{t-1}) has the expected negative sign with statistical significance. It implies that the deviation of variables (represented by the error-correction term) has a significant feedback effect on economic growth that bears the burden of short-run adjustment to bring about the long-term equilibrium. Additionally, the error-correction model also helps us distinguish between the short-term and long-term Granger causality. The error-correction term stands for long-term relations among the variables. The coefficient of ECM_{t-1} is equal to −0.2436, which is statistically significant, implying that a profound long-term relationship exists between Ln BPSC and Ln Y, and deviation to bring about the long-term equilibrium is corrected by 24.36 percent each year. It supports that bank's credit to the private sector is positively and robustly contributing to the economic development of the country. Also, contemporaneous change in Ln BPSC has profound positive short-run feedback effects on the economic growth of the country, as reflected in its coefficient and associated *t*-values. On the other hand, lagged change of Ln BPSC has also a short-term positive but subdued effect on the economic growth as it is evident from its coefficients and insignificant associated *t*-value. The results of the 'F' tests, that is, 12.37 also support the joint significance of the lags of each of the differenced variables. The Durbin-Watson value or DW-value at 1.65 indicates a mild positive autocorrelation, which is likely to be inherent in time-series data. The adjusted-R^2 shows that about 69 percent of Bangladesh's economic growth is explained by bank financing to the private sector. The optimum lag-lengths are determined by the Akaike information criterion (AIC) (Granger 1969).

The impact of stock market development on the economic growth of the country is also examined (Table 5.15, Column 2). As a long-run relationship does not exist between Ln Y and Ln CAPI according to a prior estimation of the co-integrating relationship between these two variables, the VAR model is estimated. According to Column 2, subdued net positive short-term effect is noticeable from Ln CAPI to Ln Y, as the respective sum of the lagged coefficients of variables is positive. This is supported by *F*-statistics, although the associated *t*-value of coefficients of each variable is statistically insignificant. The DW-value at 1.99 indicates a near absence of autocorrelation.

For knowing the impact of both the banking and equity market together on economic development, it is found from the vector error correction (VEC) that the estimated coefficients of error-correction terms are negative, but statistically insignificant (Table 5.15, Column 3). It means that long-run causal flows jointly from the banks' private sector credit and stock market development to Bangladesh's economic growth have been evident. However, this flow of relationship is weak as *t*-value is less than 2, meaning that the Bangladeshi financial system comprising both banking sector and the stock market is not still a strong promoter of its economic growth, although banking development is alone robustly associated with economic development (Table 5.15, Column 1). But in the case of short-term interactive relationship, it is evident that bank finance to the private sector in contemporaneous level shows a robust short-term positive causal effect to economic growth. The adjusted-R^2 discloses a significant explanatory power of the model. The *F*-statistic is also quite significant. The DW-value shows near no-autocorrelation.

Table 5.15 Impact of financial sector development of Bangladesh on economic growth

Variables	*(1)* Δ *Ln* Y*(−1)*		*(2)* Δ *Ln* Y*(−1)*		*(3)* Δ *Ln* Y*(−1)*	
	Coefficients	*Prob.*	*Coefficients*	*Prob.*	*Coefficients*	t-*statistics*
Constant	0.097691	0.0000	0.002200	0.0777	0.002019	0.1129
ECM_{t-1}	−0.243625***	0.0017			−0.015350	0.1149
Δ Ln $\Upsilon(-1)$	0.157078	0.1504	0.949650***	0.0000	0.923078***	0.0000
Δ Ln $\Upsilon(-2)$	−0.234394***	0.0012	−0.041741	0.7180	−0.007024	0.9538
Δ Ln BPSC	0.171165**	0.0198			0.091808***	0.0023
Δ Ln BPSC(−1)	0.008942	0.8995			−0.077232**	0.0449
Δ Ln CAPI			0.003312	0.4631	−0.001513	0.6258
Δ Ln CAPI(−1)			−0.000146	0.3998	0.001710	0.6576
Δ Ln CAPI(−2)			3.64E-15	0.9704	-9.20E-05	0.9825
Δ Ln CAPI(−3)			0.001577	1.0000	−0.000145	0.9737
Δ Ln CAPI(−4)			0.003312	0.6353	0.003728	0.8239
R-squared	0.688446		0.812567		0.823671	
Prob (*F*-statistic)	0.000002		0.000000		0.000000	
Durbin–Watson stat	1.647135		1.998560		1.912661	

Column 1: $\text{Ln } \Upsilon_t = \alpha + \beta_1 \text{ Ln BPSC}_t + e_t$

Column 2: $\text{Ln } \Upsilon_t = \alpha + \psi_1 \text{ Ln CAPI}_t + e_t$

Column 3: $\text{Ln } \Upsilon_t = \alpha + \beta_2 \text{ Ln BPSC}_t + \beta_3 \text{ Ln CAPI}_t + e_t$

where, Υ = GDP of Bangladesh at current prices, BPSC = Banks' private sector credit and CAPI = Market capitalization in stock exchanges. All variables are converted into natural logs

Note: ** indicates singnificant at 5% level, *** indicates singnificant at 10% level

Conclusion

The banking and non-banking financial institutions in Bangladesh have attained a reasonable level of progress and stability since 1971. This is also substantiated by the findings of the empirical analysis done in this chapter. Besides long-term relationships, contemporaneous change in banks' credit to the private sector has profound positive short-run feedback effects on economic growth. It indicates that credit from banks and NBFIs to the private sector is both positively and robustly contributing to the economic development of the country. To keep it up, Bangladesh Bank, as well as financial institutions, has to work together on it relentlessly, especially to bring down the NPL ratio. Moreover, financial inclusion is required to be continued and strengthened, which will help maintain price stability and financial stability; and achieve sustainable development goals by the stipulated time frame of 2030. Additionally, making the equity market a regular source of finance for the real economy is a must for sustainable economic development. But the empirical analysis of this study indicates a moderate contribution of the equity market to economic development. The findings of the analysis indicate that stock market development has a subdued net positive short-term effect on economic growth. The bond market, particularly the corporate bond market, is almost non-existent in Bangladesh. Several measures are required to be undertaken in this respect. Ensuring smooth operation of primary and secondary markets, increasing financial literacy among investors, minimizing volatility of the market, expanding issuer base, creating both individual and institutional investors, enhancing efficiency of the brokerage house, adding innovative financial services, initiating knowledge-based trading, rationalizing cost of generating funds and costs of funds, lessening formalities involved and required documents, introducing shelf registration system are some of them to name and suggest here to uplift the securities market to the desired level so that it can have substantial contribution to the economic growth of Bangladesh.

Notes

1. SDBs are also known as Development Financial Institutions (DFIs).
2. Some banks act as Primary Dealers (PDs), whereas the remaining are Non-primary Dealers (NPDs).

3. Of the two bonds in the pipeline, one will be issued by PRAN Group as SUKUK bond, and the other will be issued by Ashugonj Power Limited as a public issue.
4. As the bond market is almost non-existent in Bangladesh, this component of the financial sector was not considered here for empirical analysis.
5. All variables are converted into natural logs.
6. The outputs of unit root and co-integration tests are not reported here for saving space.

References

Abedin, Z. (1990). Commercial banking in Bangladesh: A study of disparities of regional and sectoral growth trends (1846–1986). Dhaka: National Institute of Local Government.

Ahmed, S. (2018). Bond market analysis of Bangladesh. Retrieved November 23, 2019, from http://dspace.bracu.ac.bd/xmlui/bitstream/handle/10361/11478/15104097_BBA.pdf?sequence=1&isAllowed=y.

Asian Development Bank (ADB). (2017, June). Asian bond monitor, emerging East Asian local currency bond markets: A regional update. *ADB*. Retrieved August 8, 2019, from https://asianbondsonline.adb.org/documents/abm_jun_2017.pdf.

Asian Development Bank. (2019, June). Asian bond monitor, emerging East Asian local currency bond markets: A regional update. *ADB*. Retrieved August 8, 2019, from https://asianbondsonline.adb.org/documents/abm_jun_2019.pdf.

Bangladesh Bank (BB). (1973). *Bangladesh Bank annual reports FY 1972–1973*.

Bangladesh Bank. (2011). *Bangladesh Bank annual reports FY 2010–2011*.

Bangladesh Bank. (2016). *Bangladesh Bank annual reports FY 2015–2016*.

Bangladesh Bank. (2018a). *Bangladesh Bank annual reports FY 2017–2018*.

Bangladesh Bank. (2018b). Monthly economic trends, October 2018.

Bangladesh Securities and Exchange Commission (BSEC). (2009). *Annual Report 2008–09*.

Bangladesh Securities and Exchange Commission. (2015). *Annual Report 2014–15*.

Bangladesh Securities and Exchange Commission. (2018). *Annual Report 2017–18*.

Dickey, D. A., & Fuller, W. A. (1981). Likelihood ratio statistics for autoregressive time series with a unit root. *Econometrica, 49*, 1057–1072.

Granger, C. W. J. (1969). Investigating causal relations by econometric models and cross-spectral methods. *Econometrica, 37*(3), 424–438.

Johansen, S. (1991). Estimation and hypothesis testing of cointegration vectors in Gaussian autoregressive models. *Econometrica, 59*, 169–210.

Johansen, S., & Juselius, K. (1990). Maximum likelihood estimation and inference on cointegration with applications to the demand for money. *Oxford Bulletin of Statistics, 52*, 169–210.

Johansen, S., & Juselius, K. (1992). Testing structural hypothesis in multivariate cointegration analysis of the PPP and VIP for the U.K. *Journal of Econometrics, 53*, 211–244.

Kwiatkowski, D., Phillips, P. C. B., Schmidt, P., & Shin, Y. (1992). Testing the null hypothesis of stationarity against the alternative of a unit root. *Journal of Econometrics, 54*, 159–178.

Moral, M. L. H. (2012). Banking sector reforms in Bangladesh: Measures and economic outcome. *Bangladesh Journal of Political Economy, 28*(1), 79–122.

Pesaran, M. H., Shin, Y., & Smith, R. (2001). Bounds testing approaches to the analysis of level relationships. *Journal of Applied Econometrics, 16*, 289–326.

Rahman, A. (2016). *Inclusive finance and sustainable development.* Occasional speeches of Bangladesh Bank Governor on 12 November at Bangladesh Institute of Bank Management (BIBM), Dhaka.

CHAPTER 6

Access to Finance for Inclusive Development: Recent Evidence from Bangladesh

S. M. Sohrab Uddin, Mohammad Zoynul Abedin, and Nahid Afroz

Introduction

In all influential economic entities, Financial Inclusion (FI) aids in enhancing earning potential, accumulating savings, availing credit, facing financial emergencies, and fighting poverty in a better way. Recent development theories also advocate for the equitable allocation of finance as a means to ensure sustainable economic growth. Although a growing body of research

S. M. S. Uddin (✉)
Department of Finance, Faculty of Business Administration, University of Chittagong, Chattogram, Bangladesh
e-mail: sohrab@cu.ac.bd

M. Z. Abedin
Collaborative Innovation Center for Transport Studies, Dalian Maritime University, Dalian, China

Department of Finance and Banking, Hajee Mohammad Danesh Science and Technology University, Dinajpur, Bangladesh

N. Afroz
Credit Rating Agency of Bangladesh (CRAB), Chattogram, Bangladesh

M. K. Barai (ed.), *Bangladesh's Economic and Social Progress*,
https://doi.org/10.1007/978-981-15-1683-2_6

is directed to link FI as one of the mainstays of global development, a very few of them offer a country-based perspective. Against this backdrop, this chapter aims to assess the degree of FI along with its contribution toward inclusive development, and provide some feasible way-out for including mass people within the formal financial network.

The FI is defined as the process of including the unbanked populace within the network of the formal financial system at an affordable cost and in a sustainable way. The United Nations (UN) blue book defines FI as "the access to credit for all 'bankable' people and firms, to insurance for all insurable people and firms and savings and payment services for everyone" (UN 2006: 1). From Bangladesh's perspective, the policy directives issued by the Bangladesh Bank (Table 6.5 in the Appendix), the central bank of the country, indicate FI as access to financial service from officially regulated and supervised entities, including licensed commercial banks, financial institutions, microfinance institutions (MFIs), and co-operatives; and official entities, including post offices, money transfer, insurance, and national savings bureau. This definition implies that inclusion should be through mainstream financial institutions, and the supply of credit from local moneylenders is excluded from the purview of FI. A person will be counted as financially included if she/he has an account with any formal financial institution, which provides her/him an opportunity of adequate and timely essential financial services, including savings, credit, insurance, payments or money transfer, and remittance transfer at an affordable, minimum, or low cost. FI, along with its minimum service provision, includes financial literacy of the beneficiary (Subbaro 2013), which involves the awareness of services and facilities provided by the respective financial institution. Besides, access to financial services, knowledge on commercial products and their usage are imperative for sound FI.

Moreover, Bangladesh is one of the emerging economies in South Asia that has shown a keen interest in bringing its population under formal financial network. With a combined and continued effort of the government through the central bank, at present 75 percent of the country's total population has access to the formal financial network. Like other parts of the world, Bangladesh is also advancing on the path with the help of technological innovation. In 2017, the number of mobile money account had experienced a growth of 33 percent, when the same for commercial bank account has been only 8 percent (Bangladesh Bank 2017).

Studies related to FI recognize dimensions of financial exclusion, such as outreach gap, gender gap, income gap, and so on. Generally, rural areas of developing countries often lag in FI due to the remoteness or a weak communication system. However, special attention by public authorities, technological advances, rapid urbanization, and so on has narrowed the rural-urban gap in the financial service sector. Also, an increasing number of internal immigrants from rural areas clogging in city slums are giving birth to another financially excluded stratum. While the area-based exclusion is reducing to a satisfactory level, the gender-based exclusion is still at large. Male domination in economic affairs has forced women to avoid financial institutions for an extended period. Studies reveal women's access to finance has a positive correlation with the improvement of family health, income, and education. Nonetheless, the gender-biased focus of non-governmental organizations (NGOs) and MFIs from the late 1970s and ease of access to finance through technological breakthroughs have influenced women's inclusion in the formal monetary chain. Then, women are slow to adopt technological advances like ownership of mobile phones and internet subscriptions, which again impedes their integration in digital FI.

In any case, FI can be measured by using different indicators such as number or percentage of account ownership, access to Automated Teller Machine (ATM) per 1000 square kilometers, and domestic credit, savings, and investment as percentage of gross domestic product (GDP) (Kim et al. 2018; Neaime and Gaysset 2018). Also, the FI is assessed applying indicators being measured the extent of transactions and usage of financial services in each bank account. As well, the technological advances have opened a new avenue for the measurement of FI. The number of Mobile Financial Service (MFS) accounts, agents, and agent outlets per 100,000 people or per 1000 square kilometers are popular indicators of digital financial integration. Then, the development agencies like the International Monetary Fund (IMF), the United Nations Development Programme (UNDP), and the World Bank have developed separate FI indexes, using distinct methodologies. The FI index used by the IMF summarizes the condition of FI in a particular country by combining geographical outreach and usage trends. By applying the weighted-geometric functional aggregator, the composite index ranks a state from zero to 100, that is to say, from the least financially included state to the highest level of inclusion (Amidzic et al. 2014).

The rest of the chapter is organized as follows: section 'Literature Review' introduces the related literature concentrating on different aspects of FI; research method is in section 'Data and Methods'; section 'FI Condition in Bangladesh' provides a discussion on FI condition in Bangladesh; section 'FI Efforts and Contribution to Inclusive Development' portrays FI efforts with particular contribution to inclusive development; section 'Technological Dimension in FI' scrutinizes the technological dimension in FI; and lastly, section 'Conclusion and Policy Recommendations' concludes the study with some policy implications.

Literature Review

As a part of access to finance, Zins and Weil (2016) identify gender, financial health, educational qualification, and age of the borrowers as determinants of FI in a study on 37 African countries. Wang and Guan (2017) offer a comprehensive discussion on measurement, effect, and influencing factors of FI. Their study identifies income level, education, and use of communication tools, financial depth, and banking health status as explanatory variables to inclusion. In parallel, Loyaza and Ranciere (2006) and Kim et al. (2018) have identified a positive correlation between FI and economic growth. Allen et al. (2016) find that FI results in lower account costs, greater proximity to financial intermediaries, stronger legal rights, and more politically stable environments, and as such setting suitable conditions for development. They reveal that users of financial services are less prone to income shocks and usually their household spending tends not to drop compared to those who do not have financial access (Karlan et al. 2016).

Besides, Koker and Jentzsch (2013) point out that the application of formal financial network, instead of cash-based informal mechanism ensures transparency and reduces corruption of the public system. Since these channels are under continual monitoring of the supervisory body, the possibility of tax evasion, money laundering, and other financial crimes can be reduced largely. Later on, Neaime and Gaysset (2018) use the Generalized Moment Method to identify the impact of FI in the financial stability of the Middle East and North African (MENA) region. The study finds a positive effect of inclusion in reducing income inequality in the region. Moreover, an evolving area of literature has been attributed to analyze FI using technological channels. For instance, Akhter and Khalily (2017) explain the impact of MFS on the FI scenario of Bangladesh. They have identified the positive effect of MFS on FI in the form of reduced transaction cost and service time.

The existing literature, attributed to FI or the impact of FI on development within the South Asian region, is predominantly concentrating on India and Sri Lanka. The study of Iqbal and Sami (2017) investigates the role of the banking sector on inclusion and identifies a positive and significant impact of the number of bank branch and credit-deposit ratio on GDP, but an insignificant effect of the growth of ATMs in India. Similarly, Gatto and Akhtar (2015), Hassan (2015), Yadav and Sharma (2016), Ghosh and Vinod (2017), Lal (2017), and Rastogi (2018) focus solely on the inclusion scenario of India. On the other hand, the study of Tilkaratna (2016) investigates household level data of inclusion and examines the reasons for using the services of multiple financial institutions in Sri Lanka. Among the cross-country studies, the study of Sehrawat and Giri (2016) examines the causal relationship between financial sector development and poverty reduction in South East Asian countries employing modern econometric techniques. In the same way, Arora (2012) covers a detailed three-stage methodological approach to examine the link between financial development and educational development in 21 developing countries of Asia

For Bangladesh, financial innovation and initiatives undertaken by the central bank and support of scheduled commercial banks have a significant impact on accelerating FI. Supported by the national financial strategy, Bangladesh is on the top of the list of highly FI growth countries among its low-income geographical competitors (IMF 2015). However, one-fourth of its adult population still remains unbanked (Akhter and Khalily 2017). Khalily (2016) also examines the structure of the financial market, financial regulation, and financial literacy along with its impact on FI. Using the Logit Regression Technique on the household level data, he identifies a moderate level of financial literacy with a positive impact on inclusive finance in Bangladesh. Siddik et al. (2014) undertake behavioral research with a particular focus on factors influencing behavioral intention to adopt or continue using mobile banking in Bangladesh. Among the 13 analyzed factors, perceived financial cost, perceived risk, and subjective norm are found to be the most influential in shaping people's behavior toward mobile banking.

Evidently, financial exclusion or obstacles to FI has remained a gray area in the financial literature. The socio-economic background of the people becomes the most significant determinant in this regard. This chapter aims to consider that in the context of Bangladesh and tries to link to its development condition. In our view, FI literature should cover the dimensions of financial exclusion, such as outreach gap, gender gap, income gap, and so on. Generally, rural areas of developing countries often lag in terms of FI due to remoteness or poor communication system. On the whole, FI in developing nations is targeted at a weaker section of the population, who involuntarily excludes from the financial chain. It might be hindered by either supply side (financial institution) related barriers or demand side (customer) related obstacles. Financial institutions may impose restrictions on FI through their outreach, inappropriate product design, higher cost of service, and approach to lower-income customers (World Bank 2008, 2018a; Choudhury 2014). So, unlike the above studies, this chapter adopts a comprehensive focus covering the link between FI and different development dimensions of Bangladesh.

Data and Methods

The study has been undertaken to capture the impact of financial access on the development of Bangladesh. The data and feature set are retrieved from different reliable sources like the IMF and World Bank databases. Data specific to FI, for example, ATMs per 100,000 adults, bank branches per 100,000 adults, deposit accounts per 1000 adults, and loan accounts per 1000 adults are calculated based on data extracted from the Financial Access Survey database of IMF (IMF 2018). Measures of financial development such as age dependency ratio, GDP growth, savings rate, consumption growth, and unemployment ratio are retrieved from World Development Indicators database of World Bank (World Bank 2018b); the two indices of inclusion and development, namely the Financial Development Index (FDI) and Financial Institutional Access Index (FINAI) are obtained from the IMF database. The period spans from 2004 to 2017 and for the technological dimension, the sample period covers 2010–17 due to data unavailability. A series of supportive tables and graphs are used to supplement the discussion.

FI Condition in Bangladesh

Initiated by Bangladesh Bank and supported by the government and policy-making authorities, Bangladesh is pacing toward FI of its population since its independence. However, the inclusion effort got momentum in recent decades to match with the global progress in the area. Table 6.1

Table 6.1 An insight to FI condition in Bangladesh from 2004 to 2017

Year	*Deposit account per 1000 adults*[a]	*Depositors per 1000 adults*[a]	*Loan account per 1000 adults*[a]	*Borrowers per 1000 adults*	*Branches per 1000 sq. Km*	*ATMs per 1000 sq. Km*	*ATMs per 100,000 adults*	*Policy holders per 1000 adults*	*Life Insurance Policy holders per 1000 adults*
2004	1252.84	1066.96	794.06	451.92	2654.77	0.88	0.13	28.47	26.08
2005	1389.52	1196.74	894.05	506.47	2738.93	1.41	0.20	34.52	32.07
2006	1511.80	1306.93	989.98	560.04	2864.16	2.54	0.34	37.71	34.91
2007	1483.932	1268.08	1002.57	580.96	2939.28	3.73	0.50	46.09	43.11
2008	1573.69	1335.95	1050.50	607.31	2985.33	6.27	0.82	52.22	49.13
2009	1608.54	1361.90	1048.30	602.09	3134.70	9.73	1.25	57.49	53.83
2010	1789.28	1493.81	1069.93	610.33	3208.55	16.29	2.05	64.90	60.79
2011	1895.18	1767.42	1035.42	576.89	3339.06	29.17	3.60	161.29	152.28
2012	1919.10	1862.56	998.76	556.46	3458.71	32.40	3.92	156.81	147.44
2013	1991.57	1815.92	1020.44	569.47	3478.50	40.51	4.81	154.11	144.42
2014	2059.98	1845.25	1017.53	571.48	3525.55	48.08	5.61	152.35	143.11
2015	2168.79	2078.67	1045.75	595.86	3507.96	60.22	6.89	139.13	128.54
2016	2281.61	2183.61	1088.97	619.66	3378.63	69.29	7.78	136.64	125.45
2017	2400.78	2288.60	1117.24	636.83	3345.65	73.15	8.07	134.41	121.95

Source: Constructed by the authors based on IMF (2018)

Notes: The indicators measure access in any bank or non-bank formal financial institution

[a]Overlapping is possible in calculation of deposit and loan indicators

offers an insight into major FI indicators in Bangladesh from 2004 to 2017 by illustrating popular indicators of inclusion.

The first indicator, deposit account per 1000 adults, is a measure of account penetration by the eligible populace. The table shows that Bangladesh has almost doubled (from 1252.84 to 2400.78) its achievement in account penetration within the last 14 years. The growth has been noted as a gradual progression during the assessment period. Secondly, a similar measure, depositors per 1000 adults shows the proportion of included population out of the total bankable population. Bangladesh has registered the highest growth (18.32 percent) in this indicator from previous fiscal in 2015.

Affordable credit is the following provision for FI. In popular FI literature, a measure of credit access is the loan account per 1000 adults. Bangladesh has been able to register regular growth in loan coverage with a pause in 2011–12. In 2017, the loan account per 1000 adults reached 1117.24, recording 11.86 percent growth in the last five years. Another similar measure, borrower per 1000 adults, offers an overview of loan coverage to all bankable adults. The table also shows that the country had experienced almost 7.07 percent annual growth until 2010, when borrower coverage dropped from 610.33 to 576.89. However, after three consecutive bad years, Bangladesh recovered from this depression to see an increase in the indicator for the last four years.

The indicators discussed so far provide a broad-based overview without focusing on usage or area-based scenario. The next measure, branches per 1000 square kilometers, however, offers an area wise coverage of formal financial institutions. Until 2013, banks and financial institutions, specifically MFIs, were spreading their network to the farthest corner of the country. Nevertheless, the high operational cost of the established network forced the formal financial institutions to rethink their decision. Accordingly, credit unions, financial co-operatives, and other depository corporations stepped back by shutting some branches from 2014, reflecting a decrease in branch coverage.

The next provision for inclusion is payment or transfer facility. ATM technology has made it super easy to withdraw or transfer money from deposit accounts, hence recognized as one of the significant yardsticks for inclusion. In Bangladesh, commercial banks and a few non-bank financial institutions (NBFIs) offer ATM services. For better coverage and customer service, banks have joined the consortium, whereby even small banks without self-ATM service can allow their customers to use their cards in ATM booths of other banks. As shown in Table 6.1, Bangladesh registered an explosive growth in ATMs per 1000 square kilometers, 82.8 times in 13 years. The dataset reveals that from 2004 to 2011, ATM coverage has been increased annually at an average rate of 65 percent. Afterward, the growth normalized with 6 percent to 25 percent yearly growth in the last seven years. This rate can be explained by the already established network, connection to national fund transfer network, and introduction of other more comfortable financial technology, like agent banking. Another measure of ATM usage is ATMs per 100,000 adults. Though ATM usage is still very low, the progress of almost 64.49 times in the last 13 years shows some rays of hope. Debit card facility with every deposit account, low cost or free of cost fund transfer, and growing awareness of financial technologies can be the catalyst for an increase in ATM access and usage.

Lastly, access to insurance is one of the widely accepted measures of inclusion. This section includes two indicators for measurement of insurance: policyholders per 1000 adults and life insurance policyholders per 1000 adults. Both indicators reflect gradual growth up to 2011. However, after 2011, the insurance industry experienced sluggish growth with the largest decline in 2015, when the number of insurance policies declined by 1,181,031 policies from the previous year (IMF 2018). Moreover, life insurance access followed a similar trend, or more precisely, the life insurance coverage registered 19.91 percent decline, while insurance coverage, in general, experienced a 16.67 percent decrease in the last seven years. No noticeable regulatory improvement, as well as the reluctance of general people toward insurance, offer challenges to the inclusion in Bangladesh through insurance.

Financial Exclusion

Nonetheless, the reasons for the exclusion of one-fourth of the population in Bangladesh should be addressed with significant attention. FI literature usually recognizes three primary forms of exclusion, namely area-based, gender-based, and income-based. All three kinds exist in Bangladesh in different proportions. Table 6.2 provides a summary of available statistics on exclusion areas.

Due to remoteness and high operational cost of maintaining small branches at distant locations, private commercial banks are often found unwilling to establish branches in rural areas. NGOs and MFIs have

Table 6.2 Area and gender-based FI in Bangladesh (2004–17)

Year	*Rural branches*	*Rural branches (% of total)*	*Male borrowers per 1000 adults*	*Female borrowers per 1000 adults*	*Deposit accounts owned by men per 1000 adults*	*Deposit accounts owned by women per 1000 adults*	*Male depositors per 1000 adults*	*Female depositors per 1000 adults*	*Loan accounts owned by men per 1000 adults*	*Loan accounts owned by women per 1000 adults*
2004	3724.00	59.10	n/a	n/a	n/a	n/a	n/a	n/a	n/a	n/a
2005	3764.00	58.80	n/a	n/a	n/a	n/a	n/a	n/a	n/a	n/a
2006	3834.00	58.40	n/a	n/a	n/a	n/a	n/a	n/a	n/a	n/a
2007	3894.00	58.00	n/a	n/a	n/a	n/a	n/a	n/a	n/a	n/a
2008	3981.00	57.80	n/a	n/a	n/a	n/a	n/a	n/a	n/a	n/a
2009	4136.00	58.30	n/a	n/a	n/a	n/a	n/a	n/a	n/a	n/a
2010	4393.00	57.40	n/a	n/a	n/a	n/a	n/a	n/a	n/a	n/a
2011	4551.00	57.20	n/a	n/a	n/a	n/a	n/a	n/a	n/a	n/a
2012	4760.00	57.20	n/a	n/a	n/a	n/a	n/a	n/a	n/a	n/a
2013	4962.00	57.10	n/a	n/a	n/a	n/a	n/a	n/a	n/a	n/a
2014	5150.00	57.00	n/a	n/a	n/a	n/a	n/a	n/a	n/a	n/a
2015	5187.00	56.80	39.67	8.76	274.73	117.01	251.18	103.06	41.46	8.83
2016	5360.00	56.70	37.60	8.72	289.81	130.16	254.49	117.57	39.10	9.07
2017	5501.00	56.60	52.80	10.89	458.38	209.02	411.91	192.45	55.17	11.02

Source: Constructed by the authors based on Bangladesh Bank (2011, 2015, 2017) and IMF (2018)

stepped into this gap since the late 1970s by spreading their network in remote rural places in tiny community houses or small branch offices with meager operational expenses. However, the ultra-poor and middle class are left unreached either for their inability to initiate income-generating entrepreneurship or their doubt in any financial institutions other than the bank. Cases of irregularities in non-bank financial sectors due to lack of specific regulation are also responsible for such confusion. Nevertheless, the instruction of Bangladesh Bank for commercial banks to make a rural-urban branch network to 1:1 successfully triggered a change. In 2010, the percentage of rural branches of commercial banks in terms of total branches stood at 59.8 percent (Bangladesh Bank 2011). Table 6.2 indicates the number of rural branches has increased gradually over the last decade; however, such progress was not enough to keep the decreasing proportion of rural branches in balance. After more than four decades of continuous attention to rural branch expansion, banking authorities are now concerned with more cost-effective usage of their network. Also, rapid urbanization and internal migration to big cities are making it unnecessary to establish more rural branches. Moreover, such a move is not considered detrimental to inclusion as a successful launching of financial technologies is reducing the outreach gap to a minimal level, even at a lower cost.

Also, a significant gender-based gap exists in FI in Bangladesh. Women are deprived of economic power for long, which results in the exclusion of a significant portion of the bankable population in formal financial chains. However, increased participation in economic activities along with particular attention by policy-making authorities have contributed to bridging the gap. Moreover, the gender-biased focus of NGOs and MFIs and Bangladesh Bank's provision for women entrepreneur's loan have made progress in credit access to female borrowers. Table 6.2 shows that the deposit account holdings by women in commercial banks per 1000 adults are 2.19 times less than that of men in 2017. The gap in the deposit account is ever-widening (157.72 in 2015 and 249.36 in 2017), a point of concern. Nevertheless, the number of female depositors is on the rise, with a reduced gap over the last three years (2.43 times to 2.14 times).

Again, a gender gap exists both in the number of loan accounts and borrowers. While the number of loan account holding of men was 4.69 times higher than their female counterparts in 2015, it went up to 5.00 times after two years. Similarly, the gender gap in the number of borrowers also has been increased by 35.62 percent in the last two years. Though such statistics only cover deposit and loan in commercial banks and leave large gender-biased coverage of MFIs, the banking authority still requires scrutinizing the reasons behind such increasing gender gap even after significant allocation for women borrowers.

Lastly, the income gap is considered to be another major reason for exclusion. Low-income people in Bangladesh often find it difficult to be included in the formal financial network. Reasons for this could be attributed to low or no savings, lack of proper identification for opening account, complex procedure for account opening or credit approval, unfamiliarity with banking procedures, lack of confidence in financial institutions other than the bank, difficulties in fund withdrawal, comfort in cash transactions, and so on. Though no particular statistics are available of this excluded stratum, by analyzing the economic condition of the country, it can be said that a significant income gap persists. The specific attention of NGOs and MFIs along with poverty alleviation programs by national and international entities has contributed to the inclusion of a major portion of low income excluded strata. At present, agent banking facility with its low service charge, easy transaction procedure, and vast outlet network have been successful in accessing this particular excluded group.

Besides the forms of exclusion discussed above, religious exclusion is also prevalent to some extent. About ninety percent of the population in Bangladesh is Muslim, among whom a small portion still excludes themselves from the conventional financial network for religious reasons. Islamic *Sha'riah* (Islamic law) prohibits transactions having any association with *Riba* (interest) causing concerned Muslims to refrain from the regular financial network. Again, another excluded stratum is emerging at present due to rapid internal migration. A large number of slum residents and people with no specific residence in big cities are the members of this group. Though not addressed formally, such group constitutes a significant portion of the excluded population and is difficult to reach. Particular focus and initiative are required to offer financial access to this group.

FI Efforts and Contribution to Inclusive Development

Since the liberation of Bangladesh, the government, Ministry of Finance (MoF), Bangladesh Bank, local government bodies, and development agencies have been working jointly or individually to integrate the entire population in the formal banking network. Nationalization of all banks after liberation was the first step toward that goal. Nationalized banks have been engaged in establishing rural branch network and disbursing rural agricultural credit. Such branches were basically engaged in disbursing crop loans to farmers at regulated rates, which were insufficient to cover the financing cost of rural lending to micro borrowers. Here again, landless illiterate villagers, unable to handle the paperwork, have been left unreached. At the same time, a surge in establishing mutually owned co-operative societies took place. The co-operative movement, though supported by the government for its potential to alleviate poverty, was soon captured by the rural elites. Ironically, the rural elite reaped the initial benefits of government patronage. But they strongly refuted the co-operative initiative, fearing the dilution of their control over the masses.

However, the mid-1970s observed a breakthrough for inclusion from the emergence of Grameen Bank and many similar MFIs. By targeting the poorer segment of the population, such entities have been partially successful in imparting minimal financial literacy, improving awareness to education, and better living standards as well as women empowerment. However, the hardcore poor segment, unwilling to be involved in entrepreneurial activities, remained unreached once again. Also, a 'missing middle' emerged from the MFI movement, who passed the microcredit threshold but not yet eligible for bank loans.

Against this background, Bangladesh Bank started structured FI efforts. In 2010, the central bank instructed all scheduled banks to introduce No Frills Account (NFA) for farmers, garment workers, freedom fighters, social safety net receivers, and other marginal segments of the population for mass financial integration. Such an account enables the account holder to avail free of charge bank account facility by depositing only BDT 10. At present, 17.07 million NFAs are functional in different banks in the country (Bangladesh Bank 2018) with a growth of 92.43 percent in seven years. Besides NFAs, Bangladesh Bank instructed all scheduled banks to introduce school banking and working-children banking since 2010 and 2014, respectively. According to Bangladesh Bank (2018), a total of 15.40 million school-banking accounts have been opened in FY 2018 in all scheduled commercial banks. Moreover, Bangladesh Bank has issued directives to make the rural-urban branch ratio of commercial banks to 1:1 in 2011 for reducing the outreach gap in banking. Another directive issued by the same in 2017, instructs all scheduled banks mandatorily to establish 50 percent of their new branches in rural areas. As of 2017, the percentage of rural branches to total commercial bank branches stood at 52.80 percent.

Bangladesh Bank has been acting through issuing regulations, and offering refinances for such credits to affect the FI situation. In 2009, Bangladesh Bank introduced BDT 5 billion refinance scheme for agricultural credit to landless sharecroppers (Bangladesh Bank 2012). Up to 2013, BDT 5770 million was disbursed to 481,000 sharecroppers under this scheme (Bangladesh Bank 2012). To reduce the gender gap in lending, the central bank issued directives for the introduction of women entrepreneur loans in 2010. A refinance fund is also introduced in 2014 under this scheme, whereby women entrepreneurs can avail 100 percent of manufacturing loans. Moreover, 15 percent of small and medium enterprise (SME) credit is allocated for women entrepreneurs since 2014. In a circular issued in February 2015, Bangladesh Bank directed all scheduled banks to initiate the Women Entrepreneur Development Unit for better service to female entrepreneurs (see Table 6.5 in the Appendix).

Besides the issuance of such directives for access to deposit and credit facility, the central bank initiated a few financial literacy programs individually and through scheduled banks. Such initiatives include joint projects with the Ministry of Education, social media marketing, educative commercials, and so on. Also, directives are issued to all scheduled banks for offering minimal financial education to their customers through informative brochures, posters, and interactions. Moreover, the introduction of financial technologies, like ATM in 1994, online banking in 2009, mobile banking in 2011, and agent banking in 2014, are regarded as milestones for FI in Bangladesh.

Nonetheless, including the entire population in the formal financial chain itself is not enough. Rather, it should be done in a sustainable way directed and aligned toward the socio-economic development of the included populace. Academics, development agencies, and policymakers affirm a positive correlation of FI with growth. Using comparative development statistics of the World Bank and IMF, the developmental effects of chronological FI efforts starting from 2010 have been portrayed in Table 6.3 for the period of 2004–17.

Four more parameters of development are shown in Table 6.3. Firstly, the GDP growth rate refers to the annual growth rate of the total marketable goods and services produced in a particular period in a specific region.

Table 6.3 Development condition of Bangladesh (2004–17)

Year	*FDI in %*	*FINAI in %*	*Real GDP growth rate (% change)*	*Age dependency ratio*	*Savings (% of GDP)*	*Household consumption Growth*
2004	14.25	7.79	6.1	64.37	21.19	5.97
2005	14.22	7.76	6.3	63.13	21.06	6.73
2006	12.48	7.87	6.9	62.24	21.44	7.05
2007	13.58	7.98	6.5	61.29	20.75	7.43
2008	17.21	8.18	5.5	60.29	19.19	3.98
2009	17.73	8.61	5.3	59.27	20.33	2.29
2010	19.03	9.27	6.0	58.24	20.81	4.60
2011	18.21	10.20	6.5	57.07	20.62	6.49
2012	16.54	10.57	6.3	55.97	21.22	4.11
2013	18.03	11.17	6.0	54.89	22.04	5.13
2014	17.93	11.75	6.3	53.76	22.09	4.01
2015	18.06	12.50	6.8	52.58	22.16	5.82
2016	17.93	13.00	7.2	51.47	24.98	3.00
2017	n/a	n/a	7.1	50.30	25.33	7.43

Source: Constructed by the authors based on Bangladesh Bank (2018), IMF (2018) and World Bank (2018b)

As shown in Table 6.3, the GDP growth rate indicates an interesting data pattern with the highest growth rate from previous fiscal registered in 2010 (FI initiation year). Besides, the second-highest growth rate (7.94 percent) from previous fiscal in post FI initiation period recorded in another milestone year 2014 (agent banking initiation year), points to an association between development condition and FI efforts in Bangladesh. Nonetheless, the age dependency ratio refers to an age-population ratio and provides the proportion of dependent (aged 0 to14 and above 65) and working (aged 15 to 64) residents. It measures monetary strain on employed inhabitants, and for the sample period, it ranges from 50.30 to 64.37. Age dependency declines annually by 2.04 percent after 2010 compared to a yearly average growth rate of 1.88 percent, clearly evidencing a significant improvement in the FI initiation period. Moreover, consumption growth indicates the annual percentage change in household consumption. Though the consumption growth is influenced by many macroeconomic factors other than inclusion, the average growth rate of 31.53 percent from (2010–17) compared to a negative growth rate of 13.19 percent in the pre-initiation period definitely shows the path. Lastly, the savings parameter refers to the percentage of savings in terms of

GDP. The highest yearly growth is recorded in 2015 (12.72 percent), when all major financial technologies, including ATMs, mobile banking, agent banking, and online banking, are in force. Also, the yearly growth rate of 2.86 percent from 2010 to 2017 indicates better saving capacity compared to the pre-FI initiation period (negative yearly growth rate of 0.72 percent), establishing a vital link between FI and development condition of the country. Figure 6.1 summarizes the above discussions highlighting the relationship between FI initiatives and the development scenario of Bangladesh.

Figure 6.2 displays FDI and FINAI for Bangladesh from 2004 to 2016. FINAI is a composite index developed by IMF to measure the inclusion condition of a region. The figure shows that Bangladesh has been experiencing a gradual improvement in FI for the last twelve years except in 2005. From 2004 to 2009, the FINAI has registered an average growth rate of 2.04 percent, while the rate reached a yearly average of 6.07 percent

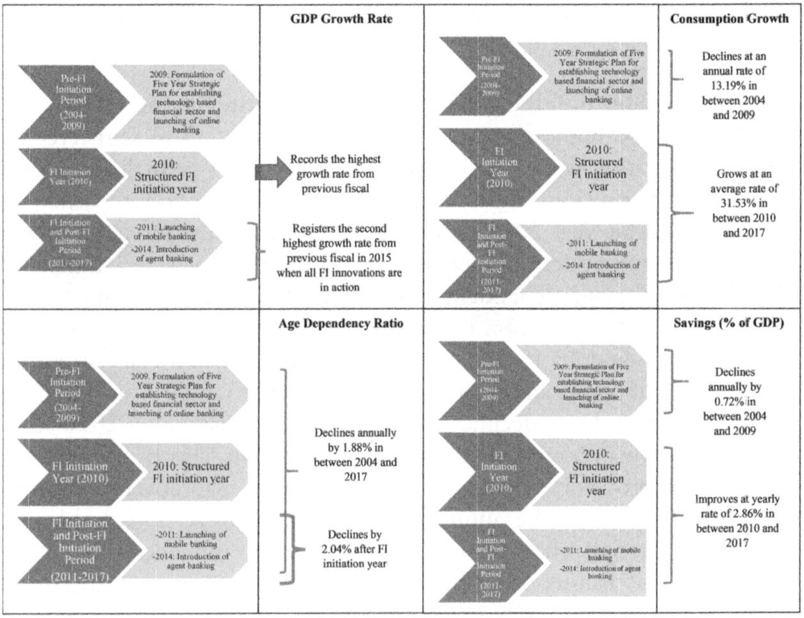

Fig. 6.1 Relationship between FI initiative and development. (Source: Constructed by the authors)

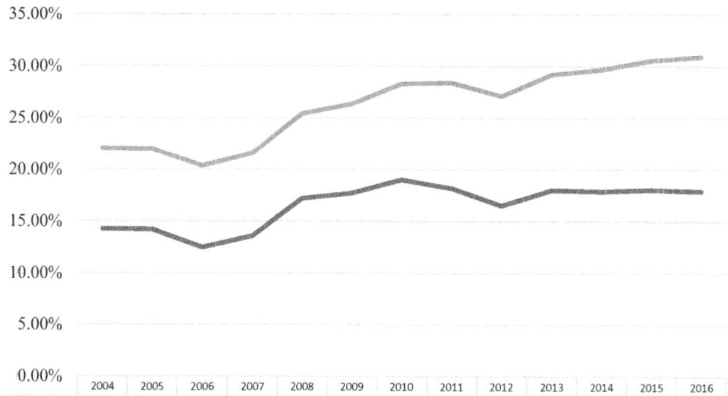

	2004	2005	2006	2007	2008	2009	2010	2011	2012	2013	2014	2015	2016
Financial Institution Access Index	7.79%	7.76%	7.87%	7.98%	8.18%	8.61%	9.27%	10.20%	10.57%	11.17%	11.75%	12.50%	13.00%
Financial Development Index	14.25%	14.22%	12.48%	13.58%	17.21%	17.73%	19.03%	18.21%	16.54%	18.03%	17.93%	18.06%	17.93%

Financial Development Index   Financial Institution Access Index

Fig. 6.2 Comparative analysis of FDI and FINAI from 2004–16. (Source: Constructed by the authors based on IMF 2018)

since 2010. At the same time, the FDI shows a much fluctuated trend. Though FDI stands at a better position with 25.86 percent growth in the last twelve years, the path of progression has not been smooth and no footprint of time is clear with inclusion efforts. A growth rate of 7.34 percent in FDI is recorded in 2010 (FI initiation year) from that of previous fiscal. However, the yearly average growth rate of 5.22 percent in the pre-FI initiation period (2004 to 2009) compared to only 0.33 percent of the post-initiation period (2010–16) is a concern for policymakers trying to align FI efforts with development goals.

Technological Dimension in FI

The journey toward the path of financial technology in Bangladesh began in 1994 with the installation of first-ever ATM by Standard Chartered Bank, one of the foreign-owned commercial banks. At present, the country is advancing in line with the rest of the world through extensive usage of innovative financial technologies, like online banking, mobile banking, and agent banking.

In 2009, Bangladesh Bank formulated a five-year strategic plan (2010–14) to develop an information technology-based financial sector. Consequently, Bangladesh Automated Clearing House (BACH),

Bangladesh Electronic Fund Transfer Network (BEFTN), and Real-Time Gross Settlement (RTGS) came into operation to make inter-bank fund transfer easier and faster. In the same year, commercial banks initiated online banking services on a small scale. Online banking, internet banking, or any-branch banking allows a user to avail of essential banking services, like fund transfer, balance query, and account statement request through internet service. Currently, 75.10 percent (Table 6.4) of all commercial banking branches offer online banking services at an annual charge of BDT 0 to BDT 300. According to Bangladesh Telecommunication Regulatory Commission (BTRC 2018), the number of active internet subscribers is recorded at 80.48 million in 2017. The growing usage of the internet can trigger the inclusion of the excluded population in the active financial chain at a very low cost.

Moreover, mobile banking, initiated in 2011, offers the most popular tool for digital financial integration. With very little paperwork, a mobile money account can be opened free of cost at nearby small agent outlets or staying at home. Such accounts offer cash out, cash payment, fund transfer, mobile recharge, bill payment, and balance inquiry facilities with a low charge from the mobile phone. Due to the ease of operation and minimal financial literacy requirement, mobile banking has experienced explosive growth of 2924.17 times in its six years of operation. In 2017, more than 1875.64 million transactions were recorded in 481,081 mobile money outlets (Bangladesh Bank 2018). The rapid growth of mobile technology, availability of mobile phones, lack of banking paperwork, and easy procedure of mobile banking have appealed to all classes of the population. As such, 14.48 percent of mobile phone users have a mobile money account presenting a lucrative opportunity for mass digital integration feasibly.

The introduction of agent banking was an epoch-making financial technology innovation in the banking sector. Since 2014, agent banking allows commercial banks to serve customers in distant places without setting up costly branch offices. The commercial banks, under the agent banking guidelines (Table 6.5 in the Appendix) issued by Bangladesh Bank, permit local retail agents to offer small-scale banking services to agent banking account holders. Such an account allows cash withdrawal and deposit, fund transfer, bill payment, and remittance withdrawal, incurring a small charge. As of FY 2018, 1.78 million agent banking accounts have been functional under 4136 retail agent outlets. Moreover, BDT 35.14 billion worth of remittances had been withdrawn using agent banking channels (Bangladesh Bank 2018).

Table 6.4 Digital financial integration from 2010 to 2017

Year	*Number of ATMs*	*Number of cards*	*Active mobile money accounts*	*Mobile money agent outlet*	*Mobile money transactions: number*	*Non-branch retail agent outlets*	*Agent banking account**	*Online banking branches*
2010	2121	n/a	n/a	n/a	n/a	n/a	n/a	n/a
2011	3797	n/a	7,186.00	2551.00	229,592.00	n/a	n/a	n/a
2012	4217	n/a	524,970.00	20,822.00	9,944,688.00	n/a	n/a	n/a
2013	5273	n/a	4,892,646.00	131,829.00	228,977,230.00	n/a	n/a	47.00
2014	6259	8.42	9,498,627.00	240,213.00	547,601,792.00	118.00	n/a	51.90
2015	7839	9.24	12,793,758.00	243,042.00	1,239,144,775.00	448.00	0.26	68.10
2016	9019	10.89	15,799,130.00	355,778.00	1,471,277,139.00	1710.00	0.54	72.70
2017	9522	12.56	21,013,056.00	481,081.00	1,875,640,183.00	4136.00	0.87	75.10

Source: Constructed by the authors based on Bangladesh Bank (2018), IMF (2018), and World Bank (2018b)

Notes: Number of cards are in million. Online banking branches are in %

*Agent banking accounts are in million

Such growing usage of financial technologies presents vast potential for FI in a sustainable way and at a reduced cost. A large portion of the population excluding themselves from the formal financial chain for the remoteness of the location, unfamiliarity with banking procedure, and high charge of banking now find it comfortable to do transactions using their agent banking or mobile banking account. Women who used to avoid banking channels for distance and social taboo can smoothly perform agent banking transactions from their house or nearby retail outlets. With the growing popularity of mobile money accounts involving small processing fees and widespread agent networks, people of different income groups, particularly the low-income group, are becoming interested in banking. Currently, 95 percent of the population in Bangladesh is mobile phone users, while only 75 percent of the population is included in the formal financial chain (BTRC 2018). Such statistics show hope to policymakers for using mobile phones as a possible digital FI tool in mobile banking and agent banking. However, the agent banking money transfer charges are still very high compared to formal banking fund transfer charges. Moreover, the security issue in using financial technology needs to be addressed as only a small portion of our population is financially literate.

Conclusion and Policy Recommendations

The journey of Bangladesh from a 'bottomless basket' to one of the monetarily powerful economies has been supported by integrating income from all levels of the population. Various initiatives established Bangladesh as the highest financially supportive country among low-income countries, covering 75 percent of its population in the formal financial chain. In line with the growing interest in FI worldwide, the government of Bangladesh has combined its effort to structure the inclusion agenda. Also, the robust growth of financial technology, especially agent banking, internet banking, and mobile banking services, has shown an avenue to reach the unbanked in a cost-effective and sustainable way. Keeping the explosive growth in financial access and financial innovation in consideration, this chapter aimed at exploring the FI scenario in Bangladesh with a specific focus on its contribution to development. Discussions on FI parameters, chronological FI efforts, and their impacts on development indicators were conducted. Finally, the technological dimension of FI, along with its potential to include the unbanked in the formal financial chain in a cost-effective way, has been covered.

The study suggests Bangladesh has impressively advanced to offer access to deposit and credit facilities with a significant link to development indicators. Again, groundbreaking progress in financial technology in the last seven years indicates the potential of such FI channels for the inclusion of the unbanked in a feasible way. However, decreasing the rural branch ratio, the ever-widening gender gap in inclusion, and continually declining insurance policy may hinder the success in financial integration.

A few policy recommendations can be offered. Since the growth of deposit accounts, loan availability, and the branch network establishment is found satisfactory, the disadvantaged and marginal excluded segment should be targeted instead of the broad-based increase goal. The growth in card-based payment is still very low for lack of financial literacy in operating ATMs. Commercial banks need to consider imparting minimum ATM usage knowledge to their customers for offering quicker fund transfer facility. Reasons for subsequent fall in insurance policy holding should be identified, and provision for micro-insurance should be introduced on a large scale. While targeting the existing inclusion gaps, the possibility of FI technological exclusion should also require to be considered. Moreover, the female-biased inclusion initiatives are highly recommended for putting a stop to ever-widening gender gaps. Also, the *Sha'riah* based FI mechanism should be employed to reach the religiously excluded strata. Well-structured initiatives from the concerned authorities, namely MoF and Bangladesh Bank, are suggested to link the impact of inclusion aligned with poverty alleviation, equality, economic growth, and quality education. Likewise, financial innovations in Bangladesh should be affiliated with mainstream financial institutions to reach all segments of the population through a formal and safer channel.

Appendix

Table 6.5 List of directives issued by Bangladesh Bank

Provision of NFA issued in January, 2010
Farmers, readymade garment workers, underprivileged segment of population, and beneficiaries of social safety net programs are eligible to open NFA account with only BDT 10 as initial deposit in any state-owned commercial bank or financial institution, and scheduled private commercial banks involving no service charge.
Guidelines on MFS for the banks issued vide DCMPS (PSD) circular letter no.11 on December 20, 2011
Bangladesh Bank has approved some basic MFS, including inward remittance disbursement, cash in or cash-out, and cash payment through own mobile money account for FI of the unbanked.
Comprehensive guidelines on School Banking issued in 2013 through GBCRD circular no. 7
Bangladesh Bank advised all scheduled banks to start school banking from 2010 to broaden and deepen base of FI, including students aged under 18. Any student aged between 6 and 18 years can open school-bank account operated through parents or legal guardians with a minimum initial deposit of BDT 100, without charging any service fees other than government charges. As soon as account holder is of age, the account will be converted into a regular savings account.
Guidelines on Agent Banking for the banks issued vide PSD Circular no. 05 on December 09, 2013
Agent banking presents safe, secure, and smooth alternative delivery channel of financial services for the non-privileged, underserved, and poor segment of the population, especially from geographically remote locations where branch establishment is extremely difficult or infeasible. An agent offers some basic banking services, including cash deposit, withdrawal, fund transfer, and bill payment complying regulatory issues, infrastructure requirement, customer protection arrangements, and risk mitigation issues as per the guideline.
Banking for Working/Street Children introduced in March, 2014
All banks are advised to open custodial accounts with NGOs by depositing minimum BDT 10 as initial balance without any service charge or fees. By signing bilateral agreements, NGOs agree to be fully responsible for co-operation between the bank and clients.
Refinance scheme for BDT 10 account holders introduced in May, 2014
To ensure FI of underprivileged, a revolving refinance fund of BDT 2 billion has been introduced with the highest limit of refinancing facility of BDT 50,000 under this scheme, offering interest subsidy provided by participating banks under certain conditions.
Guidance note for approval and operation of Agent Banking activities for banks issued in June, 2014
The guidance note provides a clear framework covering approval requirements, agent selection, and approval procedure of launching agent banking. Banks are instructed to maintain the ratio of rural and urban outlets to 2:1 for ensuring inclusive growth.

(*continued*)

Table 6.5 (continued)

Initiatives on Financial Education introduced in 2014

Bangladesh Bank has undertaken the following initiatives to promote financial literacy:

- Development of a web-link titled 'Financial Literacy' in Bangladesh Bank webpage
- Creation of a dynamic and interactive web portal
- Broadcasting of television and radio commercials, and awareness-creating press layouts
- Joint project with the Ministry of Education to conduct Financial Literacy and Education (FLE) program at school and college levels.

Circular on the establishment of 'Women Entrepreneur Development Unit' issued in February, 2015

- All scheduled banks and financial institutions are instructed to open 'Women Entrepreneur Development Unit' for providing all sorts of services to women entrepreneurs on a priority basis and more effectively and efficiently through dedicated desk/help desk.
- Appointment of women officials in 'Women Entrepreneur Development Unit' has been given priority.

Guidelines for Banks on Financial Literacy issued in 2014

Banks are instructed for designating focal point/contact person in each bank for financial literacy issues, developing descriptions of bank's products and services in simple language, developing an interest calculator, constructing a page containing frequently asked questions, and option for query and complaints.

Refinance Scheme for Women Entrepreneurs issued in 2014 and updated in each fiscal year

- Banks are required to reserve 15 percent of total SME funds exclusively for women entrepreneurs at a lending rate within 9 percent (bank rate + maximum 4 percent spread) for women entrepreneurs under the scheme;
- Banks and NBFIs are instructed to sanction at least BDT 2.5 million to women entrepreneurs with a personal guarantee but without collateral under refinance facilities.

Amendment to BDT 10 Refinance Scheme issued in January, 2016

All scheduled banks have been instructed to comply with the following procedures to bring dynamism in the disbursement and recovery process:

Banks may determine one or more installments in its sole discretion to recover entire loan in case of a loan disbursed directly to the consumer level for sectors stated in the agricultural credit policies. For disbursement of up to BDT 50,000 under this scheme, no credit information bureau (CIB) report will be required.

Agricultural and Rural Credit Policy and Program issued for the fiscal year 2017 issued in July, 2016

- Scheduled banks can disburse agriculture and rural credit through their agent banking channels in addition to ongoing agricultural credit program.
- Receipt of loan applications, primary scrutiny, disbursement, and collection can be made through agents, while loan appraisal, approval, and supervision should be conducted by the respective bank and a maximum 0.5 percent service charge can be credited to agents' account from borrower's account through the bank.

Instruction on setting sustainable finance unit in all scheduled banks issued in December, 2016

(continued)

Table 6.5 (continued)

All banks and financial institutions are instructed to open a separate unit in the head office to ensure corporate social responsibility (CSR) activities to support the achievement of sustainable developments goals (SDGs). A committee is to be formed in each bank led by seniormost deputy-managing director to supervise planning and monitoring of sustainable banking related activities.
Maximum ceiling for Agricultural and Rural Credit issued in June, 2017
Maximum lending rate for agricultural and rural credit is set at 9 percent effective from July, 2017.
Prudential guidelines for Agent Banking operation in Bangladesh issued in September, 2017
The guideline covers operational aspects of agent banking, including approval procedure, contractual area and permissible activities, the responsibilities of banks, and the agent assessment process not stated in previous guidelines and guidance notes.

Source: Constructed by the authors based on different orders and statues issued by Bangladesh Bank and various annual reports of Bangladesh Bank

References

Akhter, N., & Khalily, M. A. B. (2017). *Impact of mobile financial services on financial inclusion in Bangladesh*. Working Paper No. 52. Institute for Inclusive Finance and Development (InM).

Allen, F., Demirguc-Kunt, A., Klapper, L., Soledad, M., & Peria, M. (2016). The foundations of financial inclusion: Understanding ownership and use of formal accounts. *Journal of Financial Intermediation, 27*, 1–30. https://doi.org/10.1016/j.jfi.2015.12.003

Amidzic, G., Massara, A., & Mialou, M. (2014). *Assessing countries' financial inclusion standing—A new composite index*. IMF Working Paper 14/36. Retrieved December 20, 2018, from https://www.imf.org/external/pubs/ft/wp/2014/wp1436.pdf.

Arora, R. U. (2012). Financial inclusion and human capital in developing Asia: The Australian connection. *Third World Quarterly, 33*(1), 179–199.

Bangladesh Bank. (2011). *Annual Report 2010–2011*. Retrieved December 15, 2018, from https://www.bb.org.bd/pub/publictn.php.

Bangladesh Bank. (2012). Bangladesh Bank: Comparative scenarios of financial inclusion and other changes (2002–05 vs. 2009–12). Retrieved December 15, 2018, from https://www.bb.org.bd/pub/publictn.php.

Bangladesh Bank. (2015). *Annual Report 2014–2015*. Retrieved December 15, 2018, from https://www.bb.org.bd/pub/publictn.php.

Bangladesh Bank. (2017). *Annual Report 2016–2017*. Retrieved December 15, 2018, from https://www.bb.org.bd/pub/publictn.php.

Bangladesh Bank. (2018). *Annual Report 2017–2018*. Retrieved December 15, 2018, from https://www.bb.org.bd/pub/publictn.php.

Bangladesh Telecommunication Regulatory Commission (BTRC). (2018). License and Statistics. Retrieved February 22, 2019, from http://www.btrc.gov.bd/telco/internet.

Choudhury, T. A. (2014). Financial inclusion in Bangladesh: Background, issues, regulatory measures and challenges. Bi-Annual Conference of BEA held during November 22–22, 2014 at Dhaka.

Gatto, M. A., & Akhtar, S. M. J. (2015). The development of India's financial inclusion agenda—Some lessons for Pakistan. *The Pakistan Development Review, 54*(4), 569–584. Part II (Winter 2015).

Ghosh, S., & Vinod, D. (2017). What constrains financial inclusion for women? Evidence from Indian micro data. *World Development, 92*, 60–81.

Hassan, A. (2015). Financial inclusion of the poor: From microcredit to Islamic microfinancial services. *Humanomics, 31*(3), 354–371. https://doi.org/10.1108/H-07-2014-0051

International Monetary Fund (IMF). (2015). Financial Access Survey. Statistics Department.

International Monetary Fund (IMF). (2018). Financial Access Survey. Retrieved February 16, 2019, from https://data.world/imf/financial-access-survey-fas.

Iqbal, B. A., & Sami, S. (2017). Role of banks in financial inclusion in India. *Contaduría y Administración, 62*(2), 644–656.

Karlan, D., Kendall, J., Mann, M., Pande, R., Suri, T., & Zinman, J. (2016). *Research and impacts of digital financial services*. NBER Working Paper No. 22633. Faculty Research Working Paper Series.

Khalily, M. A. B. (2016). *Financial inclusion, financial regulation, and education in Bangladesh*. ADBI Working Paper 621. Tokyo: Asian Development Bank Institute. Retrieved from https://www.adb.org/publications/financial-inclusion-financial-regulation-and-educationbangladesh.

Kim, D.-W., Yu, J.-S., & Hassan, M. K. (2018). Financial inclusion and economic growth in OIC countries. *Research in International Business and Finance, 43*, 1–14.

Koker, L. D., & Jentzsch, N. (2013). Financial inclusion and financial integrity: Aligned incentives? *World Development, 44*, 267–280. https://doi.org/10.1016/j.worlddev.2012.11.002

Lal, T. (2017). Impact of financial inclusion on poverty alleviation through Cooperative Banks. *International Journal of Social Economics, 45*(5), 808–828. https://doi.org/10.1108/IJSE-05-2017-0194

Loyaza, N., & Ranciere, R. (2006). Financial development, financial fragility, and growth. *Journal of Money, Credit, and Banking, 38*(4), 1051–1076.

Neaime, S., & Gaysset, I. (2018). Financial inclusion and stability in MENA: Evidence from poverty and inequality. *Finance Research Letter, 24*, 230–237. https://doi.org/10.1016/j.frl.2017.09.007

Rastogi, S. (2018). Financial inclusion and socioeconomic development: Gaps and solution. *International Journal of Social Economics, 45*(7), 1122–1140. https://doi.org/10.1108/IJSE-08-2017-0324

Sehrawat, M., & Giri, A. K. (2016). Financial development and poverty reduction: Panel data analysis of South Asian countries. *International Journal of Social Economics, 43*(4), 400–416. https://doi.org/10.1108/IJSE-04-2014-0069

Siddik, M. N. A., Sun, G., Yanjuan, C. U. I., & Kabiraj, S. (2014). Financial Inclusion through Mobile Banking: A Case of Bangladesh. *Journal of Applied Finance & Banking, 4*(6), 109–136. ISSN: 1792-6580 (print version), 1792-6599 (online) Scienpress Ltd, 2014.

Subbaro, D. (2013). Keynote address in India-OECD-World Bank Regional Conference on financial education. *RBI Monthly Bulletin.*

Tilkaratna, G. (2016). Financial inclusion in Sri Lanka: Current status and issues. In S. Gopalan & T. Kikuchi (Eds.), *Financial inclusion in Asia*. Palgrave Macmillan, Studies in Impact Finance. https://doi.org/10.1057/978-1-137-58337-6_6.

United Nations. (2006). *Building inclusive financial sector for development.* UN Publication Number: E.06.II.A.3; ISBN: 92-1-204251-1.

Wang, X., & Guan, J. (2017). Financial inclusion: Measurement, spatial effects and influencing factors. *Applied Economics, 49*(18), 1751–1762.

World Bank. (2008). *Finance for all? Policies and pitfalls in expanding access.* A World Bank Policy Research Report. https://doi.org/10.1596/978-0-8213-7291-3.

World Bank. (2018a). *The Global Findex database 2017: Measuring financial inclusion and the fintech revolution.* https://doi.org/10.1596/978-1-4648-1259-0

World Bank. (2018b). World Development Indicators. Retrieved February 16, 2019, from https://datacatalog.worldbank.org/dataset/world-development-indicators.

Yadav, P., & Sharma, A. K. (2016). Financial inclusion in India: An application of TOPSIS. *Humanomics, 32*(3), 328–351. https://doi.org/10.1108/H-09-2015-0061

Zins, A., & Weil, L. (2016). The determinants of financial inclusion in Africa. *Review of Development Finance, 6*(1), 46–57.

CHAPTER 7

Development Dynamics of Remittances in Bangladesh

Munim Kumar Barai

Introduction

The economic globalization that began in the 1980s led to a rapid international rise in demand for skilled and unskilled workforce due to an increase in global economic activities. That paved the way for many people, including that of the developing countries, to move to overseas destinations (Castles and Davidson 2000) to earn their livelihood. As a result of this growth in outward movements of the workforce, the volume of inward remittances accelerated to become a regular and substantial source of resource transfer. Also, societies all over the globe are going through radical changes because of a steady increase in migration (United Nations 2017) and direct and indirect socioeconomic impacts of remittances.

An earlier version of the paper has appeared in the *Sage Open* in 2012. But this chapter has been thoroughly revised and updated to make it contemporary.

M. K. Barai (✉)
Graduate School of Management, Ritsumeikan Asia Pacific University,
Beppu, Japan
e-mail: baraimk@apu.ac.jp

M. K. Barai (ed.), *Bangladesh's Economic and Social Progress*,
https://doi.org/10.1007/978-981-15-1683-2_7

Bangladesh is a beneficiary of the spillover effect of the economic globalization as workers, mostly semi-skilled and unskilled, started migrating to various labor deficit zones. Indeed, this was a welcome relief for Bangladesh as its development strategies could not cope with the growing demand for employment from a fast-growing population. The consequence of the multi-directional relocation of people, both temporary and permanent, was the quick rise in remittances in the economy.

In a broader frame, the migration of the labor force from Bangladesh may be explained by different pull and push factors.[1] However, over time, a compositional shift seems to have taken place in migration as temporary workers now form the overwhelming part of its total migration. This short-term migration has, again, remained mostly Asia-centric due to the fast expansion of demand for workforce in many economies within the region. As we know, massive investments in infrastructures in the Middle Eastern countries induced by petrodollars[2] necessitated some of the Arab states to look for external workforce since the mid-1970s. On the other hand, rapid economic development of the newly industrialized economies (NIEs)[3] in the 1980s and 1990s coupled with the Japanese need created a high demand for cheap foreign labor in the East and Southeast Asian region (Cruz 2005: 23). Both these economic events created scope for short-term employment opportunities for workers of many labor-surplus countries, including Bangladesh. The World Bank's Migration and Remittances Data for 2017 estimated that Bangladesh has a total stock of 7.8 million migrants worldwide (World Bank 2018), equivalent to about 4.9 percent of its total population, up from 5.38 million migrants in 2010 (World Bank 2010: 58). A significant portion of them is now based in Asia, particularly in the Middle East and the East and Southeast Asia. However, the direction of permanent migration from Bangladesh remains mostly to the West and other developed countries in the world, though a gradual shift is also taking place as more migrants are heading toward developing economies.

As a parallel development, the flow of inward remittances accelerated to become a regular and substantial source of resource transfer to Bangladesh. However, remittances were trivial in size until 2000 and had little developmental relevance. But remittances now stand many folds to its foreign direct investment (FDI) and official development assistance (ODA) combined. According to the World Bank, the estimated remittances to Bangladesh have reached US$ 15.9 billion in 2018, making it the eighth largest remittance recipient in the world (World Bank 2018). Indeed, a regular and high flow of remittances has upended the developmental significance of remittances, both in social and economic sectors, in the eyes of the policy strategists.

However, linking the development impacts of remittances with the socioeconomic variables in the recipient economy is mainly dependent on the pattern of uses by the beneficiaries. In other words, the development linkages of remittances may be examined by their uses for consumption, savings, education, healthcare, businesses, assets holding, debt redemption, and so on of the recipient households. Though establishing such an association is acknowledged to be complicated, researchers have been giving more attention to this aspect in recent years. For a country like Bangladesh, the developmental importance of remittances on economic and social sectors seems to have a strong basis when we find the argument that in less financially developed countries remittances promote growth and present an alternative mode of investment financing (Giuliano and Ruiz-Arranz 2009).

The objective of this chapter is to argue and present the economic and social impacts of remittances in Bangladesh in five more sections including literature review, the methodology of impact computations, picture of Bangladesh's migration and remittances and their directional and compositional changes, development dynamics of remittances in terms of socio-economic impacts in Bangladesh and conclusions.

Remittances and Development: Evidence in Literature

In most cases, first-round effects of remittances on economic development are felt at the households of the migrants (Taylor and Wyatt 1996) when we find remittances move as person-to-person flows, targeted to the needs of the recipients most of the time (Ratha and Mohapatra 2007: 1). Remittances bring additional money to the recipient households to spend on higher consumption, better access to education and health services, improved housing and living conditions, and employment of resources in productive activities (Thao 2009). Bahadir et al. (2018) found that remittances impact entrepreneurs' ability to increase investment and labor demand leading to a subsequent reduction of labor supply. Assuming remittance as a source of household income, *ceteris paribus*, Javaid (2017) finds that an increase in remittances shifts the budget constraint outward for the receiving families, leading to a positive impact on the household consumption. Using the Household Income and Expenditure Survey (HIES) data of 2010, Syed and Hossain (2016) estimated the impact of remittance to households. Their ex-ante and ex-post remittance evaluation of households allowed them to see the changes in household consumption. They conclude that remittances are used for both human investment and direct consumption.

In the end, workers' remittances complement national savings to form a bigger pool of resources available for investment (Solimano 2003; Carling 2004; Ghosh 2005). Hugo (2003: 5) argues that remittances represent a substantially higher redistribution of wealth than FDI and ODA, mainly because of the absence of any conditionalities (attached to ODA) and repatriation possibilities (of FDI). At the macro level, these culminate in a chain of increase in aggregate demand-output-income, affecting the growth of the economy at the end. The sustainability of the process could be debated though, as the development effects cannot be a permanent feature unless the commitment of migrants to remittances is institutionalized. This still is a problem in Bangladesh as the use of unofficial channels[4] for sending remittances is popular, making the institutionalization process a bit difficult. However, Aggarwal et al. (2011) and Grigorian and Melkonyan (2012) find that remittances through financial institutions create bank deposit and credit which could be put into financial intermediation process to benefit the economy.

Many empirical and analytical works have examined the impact of remittances on the incidence of poverty, inequality, and economic growth position, particularly in developing countries. Adams (1991), for example, finds that though remittances reduced poverty by a small margin in Egypt, their overall impact on the income distribution was negative. In his analysis for Pakistan in 1992, Guatemala in 2004 and Ghana in 2006, Adams concludes that remittances slightly reduced poverty but their overall impact on income distribution was negative (cited in Pfau and Long 2007). But Taylor and Wyatt (1996) find that remittances reduce inequalities in rural Mexico. Adams and Page (2005), Lopez-Cordova (2005), Maimbo and Ratha (2005), Acosta et al. (2006), Yang and Martinez (2006), Ozden and Schiff (2006), Brown (2008), and so on, have important studies in this context. However, studies that investigated the impact of remittances on poverty and inequality form no single uniform standpoint and have depicted a mixed picture. Except for the real ground situations, the disuniformity could happen because of the underlying methodology to which poverty and inequality are highly sensitive (Acosta et al. 2006). Acosta et al. show that in Latin American countries, the proportion of the poor is reduced by 0.4 percent for a one percentage point increase in remittance to gross domestic product (GDP) ratio.

On the link between remittances and growth, studies suggest mixed evidence. Jongwanich (2007), for example, finds that remittances raise income and have a significant impact on poverty reduction in developing Asia and Pacific countries, though their impact on growth is marginal. While Barajas et al. (2009) find no growth effects of remittances; a study by Catrinescu et al. (2006) shows a weak positive impact of remittances on long-term macroeconomic growth. But Vargas-Silva et al. (2009) summarize that fixed-effect and random-effect estimations indicate remittances affect the real annual GDP per capita growth of home country positively. Their findings signify that a 10 percent increase in remittances as a portion of GDP should lead to about a 0.9–1.2 percent increase in the growth of output in an economy. From the viewpoint of Bangladesh, the Philippines, Tajikistan, and so on, this is a significant figure as remittances account for more than 10 percent of their GDP. Several studies like Barua et al. (2007), Bruyn and Kuddus (2005), Deb (1986), Das (1981), the World Bank (2006), and so on have tried to find the relationship of remittances with socioeconomic development in Bangladesh. Their findings support a positive association between them. Moreover, Wadood and Hossain (2017) reveal the interesting aspect that in case of Bangladesh, the potential diminishing in labor supply due to migration may help decrease the pressure in the domestic labor market from the high rate of unemployment, resettle the market wage and offer an outlet for workers who might otherwise present serious domestic problems.

Several studies like Akkoyunlu and Vickerman (2000), Solimano (2003), Rapoport and Docquier (2003) and so on have raised the possible "Dutch Disease"[5] effect of remittances, whereby an appreciation of the real exchange rate of the domestic currency due to inflow of large sum of remittances could lead to a rise in the price of exportable commodities. This may erode the competitiveness of the domestic products in the international markets and thus jeopardizes the development of the tradable goods sector. Empirical studies of Amuedo-Dorantes and Pozo (2004), Rajan and Subramanian (2005), and Lopez and Molina (2006) use cross-country data to document the real exchange appreciation following flows of remittance (cited in Acosta et al. 2007). Also, the negative impacts of remittances on the labor supply of El Salvador and Mexico have been documented by Acosta (2006) and Hanson (2007). This happens as remittances may create a dependency syndrome among the recipients and may particularly affect rural development and change (Thao 2009: 8). Acosta et al. (2007) examine whether an increase in remittances causes Dutch disease effects in Salvador, a small open Latin American economy with a large flow of remittances. The findings of their study generally suggest that the inability of the Salvadorian economy to absorb remittances leads to the realization of the Dutch disease phenomenon under three of the cases considered: "one where remittances are exogenously determined, another where remittances are countercyclical, and finally the case where remittances act like capital inflows" (Acosta et al. 2007: 22). A study on Pakistan shows the existence of Dutch Disease as a consequence of remittances suggests monetary and directive measures to overcome the decline in competitiveness of the tradable sector (Makhlauf and Mughal 2013). For Bangladesh, the effects of such a "disease", if any, need to be examined further.

Impact Assessment Methodology

This study refers to the international transfer of funds by migrants or emigrant diasporas to the home country, through official channels, from the country where they work or live in as remittances. So, inward transfers by both temporary and permanent migrants are taken into account. Moreover, temporary migration is characterized by employment with specific short-term job contacts and returning home of the workers after completion of the contract period. In the case of Bangladesh, most short-term migrants abroad are from rural areas and poor (Hasan 2006: 19). Permanent migration, on the other hand, takes place when one migrates with a permanent change in usual residence so that the relocation becomes a lasting one. The permanent migrant is supposed to hold no intention to return for living in the future to the land s/he is leaving. People from well off households form most permanent migrants abroad.

Presumably, remittances sent by the Bangladeshi migrants go first to households, as remittances are fundamentally person-to-person flows. However, remitted amounts ultimately join the mainstream economy by way of consumption and investment expenditures. For instance, migrants can invest remittances in different government savings schemes like non-resident Foreign Currency Deposit, US Dollar Investment Bond, US

Dollar Premium Bond, Wage Earners' Development Bond, and so on, where they have the right to take the invested amount out of the economy again. But these investments at the end are mostly liquidated in the Bangladesh economy. There is little evidence to show that migrants channel their invested amounts significantly out of the economy again.

The chapter has primarily been based on secondary sources of information and the socioeconomic impacts analysis is broad as the effects of remittances may become apparent from immediate to medium to long term. It recognizes the economic and social impacts of the unofficial transfer of remittances but does not deploy any effort to present the effects of unofficial transfer in the economy because of the practical difficulties in quantifying the amount accurately. Moreover, the chapter takes the Keynesian Multiplier[6] method for measuring the GDP impact of remittances. In accepting this, the chapter ignores the criticisms of the multiplier by various economists as it is not based on any government investment or deficit financing. On the contrary, remittances in Bangladesh form a net surplus source of finance, and the GDP creation impact of remittances is perceptible (Fig. 7.1).

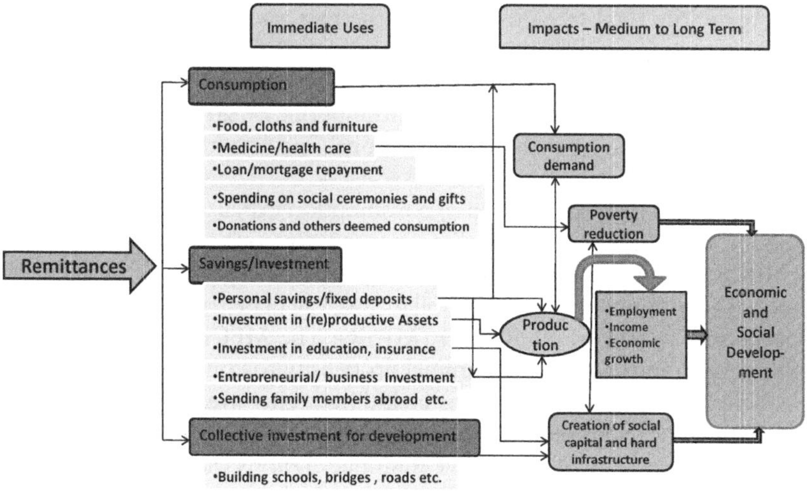

Fig. 7.1 Socioeconomic development linkages of remittances. (Source: Author's construction)

Remittance spending by the recipients has been divided here into two broad categories: consumption and investment. The broad-head consumption includes the recipients' expenses on items like food, clothes and furniture, medical treatment, repayment of loans, home construction/repair, social ceremonies, gift or donation, and others. Treating expenses for home construction/repair as consumption expenditure may be debated because of the perceived indirect backward and forward linkage effects. But our discussion on the home construction/repair expense out of remittances takes the view that this expense does not generate any direct income as a return.

Moreover, in most cases, the recipient households are typically dependent on the remittance for their living, so any expenses on home construction/repair turn out to be merely consumption expenditure. The rest of the uses of remittances are treated as saving or investment. The major items included in this category are the business investment, savings/fixed deposit, purchase of agricultural and homestead land, the release of mortgaged land or taking mortgage of property, education cost, community development investment, and sending family members abroad. The second grouping is based on the consideration that all these uses have potential short- and long-term returns to the users themselves and or to the society.

Again, the total weighted value of the two categories of expenditures, namely, consumption, and investment is assigned to as one. In the end, the household remittance income function becomes as $y = c + s$ or $y = c + i$, where y = remittance income, c = consumption, s = saving, and i = investment. From this, we draw the national income/output function as $Y = C + S$ or $Y = C + I$, as $S = I$.

Out of the two, the portion of consumption expenses has been used to obtain the value of marginal propensity to consume of remittances (MPCR). Expressed in decimal point, this is the percent equivalent of money used for consumption. Similarly, we calculate the value of marginal propensity to save of remittances (MPSR). The MPCR is expected to be different from the national marginal propensity to consume (MPC) value in Bangladesh for several reasons including higher average income of the remittance recipient households.

Finally, the value of remittance multiplier (*rm*) is calculated to find the GDP contribution of remittances, measured in terms of the aggregate amount of GDP added or created by remittances. This is the GDP effect of the investment made by remittances. The value of *rm* is calculated by using MPCR or MPSR. So, the formula used for calculation of remittance multiplier is $rm = (\Delta YR)/(\Delta IR) = 1/(1 - \text{MPCR})$ or $1/\text{MPSR}$, where ΔYR = change in income induced by remittances and ΔIR = change in remittances – investment. In this study, the MPCR and MPSR have been calculated from the study of Siddiqui and Chowdhury (2003). We accept the values of MPCR, MPSR, and *rm* as constant to calculate the approximate the GDP contribution of remittances from 1976 to 2016.

Migration and Remittances

In a broader frame, migration of the labor force from Bangladesh may be explained by various pull and push factors. However, over time a compositional shift seems to have taken place in migration from Bangladesh, particularly between pre- and post-independence phases, as temporary migration of workers now form the overwhelming part of its total migration. Nonetheless, before dealing with development impacts of remittances in Bangladesh, a brief preview of the direction of gross migration from Bangladesh and growth in remittances in its economy over the last four decades starting from 1977 may be helpful.

Figure 7.2 depicts the picture of flows of migration and remittances in Bangladesh since 1977–2016, which may also help understand the

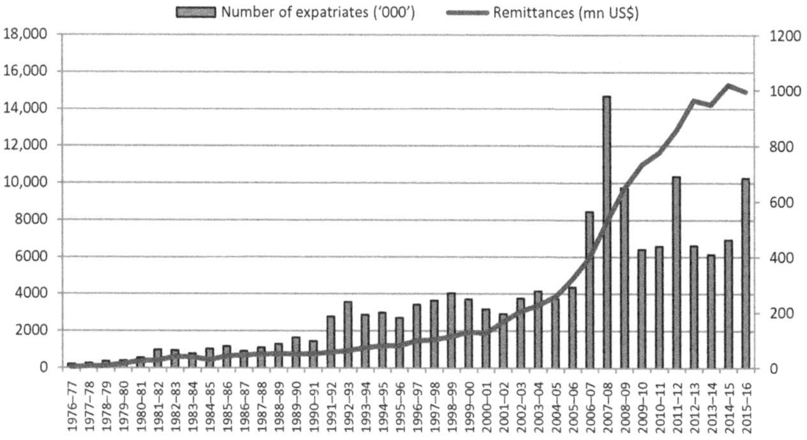

Fig. 7.2 Migrations from and remittances in Bangladesh, 1976–2016. (Source: Constructed. Data from the Ministry of Finance 2018)

developmental importance of remittances in the economy. On record, the migration figure touched the highest number of 981,000 in 2007–08 from a tiny base of 14,000 in 1976–77. But the Great Financial Crisis of 2008 seems to have affected the outflow of people up to 2014–15 with a temporary surge in 2011–12. However, the migration figures for the last two available years between 2014 and 2016 have shown some improvement. So, an analysis of the growth of migration during the sample period shows three distinctive phases: (i) a relatively slow growth from 1976 to 1990, (ii) doubling of the figure in 1991–92 from where the annual migration nearly stagnated to that level till 2005–06, and (iii) fluctuations in growth since the peak of 2007–08.

Based on the World Bank (2018) data, we have prepared Appendix Fig. 7.6 to show the destination-wise cumulative distribution of migrants. The directional distribution shows that the Middle East countries like the Kingdom of Saudi Arabia (KSA), the United Arab Emirates (UAE), Kuwait, Oman, Bahrain, Qatar and Libya in Africa are prime destinations for Bangladeshi workers. These countries together absorbed about 70 percent of the cumulative total and the KSA alone accounted for 45 percent. Besides, Malaysia has emerged as the third largest destination for Bangladeshi workers, pulling about 10 percent of the cumulative total. Singapore, the USA, the UK, and Canada are also significant destinations (Fig. 7.3). India, however, is a notable omission in the government list of Bangladesh, though unofficially it houses the highest number of (economic) migrants from Bangladesh, totaling about 3.1 million in 2017 (World Bank 2018).

While dealing with remittances, we find that Bangladesh does not maintain any segregated records for inflows from permanent migrants and temporary workers abroad. The segregated figures could have provided a better picture of the contribution of the temporary and permanent migrants to the transferred amounts. Nonetheless, Fig. 7.2 indicates that growth in remittances took place in tandem with the number of outgoing migrants during the period. The figure that began with an amount of $ 49 million in 1976–77 reached $9689 million in 2008–09, registering about 198 times increase during the period. However, the worldwide recession in 2008–09 seems to have affected the number of migrants from Bangladesh, as indicated by a sudden decline in 2009, though remittance inflows during that time got increased. Interestingly, remittances growth in Bangladesh followed a similar global pattern for the developing, underscoring a cherished area of wealth transfer where the developing countries

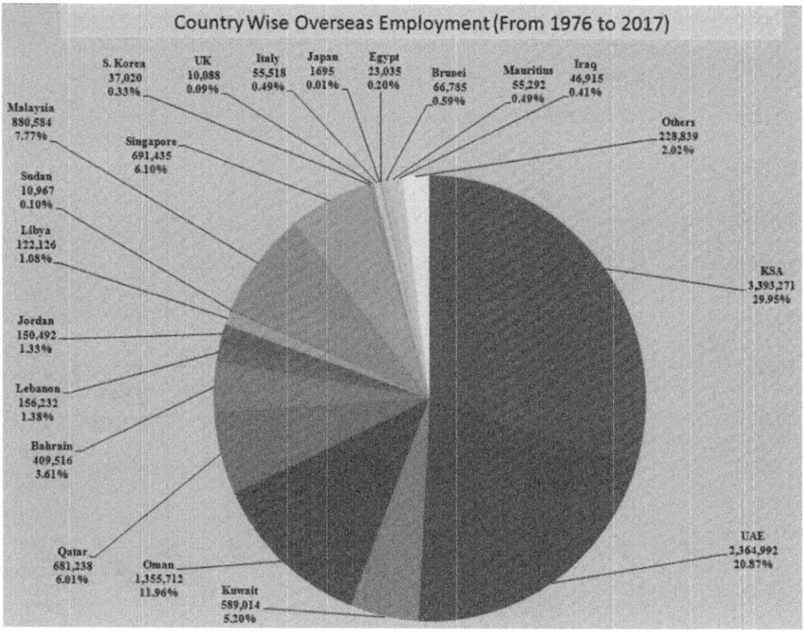

Fig. 7.3 Country-wise overseas employment (1976–2017). (Source: http://www.old.bmet.gov.bd/BMET/viewStatReport.action?reportnumber=34)

have an absolute advantage and have tremendously outpaced the developed countries (Barai 2012).

Figure 7.4 shows us the cumulative inflows of remittances from various countries to Bangladesh from 1980–81 to 2015–16. The importance of KSA in particular and other Middle Eastern counties, in general, could be understood for remittance inflows in Bangladesh. During the period, the KSA alone was responsible for 33.0 percent of the total remittances. Though the USA and the UK do not host many Bangladeshi short-term workers, their cumulative shares highlight the role of permanent migrants in remittance transfers. Though Malaysia hosts a large number of Bangladeshi workers, the cumulative figure of remittances that country constitutes is only 5.8 percent of the total. Possible explanations for this smallness could be as follows: (a) migration to Malaysia from Bangladesh is a late phenomenon, (b) the jobs of the Bangladeshi workers are mostly requiring lower skill and hence financially less rewarding, and (c) the

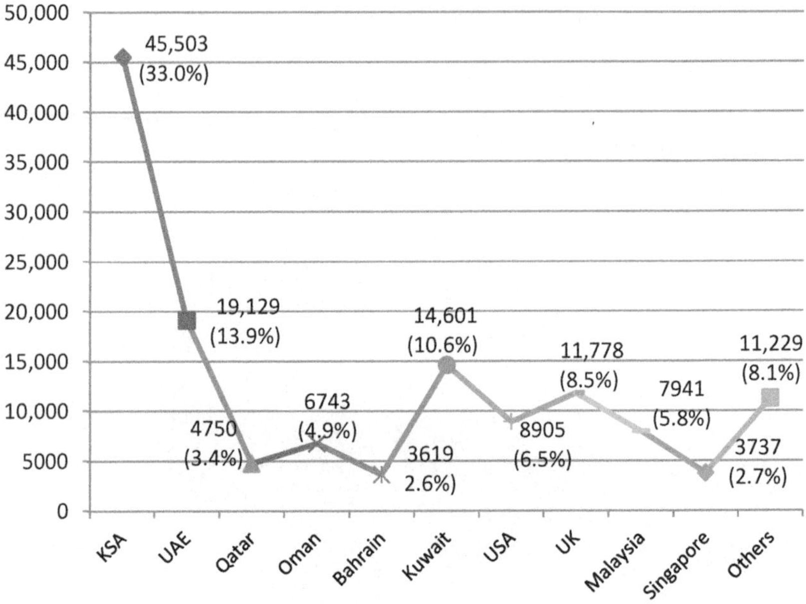

Fig. 7.4 Bangladesh—origins of remittance inflows from 1980–81 to 2015–16 (cumulative, million US$). (Source: Constructed. Data from the Ministry of Finance 2018)

migrants might be using unofficial channels more for sending remittances from Malaysia. A number of reasons may be behind the use of *hondi* channels, including the presence of a higher number of illegal workers, their low level of education, convenience, and so on.

A pertinent question arises—what are the tentative motives of migrants for sending remittances to Bangladesh? Knowing the answer is indeed important as underlying motives for sending remittances also influence the pattern of uses by the recipient households. The use pattern of remittances, in turn, affects socioeconomic development variables at the macro level. Keeping this linkage in mind, we find that there are primarily four groups of motives for sending remittances by the migrants. These are—altruistic motive, portfolio motive, loan repayment motive, and co-insurance motive. Most important of all is the altruistic motive where migrants are guided by the concerns for the wellbeing of the family members for sending remittances back home. On the other hand, income differential, the desire to return because of the temporary nature of migration, self-interest, and so on, may motivate migrants to direct remittances on investment and savings (Medina and Cardona 2010). Barua et al. (2007: 5) identify altruistic motive as the major determinant of remittances in Bangladesh. But we argue that remittances by temporary workers are broadly altruistic and portfolio in nature, while for permanent migrants they could mostly be guided by altruistic motives. This is because remittances sent by the permanent migrants are basically for the welfare concerns of the recipients as the migrants do not intend to establish a future for themselves in their country of origin. On the contrary, most of the temporary workers work in a different country for their livelihood but see their future in the country where they have come from. So, they send their earnings back to the country they tend to belong for a future with both altruistic and portfolio motives.

The discussions above, however, do not highlight some critical aspects of external migrations and remittances of Bangladesh. *First*, the USA and the UK as sources of transfer of remittances indicate that the Bangladeshi diasporas or permanent migrants play a significant role in the flow of remittances. This may be realized when we see that during 1980–81 to 2008–09, more than 20 percent of the cumulative total of remittances came from these two countries. An inclusion of remittances from the same type of migrants from Canada, Australia, Japan, and other countries will push their relative share further up. *Second*, the gender-wise statistics of external migration indicate that migration has remained mostly a male affair. *Third*, Bangladesh is still facing a problem with the mode of transfer of money earned by the migrants abroad. This is mainly because of the preference of workers to send remittances through informal channels, popularly known as *hondi*. According to Siddiqui (2004: 9–10), "Hundi refers to the illegal transfer of resources outside the international or national legal foreign currency transfer framework. Organized groups based in diverse cities such as London, New York, Dubai, Kuala Lumpur, and Singapore conduct hundi operation through their partners in Bangladesh or the region." The *Global Economic Prospect* (GEP) *2006* of the World Bank estimated that as much as 56 percent of remittances were directed through informal channels in Bangladesh. In their study Siddiqui and Chowdhury (2003), however, find that 40 percent of the total volume of remittances had been channeled through hundi. Nevertheless, we believe that this problem has subsided a bit since then as there has been an improvement in the remittances receiving infrastructure up to the rural level. This seemed to have helped increase the use of formal channels for transferring remittances, but the problem persists. *Finally*, migration to India is never recognized in Bangladesh because of the political sensitivity of the issue and illegal routes used by the people for crossing the border. Remittances from these people most likely follow the unofficial routes and the economic contribution of this flow remains unaccounted for. In our view, this is not only increasing the *hondi* transfer, but also perhaps abetting the cross-border smuggling by supplying finance for such trade.

Utilization and Development Dynamics of Remittances

The development impacts of remittances may be assessed by effects remittances have on various short- and long-term micro and macro socioeconomic variables. Again, these impacts are more in developing countries with higher poverty incidence and lower financial development density (Jongwanich 2007; Giuliano and Ruiz-Arranz 2009). The remitters, who were mostly unemployed in their home countries, have now jobs in overseas places. This may create limited employment opportunities for others in the home country. Likewise, the remittances they are sending back may help employment generation domestically as well. The latter happens through the reinforcement of remittances-induced national savings, capital accumulation, and investment (Barua et al. 2007). So, the direct, trickle-down, and indirect benefits of remittances could be significant in aggregate for many of the developing countries.

We argue that the development impacts of remittances on the economy and society are affected by the manner remittances are used. We may, however, examine the linkage between remittances and development following the flow-paths in Fig. 7.3. The figure lines up the present use of remittances and links the consequential social and economic effects in the medium to long term. Once received, remittances are used in the forms of consumption, saving, and investment by the recipients individually and collectively. The savings out of remittances can promote them to initiate some entrepreneurial activities for further accumulation of capital. In the process, remittances also help develop soft power[7] of the individual beneficiaries. So, what essentially begins as short-term micro-level benefits to individuals and households ultimately becomes a macro-level influencer of economic forces in the medium to long term to benefit the whole economy.

Uses of Remittances and Impacts on Socioeconomic Factors in Bangladesh

In analyzing the transfer and utilization dynamics of remittances Bruyn and Kuddus (2005) find that remittances inflows in Bangladesh happen mostly in the forms of (i) transfer to family and friends, and (ii) transfer to save or invest; and not much in the forms of (iii) transfer to charity or community development, and (iv) collective transfer to charity or community development. So, the impact assessment mainly centers on the first two types of transfers. Sensibly, in those two types of transfers, the recipients are often the father, mother, spouse, other family members or even relatives of near and far.

But how do recipient households in Bangladesh use the remittances they receive? Most of the studies that explored the dynamics of remittances utilization have divided various uses of remittances into two categories, for example, productive and non-productive expenditures. The terminologies used are instructive of their meaning. Those uses of remittances are considered productive, which have been used on assets that increase productive capacity and bring income to households. The other uses, on the contrary, are non-productive as they do not help accumulate capital or generate further income for them. In this study, we have, instead, grouped the uses of remittances under two separate categories, for example, consumption and investment to mean non-productive and productive expenditures, respectively. This has been done to use their aggregate values to calculate the remittance multiplier (*rm*) for Bangladesh.

To have a better picture of the uses of remittances in Bangladesh, we have summarized the findings of Siddiqui and Chowdhury (2003) in Table 7.1. We have also included the results of Bruyn and Kuddus (2005) on the same table to offer a comparative position on some of the uses. It should be noted that the study of Bruyn and Kuddus compiles remittance uses data from 21 studies, including that of Siddiqui and Chowdhury (2003). Column three in the table has averaged out the range of minimum and maximum percent of uses for respective heads from the study of Bruyn and Kuddus. Technically, the figures in column three give a view on the central tendency of uses of remittances in those studies and amplify the fact that their findings on consumption and the investment uses of remittance draw nearly a similar picture as has been found by Siddiqui and Chowdhury (2003).

In this study, we tend to focus more on the findings of Siddiqui and Chowdhury (2003) since we have accepted their results as the base for

Table 7.1 Bangladesh—patterns of utilization of remittances

Purposes	*Study I[a] (%)*	*Study II[b] (Average, %)*
Food and cloths (Consumption)	20.45	28
Medical treatment	3.22	2
Children education	*2.75*	2.5
Agricultural land purchase	*11.24*	21.5
Homestead land purchase	*0.96*	
Home construction/repair	15.02	16
Release of mortgage land	*2.24*	
Taking mortgage of land	*1.99*	
Repayment of loan (for migration)	10.55	14.5
Repayment of loan (other purposes)	3.47	
Investment in business	*4.76*	2.5
Savings/fixed deposit	*3.07*	5
Insurance	0.33	
Social ceremonies	9.07	5
Gift/donation to relatives	0.94	
Send relatives for pilgrimage	0.92	
Community development activities	*0.09*	
Sending family members abroad	*7.19*	3.5
Furniture	0.69	
Others	1.05	

Sources: Constructed. [a]Siddiqui and Chowdhury (2003) and [b]Bruyn and Kuddus (2005)
Study I: Consumption = 66 percent; investment = 34 percent

grouping uses of remittances into consumption and investment and further analysis. They surveyed a total of 100 remittance-receiving households in two administrative blocks in two districts of Bangladesh and another 20 labor-remitters in the UAE. For our study, they have formed the basis for calculations of the values of MPCR, MPSR, and *rm*.

To get the consumption estimate of remittances, we now add the recipients' expenses on items like food and clothes, medical treatment, home construction/repair, repayment of loans, insurance, social ceremonies, gift or donation, sending relative for pilgrimage, furniture, and others. Broadly, uses in Table 7.1 together constitute the percentage of remittances used for consumption by the surveyed households. On the other hand, all uses in business investment, savings/fixed deposit, purchase of agricultural and homestead land, the release of mortgaged land or taking mortgage of land, education cost, community development investment, and sending family members abroad have been added together to calculate the percentage of remittances used for investment. Differences in opinions may

Table 7.2 Impacts of remittances at household and community levels

Major indicators	*Positive impact of remittances*
Nutrition	Allow families of migrants to meet basic nutritional needs
Living condition and Housing	Living condition and housing improved
Education	More investment for education of children
Healthcare	Increased investment for healthcare
Social security	Social security for elderly people increased
Investment	Increased investment in business or income-generating activities

Source: Hasan (2006), modified from Bruyn and Kuddus (2005)

exist on the reasoning for identifying the various uses with either one of the groups, but we have reasoned our own for the kind of grouping and clubbing the uses into them. However, by adding all the values into two groups, we find about 66 percent of the remittances in Bangladesh are used for consumption and the rest 34 percent are for investment from the study of Siddiqui and Chowdhury (2003).

As mentioned, various consumption and investment uses of remittances have short- and long-term socioeconomic benefits at the household level. They ultimately go beyond to affect the community and national economy. In this regard, Table 7.2 lists some major social and economic indicators and impacts of remittances on them at household and community levels in Bangladesh. Indicators like nutrition, living condition and housing, education, healthcare, social security, and investment of the recipient households have been positively affected by remittances. The correlation between these benefits and remittances needs a bit of explanation. As we may understand, the poverty profile of the migrants is important for the social benefits appraisal of remittances, because the impact of remittance income on poverty reduction is expected to be more on the poorer households. In Bangladesh, most of the short-term migrant workers are from poor families of rural areas. So, in most of the cases, remittances form an important part of the household earnings of the recipients and could constitute 51–70 percent of the households' earnings on an average (Siddiqui and Chowdhury 2003; Mahmood 1991). Afsar et al. (2002) in their survey found that the household income of the migrants increases by 55 percent, once they start sending remittances.

So, this enhanced income helps loosen the financial constraints of the recipient families, allowing them to spend more on consumer durables, non-durables, healthcare, physical living condition, and so on. Investment in education, income-generating assets, and social security measures also get increased. Thus, remittance income in the short and long term not only protects the recipients from negative income shock but also contributes to poverty reduction and economic growth (Hasan 2006: 19–20). This is corroborated by the *Global Economic Prospects 2006*, which suggests that remittances in Bangladesh have helped the poverty headcount ratio decline by 6 percentage points from 1990 to 2006 (World Bank 2006).

Remittances and the Macroeconomy of Bangladesh

Remittances now represent an important external source of finance for Bangladesh and the tentative impacts on macroeconomic development cannot be ignored. Figure 7.5 gives us a clear view of the growing importance of remittances while compared to GDP, external debt, imports, exports, and FDI flows in the economy, all figures presented at the current price. The importance is increasing rapidly since 2000.

Let us take some comparative figures of remittances in perspective. Results for 2000 show that workers' remittances amounted to 4.2 percent of GDP, 29.7 percent of exports, 12.4 percent of external debt, 699.3 percent of FDI, 23.4 percent of gross domestic savings, and 21.6 percent

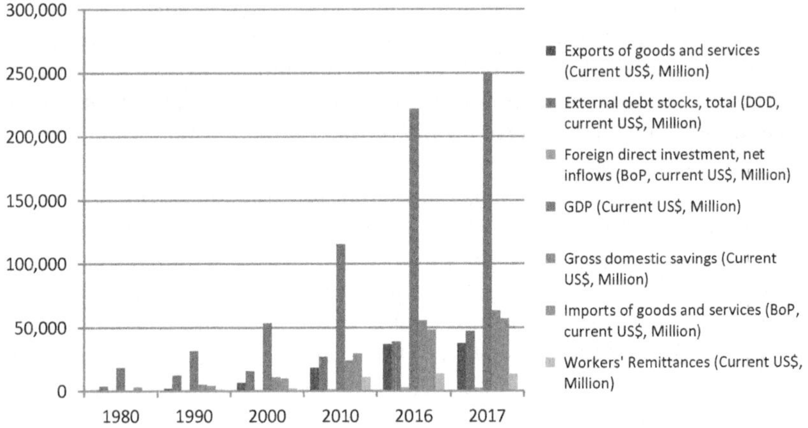

Fig. 7.5 Bangladesh—remittances and major macroeconomic indicators, 1980–2017. (Source: Constructed. Data from the World Bank 2018)

of imports. While the respective figures stood as 9.4, 58.7, 40.4, 880.7, 45.2, and 36.8 percent in 2010. In 2017, the relative positions of remittances against those macro variables seem to have not changed much from those of 2000 as workers' remittances amounted to 5.4 percent of GDP, 35.9 percent of exports, 28.5 percent of external debt, 627.5 percent of FDI, 21.3 percent of gross domestic savings, and 23.8 percent of imports (based on GDP figures and data presented in Fig. 7.5).

The critical factor is the relative position of remittances against external debt and imports. Bangladesh has remained a trade deficit country in most of the years since independence, but in the years onward from 2000, it has been continuously posting current account surplus (the gap between exports and imports of goods, services, and unrequited transfers), mainly because of remittance income. Notably, remittances have emerged to be the single largest source of net factor income source from abroad, contributing to offset the pressure of deficit of merchandise trade and to service external debt. As a result of the surplus of the current account, regular debt servicing, GDP growth, and so on, Bangladesh has bettered its international credit rating as well. For about a decade, Bangladesh is maintaining stable sovereign ratings (Moody Ba3, S&P BB-, and Fitch BB-) in the list of top-rating agencies in the world (Countryeconomy.com 2019).

This brings us to the important task of assessing the contribution of remittances to GDP creation in Bangladesh. In doing so, we need to know the MPC for Bangladesh. Ghosh (2010) identifies that MPC on average is higher in rural areas than in urban areas, and their average figures were 0.74 and 0.65, respectively, in 2005. We have already estimated from Siddiqui (2004) that 66 percent of remittances received have been used for consumption, while the rest 34 percent is invested. So, we consider the "marginal propensity to consume" of remittance and "marginal propensity to save" of remittance values of remittances as 0.66 and 0.34, respectively. Thus, our estimated MPCR looks to be close to the national average of MPC for Bangladesh. Moreover, the MPC of the remittance recipient households may be a bit lower even in the rural areas, given the kind of "elitism" they attain because of higher average income and exposure to cross-border culture.

Appendix Table 7.3 has been prepared to estimate the GDP creation impact of remittance income by using remittance multiplier (*rm*) value as 2.94, calculated on the MPCR value of 0.66. The MPCR value of 0.66 has been derived from the consumption uses of remittances from Siddiqui and Chowdhury (2003). The standard multiplier equation, $m = (\Delta Y)/(\Delta I) = 1/$

(1 – MPC) has been applied with modification in MPC to make it MPCR and MPS to MPSR. By any measure, this was a substantial contribution. The table shows that remittances created about US$ 1 billion (or 5.5 percent) of GDP in 1980. But with a rapid increase of remittances since saw the contribution went up to 31.1 percent in 2012 and subsequently going down 15.9 percent of GDP in 2017.

An effort to calculate the national MPC and using that value in the equation shows a bigger level of GDP impact of remittances for Bangladesh. For instance, by regressing total consumption on nominal GDP for a data period of 1981–2017, the MPC of turns out to be 0.84. But when the regression is done on the first difference of the same data, the national MPC becomes 0.77. The second result is more appropriate than the first one, as the level form data have unit roots. If an MPC of 0.77 is accepted, then both the GDP contribution and the share in GDP of remittances go further up for Bangladesh. Had all remittance transfers to Bangladesh been channeled through official routes, the GDP impact could have been translated further up.

Have remittances adversely impacted the external competitiveness of export trade by putting appreciating pressure on Bangladeshi Taka (BDT), the local currency? It is indeed not; as the economy has so far been able to avoid the "Dutch Disease" effects of remittances at a macro level due to a continuous depreciation of BDT against the major international currencies over time. For example, while US$1 could buy BDT 34.57 in 1990, it could trade against BDT 75.00 in 2011. Interestingly, the depreciation has accelerated since 2003 when Bangladesh adopted a fully floated exchange rate. In other words, BDT has lost substantial exchange power during this time. Moreover, the export basket of Bangladesh is still small and is dominated by the ready-made garment (RMG) products. To substantiate, the contribution of the RMG sector alone hovers around 75–80 percent of total exports in every year. Importantly, the sector employs a workforce that has a large pool of labor supply, and very few of them are remotely linked to the direct benefits of remittances. Furthermore, the domestic value addition in the sector is also increasing through backward and forward linkages of internal resources, and the utilization of import components is declining. All these together have an insulating effect on the most crucial export sector to remain internationally competitive even during the recession in 2008–09.

But there are "quasi" Dutch Disease effects present in the remittance-related segments of the economy. It is apprehended that remittances may have contributed to the creation of dependency syndrome among a section of the recipients (Bruyn and Kuddus 2005). Such a syndrome usually inspires intentional unemployment which could affect the allocation of human resources necessary to the development of domestic industries. This may be one of the important reasons that some of the zones which have the most remittance inflows within Bangladesh have fewer industrial activities. Moreover, superficial signs of inflation are visible in those "pockets of remittances" as prices of housing, land and properties, some food items, and so on, are relatively higher than the national average. This robs part of the transferred resources that could have otherwise been used for productive purposes.

Conclusion

This chapter reveals the magnitude and direction of migration and remittances and the ways remittances are impacting development of the society and economy. Plausibly, Bangladesh will remain a labor export franchise in the foreseeable future because of its low level of economic development and a huge surplus labor force which is always ready to fly. So, remittances should continue to rise in the economy if the outmigration continues.

As we have seen, migration from Bangladesh is more diverse in terms of destinations. However, an improvement in the composition of female workers abroad could enhance the economic empowerment of their families and the returnee female migrants at the end. Moreover, Bangladesh still needs to improve its remittance delivery infrastructure so that migrants avoid informal channels for sending remittances back home. That could help diminish the growth of the unofficial economy by reducing the unrecorded inflows. It may also minimize the problem of superficial inflation visible in the zones which have most migrants outside the country.

The recipients of remittances use their remittance income for a wide range of purposes, of course, a substantial portion for consumption. Because of the higher density of poverty, MPC of remittances is expected to remain high in the future too. That will keep the investment multiplier value of remittance higher. For a better picture of the remittance-beneficiaries, the household living standard survey in Bangladesh should identify the population who are benefitted by remittances in every quintile.

Remittances now weigh more importantly against many other macroeconomic variables. By offsetting the pressure of deficits of the merchandise trade balance, remittances have helped Bangladesh improve international credit rating. Moreover, a significant contribution of remittances to GDP creation makes it more important for the socio-economic development of Bangladesh. Though the quasi Dutch Disease effects of remittances may have affected some small segments of the economy, Bangladesh has so far been able to avoid the "Dutch Disease" effects on the real exchange rate. It seems that remittances have not added any appreciating pressure to make export trade costlier. Rather, the continuous depreciation of BDT over the time has warded off possible impacts on the export trade. However, it is plausible to argue that the depreciation could have been much higher with a much lower remittance inflow.

Appendix

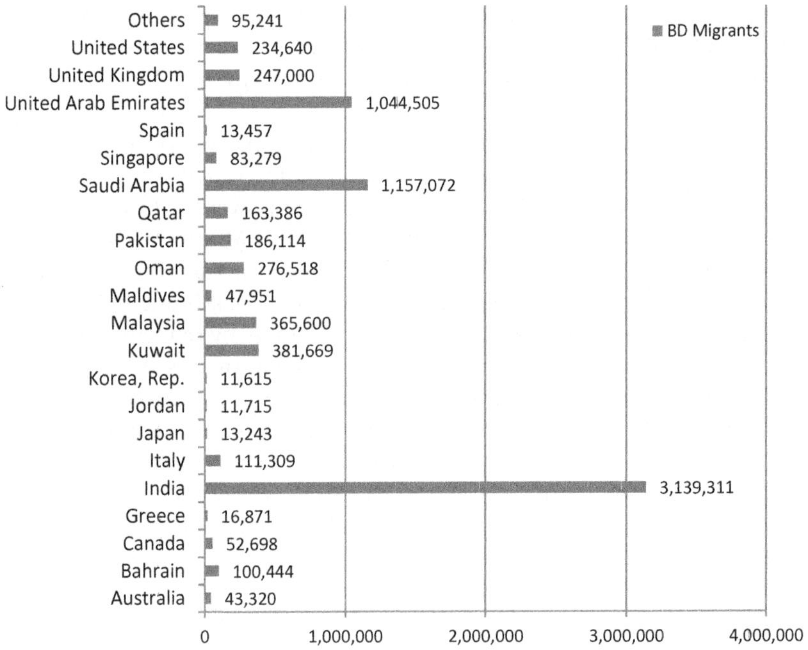

Fig. 7.6 Destinations of Bangladeshi migrants and workers, 2017 (cumulative figures). (Source: Constructed. Data from the World Bank 2018)

Table 7.3 Bangladesh—GDP creation by remittance, 1976–2017

Year	*GDP (Current-US$ mn)*	*Remittances (Current-US$ mn)*	*GDP Creation of Remittances MPCR = 0.66*	*GDP Creation of Remittances MPCR = 0.77*	*GDP Share of Remittances @ MPCR = 0.66 and* rm = *2.94*	*GDP Share of Remittances @ MPCR = 0.77 and* rm = *4.565*
1980	18,138	339	997	1474	5.5	8.1
1981	20,250	381	1120	1657	5.5	8.2
1982	18,525	527	1549	2291	8.4	12.4
1983	17,609	642	1887	2791	10.7	15.9
1984	18,921	501	1473	2178	7.8	11.5
1985	22,278	503	1479	2187	6.6	9.8
1986	21,774	576	1693	2504	7.8	11.5
1987	24,298	748	2199	3252	9.1	13.4
1988	26,579	764	2246	3322	8.5	12.5
1989	28,782	758	2229	3296	7.7	11.5
1990	31,598	779	2290	3387	7.2	10.7
1991	30,957	769	2261	3343	7.3	10.8
1992	31,709	912	2681	3965	8.5	12.5
1993	33,167	1010	2969	4391	9.0	13.2
1994	33,769	1150	3381	5000	10.0	14.8
1995	37,940	1200	3528	5217	9.3	13.8
1996	46,438	1350	3969	5870	8.5	12.6
1997	48,244	1531	4500	6655	9.3	13.8
1998	49,985	1606	4723	6984	9.4	14.0
1999	51,270	1810	5322	7870	10.4	15.4
2000	53,370	1969	5790	8563	10.8	16.0
2001	53,991	2100	6175	9132	11.4	16.9
2002	54,724	2860	8410	12,436	15.4	22.7
2003	60,159	3192	9384	13,877	15.6	23.1
2004	65,109	3582	10,530	15,572	16.2	23.9

(*continued*)

Table 7.3 (continued)

Year	*GDP (Current-US$ mn)*	*Remittances (Current-US$ mn)*	*GDP Creation of Remittances MPCR = 0.66*	*GDP Creation of Remittances MPCR = 0.77*	*GDP Share of Remittances @ MPCR = 0.66 and* rm = *2.94*	*GDP Share of Remittances @ MPCR = 0.77 and* rm = *4.565*
2005	69,443	4642	13,649	20,184	19.7	29.1
2006	71,819	5428	15,957	23,598	22.2	32.9
2007	79,612	6562	19,293	28,532	24.2	35.8
2008	91,631	8941	26,285	38,872	28.7	42.4
2009	102,478	10,521	30,931	45,742	30.2	44.6
2010	115,279	10,850	31,900	47,175	27.7	40.9
2011	128,638	12,071	35,489	52,483	27.6	40.8
2012	133,356	14,120	41,512	61,389	31.1	46.0
2013	149,990	13,867	40,769	60,291	27.2	40.2
2014	172,885	14,988	44,063	65,163	25.5	37.7
2015	195,079	15,296	44,969	66,502	23.1	34.1
2016	221,415	13,574	39,908	59,018	18.0	26.7
2017	249,724	13,498	39,685	58,688	15.9	23.5

Source: Constructed. Data from World Bank (2019)

Notes

1. As the terms may indicate, push factors are located in the country of origin from where people try to move out, whereas pull factors are present in the country of destinations where they try to move to. Political turmoil and oppression, civil unrest, armed violence, wars, natural disasters, dire economic conditions, and so on could play as push factors. Interestingly, failure of the domestic country to respond to some major events sufficiently quickly was responsible more for many major migrations in the past. On the other hand, the attractions for jobs, public merit goods such as better education, healthcare system, protection of rights and human security, a higher standard of living, quality consumption commodities, and so on in the foreign lands too could pull people to migrate.
2. Petro-dollar is an outcome of the rise in oil prices because of crisis in the 1970s due to the Arab–Israeli War and the subsequent oil-boom in the Middle East countries like the KSA, UAE, Kuwait, Iraq, Oman, Iran, and so on.
3. South Korea, Singapore, Taiwan, Hong Kong, Malaysia, and Thailand are sometimes referred to as newly industrialized economies (NIEs) or Asian tiger economies. Now newly industrialized countries (NICs) are found all over the world.
4. A number of means are used to remit money unofficially like hundi, where an organized group is engaged to collect remittances from the migrants and deliver them to the migrants' households back home, through friends and coworkers, hand carry, and so on.
5. In the 1960s, the Netherlands experienced a vast increase in its wealth after discovering large natural gas deposits in the North Sea. Unexpectedly, this ostensibly positive development had serious repercussions on important segments of the country's economy, as the Dutch guilder (Dutch currency) became stronger, making Dutch non-oil exports less competitive. This syndrome has come to be known as "Dutch disease" (Thao 2009: 8).
6. Richard Kahn introduced Keynesian Multiplier (KM) in the 1930s. Simply put, KM "states that an increase in private consumption expenditure, investment expenditure, or net government spending (gross government spending—government tax revenue) raises the total Gross Domestic Product (GDP) by more than the amount of the increase" (CFI 2019).
7. Soft power at the individual level comprises one's skills and abilities to learn, innovate, become competitive, and influence others. The power makes one tolerant and resilient and gives strength and affinity to the authority. Soft power has an association with entrepreneurship and leadership abilities of people or enterprises.

References

Acosta, P. (2006). Occupational choice, migration and remittances in El Salvador. *Mimeo*. Washington, DC: The World Bank.

Acosta, P., et al. (2006). What is the impact of international remittances on poverty and inequality in Latin America. In *The World Economy 2006*. Washington, DC: World Bank.

Acosta, P., et al. (2007, April). *Remittances and the Dutch disease, Federal Reserve Bank of Atlanta*. Working Paper 2007–08.

Adams, R. H. (1991). *The effects of international remittances on poverty, inequality, and development in rural Egypt*. Research Report No. 86. Washington, DC: International Food Policy Research Institute.

Adams, R. H., & Page, J. (2005). Do international migration and remittances reduce poverty in developing countries? *World Development, 33*, 1645–1669.

Afsar, R., Yunus, M., & Islam, A. B. M. S. (2002). *Are migrants after the "Golden Deer"? A study on the cost-benefit analysis of overseas migration by the Bangladeshi labour*. Dhaka: IOM Regional Office for South Asia.

Aggarwal, R., Demirgüç-Kunt, A., & Martínez Pería, M. S. (2011). Do remittances promote financial development? *Journal of Development Economics, 96*(2), 255–264.

Akkoyunlu, S., & Vickerman, R. (2000). Migration and the efficiency of European labour markets. In J. Bröcker & H. Herrmann (Eds.), *Spatial change and interregional flows in the integrating Europe—Essays in honour of Karin Peschel Heidelberg* (pp. 157–170). Physica-Verlag.

Amuedo-Dorantes, C., & Pozo, S. (2004). Workers' remittances and the real exchange rate: A paradox of gifts. *World Development, 32*, 1407–1417.

Bahadir, B., Chatterjee, S., & Lebesmuehlbacher, T. (2018). The macroeconomic consequences of remittances. *Journal of International Economics, III*, 214–232.

Barai, M. K. (2012). Socioeconomic impacts of remittances: A comparative study of Bangladesh and Vietnam. *Asia Pacific World, 3*(1), 110–139.

Barajas, A., Chami, R., Fullenkamp, C., Gapen, M., & Montiel, P. (2009). *Do workers' remittances promote economic growth?* IMF Working Paper No. 09/153. Washington, DC: International Monetary Fund.

Barua, S., Majumder, M. A., & Akhtaruzzaman, M. (2007). *Determinants of workers' remittances in Bangladesh: An empirical study*. Working Paper Series: WP 0713. Dhaka: Policy Analysis Unit of Bangladesh Bank.

Brown, R. (2008). A comparative econometric assessment of the effects of migrants' remittances on income and welfare in Armenia, Azerbaijan, the Kyrgyz Republic and Tajikistan. In *Regional technical assistance on remittances and poverty in Central Asia and South Caucasus*. ADB Economics Working Paper Series No. 182. Asian Development Bank.

Bruyn, T. de, & Kuddus, U. (2005). *Dynamics of remittance utilization in Bangladesh.* IOM Migration Research Series No. 18. Geneva: International Organization for Migration.

Carling, J. (2004). *Policy options for increasing the benefits of remittances.* Working Paper No. 8. University of Oxford: Centre on Migration Policy and Society.

Castles, S., & Davidson, A. (2000). *Citizenship and migration: Globalization and the politics of belonging.* New York: Routledge.

Catrinescu, N., Leon-Ledesma, M., Piracha, M., & Quillin, B. (2006). Remittances, institutions, and economic growth. *World Development, 37*(1), 81–92.

CFI. (2019). *Keynesian multiplier.* Retrieved April 29, 2019, from https://corporatefinanceinstitute.com/resources/knowledge/economics/keynesian-multiplier/.

Countryeconomy.com (2019). Sovereigns ratings list. Retrieved April 29, 2019, from https://countryeconomy.com/ratings.

Cruz, G. T. (2005). Migration in the Asian Region: Retrospect and prospects. *World Mission, XVI*(3), 22–26.

Das, H. K. (1981). Impact of migration and money remittances on the economy of developing nations: A case study of Bangladesh. *Journal of the Institute of Bankers Bangladesh, 13,* 57–69. Dhaka.

Deb, N. C. (1986). Consumption pattern in rural Bangladesh. *The Bangladesh Development Studies, XIV*(1), 1–25.

Ghosh, B. (2005). Economic effects of international migration: A synoptic overview. In *World Migration 2005* (pp. 161–183). Geneva: International Organization for Migration.

Ghosh, B. K. (2010). Rural-urban consumption patterns in Bangladesh. *International Review of Business Research Papers, 6*(4), 30–47.

Giuliano, P., & Ruiz-Arranz, M. (2009). Remittances, financial development, and growth. *Journal of Development Economics, 90,* 144–152.

Grigorian, A. D., & Melkonyan, A. T. (2012). Microeconomic implications of remittances in an overlapping generations model with altruism and a motive to receive inheritance. *Journal of Development Studies, 48*(8), 1026–1044.

Hanson, G. H. (2007). Emigration, labor supply, and earnings in Mexico. In NBER: *Mexican immigration to the United States* (pp. 289–328). National Bureau of Economic Research, Inc.

Hasan, R. A. (2006). *Harnessing remittances for economic development of Bangladesh.* Working Paper Series No. 1. Dhaka: INAFI Bangladesh.

Hugo, G. (2003). *Migration and development: A perspective from Asia.* Migration Research Series No. 14. Geneva: International Organization for Migration.

Javaid, W. (2017). Impact of remittances on consumption and investment. Case study of Tehsil Sargodha, Punjab, Pakistan. *Journal of Finance and Economics, 5*(4), 156–163.

Jongwanich, J. (2007). *Workers' remittances, economic growth and poverty in developing Asia and the pacific countries.* Working Paper WP/07/01. Bangkok: United Nations Economic and Social Commission for Asia and the Pacific. Retrieved from www.unescap.org/pdd/publications/workingpaper/wp_07_01.pdf.

Lopez, H., & Molina, L. (2006). Remittances and the real exchange rate: Are there reasons to be concerned about Dutch disease in Latin America? *Mimeo.* The World Bank.

Lopez-Cordova, E. (2005). *Globalization, migration and development: The role of Mexican migrant remittances.* INTAL/ITD Working Paper No. 20. Washington, DC: Inter-American Development Bank.

Mahmood, R. A. (1991). Bangladeshi returned migrants from the Middle East: Process, achievement and adjustment. In G. Gunatilleke (Ed.), *Migrants to the Arab world: Experiences of the returning migrants* (pp. 238–289). Tokyo: United Nations University Press.

Maimbo, S., & Ratha, D. (2005). *Remittances: Development impact and future prospects.* Washington, DC: World Bank.

Makhlauf, F., & Mughal, M. (2013). Remittances and Dutch disease in Pakistan: A Bayesian approach. *Journal of Economic Development, 38*(2), 67–97.

Medina, C., & Cardona, L. (2010). The effects of remittances on household consumption, education attendance and living standards: The case of Colombia. *Lecturas de Economía, 72,* 11–43.

Ministry of Finance (MoF). (2018). *Bangladesh Economic Review 2018.* Dhaka: Government of Bangladesh.

Ozden, C., & Schiff, M. (2006). *International migration, remittances, and the brain drain.* Washington, DC: World Bank.

Pfau, W. D., & Long, G. T. (2007). Remittances in Vietnam during economic integration: Characteristics and impacts on household welfare. Paper presented at The Third Vietnam Development Forum—Tokyo, *Conference on the Development of Vietnam at National Graduate School for Policy Studies,* Tokyo, Japan, June 2.

Rajan, R., & Subramanian, A. (2005). Aid and growth: What does the cross-country evidence really show? *The Review of Economics and Statistics, 90*(4), 643–665.

Rapoport, H., & Docquier, F. (2003, June). The economics of migrants' remittances. In L. A. Gerard Varet, S. C. Kolm, & J. Mercier Ythier (Eds.), *Handbook on the economics of reciprocity, giving and altruism.* North Holland.

Ratha, D., & Mohapatra, S. (2007). Increasing the macroeconomic impact of remittances on development. Berlin: Note prepared for the G8 Outreach Event on Remittances. November 28–30.

Siddiqui, T. (2004). *Efficiency of migrant workers' remittances: The Bangladesh case.* Manila: Asian Development Bank.

Siddiqui, T., & Chowdhury, R. A. (2003). *Migrant worker remittances and microfinance in Bangladesh*. Dhaka and Geneva: International Labour Organization.

Solimano, A. (2003, October). *Remittances by emigrants: Issues and evidence*. Santiago, Chile: Economic Development Division.

Syed, N. W., & Hossain, M. A. (2016). Microeconomic impact of remittances on household welfare: Evidences from Bangladesh. *Business and Economic Horizons, 13*, 10–29.

Taylor, J. E., & Wyatt, T. J. (1996). The shadow value of migrant remittances, income and inequality in a household-farm economy. *Journal of Development Studies, 32*, 899–912.

Thao, N. M. (2009). *Migration, remittances, and economic development: Case of Vietnam*. Hanoi: Central Institute for Economic Management. Retrieved March 22, 2019, from http://www.trf.or.th/TRFGallery/Upload/Gallery/Documents/Files/1000000027.pdf

United Nations. (2017). *International Migration Report 2017*. New York.

Vargas-Silva, C., Jha, S., & Sugiyarto, G. (2009). *Remittances in Asia: Implications for the fight against poverty and the pursuit of economic growth*. Working Paper Series No. 182. Manila: ADB Economics.

Wadood, S. N., & Hossain, M. A. (2017). Microeconomic impact of remittances on household welfare: Evidence from Bangladesh. *Business and Economic Horizons, 13*(1), 10–29.

World Bank. (2006). *Global economic prospects 2006*. Washington, DC: World Bank.

World Bank. (2010). *Migration and remittances factbook 2011*. Washington, DC: Migration and Remittances Unit, World Bank.

World Bank. (2018). Migration and remittances data. Retrieved December 27, 2018, from http://www.worldbank.org/en/topic/migrationremittancesdiasporaissues/brief/migration-remittances-data.

World Bank. (2019). *World Development Indicators 2018*. Washington, DC: World Bank.

Yang, D., & Martinez, C. (2006). Remittances and poverty in migrants' home areas: Evidence from the Philippines. In C. Ozden & M. Schiff (Eds.), *International migration, remittances and the brain drain*. Washington, DC: World Bank.

PART IV

Economic Sectors and Development

CHAPTER 8

Agricultural Development and the Rural Economy: The Case of Bangladesh

Mohammad Dulal Miah, Rashedul Hasan, and Helal Uddin

Introduction

The idea that society is becoming 'post-industrial' is perhaps the most influential in a broader intellectual circle of the day. The term 'post-industrial society,' coined by Daniel Bell, is used to describe a series of contemporary macro-social changes that were occurring as early as the 1950s. For Bell (1973) the common traits of post-industrial society are a new class of ruling elite, the movement of the labor force into service sectors, technology as the driving force of change, and the theory as the most important type of knowledge. The service sector, in the post-industrial

M. D. Miah (✉)
Department of Economics and Finance, University of Nizwa, Nizwa, Oman
e-mail: dulal@unizwa.edu.om

R. Hasan
Faculty of Business, Communication, and Law, INTI International University, Nilai, Malaysia

H. Uddin
Ritsumeikan Asia Pacific University, Beppu, Japan

M. K. Barai (ed.), *Bangladesh's Economic and Social Progress*,
https://doi.org/10.1007/978-981-15-1683-2_8

society, gradually takes the place of the industry as the new engine of growth which grows at a faster pace than the manufacturing sector. Agriculture is an insignificant sector in the post-industrial countries and contributes only a tiny fraction to the gross domestic product (GDP). Bell's account sheds important light on the significance of the service sector in the post-industrial stage of countries, no doubt. However, he has also argued that a growing service sector does not wholly displace the agrarian and industrial worlds because they are the building blocks of transition from agrarian to post-industrial phase.

The transition from one stage to another requires higher productivity. In an orderly fashion, a society passes through several stages such as primitive, pre-take-off, take-off driving to maturity, and the stage of mass consumption (Rostow 1960). In the primitive or traditional stage, an economy is dominated by agriculture where appropriate technology is either not available or not applied systematically. However, a change in the major characteristics of the primary sector embraces societies in the process of transition driving toward industrialization (secondary sector). An industrial society, however, tends to transit to 'post-industrial society' because there is a universal tendency that the trade and services (tertiary sector) grow more swiftly than either primary or secondary sector. As per this growth account, countries strive to achieve economic growth basically by advancing to the 'service or tertiary society.' In this sense, the development strategy of underdeveloped economies depends largely on the transition from agrarian to industrial society.

The process of this economic transition has been spelled out well by the 'structural theory.' The theory states that a dynamic transformation from traditional agriculture- dominant economy to modern industrial society takes place if the agriculture sector is modernized through improved technology and productivity (Adelman 1984). The critical issue for countries relying predominantly on agriculture is to increase agricultural income which is linked to raising the productivity of labor. The rise of productivity would presumably bring a revolutionary demand for industrial output in two ways. First, the demand for modern agricultural machinery and tools increases. Second, the modernization of agriculture leads to increased productivity and the release of the agriculture labor force from the primary sector to be employed in the industry. Without the basic foundation laid by agriculture through increased productivity, which in turn, leads to augmented demand for the industrial product, the industrialization of developing economies is highly unlikely.

In this chapter, we will revisit the trend of agriculture development in Bangladesh, in particular, the adoption of modern technology and its impact on the productivity of labor. Bangladesh is at a crucial development stage and is considered one of the next 11 (N-11) emerging countries after Brazil, Russia, India, China, and South Africa (BRICS). According to the projection of PricewaterhouseCoopers [PwC] (2015), Bangladesh has the potential to emerge as the 29th largest economy by 2030 and 23rd by 2050 (based on purchasing power parity). The report further projects that the GDP of the country is expected to grow at 5.1 percent for the period 2014–50, third-highest following only Nigeria (5.4 percent) and Vietnam (5.3 percent). However, PwC's supposition that emerging economies have stronger potential growth than the advanced countries relies on the assumption that those emerging economies '...continue to follow broadly growth-friendly policies.'

Modernizing agriculture and increasing farm wage are the keys to these growth-enhancing policies as far as Bangladesh is concerned because agriculture still occupies a dominant place in the economy although its role has been gradually declining in recent years. Thanks to its arable land and natural ambient, the country has earned self-sufficiency in food grain production for its large population that played a critical role in eradicating rural poverty.

Structural Shift Through Agrarian Development

Structure, in the context of development economics, refers to the relative importance of sectors in terms of producing and contributing to the growth of a country. The structural shift in this sense means to imply the change of economic epicenter from one sector to another. In particular, the primary change in structure emphasized in the classical development literature embodies a paradigm shift from the traditional sector (agriculture) to industry (Bairoch 1973; Johnston and Mellor 1961). The fundamental driver of this change is the increase in productivity of the traditional sector. Higher agriculture productivity eventually leads to the release of the labor force engaged in agriculture. Such a movement of labor from agriculture to the modern industrial sector is referred to as the 'labor push' hypothesis (Alvarez-Cuadrado and Poschke 2011). Based on this presumption, the classical development paradigm perceives agricultural growth as an engine for structural transformation and thereby industrialization.

Empirical evidence on which the classical theory often relies can be traced back to the industrial revolution. The industrial revolution was preceded by agricultural growth in some countries, including England, Japan, and the USA. For instance, the USA employed about three-fourths of its labor force in agriculture, which contributed more than half to the GDP in 1800 (Alvarez-Cuadrado and Poschke 2011). In 2000, less than 2 percent of the labor force remained in the agricultural sector and the share of agricultural production in GDP fell below 2 percent. Over these two centuries, US output per capita increased more than 25 times. Japan employed about 65 percent of its labor force in agriculture even as late as 1900 when the modern industry had begun to expand substantially. At the same time, agriculture's contribution to GDP accounted for 38 percent. The share of agriculture to GDP declined to a minuscule 1.5 percent whereas the share of the labor force employed in the sector plummeted to 5 percent.

This structural school further draws evidence from the rise of Asian tigers, including South Korea and Taiwan. Lipton and Longhurst (2011) argue that this classical paradigm was successfully implemented in Asia in the 1960s and 1970s, where the Green Revolution averted major famines and simultaneously facilitated industrialization. Their development was arguably facilitated by land reforms leading to the rapid productivity increase in smallholder farming.

The basic premise of this school is that a dynamic transformation from the traditional agriculture-dominant economy to the modern industrial society is feasible if agriculture is modernized through modern technology, which in turn, leads to increased productivity. The effect of an increase in productivity will be seen by the rise of the purchasing power of the agrarian population. The demand for non-farm products will rise, as a result. Increased demand will pave the way for industrialization. This hypothesis is labeled as the 'demand-driven' strategy of development (Adelman 1984). Adelman stresses that the role of increased agricultural productivity via technological innovation and increased investment in raising rural incomes for 'agricultural-demand-led-industrialization' (ADLI) is critical for agro-based economies.

Given the institutional link of the agriculture sector to the rest of the economy, a stimulus to agricultural activities is expected to induce strong demand and thereby, foster industrial expansion. Vogel (1994) applies the Social Accounting Matrix (SAM)—aggregate structural interrelationships among the various agents of an economy—to identify the importance of agriculture on industrialization and finds that at the low level of development, agriculture possesses strong backward links to non-agriculture activities possibly so high that a $1 expenditure in agriculture generates $2.75 in induced demand in non-agriculture sector and the link continues to increase during the course of development. The surplus, linkage, and market contributions of agriculture, and the associated multiplier effects could accelerate growth in the rest of the economy above the rate of growth in agriculture, leading to a relative decline of the agricultural sector in employment and GDP. The role of agriculture in development was thus measured in its support to the acceleration of growth in the rest of the economy, principally industry, with the relative decline of agriculture.

Despite its glorious role in the early stage of industrialization of advanced nations, the role of agriculture in the classical development paradigm was neglected for about 20 years (De-Janvry 2010). During the period 1985–2005, agriculture was seen as a sunset industry and not competitive for public investment. This resulted in a sharp decline in public investment and overseas development assistance going to agriculture, and dismantlement of many of the support agencies to agriculture, including agricultural development banks and parastatal marketing agencies. Besides, agriculture was no longer seen as the most effective approach to achieve industrialization that could better be obtained through Open Economy Industrialization strategies based on international financial capital movements, foreign direct investment, international transfers of technology, and economies of scale in urbanization (Rodrik 2006). De-Janvry (2010) attributes this demise to the drawback of new development paradigm, which fails to conceptualize the role of agriculture in development adequately. Moreover, the success of agriculture should be seen beyond what the market can achieve. For example, the conventional measure of development rarely considers such factors as poverty reduction, sectoral disparities, gender equity, and intergenerational sustainability in resource use. These parameters are developed most often than not with the development of agriculture, which entails that social choices must be made in weighing various development outcomes of agriculture not merely its contribution to wealth accumulation (De-Janvry 2010).

To this point, agriculture has been able to attract widespread attention from scholars and policymakers in the question as to how sustainable development of developing economies can be achieved and sustained in a time when rural-urban disparities have widened, the gap between the rich and poor has heightened, and environmental degradation has been at the peak. Lo (2012) examines Chinese economic growth through the lens of

Marxian egalitarian patterns of income distribution. The growth acceleration of the Chinese economy so far has facilitated by two necessary conditions. First, the process of structural change involved both an expansion of the share of industry in the economy and the leading role of a wide range of mass-production of industries. Second, the egalitarian pattern of the income distribution, which underpinned mass consumption has induced investment and overall expansion of demand (Suzuki and Miah 2017). Low's analysis throws a clear light on the fact that sustainable development of the Chinese economy critically depends on the equitable distribution of income. The economic acceleration of a growing economy is prone to disruption if the bottom of the population pyramid remains economically destitute.

Chakravarty (1979) scrutinizes strategies for Indian economic growth. He favors agriculture-first strategy as a sustainable approach for industrialization. He argues that the desirability, as well as the feasibility of an export-led industrialization strategy in a slow-growing economy, will not be realized unless the agriculture sector is reinvigorated. The long-term growth must primarily be based on the expansion of internal rather than external demand. Similarly, Storm (1995) supports a policy that an increase in agricultural production and income is likely to improve industrial performance because they expand the size of the domestic market. Thus, the industrialization of countries with a low economic base can mainly be sustained by the expansion of the agriculture sector.

Scholars in the context of Bangladesh argue that the development strategy of the country depends mainly on the development of agriculture. For example, Faruqee (1998) and Palmer-Jones (1999) advocate strategies that focus on the promotion of the agriculture sector. By the same token, Ali (2007) contends that social change will not occur until food security is achieved and farm income increases to raise people's aspiration level. Such a mechanism for boosting agro-productivity is coined as a 'green revolution' in the existing literature (Alauddin and Tisdell 1995; Hossain 1991).

Green revolution in agriculture gives a strong stimulus to non-farm employment through consumption linkage (Hossain 1988). Modern large-scale agriculture requires industrial products as inputs and raw materials which means that the demand for service and non-farm products increases leading to the creation of new job opportunities in the non-farm sector (Alauddin and Tisdell 1995). At the same time, the wage rate in the non-farm sector increases. Increased income in both farm and non-farm sectors brought by the green revolution will be followed by an accumulation of capital. Such capital accumulation facilitates capitalist development leading to the rise of investment in agriculture and industry.

Most underdeveloped economies have failed to make this transition due to various structural obstacles. William Arthur Lewis' two-sector model can help identify these obstacles. Lewis (1954) argues that most developing economies can be characterized by the presence of dominant agriculture or the traditional sector and a small capitalist class. The traditional sector usually absorbs a considerable labor force which works even at subsistence wage rate. The overall population is so large relative to the capital and natural resources that marginal productivity of labor is insignificant or zero. This induces rural employers to employ more labor at subsistence wage and expand the sector as long as subsistence labor is available. As a result, the rural traditional sector is incapable of generating reproducible capital as well as capital accumulation. On the other hand, subsistence wage restricts workers' capability to save for non-farm consumption and thereby improve their situation from subsistence to surplus level. This situation is labeled as a 'vicious-circle' or low-level equilibrium trap.

In contrast, the urban capitalist sector is small and growing. Capitalists recruit labor until the marginal wage equals to marginal productivity. At this stage, capitalists enjoy huge surplus as profit, which can be expanded for further investment. Given the abundance of the labor force in the traditional sector, the expansion of industrial activities seems to be easier as long as investible capital is available. Recruiting additional labor force for the industry, however, does not negatively affect agriculture productivity. This process not only accelerates industrialization but also increases labor productivity in the traditional sector and continues until the labor surplus disappears. From this view, Lewis argues that the center for economic development is the rapid accumulation which can be facilitated by altering income distribution to saving.

It is thus, imperative to examine the extent to which agriculture growth in Bangladesh has been able to help industrialize the country and disrupt the dual-economic structure mentioned in Lewis. This chapter aims to accomplish this objective. Moreover, as mentioned earlier, it would be unrealistic to assess the contribution of agriculture through the lens of market-determined yardsticks. Thus, we also focus on assessing the contribution of agriculture to improve complementary social parameters.

Structural Transformation in Bangladesh

The economy of Bangladesh fits the typical Lewis paradigm. The country is characterized by the existence of a dual system—the dominant agriculture sector and the urban small capitalist class. As of 2016, 65 percent of the total population lived in the rural area where the crucial means of livelihood is agriculture, which is even vulnerable to natural calamities. In 1972, agriculture contributed about 60 percent of the total GDP, which has been declining over the years (Fig. 8.1). The tertiary or service sector is taking the place of declining agriculture sector whereas the contribution from the industrial sector is still very low. In 2016, more than half (56.46 percent) of the total GDP was the contribution of the service sector whereas industrial contribution accounted for 28.77 percent and 14.77 percent was the contribution of agriculture. The labor participation rate is little more than half (58.5 percent) of the total population majority of which are employed in the agriculture sector. Of the total employed labor force, 43 percent is absorbed by the agriculture sector, 20 percent by the industry, and 37 percent by the service sector (Asian Development Bank [ADB] 2017). Annual value added per worker in agriculture is US$389 whereas the respective figures for industry and service sectors are

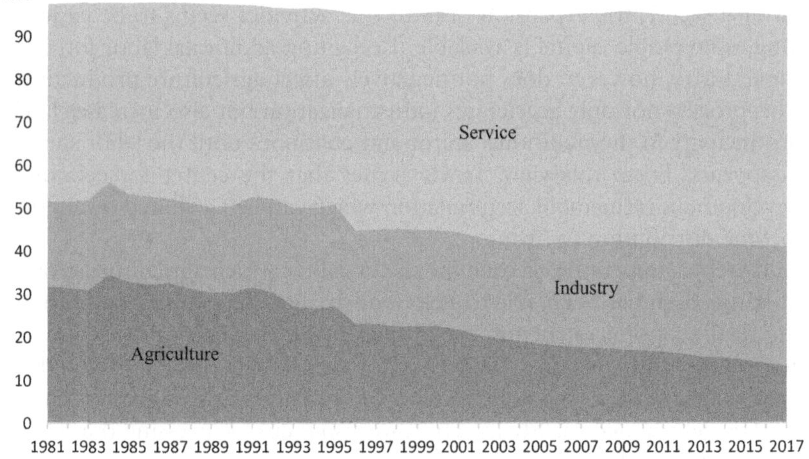

Fig. 8.1 Composition GDP (%). (Source: World Bank, WDI, online version)

$1772 and $1389 (in 2000 price). The growth rate of the gross value added by agriculture averaged 2.32 percent in 1980–90, which rose to 5.27 percent in 2000–10 before declining to 3.42 percent during the period 2011–16. Respective statistics for the industry were 4.79, 7.17, and 9.5 percent (ADB 2017). The value addition of the service sector grew at an average rate of 3.47 percent from 1980 to 1990 and 6.00 percent from 2011 to 2016. These statistics make it evident that a structural transformation is in progress.

Figure 8.2 portrays the historical data of the average growth rate of GDP and agriculture. It is observed that the GDP growth rate shows an upward trend during the observed period. Since the mid-2000s, the GDP growth rate surpassed 5 percent mark. The graph also shows that the agriculture growth rate paralleled the GDP growth rate until the mid-2000s. At times, the trend of agriculture growth exceeded the trend of GDP growth. However, since the mid-2000s, the momentum of agriculture growth halted and nosedived by about 1 percent between the period 2001–10 and 2011–17.

According to the structural shift theory, the contribution of agriculture to GDP and the labor force employed in agriculture declined as the per

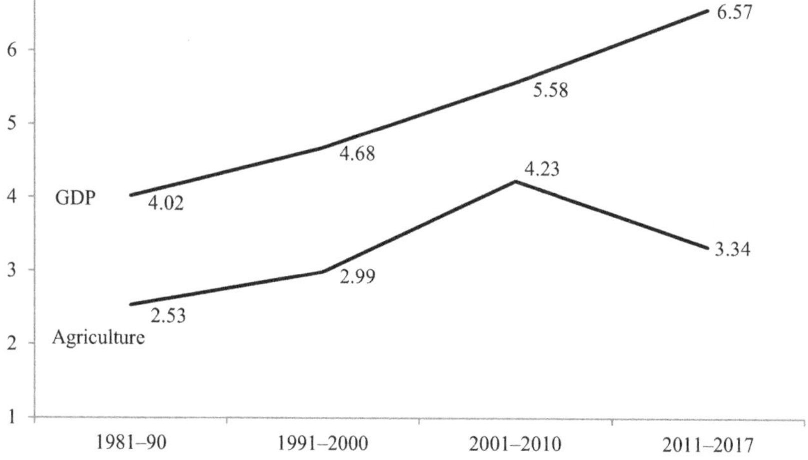

Fig. 8.2 Growth of GDP and agriculture (%). (Source: World Bank, WDI, online version)

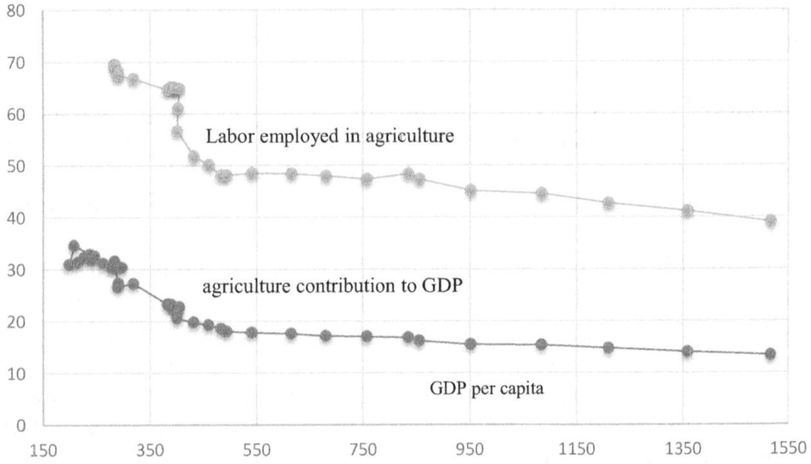

Fig. 8.3 Structural shift in the economy. (Data source: World Bank, WDI, online version)

capita income kept rising. Figure 8.3 shows these statistics. The structural shift continued to accelerate until per capita income reached US$550 mark. Since then, per capita income rose to US$1550, but the contribution of agriculture to GDP remained almost the same. The same is true for the labor force employed in agriculture (see Fig. 8.4). Labor employed in agriculture declined from 70 percent in 1991 to 48 percent in 2005, a decline of about 29 percent. However, the drop plummeted to 3 percent in the following decade, much slower than its preceding decade.

The Impact of Agriculture on Development

The potential of agriculture to reduce poverty is rarely contextualized in terms of the farm household, or the share of agriculture in household income, or the livelihood strategies that rural households have used to eradicate poverty (Harris and Orr 2013). Debates about the potential of rainfall based agriculture in reducing poverty have allowed the exploration of development strategies focusing on smallholder agriculture that has the ability to increase productivity and cope with natural disasters (Eskander and Barbier 2016). Bangladesh is one of the most disaster-prone countries due to its geographic location and land characteristics. Natural disasters

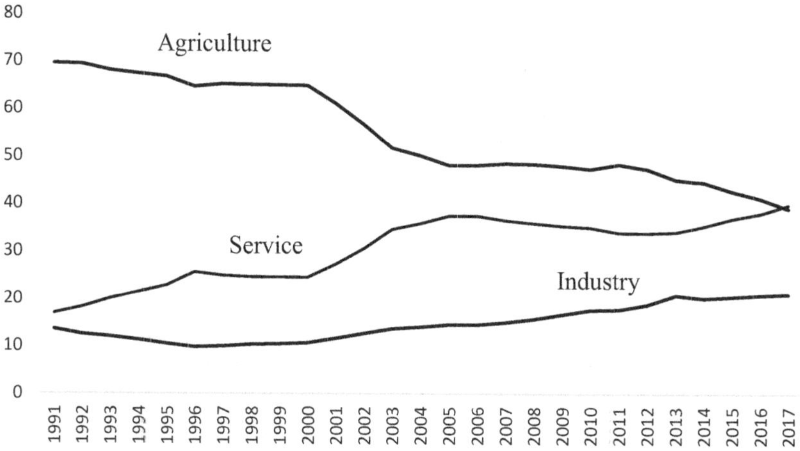

Fig. 8.4 Labor employed. (Data source: World Bank, WDI, online version)

such as floods which affect mostly the coastal region and cyclones that affect the northern regions are common. The 1991 cyclone not only caused the deaths of 138,000 people but also reduced agricultural and industrial production in the coastal area of Chittagong (Huq et al. 2015). Small-scale farmers depend heavily on agriculture, and such disasters can limit their ability to invest in defensive measures. Consequently, natural disasters often force rural households and farmers to resort to selling off productive assets such as agricultural land (Duflo 2003 cited in Eskander and Barbier 2016).

In addition, many rural households continue to seek off-farm work in either agricultural or non-agricultural employment (Mueller and Quisumbing 2011) and participate in the land rental market (Ward and Shively 2011). The average farm size is estimated at 0.24 hectares per rural household (Rapsomanikis 2015) in Bangladesh, which is one of the smallest average farm sizes globally. In such a situation, many farmers rely on the informal land rental market to better manage and utilize the available land. The impact of participation in the land rental market among rural households in Bangladesh is explored by Eskander and Barbier (2016). They report that such practices allow farmers to mitigate the adverse effects of the disaster on agricultural yield and thereby, rural poverty. In this section, we assess the impact of agriculture on development and poverty eradication.

Agricultural production in Bangladesh takes place on small family firms in various cropping seasons. Primary reasons for such agricultural practice can be attributed to the factor that the majority of the rural poor are landless farm or non-farm laborers or smallholders. Given the high population density, the government of Bangladesh encourages agricultural intensification and mechanization that could result in increased production and self-sufficiency (Mainuddin and Kirby 2015). Several mechanisms adopted by the government include a reduction in import tariffs on selected agricultural machinery, and the development of subsidiary programs to partially offset fixed costs of production (Mottaleb et al. 2016). The use of agriculture machinery increased as a result (Table 8.3). In particular, the use of two wheels tractors as well as a shallow tube well increased tremendously until 2006. The rate of increase, however, halted in the subsequent period.

All these measures have helped the country to experience the boost of agriculture products, especially since the last decade of the twentieth century. This has facilitated the country to dream for the status of 'middle-income' country by 2021. Although ambitious, the dream can be realized if the GDP growth rate can be maintained little more than 7 percent, which is not infeasible given the natural and economic microstructures of the country. Thanks to the modest GDP growth rate in the last couple of decades, the extreme poverty of the country declined sharply (Fig. 8.5).

Table 8.3 Regression statistics

Variables	*Coefficient*	*Std. Error*	*t-statistic*	*Prob.*
C	1.334	1.030	1.296	0.222
Agriculture	0.200	0.046	4.323	0.001
Service	0.024	0.209	0.113	0.912
Industry	0.320	0.066	4.850	0.001
Trade openness	3.928	1.714	2.292	0.043
Remittance	−14.146	5.860	−2.414	0.034
Inflation	0.105	0.066	1.584	0.141
Adjusted R^2	0.847	Durbin-Watson stat.	1.988	
S.E of regression	0.288	Probability	<0.001	
F-statistic	16.697			

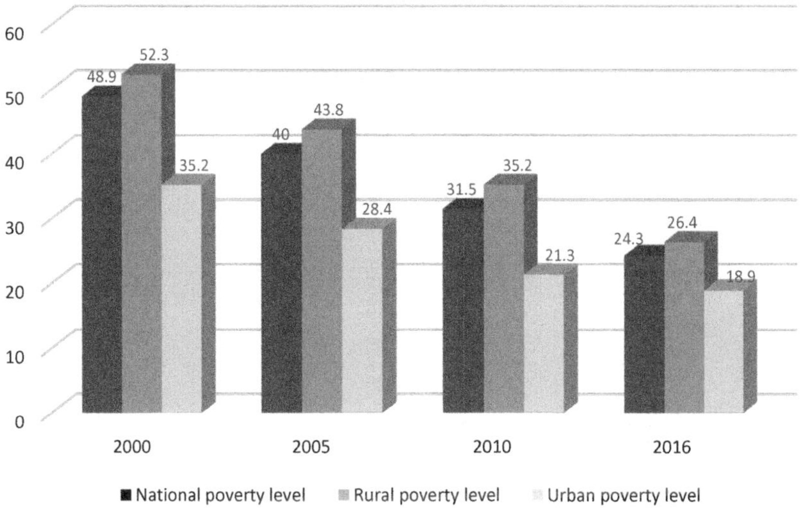

Fig. 8.5 Poverty rate (%). (Data source: Bangladesh Bureau of Statistics)

Poverty, both rural and urban, declined to half from 2000 to 2016, which is presumably a laudable achievement of the country.

Table 8.1 provides information on agricultural development in Bangladesh from 2000 to 2016. We see from the evidence presented in Table 8.1 that both the share of male and female employment has a decreasing pattern which has a toll on the value added by agriculture, forestry, and fisheries to the GDP. The percentage of arable land and agricultural land has not been reducing in comparison. Thus, we agree with the findings of Mueller and Quisumbing (2011) that the rural population has been seeking off-farm activities to earn a living. It is interesting to find that despite the decreasing engagement of rural population in agriculture, the livestock, food, and crop production has seen the highest score in 2016. Such achievement can be attributed to government efforts to modernize agricultural production through the use of the latest technologies and better quality of fertilizers, and implementing policy initiatives to provide access to finance for the agricultural sector. We discussed the pattern of fertilizer usage and the importance of agricultural finance toward agricultural development in detail in the latter part of the study.

Table 8.1 Agricultural developments in Bangladesh during 2000–16

Year	*2000*	*2001*	*2002*	*2003*	*2004*	*2005*	*2006*	*2007*	*2008*	*2009*	*2010*	*2011*	*2012*	*2013*	*2014*	*2015*	*2016*
Employment in agriculture (percent of the population)																	
Male	60.69	57.24	53.56	49.58	45.87	41.99	41.94	42.15	42.01	41.63	40.93	42.84	42.88	42.04	38.90	34.70	32.91
Female	78.79	73.88	67.11	58.79	64.17	68.21	68.19	68.35	67.82	66.95	65.53	63.73	59.52	53.44	59.44	63.45	62.13
Agri VA	22.72	21.85	20.58	19.81	19.27	18.57	18.03	17.81	17.60	17.10	17.00	16.81	16.18	15.49	15.35	14.78	14.05
Land dimension (percent of land area)																	
percent Arable	64.15	63.79	63.40	63.21	62.56	60.77	60.54	60.04	59.94	59.89	59.85	58.98	58.92	58.98	58.92	59.40	59.65
percent Agri Land	72.21	72.24	71.85	71.66	71.62	71.53	71.29	71.18	71.08	71.03	70.99	70.12	70.06	69.97	69.90	70.39	70.63
Production Index (agricultural production for each year relative to the base period 2004–06)																	
Livestock[a]	84.31	86.28	90.14	93.56	95.83	101.1	103.0	105.6	108.9	108.5	114.3	117.9	122.6	124.4	130.2	135.2	135.8
Food[b]	89.90	87.89	90.42	92.95	90.98	102.9	106.1	112.0	120.2	121.3	128.5	131.7	132.4	135.0	140.9	141.7	145.3
Crop[c]	90.60	88.29	90.56	92.86	90.29	103.0	106.6	113.0	122.1	123.0	130.5	135.0	135.5	138.1	142.4	142.7	146.4
Fertilizer use (kilograms per hectare of arable land)																	
Fertilizer	–	–	188.64	160.27	170.67	197.75	193.19	184.41	200.06	188.85	212.96	255.76	260.44	254.60	279.22	298.97	289.40

Source: World Bank

[a]Livestock production index includes meat and milk from all sources, dairy products such as cheese, and eggs, honey, raw silk, wool, and hides and skins

[b]Food production index covers food crops that are considered edible and that contain nutrients. Coffee and tea are excluded because, although edible, they have no nutritive value

[c]Crop production index shows agricultural production for each year relative to the base period 2004–06

Empirical Investigation

Historical evidence suggests that the transition from agrarian to an industrialized and service-based society has resulted in the economic development of most developed countries (Katircioglu 2006). However, development economists argue that agriculture and the rural economy need to play a dynamic role in the economic development process of developing countries. Gunner Myrdal argues that it is the agricultural sector that the battle for long-term economic growth will be won or lost. Owens et al. (2003) indicate that agricultural development can lead to an increase in income and reduction of hunger that could lead to the improvement of other measures of well-being in many parts of the developing world.

Economic growth, however, does not solely depend on the contribution of a single sector, and therefore, one should model all potential determinants of economic growth to have a better understanding of the growth process. The Central Bank of Bangladesh follows the divisions of economy proposed by Fisher (1939) and reports the contribution of agriculture, industry, and service, to the GDP of Bangladesh. As mentioned earlier, the service sector gradually takes the place of the sector as the engine of growth, which is the common trait of a post-industrial society (Bell 1973). Gani and Clemes (2010) report a positive and statistically significant correlation of service growth to per capita gross domestic product growth for Pacific Island countries. Besides the three sectoral contributions as independent variables, this study has utilized several control variables. Trade openness is introduced based on the findings of Tahir and Khan (2014). While studying the contribution of the service sector to economic growth, Gani and Clemes (2010) have adopted inflation as a control variable. Finally, remittance is included by following the study of Catrinescu et al. (2009) as the authors find that remittances exert a weakly positive impact on long-term macroeconomic growth. Accordingly, the single-equation framework proposed here is represented by Eq. (8.1)

$$gdpg_t = \beta_0 + \beta_1 agr_t + \beta_2 ser_t + \beta_3 ind_t + \beta_4 trd_t + \beta_5 rem_t + \beta_6 \inf_t + \mu_t \quad (8.1)$$

The dependent variable *gdpg* measures the growth of GDP at constant market prices, *agr* is the contribution of the agriculture sector to the GDP, *ser* is the contribution of the service sector to the GDP, *ind* is the contribution of large-, medium-, and small-scale industry to the GDP, *trd* is the trade share in GDP, *inf* is the rate of inflation measured by the growth rate of consumer price index and *rem* is the total remittance share in GDP.

Data used in this study are annual figures covering the period 2000–17; variables that are measured in US Dollar (USD) are constant at 1996 prices. Data are collected from the published annual reports of Bangladesh Bank, the Central Bank of Bangladesh. Levin et al. (2002) and Im et al. (2003) panel unit root tests are employed to test the integration level and the possible co-integration among variables as they have higher power than unit root tests based on individual time series. Ordinary least square regression is conducted to test the validity of Eq. (8.1) presented earlier.

Results and Discussion

Panel unit root testing emerged from time series unit root testing. The limited power of individual unit root tests in rejecting the null hypothesis in the unit root has resulted in too many unit roots in time series data. Therefore, this study has utilized the panel unit root tests proposed by Levin et al. (2002) and Im et al. (2003). Levin et al. (2002) propose a test which has an alternative hypothesis that the ρ_i are identical and negative. Im et al. (2003) allow a general alternative to Levin et al. (2002). According to Im et al. (2003), the ρ_i can vary and some individuals can have a unit root. Results of unit root tests are provided in Table 8.2. It can be noticed from Table 8.2 that each time series became stationary at first difference in both methods.

The regression results based on the ordinary least-square estimation method are reported in Table 8.3. The regression results regarding the

Table 8.2 Unit root test results

Method	*Level*		*1st difference*	
	Statistics	*Probability*	*Statistics*	*Probability*
Individual intercept				
Levin, Lin & Chu	−3.120	0.001	−10.882	0.000
Im, Pesaran & Shin	−1.191	0.028	−8.288	0.000
Individual intercept and trend				
Levin, Lin & Chu	−3.340	0.000	−8.975	0.000
Im, Pesaran & Shin	−0.728	2.332	−6.754	0.000

impact of agricultural development and economic growth for developing economies are consistent with both economic theory and empirical literature. The variable used for agricultural development is significantly related to economic growth represented by the growth of the gross domestic product. The service sector, however, has an insignificant relationship with the economic development of Bangladesh. The regression model is statistically significant ($p < 0.001$) and explains 84.7 percent of variations of economic growth. The positive effect of agricultural contribution to GDP shows that it is an important determinant of economic development. The positive influence of trade openness on economic growth suggests that exports are drawn into a highly productive agricultural sector. Remittance has a negative impact on economic growth which suggests that the amount of remittances sent by foreign workers is not contributing to longer-term growth by building human and financial capital.

Constraints to Agriculture-Led Industrialization

Bangladesh has transformed agriculture since the early 1970s, improving the total food grain production from 10 million tons in 1972–73 to 35 million tons in 2012–13 to feed the growing population (Hossain and Bayes 2009). A smooth transition to a more productive, climate-resilient, and diversified economy for Bangladesh requires agricultural to play an expanding role in the transformation process. According to the report published by the Centre for Policy Dialogue (2018), the contribution of agriculture to growth has been declining over the years (see also Figs. 8.1 and 8.2). This section will shed light on the primary constraint to agriculture growth. In particular, the emphasis is placed on how demand-led industrialization can be accelerated.

As mentioned before, demand-driven strategy for industrialization emphasizes on increasing demand for local goods and services. This, in turn, will stimulate production and thereby income for a large population. The income-consumption spiral will accelerate GDP growth as far as the domestic producers can satisfy the rising demand. As shown in Fig. 8.4, more than 40 percent of the total employable labor force is employed in agriculture. Moreover, about two-thirds of the total population of Bangladesh live in the rural area. This big chunk of the population depends directly or indirectly on agriculture income. Thus, the realization of demand-led industrialization hinges critically on boosting the income of those who are engaged with agriculture. The income of this segment is derived basically from wage income and income from agriculture output.

The wage rate, however, did not play a greater role in increasing the income of the rural population. It is observed that the labor force participation rate is almost constant in the agriculture sector. In 1983, employed labor in this sector comprised 59 percent of the total labor force, which declined to 52 percent in 2003, and 43 percent in 2016. If we assume that the labor market was in equilibrium in 1983, a declining share of agriculture to GDP in the subsequent period should have accompanied by an equivalent level of labor force decline. However, agriculture share to GDP declined by more than half from 31 percent in 1983 to 15 percent in 2016. In other words, labor force engagement over the year (1983–2016) declined by 27 percent while the share of agriculture to GDP fell by 52 percent. This assumes that technology is constant and the share of agriculture to GDP growth rate, as well as the labor absorption rate of agriculture from the pool of labor newly joined in the workforce are equal. In this case, even if we assume that there was no excess labor in the agriculture sector in 1983, it has accumulated a significant amount of excess labor over the period.

Now let us relax some assumptions. The second assumption is held in reality, loosely though. Over the period 1981–2016, GDP grew 5.2 percent on average of which agriculture contributed almost a quarter of it (5.2 percent × 24.75 percent = 1.29 percent). Meanwhile, the population increased by a little less than 2 percent, and the agriculture sector absorbed more than half of it (1.93 percent × 52.20 percent = 1 percent). This implies that the contribution of agriculture and the increased labor absorption match to some extent. But, the first assumption that technology is constant is not true. Over the years, technology has increased significantly though not overwhelmingly in the context of Bangladesh. The use of both shallow and deep-tube wells has increased manifold (Adnan 1999) along with improved technology of farming tools such as power tiller (Table 8.4).

Moreover, chemical fertilizers and pesticide consumption also increased substantially. Chowdhury and Shahabuddin (1992) report that the use of chemical fertilizers in the agriculture sector increased by about 200 percent between the periods 1965–66 and 1989–90. The rate of increase is faster in the subsequent period due to the privatization of the fertilizer market. Estimation suggests that the share of the private sector in the fertilizer market increased from less than 5 percent to more than

Table 8.4 Number of machines used for agriculture

Year	*1977*	*1984*	*1989*	*1996*	*2006*	*2008*	*2009*	*2010*	*2011*
4 wheels tractor	300	40	1000	2000	12,500	14,890	17,905	21,638	26,369
2 wheels tractor	200	500	5000	100,000	300,000	343,000	366,700	400,030	420,027
Deep tube well	4461	15,519	22,448	24,506	28,189	31,302	32,174	32,912	N/A
Shallow tube well	3045	67,103	223,588	325,360	1,182,525	1,304,973	1,374,548	1,425,136	N/A

Source: Adapted from International Development Enterprises (IDE 2012)

Note: NA stands for not available

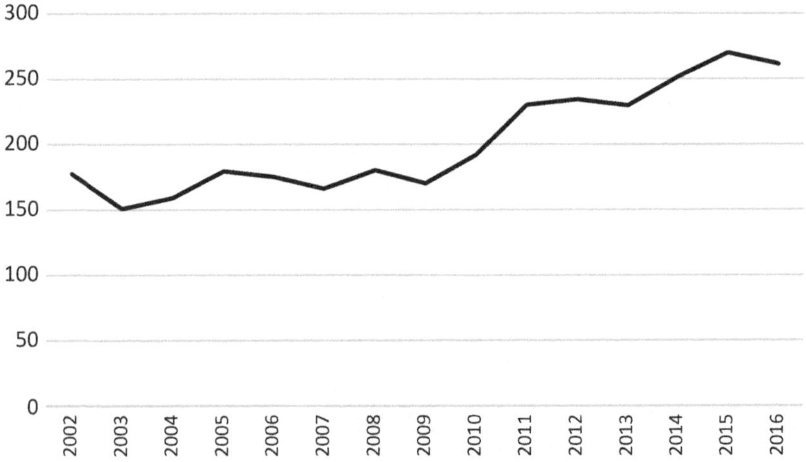

Fig. 8.6 Use of fertilizer (kg/hector). (Source: Food and Agriculture Organization of the United Nations)

90 percent over the period 1987–92 (Shahabuddin 1999). Figure 8.6 shows the use of chemical fertilizers (nitrogen, potassium, and phosphate). The figure reflects that the increasing trend of using fertilizer remained unchanged in the subsequent period. The use of increased technology, along with fertilizer, is supposed to lead to an increase in the productivity of labor. If so, a substantial share of labor should be shifted to industry to facilitate structural transformation. Although the share of agriculture to GDP has declined over the period, the labor force participation rate did not decline commensurably. This postulates that there is already excess labor in the sector. This circumstance proves Lewis hypothesis (1954) that in developing countries the primary sector is overburdened by subsistence labor.

Further insight can be derived from the change in the labor wage rate. The daily wage of human labor increased by 104 percent from 1985 to 2000, whereas the consumer price index increased by 133 percent over the same period. If we assume that subsistence earning was maintained in 1985, labors employed in the agriculture were forced to sink below this subsistence level in the subsequent period because of slicing their purchasing power. The scenario remains unchanged in the subsequent period. For example, Fig. 8.7 shows that the rate of change in wage and the CPI coin-

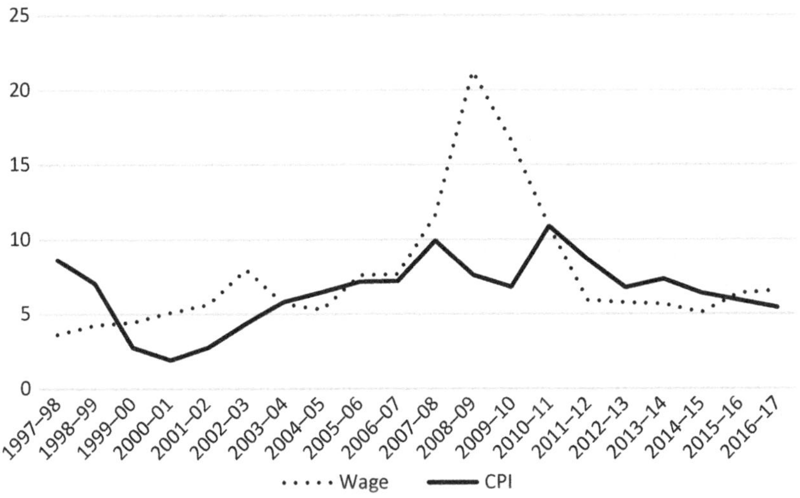

Fig. 8.7 Rate of wage change and consumer price index (%). (Source: Bangladesh Bureau of Statistics)

cided during the period 1998–2016 except for the period 2008–09, which can be considered exceptional. This implies that the real change of income of agriculture labor did not take place in the last three decades, which explains the stalemate of structural transformation.

Another critical issue on which the demand-led transformation relies is the distribution of income. The Marxian school argues that an egalitarian distribution of income is a critical prerequisite to sustain demand-led growth, an aspect which is missing from the policy agenda of the demand-driven strategy in Bangladesh. According to World Bank data, the Gini coefficient was 0.28 in 1992, which rose to 0.33 in 1996 before it finally settled at 0.35 in 2015. These statistics, however, do not reveal the real picture. Osmani and Sen (2011) provide elaborate data with detailed stratification. They show that the rise in inequality of the last decade was due to a sharp increase in the income of the richest quintile of the population compared to the others. Growth in per capita income was above the mean income only after the 80th percentile. This provides evidence that a lack of egalitarian distribution of income can be considered one of the critical reasons for the failure of demand-driven strategy in Bangladesh.

Toward a Viable Agriculture Sector

Many constraints can be regarded as critical to the development of agriculture sector in Bangladesh. The primary among them is the natural calamity resulting from climate change. Although every country has got some responsibilities toward combating climate change, Bangladesh, however, has a lot of other functions to accomplish for revitalizing its agriculture sector. Given the fact that most agriculture farms in Bangladesh are small in size (Khan 2004), they have difficulty accessing to necessary finance. Figure 8.8 provides data of finance to agriculture and fisheries. From 2002 to 2008, agriculture credit was static. There was almost no increase in agriculture credit. Since 2009, agriculture credit has been increasing.

It is expected that finance will be expanded into a growing economy. Agriculture receives a share of it, resulting in the rise of agriculture credit. However, looking at other estimation shows a different picture. The share of agriculture credit to total credit reveals that the trend is declining (Fig. 8.8). In 2002, the share of agriculture credit to total credit accounted for 12.57 percent, which fell to a sheer 5 percent in 2017.

Recently, the government of Bangladesh was very sympathetic to agriculture and hence formulated various policies conducive to agriculture growth. For example, the government has instructed all commercial banks

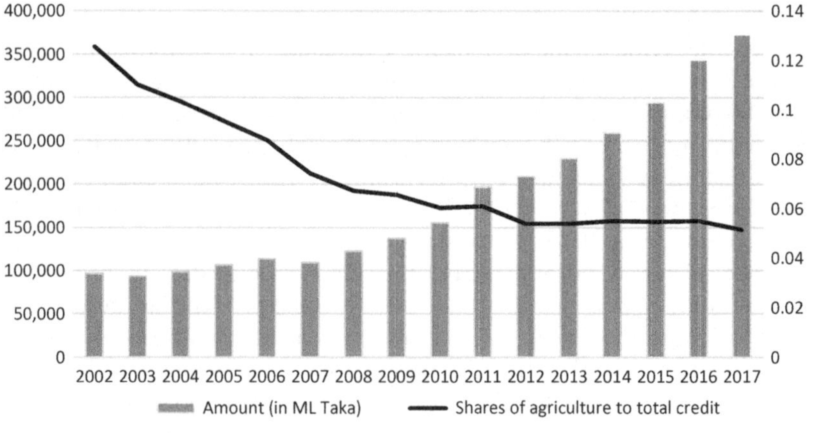

Fig. 8.8 Agriculture loan in total (left axis) and percentage of the total loan (right axis). (Source: Food and Agriculture Organization of the United Nations)

to allocate a certain percentage of their credit to the agriculture sector. If a bank fails to meet the given target, the unattainable portion of the target should be deposited to the central bank on which the central bank would pay 5 percent interest. As a result, private commercial banks have been gradually increasing their rural presence since the mid-2000s. In 2012, the government instructed all commercial banks to open at least 50 percent of the total new branches in the rural area. Between 2005 and 2010, growth in rural bank branches was about 3.4 percent, not much lower than the 4.8 percent growth in urban areas (Khandker and Koolwal 2016).

At the beginning of the 1990s, the government of Bangladesh liberalized the financial market. The interest rate on loan was determined based on the demand and supply of credit. Agriculture credit was not an exception. Subsequently, the government fixed the maximum limit for the interest of some sectors. The primary among them was the agriculture sector. Until 2010, banks charged a very high percentage on agriculture loans. In 2013, the central bank fixed a 13 percent cap for this sector, which remained unchanged until 2015. In January 2016, the rate was reduced by 2 percent to 11 percent. The rate was further revised and fixed at 10 percent in June 2016. After 1 year, the rate was again sliced to 9 percent, which again cut to 8 percent in 2018.

Although agriculture-friendly, private commercial banks have found the rate unsuitable for their profit purpose. Especially, screening and monitoring of small and micro-borrowers of the agriculture sector turned to be costly. Private commercial banks in Bangladesh have yet to develop such delicate screening and monitoring processes. Microcredit providers have already developed information technology and thereby, possess a competitive edge over commercial banks. The latter intended to take this advantage. Commercial banks sought for central bank's permission to disburse the target agriculture loan through the microcredit organizations. In this system, commercial banks transfer the amount for agriculture loans to an agent (NGO) at a rate fixed by the central banks. In so doing, commercial banks shift their duty of screening and monitoring of borrowers to the agent. Because agents undertake these activities, they charge a rate to the final borrowers above the commercial bank rate determined by the government. Since its inception, the distribution of agriculture loans through agent banking increased tremendously (Fig. 8.9).

As mentioned earlier, farm size is tiny in Bangladesh, which can be attributed to the division of land among the members of the family. Members of a family who cannot effectively find a permanent or full-

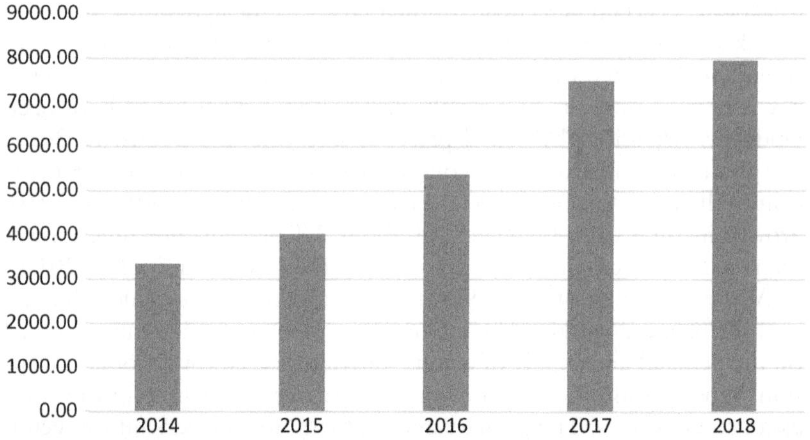

Fig. 8.9 Farm loan disbursement through NGOs (Amount in crore taka). (Source: Bangladesh Bank, year represents the fiscal year, July–June)

time employment work on their own land even if redundant for a small piece of available land. The rising population thereby adds more and more subsistence labor to the agriculture sector. This scenario is manifested in Fig. 8.10. Even though the rural population growth plummeted enormously over the years (Fig. 8.10, left axis), the share of the rural population as a percentage of the total population did not decline proportionately. Estimation shows that nearly 87 percent of rural households directly rely only on income derived from agriculture. Even though the dependency has been decreasing day by day, the rate is very minimal.

This situation has been worsened by the gradual decline of arable land. Figure 8.11 shows that both arable land and the agriculture land are declining over the years. Since 1992, the percentage of arable land declined at a higher rate than the decline of agriculture land. This can be attributed to the rise of the population, which supports our previous arguments. On the other hand, the increased need for habitat for a rising population, urbanization, and other commercial activities have caused the agriculture land to decline. The combined effect is the lower productivity per agriculture worker. Unless these issues are tackled, agriculture demand-led industrialization would be challenging to realize.

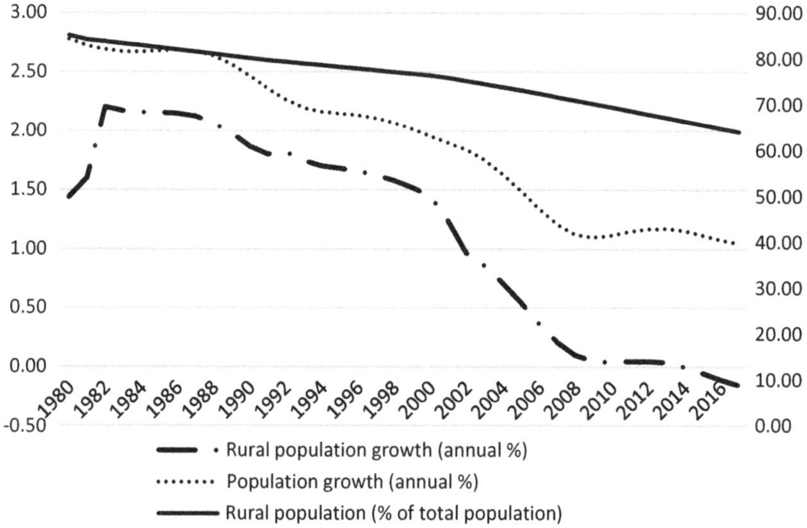

Fig. 8.10 Population growth rate (left axis), rural population (right axis). (Source: World Bank)

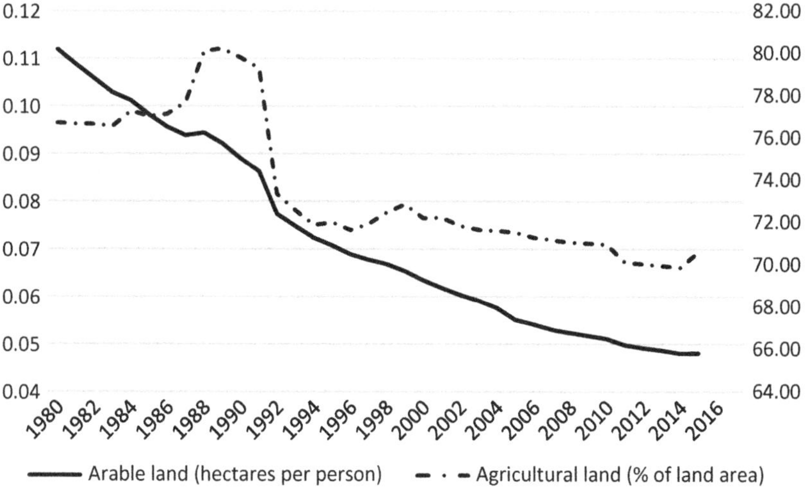

Fig. 8.11 Arable land (left axis) and agriculture land (right axis). (Source: World Bank)

Conclusion

People living in rural areas in Bangladesh depend directly or indirectly on agriculture for livelihood. One of the fundamental aspects of rural poverty can be linked to unemployment or under-employment. The contribution of agriculture to alleviating poverty in rural Bangladesh has not yet been contextualized. Government efforts have increased in recent years for agricultural intensification and mechanization to increase productivity and self-sufficiency. However, the country's dream of updating its economic status to 'developing economy' cannot be materialized by keeping its agriculture sector ailing. We, in this chapter, have attempted to examine the feasibility of agriculture to lead the industrialization of the country. In particular, we have attempted to identify critical drivers of agriculture growth and the causes of its recent slowdown. We have argued that a dynamic transformation of the country requires a shift from agriculture to industry. This transformation can be achieved by adopting the 'demand-driven' strategy, which can be materialized by modernizing the agriculture sector. A modern agriculture sector would increase the demand for farm and non-farm inputs which, in turn, is expected to lead the industrialization of the country. However, the agriculture sector of Bangladesh has failed to boost the demand for industrial products. We have identified several reasons that can explain the apparent failure of agriculture to facilitate industrialization.

First, the agriculture sector of Bangladesh has failed to promote vertical or horizontal integration or the diversification of agricultural business, resulting in a failure to raise the wage rate in the sector. Over the years, agriculture labor has sunk below the subsistence level due mainly to the fact that the consumer price index exceeded the rise of the wage rate. As a result, the subtle purchasing power of a large portion of the rural population did not facilitate increasing the demand for durable and consumable industrial products. Second, the subsistence labor joining in agriculture has worsened the situation. The contribution of agriculture to GDP has been declining over the years. However, the labor force participation rate did not decline expectedly despite the introduction of modern technology, to a limited extent, though, in agriculture. This implies that the agriculture sector is overburden by the huge accumulation of subsistence labor. Third, government initiatives did not pay off practically. Although the government has instructed all commercial banks to disburse a certain percentage of their total loan to the agriculture sector at a lower rate than the commercial rate, commercial banks have found ways to legally comply with this rule without having much impact on agriculture. Most commercial banks have transferred the amount to NGOs at a rate specified by the government. NGOs, however, charge farmers the competitive market rate, which is much higher than the government-specified cap. Fourth, the agriculture lands and the arable lands have been declining during the last two decades. In such a circumstance, agriculture productivity will remain low despite the higher intensity of agriculture cropping.

The economic development of Bangladesh depends critically on modernizing the agriculture sector instead of neglecting it because the country's natural ambient and social structure support 'agriculture first' strategy especially in the context of alleviating rural poverty and ensuring food safety which was also proved by the regression analysis. Removing the above-mentioned constraints is thus, critical toward this step. Increased use of technology, chemical fertilizers, and pesticides was followed recently. This trend should be kept moving for the increase in productivity. At the same time, subsistence labor should be released from the agriculture sector for higher productivity and income. Also, small agricultural firms in Bangladesh are facing difficulty in accessing to finance. The high-interest rate charged to this sector due to lack of capital led the poor people toward the deadly trap of microfinance. As part of the Millennium Development Goal (MDG-1) of developing the rural economy, the government should consider developing viable strategies to ensure credit among rural communities. The government can also develop strategies to increase technology use in the agricultural sector to ensure a swift transition toward industrial society. Evidence provided by this study is expected to attract research attention to further explore the significance of agricultural development as a viable poverty alleviation tool for an emerging economy like Bangladesh.

References

Adelman, I. (1984). Beyond export-led growth. *World Development, 12*(9), 937–949.

Adnan, S. (1999). Agrarian structure and agriculture growth trends in Bangladesh: The political economy of technological change and policy interventions. In R. Ben, H.-W. Barbara, & B. Sugata (Eds.), *Sonar Bangla? Agriculture growth and Agrarian change in West Bengal and Bangladesh* (pp. 177–228). New Delhi: Sage Publications.

Alauddin, M., & Tisdell, C. (1995). Labor absorption and agricultural development: Bangladesh's experience and predicament. *World Development, 23*(2), 281–297. https://doi.org/10.1016/0305-750X(94)00117-H

Ali, A. M. S. (2007). Population pressure, agricultural intensification and changes in rural systems in Bangladesh. *Geoforum, 38*(4), 720–738. https://doi.org/10.1016/j.geoforum.2006.11.028

Alvarez-Cuadrado, F., & Poschke, M. (2011). Structural change out of agriculture: Labor push versus labor pull. *American Economic Journal: Macroeconomics, 3*(3), 217–258.

Asian Development Bank. (2017). *Basic Statistics 2017.* Asian Development Bank.

Bairoch, P. (1973). Agriculture and the industrial revolution, 1700–1914. In C. Cipolla (Ed.), *The Fontana economic history of Europe: The industrial revolution* (Vol. 3, pp. 452–506). London: Collins, Fontana Books.

Bell, D. (1973). *The coming of post-industrial society: A venture in social forecasting.* Basic Books.

Catrinescu, N., Leon-Ledesma, M., Piracha, M., & Quillin, B. (2009). Remittances, institutions, and economic growth. *World Development, 37*(1), 81–92.

Centre for Policy Dialogue. (2018). *State of the Bangladesh economy in FY2017–18.*

Chakravarty, S. (1979). On the question of home market and prospects for Indian growth. *Economic and Political Weekly, 14*(30/32), 1229–1242.

Chowdhury, O., & Shahabuddin, Q. (1992). *A study of food situation and outlook of Asia: Country report on Bangladesh.* Bangladesh Institute of Development Studies.

De-Janvry, A. (2010). Agriculture for development: New paradigm and options for success. *Agricultural Economics, 41*, 17–36.

Eskander, S., & Barbier, E. (2016). *Adaptation to natural disasters through the agricultural land rental market: Evidence from Bangladesh.* Working Paper No. 266.

Faruqee, R. (1998). *Bangladesh agriculture in the 21st century.* Dhaka: University Press Ltd.

Fisher, A. G. (1939). Production, primary, secondary and tertiary. *Economic Record, 15*(1), 24–38.

Gani, A., & Clemes, M. D. (2010). Services and economic growth in Pacific Island countries. *International Journal of Development Issues, 9*(2), 113–130.

Harris, D., & Orr, A. (2013). Is rainfed agriculture really a pathway from poverty? *Agricultural Systems, 123*, 84–96.

Hossain, M. (1988). *Credit for the alleviation of rural poverty: The Grameen Bank in Bangladesh.* Dhaka: International Food Policy Research Institute in Collaboration with Bangladesh Institute of Development Studies.

Hossain, M. (1991). *Agriculture in Bangladesh: Performance, problems, and prospects.* Dhaka: University Press.

Hossain, M., & Bayes, A. (2009). *Rural economy and livelihoods: Insights from Bangladesh*. AH Development Publishing House.

Huq, N., Hugé, J., Boon, E., & Gain, A. K. (2015). Climate change impacts in agricultural communities in rural areas of coastal Bangladesh: A tale of many stories. *Sustainability, 7*(7), 8437–8460.

Im, K. S., Pesaran, M. H., & Shin, Y. (2003). Testing for unit roots in heterogeneous panels. *Journal of Econometrics, 115*(1), 53–74.

International Development Enterprises. (2012). Commercialization of Selected Agriculture Machines in Bangladesh. iDE, Dhaka. Retrieved November 21, 2018, from http://repository.cimmyt.org/xmlui/bitstream/handle/10883/3394/98527.pdf.

Johnston, B., & Mellor, J. (1961). The role of agriculture in economic development. *American Economic Review, 87*(2), 566–593.

Katircioglu, S. T. (2006). Causality between agriculture and economic growth in a small nation under political isolation: A case from North Cyprus. *International Journal of Social Economics, 33*(4), 331–343.

Khan, M. H. (2004). Power, property rights and the issue of land reform: A general case illustrated with reference to Bangladesh. *Journal of Agrarian Change, 4*(1–2), 73–106.

Khandker, S. R., & Koolwal, G. B. (2016). How has microcredit supported agriculture? Evidence using panel data from Bangladesh. *Agricultural Economics, 47*(2), 157–168.

Levin, A., Lin, C. F., & Chu, C. S. J. (2002). Unit root tests in panel data: Asymptotic and finite-sample properties. *Journal of Econometrics, 108*(1), 1–24.

Lewis, A. (1954). Economic development with unlimited supplies of labor. *Manchester School of Economic and Social Studies, 22*(2), 139–191.

Lipton, M., & Longhurst, R. (2011). *New seeds and poor people*. London: Routledge.

Lo, D. (2012). *Alternatives to neoliberal globalization: Studies in the political economy of institutions and late development*. Basingstoke: Palgrave Macmillan.

Mainuddin, M., & Kirby, M. (2015). National food security in Bangladesh to 2050. *Food Security, 7*(3), 633–646.

Mottaleb, K. A., Krupnik, T. J., & Erenstein, O. (2016). Factors associated with small-scale agricultural machinery adoption in Bangladesh: Census findings. *Journal of Rural Studies, 46*, 155–168.

Mueller, V., & Quisumbing, A. (2011). How resilient are labor markets to natural disasters? The case of the 1998 Bangladesh Flood. *Journal of Development Studies, 47*(12), 1954–1971.

Osmani, S. R., & Sen, B. (2011). Inequality in rural Bangladesh in the 2000s: Trends and causes. *The Bangladesh Development Studies, 34*(4), 1–36.

Owens, T., Hoddinott, J., & Kinsey, B. (2003). The impact of agricultural extension on farm production in resettlement areas of Zimbabwe. *Economic Development and Cultural Change, 51*(2), 337–357.

Palmer-Jones, R. (1999). The slowdown in agricultural growth in Bangladesh: Neither a good description nor a good to give. In R. Ben, B. Barbara, & B. Sugata (Eds.), *Sonar Bangla? Agriculture growth and Agrarian change in West Bengal and Bangladesh* (pp. 92–136). New Delhi: Sage Publications.

PricewaterhouseCoopers. (2015). The world in 2050: Will the shift in global economic power continues?

Rapsomanikis, G. (2015). *The economic lives of smallholder farmers—An analysis based on household data from nine countries.* Rome: Food and Agriculture Organization of the United Nations.

Rodrik, D. (2006). *Industrial development: Stylized facts and policies.* Cambridge, MA: Harvard University, John F. Kennedy School of Government.

Rostow, W. W. (1960). *The stages of growth: A non-communist manifesto.* Cambridge: Cambridge University Press.

Shahabuddin, Q. (1999). Why is agricultural growth uneven? Class and the Agrarian surplus in Bangladesh. In B. Rogaly, B. Hariss-White, & S. Bose (Eds.), *Sonar Bangla? Agriculture growth and Agrarian change in West Bengal and Bangladesh* (pp. 147–176). New Delhi: Sage Publications.

Storm, S. (1995). On the role of agriculture in India's longer-term development strategy. *Cambridge Journal of Economics, 19*(6), 761–788. https://doi.org/10.1093/oxfordjournals.cje.a035340

Suzuki, Y., & Miah, M. D. (2017). China's "New Normal": Explaining China's economic development from institutional and Marxian perspectives. In *Understanding growth, sustainability in the Asia-Pacific region* (pp. 21–41). Singapore: Palgrave Macmillan.

Tahir, M., & Khan, M. (2014). Trade openness and economic growth in the Asian region. *Journal of Chinese Economic and Foreign Trade Studies, 7*(3), 136–152.

Vogel, S. J. (1994). Structural change in agriculture: Production linkages and agricultural demand-led industrialization. *Oxford Economic Papers, 46*(1), 136–156. https://doi.org/10.1093/oxfordjournals.oep.a042116

Ward, P. S., & Shively, G. E. (2011). *Migration and land rental as risk response in rural China.* Retrieved January 21, 2019, from https://ageconsearch.umn.edu/record/103379/.

CHAPTER 9

Growth Trajectory and Developmental Impact of Ready-Made Garments Industry in Bangladesh

Kazi Mahmudur Rahman and Ehsanul Huda Chowdhury

Introduction

Since the birth of Bangladesh in 1971, socio-economic and political critics have been nothing short of cynical about the prospect of its development and some even argued that it would remain a "below poverty level equilibrium trap" (Bhattacharya et al. 2002). However, Bangladesh has progressed a long way and managed to prove the critics wrong in many respects. With 40 percent of this country's economy being affiliated with the global market through exports and imports, it is safe to say that Bangladesh has moved on from being a help-seeking nation to an actively trading one (Bhattacharya et al. 2002).

K. M. Rahman (✉)
University of Liberal Arts Bangladesh (ULAB), Dhaka, Bangladesh
e-mail: mahmudur.rahman@ulab.edu.bd

E. H. Chowdhury
Faculty of Education and Business Studies, Department of Business Studies and Economics, University of Gävle, Gävle, Sweden
e-mail: Ehsanul.Chowdhury@hig.se

M. K. Barai (ed.), *Bangladesh's Economic and Social Progress*,
https://doi.org/10.1007/978-981-15-1683-2_9

One of the prime factors of this development is the contribution of the export-oriented ready-made garments (RMG) sector to the economy. "When jute and jute goods were losing their traditional markets, with the prospect of drastic fall in foreign earnings, it was the RMG sector which came to the rescue. While the traditional export sector could not yield expected results, the RMG sector gradually injected dynamism in the export as well as in the domestic economy through backward and forward linkage economic activities" (Bhattacharya et al. 2002). Nonetheless, the journey toward this progress has not been easy, and several factors have played significant roles in achieving what this sector is today. Major RMG-supported activities, both in domestic and foreign markets, amid rapid globalization, have been responsible for narrating a story seldom seen in a developing nation.

Bangladesh, branding as a "development case" through RMG export, has been featured in various development discourses. For instance, reports from MacKenzie, the World Bank, and other sources[1] have highly commended Bangladesh's achievements through apparel dependents. Similarly, Professor Sobhan's groundbreaking concept of "moving away from aid-dependent to a trade-dependent nation"[2] and Jeffrey Sachs's (2005) "ladder discourse"[3] have argued for RMG-led development. These achievements under its belt, Bangladesh is now considered the next Asian Giant,[4] successfully moving away from the "bottomless basket"[5] case to a lower middle-income country.[6] Thus, it is a matter of great interest whether the economy of Bangladesh will continue to grow at a steady pace, sometimes even when rowing against the tide. The RMG industry has played a crucial role in materializing this growth dynamism.

For example, the current share of the industrial sector in the gross domestic product (GDP) of Bangladesh is 30.4 percent, while the agricultural sector comprises only 16 percent of the GDP (BER 2015). The contribution of the industrial sector to GDP is further expected to increase by 5 percent over the next 5 years, in which the manufacturing sector will play the leading role (Shadat et al. 2017). It is important to note that the manufacturing sector of Bangladesh is dominated largely by the RMG industries. RMG remains the single largest source of export earnings by feeding 84.5 percent of total earnings while absorbing most of the manufacturing jobs in the country (EPB 2017). At present, 4 million employees, of whom 60 percent are women,[7] are engaged in this sector. Hence, a stock-taking of this sector provides the impetus for a policy analysis perspective and guiding notes for other sectors, possibly for becoming an industrialized country.

Apart from the robust export performance, the sector has registered progress on a number of issues related to working hours, child labor, and compliance related to structural soundness and fire safety in particular, soon after the two large industrial catastrophes, namely the Tazreen Fashions fire in 2012 and the Rana Plaza disaster in 2013. Ensuring compliance (and inspection) has become a prerequisite for exporting RMG products from Bangladesh.[8] Non-compliance would have a major negative impact on exports.[9] However, after the Rana Plaza incident, by addressing the challenges of safety, compliance,[10] and maintenance, Bangladesh has emerged as a top exporter of RMG after China.[11]

Therefore, there are *drivers* or actors who have steered the fate of RMG in Bangladesh's history. There are *decks* for challenges emanating for global and national environments and *dreams* to steer the growth trajectories and branding Bangladesh around the world and positing herself into the realm of apparel exports. To carry forward discussions, this chapter is concentrated in six sections, including the introduction. While section "RMG in Bangladesh and Historical Trajectories" highlights the historical evolution of RMG and its different trajectories, section "Growth of the Sector" discusses the state of the growth of the RMG sector, section "Impacts of RMG Industry: Macroeconomic and Social Impacts" discusses the associated impacts of RMG on various sectors, section "Challenges and Avenues to Overcome" articulates global and national challenges this sector has been facing and avenues to overcome these challenges, and section "Conclusion" concludes.

RMG in Bangladesh and Historical Trajectories

Historical Evolution of RMG in Bangladesh and Current Context

In Bangladesh's economy, the RMG industry occupies a unique position after experiencing phenomenal growth during the last 37 years. Generally, an industry initially develops in response to domestic demand and then turns to export once it becomes mature. However, the RMG industry has grown as a response to the growing demand in developed countries for cheap apparel. However, one should not forget that there was a small domestic garments industry in then East Pakistan (now Bangladesh) during the 1960s which catered to the demand for apparel in what was then West Pakistan. Mercury, a company located in Karachi, sourced a few consignments of shirts during the period 1965–68 made by some tailoring outfits operating in Dhaka and then exported these to some European countries (Bhattacharya et al. 2002; Bhattacharya and Rahman 2000; Siddiqi 2005). There were a few tailoring groups in Dhaka that made a small quantity of export-quality shirts and children's wear on specific orders. However, there was little investment in this industry during those days because of the limited size of the domestic market.

The process started in the late 1970s when the Asian Tigers started looking for ways to circumvent the export quotas of Western countries. In their search, they discovered Bangladesh as a potential investment destination. A significant example of the impact of their endeavor was the collaboration of a domestic private garment firm in Bangladesh, the Desh Company, with a Korean company, Daewoo, in 1978. Daewoo, a major exporter of garments, was looking for opportunities in countries that had barely used their quotas under the Multi Fibre Agreement (MFA). As a Least Developed Country (LDC), Bangladesh had the opportunity to export garments without any restrictions, and for this reason Daewoo became interested in establishing operations in Bangladesh. As part of its global strategies, the Daewoo Corporation proposed an ambitious joint venture to the government of Bangladesh for the development and operation of tires, leather goods, cement, and garment factories (Rock 2001).

The first consignment of private sector export of garments from Bangladesh took place in 1977–78 when M/S. Reaz Garments Ltd. exported men's shirts worth 13 million French francs to a Paris-based firm (Yunus and Yamagata 2012; Vixathep and Matsunaga 2015). At that time, there were only 9 export-oriented RMG units (see Table 9.1) in Bangladesh, which went up to 22 in 1979 (Yunus and Yamagata 2012; Quddus and Rashid 2000; Mottaleb and Sonobe 2011).

By 1980, the number of firms in the industry increased to 47, but the total RMG export from Bangladesh was less than USD 1 million (Siddiqi 2005; Ahmed 2009). Despite the small export volume in the initial years, by the early 1980s, the export-oriented RMG industry was well on its way to creating history by becoming the driving force of industrial development in Bangladesh. Today the RMG industry has 4560 manufacturing units (see Table 9.2) that employ four million workers (Bangladesh Garment Manufacturers and Exporters Association (BGMEA) 2018).

Table 9.1 First set of garment factories and their production in 1982

Name of garment factory	*Yearly production capacity (million pieces)*
Desh Garments Ltd.	10.00
QuashemSarwar Co. Ltd.	8.00
Youngjons	2.00
AmbiMohon Export Ltd.	2.00
BSA Garments Ltd.	1.50
ARA Garments Factory Ltd.	1.50
Eastern Trading Co.	1.50
Hashim Garments Ltd.	1.00
Nirman Garments Ltd.	1.00

Source: Development Debate, cited in Inkpen and Choudhury (1995: 17)

Table 9.2 RMG in Bangladesh: factories and workers

Year	*No. of garment factories*	*Employment (million workers)*
1987–88	685	0.31
1997–98	2726	1.50
2007–08	4743	2.80
2017–18	4560	4.00

Source: BGMEA (2018)

Table 9.2 shows the growth of the number of factories and employees after every 10 years.

With small steps taken during the late 1970s, the RMG industry has grown in its capacity every year, and now Bangladesh has become the second largest RMG manufacturer and exporter in the world. By many measures, the RMG sector has performed spectacularly well over the past decade. Output has grown by more than 15 percent annually over the last 5 years. However, this performance originated through both external and internal factors.

Factors Which Supported the Growth of This Sector: External Linkages

While the global prominence of RMG in development discourse can be traced to the 1970s, Bangladesh began to adopt a neoliberal trade-led development strategy comprehensively from the early 1980s. Since then, the exports of the RMG sector have increased considerably, from merely USD 10 million per year in the 1980s to USD 1 billion in the first half of the 1990s. Concurrently, its female workforce also increased from a mere 0.1 million in the mid-1980s to 2 million in 2000 (Rahman et al. 2008: 34–45). The shift in emphasis to trade-led development through RMG occurred because of the opportunistic coincidence of outside interests with the interests of the local business elites who were keen to adopt the trade liberalization agenda (Quddus and Rashid 2000) as a core (national) development strategy. This coincidence of interests enabled the consolidation of condition of RMG to flourish in Bangladesh, and was further advanced by the implementation of Structural Adjustment Programs (SAPs) that followed in the 1980s as part of the conditionalities of the International Monetary Fund and the World Bank. SAPs resulted in the closing down of numerous state-owned jute factories, some of which were later transformed into export processing zones (EPZs). For the EPZs, new regulatory legislation came into place which was distinctively autonomous and different from non-EPZ factories.

The success of the RMG industry of Bangladesh is also attributed to the MFA, which provided the basis for industrialized countries to restrict imports from developing nations, especially the Asian Tigers. Import-competing firms in the developed countries justifiably feared that the rapid growth of imports from the cost-competitive developing world would threaten their jobs and the viability of their textile and clothing industry (Smith 2003). Consequently, the developed world increasingly placed restrictive protectionist measures against the import of textiles and apparel from developing countries under the auspices of the MFA, violating the principles of the General Agreement of Tariff and Trade. The MFA restrictions negatively affected the non-LDC countries such as Hong Kong, Taiwan, and the Republic of Korea, which were the main exporters of textiles and clothing. For example, in 1981, 73 percent of Korean exports of such goods were subjected to MFA quotas, and by 1987, this had risen to 97 percent (Smith 2003). On the other hand, the MFA worked as a catalyst for most of the LDCs. Since the European Union (EU) did not impose quotas on LDCs, Bangladesh acquired an advantage over non-LDCs such as Korea and Hong Kong (Green 1998). Until 1985, Bangladesh operated as a quota-free territory, a factor that greatly facilitated the early growth of the garment industry. In subsequent years, the United Kingdom (UK), France, Canada, and the United States (US) imposed quotas on the import of Bangladeshi garments as per the MFA (Rock 2001). However, after negotiations, the UK and the

French quotas were largely withdrawn and the US quotas were relaxed (Quddus 1993). The introduction of the MFA is therefore considered the key factor behind the rapid development of the Bangladesh RMG industry.

Factors Which Supported the Growth of This Sector: Internal Supports

Bangladesh continued to advance the import-substituting industrialization (ISI) policy that it had inherited during its East Pakistan period. Its relations with India and the then Soviet Union might have influenced the post-independence industrialization path. At the end of the 1970s, however, the country shifted from the ISI to the export-oriented industrialization policy, soon after the World Bank's neoliberal prescriptions and the beginning of the era of SAPs. In that period, discourses such as the merits of private trade-led development strategies emerged and proliferated, replacing the traditional state-led industrialization.

The role of successive governments in the promotion of the RMG sector in Bangladesh is quite remarkable. The first export consignment of shirts from Bangladesh was made by a state agency. During the 1980s as part of its commitment to free trade-led (neoliberal) development, the government of Bangladesh also allowed and issued licenses for importing duty-free garment machinery. To remain competitive in the global market, the Government of Bangladesh deliberately facilitated the conditions for the RMG sector to flourish by allowing production processes to also be extended to the "informal" sector through outsourcing, for example, and by not making mandatory and/or enforcing the regulatory provisions that full-fledged factories were subjected to. This meant that entrepreneurs in such cases did not have to provide the same facilities (such as maternity leave, provident funds, and gratuity) as required in other sectors such as leather and jute (Paul-Majumder 1994: 49).

One key ingredient in Bangladesh's RMG-led export growth success was an elaborate incentive package, which became a characteristic feature of the trade policy regime in the 1990s. This included duty drawbacks on imports of intermediate goods, bonded warehouse facilities to enable exporters to import intermediate inputs duty-free, and cash compensation schemes for the so-called non-traditional exports with a cash assistance rate for exporters not availing duty-drawback or bonded warehouse facilities. These incentives continue to operate (see Tables 9.3 and 9.4), although the nature and depth of coverage for some of them have changed.

Table 9.3 Policy supports—fiscal

SL. No.	*Policy support/facilities*	*RMG/textile*
1	Cash incentives on Shipped On Board (SOB) export **initial period cash incentives (1994 onwards)	4–10 percent 25 percent
2	Duty-free import of raw materials	Yes
3	Corporate tax rates	17.5 percent (for 100 percent export co.)
4	Deduction of Advance Income Tax (AIT) from export proceeds	0.7 percent
5	Income tax rebate for export	50 percent
6	Export Development Fund credit facility offered by Bangladesh bank (@ 1.5 percent + Libor)	$20 million
7	Two-step loan facility @6 percent for compliance/ retrofitting by Japan International Cooperation Agency (JICA)	Yes
8	Low-cost finance for housing of workers—@2 percent	Yes
9	Preferential working capital finance facility for textile sector at low cost	9 percent (1990–21)

Source: Authors' compilation from different sources

Table 9.4 Policy supports—non-fiscal

SL. No.	*Policy support/facilities*	*RMG/textile*
1	Renewal of general bond	Every 3 years
2	Limits/co-efficient of material imports	Case-to-case basis (by back-to-back LC)
3	Cut-off time for shipment of export goods (handover goods for carrier)	24 hours before the departure of vessel
4	Examination of import materials by customs at port	Few materials examined randomly or no examination
5	Extended bonded warehouse facilities	Single-bonded warehouse for two sister-companies within 60 km range
6	Issuing utilization permission for raw materials/packing usage by the bonder	Provided by BGMEA/Bangladesh Knitwear Manufacturers and Exporters Association
7	Utility connections	Has been provided on a priority basis

Source: Authors' compilation from different sources

Growth of the Sector

Along with the historical trajectories, understanding the dynamics of the growth of RMG is important to reveal the development path of Bangladesh. The pathways of growth are discussed in terms of export value, product concentration, historical growth path, export destination and market trend, top product exports, and transition of the industry, especially after the Rana Plaza incident.

There has been a significant decrease in the average RMG export since the Rana Plaza incident. Bangladesh registered USD 29.2 billion on RMG export in 2017. Knit export was USD 14.5 billion and woven export 14.6 billion (share almost 50 percent for both). Average RMG export growth was 16.9 percent during 2008–12 and 8.25 percent during 2013–17 (see Figs. 9.1 and 9.2). There are three primary reasons behind this decrease in the average export growth rate: (i) slow demand for apparel in the export destinations, (ii) limited non-traditional market and limited variety of products, and (iii) closure of many small RMG units—a major change after the Rana Plaza incident.

Growth rates in RMG export and export destinations have been changing since the Rana Plaza incident. The growth curve shows ups and downs over the years, and since 2013 growth has not crossed dou-

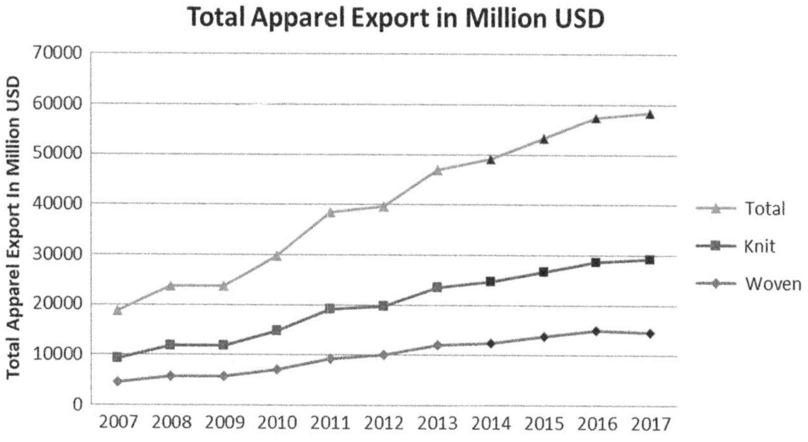

Fig. 9.1 Trend in export, share of RMG and RMG products. (Source: Calculated. Data from ITC, Trade map database & Export Promotion Bureau Compiled by BGMEA 2018)

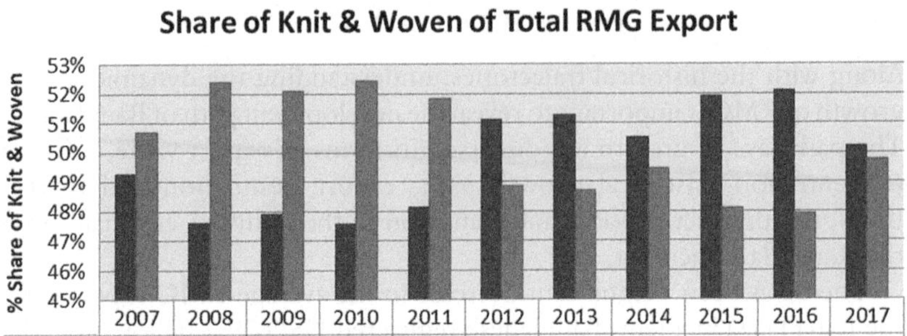

	2007	2008	2009	2010	2011	2012	2013	2014	2015	2016	2017
Woven	49%	48%	48%	48%	48%	51%	51%	51%	52%	52%	50%
Knit	51%	52%	52%	52%	52%	49%	49%	49%	48%	48%	50%

Fig. 9.2 Share of Knit & Woven. (Data Source: Calculated from ITC, Trade map database & Export Promotion Bureau Compiled by BGMEA 2018)

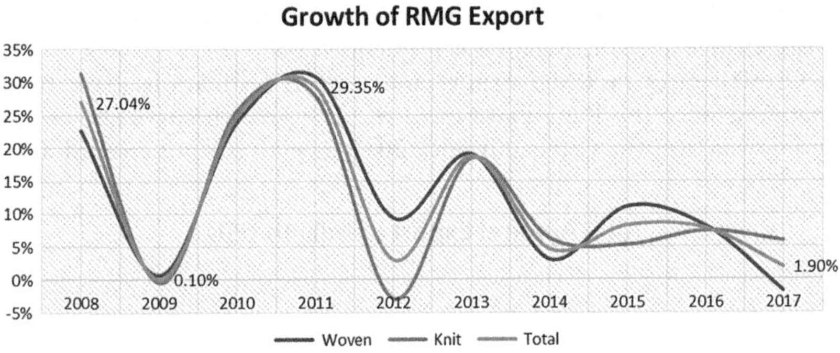

Fig. 9.3 Growth of RMG export. (Data Source: Calculated from ITC, Trade map database & Export Promotion Bureau Compiled by BGMEA 2018)

ble-digit figures. The highest growth recorded in 2011 was 31 percent. Garment exports grew by 9.11 percent year-on-year to $22.83 billion in July–March of 2017–18 (see Fig. 9.3). The composition of products has changed since 2013, especially for woven products. The demand for woven products from Bangladesh has increased in the EU market. Exports in the US market have decreased during this period and the EU holds a share of approximately 64 percent of export from Bangladesh.

Table 9.5 Non-traditional market for RMG products

Country	*Share among non-traditional destinations (%)*
Japan	17
Australia	14
Russia	9
China	9
Turkey	6
India	4
Korea Rep.	4

Source: ITC, Trade map database (2018)

Market Trend: Diversifying to Non-traditional Market

The RMG industry has not been successful in capitalizing on non-traditional markets. About 14 percent of total exports are destined for the non-traditional market. Among these, the top three countries are Japan, Australia, and Russia with 17 percent, 14 percent, and 9 percent of total non-traditional export from Bangladesh. India and China are emerging as major non-traditional markets (see Table 9.5).

Product and Price Trend of Top Five Knit and Woven Products
RMG export concentration on the top five products decreased slightly in 2016 compared to 2012. The share of the top five knit products was 79 percent in 2012 while it was 67 percent in 2016. Some other (very few) knit products have gained market share. The share of the top five woven products was 75 percent in 2012 while it was 69 percent in 2016 (see Fig. 9.4). This is a tiny improvement in terms of product diversity and market share in four years for both knit and woven. Having a diversified market for RMG products is desirable and helpful for sustainability.

Transition in the Industry

There is a shift in the RMG industry of Bangladesh concerning the size of factories. The inspection by Accord, Alliance, and the National Tripartite Plan of Action (NTPA) has caused many of the small factories to shut down their activities due to non-compliant working conditions. On the other hand, medium and large factories are increasing their production capacity by expanding factories as well as constructing new ones. Before

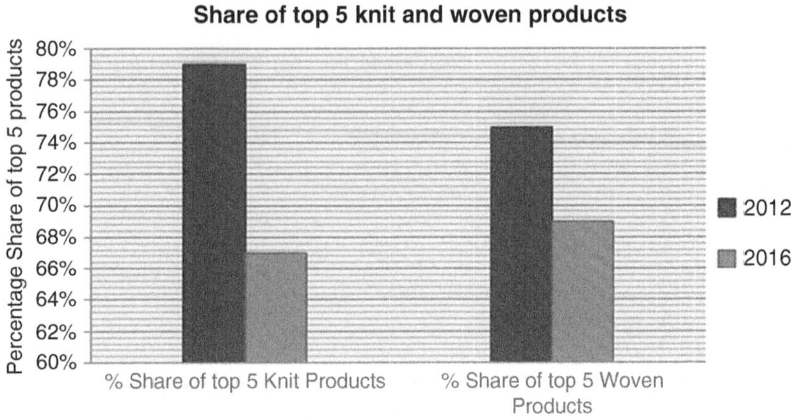

Fig. 9.4 Share of top five knit and woven products. (Source: ITC, Trade map database 2018)

Table 9.6 Number of factories according to CPD during 2017

	Enterprises	*Workers*
Small	1739 (48.36 percent)	669,403 (19.1 percent)
Medium	1592 (44.27 percent)	1,868,020 (53.0 percent)
Large	265 (7.36 percent)	963,800 (27 percent)
Total	3596 (100)	3,504,728 (100 percent)

Source: Centre for Policy Dialogue (CPD) survey (2018)

2013, there was no database on export-oriented RMG factories in Bangladesh. Although BGMEA maintained a list of their members, all of them were not export-oriented, while several factories were non-operational. According to a recent survey by CPD, there are a total of 3596 factories in Bangladesh. Of these, 45.36 percent are small, 44.27 percent medium, and 7.36 percent large in terms of workers (small <500, medium <3000, remainder are large) (see Table 9.6).

According to the Department of Inspection for Factories and Establishments (DIFE), the total number of factories is 3780. Of these, 1505 factories are under Accord inspection, 890 under Alliance inspection, 164 under inspection by both Accord and Alliance, and 1549 factories are under the scrutiny of National Initiative. Against this backdrop, it is imperative to know the impact of the RMG industry on the overall macro-economic context and also on the social sectoral point of view.

Impacts of RMG Industry: Macro-economic and Social Impacts

Macro Contributions

The RMG sector has been a robust catalyst for the development of several macro indicators, such as being a source of foreign exchange earnings, contribution to the GDP, and employment creation, especially female employment and poverty reduction. It has also contributed to creating a cohort of entrepreneurial classes along with diverse backward linkages supporting this sector. Apart from this macro contribution, it has contributed to immense social sector developments.

Foreign Exchange Earnings and Contribution to GDP
The RMG industry drives the economic growth of Bangladesh, contributing 6 percent to average annual growth since 2007. The total export earnings from the RMG industry during 2018 was USD 32.9 billion (BGMEA 2019), out of which knit export was USD 16.7 billion, and woven export was USD 16.2 billion (BGMEA 2019). The contribution of the RMG industry is equivalent to 12 percent of GDP of the country, and the local value addition in this industry was 74.6 percent during 2018 (ibid.), out of which knit export was USD 16.7 billion, and woven export was USD 16.2 billion (ibid.). Figure 9.5 shows the contribution of the RMG industry to the national export and GDP of Bangladesh between 2006–07 and 2013–14.

Employment Creation
The RMG industry of Bangladesh is fully labor intensive rather than technology oriented, and currently this industry employs four million people

Fig. 9.5 Contribution of RMG industry. (Source: Rahman and Siddiqui 2015: 7)

(BGMEA 2018). This industry provided a new lifeline to the Bangladesh economy by employing unskilled and skilled labor, especially women. At present, 3.2 million women workers are employed in this industry. The RMG industry has relieved Bangladesh from the unemployment burden by providing the largest employment avenue as an industry. Around 10 million livelihoods are directly or indirectly dependent on this industry. This industry allowed Bangladeshi women to have a new identity as industry workers. Earlier they were perceived to work at home or as agricultural workers. Therefore, this industry not only generated employment but also empowered women. This has transformed their position in their own families, as well as in society and finally in terms of social sustainability.

The growth of the RMG sector also has domino development effects on other industries in Bangladesh. They provide needed support to the RMG industry as well as creating the backward or forward linkages for the RMG industry to function efficiently. The development of the other industries related to the RMG industry also created a large employment opportunity for skilled and non-skilled people. Therefore, the RMG industry is indirectly responsible for creating employment in other industries that act as suppliers of manufactured or traded items to the RMG industry.

Empowering Women: Rise of Women's Social Power

The Bangladesh RMG industry has played a significant role in economically uplifting a large cohort of poor and vulnerable women in Bangladesh. RMG is the first industry to provide large-scale employment opportunities to rural women. This sector has uplifted the neglected section of the population, thus radically transforming the socio-economic condition of the country. In most cases, employment in the garment industry has given them the first opportunity to earn wages, which are typically several times higher than what they could have earned doing domestic service, one of the very few other job opportunities open to them. The opportunity to be employed as an RMG manufacturing worker has served as a repellent against early marriage and allowed uneducated rural women to migrate to industrial areas and become empowered. Control over income also provides women with more decision-making power at home, a voice in the social sphere, and self-esteem. Women entering the RMG industry generally find themselves in low-skill/low-wage jobs. It has often been argued that entrepreneurs in the garment industry have preferred to hire more women because of prevailing beliefs that women are nimble and

Table 9.7 Contribution of female RMG workers to the national economy

	Total RMG sector			Female RMG worker			
FY	National Export(%)	GDP (%)	Employment	worker	Worker (%)	National Export (%)	GDP (%)
2013-14	81.16	14.07	4	3.2	80	64.93	11.256
2012-13	79.61	16.57	4	3.16	79	62.89	13.0903
2011-12	78.6	16.31	4	2.88	72	56.59	11.7432
2010-11	78.14	16	3.6	2.88	80	62.51	12.8
2009-10	77.12	12.45	3.6	2.7	75	57.84	9.3375

Source: Rahman and Siddiqui (2015: 7)

patient, more conforming in nature, less likely to join trade unions, and better at sewing. Also, they are willing to accept lower wages than men. Table 9.7 shows the contribution of female RMG workers to the economy from 2009–07 to 2013–14.

Economic Growth and Poverty Reduction

The RMG industry is the first manufacturing industry in Bangladesh to create opportunities in providing jobs to low-skilled (mostly female) workers that have few paid employment alternatives. Although salaries are low by international standards, RMG manufacturing workers tend to make more money than they would in other activities—low-skill agriculture and services—in the domestic market. Thus, for millions of poor, unskilled workers, the RMG industry is a gateway to start getting out of poverty. The fact that apparel workers are mostly women is another strong link to poverty reduction, as boosting economic opportunities for women is a necessary step toward poverty reduction and development. The income generation caused by employment generation in the RMG industry and the sectors that serve as backward and forward linkages to the RMG industry has a significant impact on reducing poverty. The RMG industry has a significant effect on the GDP of Bangladesh and has contributed to the economic growth of the country since the early 1990s. The pace of economic growth increased after 2010, with GDP growing at a rate of 6.5 percent on average per year between 2010 and 2016. Similarly, the national poverty rate fell by 1.2 percentage points annually from 2010 to 2016 compared to 1.7 from 2005 to 2010. One of the reasons for the slow poverty reduction is the wage rate of the four million workers working in the RMG industry, as wages received by the workers in the RMG industry of Bangladesh are some of the lowest in the global RMG industry and far below than the credible living wage estimate.

Backward and Forward Linkages
To perform efficiently, the RMG industry required raw materials, machines, spare parts repair and maintenance services, and different other services. This need for backward and forward linkages, as well as other supports, influenced the development of backward and forward linkages sectors and other support sectors in Bangladesh. The RMG industry is responsible for developing sectors like cotton manufacturing, thread manufacturing, textile manufacturing, machine manufacturing, spare part manufacturing and importing, clothes washing and dyeing, clothes embroidery, buttons manufacturing, packaging material manufacturing, chemical manufacturing and trading, plastic products manufacturing, polybags manufacturing, zipper manufacturing, label manufacturing, and apparel designing that provides backward linkages to the RMG industry. To ensure an effective supply chain, the RMG industry is also responsible for the development of support industries like warehousing, transportation, security services, apparel quality labs, and catering services. On the other hand, buying houses, Bangladeshi fashion brands, and fashion houses are established to provide forward linkage to the RMG industry. The RMG industry not only propelled the growth of backward and forward linkage industries but also rendered large externalities by contributing to other economic activities in such areas as shipping and logistics, banking, insurance, real estate, packaging, hotels and tourism, recycling, consumer goods utility services, and inland transport communication.

Social Contributions

The RMG industry has profound welfare effects on social, household, and individual (particularly on women) levels. The benefit could come through several avenues such as social benefits by contributing to women's empowerment, higher school enrolment, and lowering childbirth and marriage rates (Heath and Mobarak 2015, kHM hereafter). According to the Asian Center for Development (2015), the average income of a poor household in Bangladesh is 8900 Bangladeshi taka (BDT) while the average family income for RMG workers is 15,720 BDT. In the case of asset ownership, 86 percent own mobile phones, 68 percent own a television, 84 percent own an electric fan, 75 percent own a home, and 28 percent have gold ornaments. About 83 percent of RMG workers can read a letter, while 71 percent can also write in Bengali, which is greater than the national average (58 percent).

For the first time since independence, many females from rural areas have started working outside of the local environment of their homes. The RMG industry accelerated change in the area of politics and economics among working-class people. If we consider the phrase "emancipation of women" from the perspective of narrowly economic terms, the RMG industry eased the way. The greatest socio-economic impact of the RMG industry has come from the female workers' movement (their disposition[12] from their rural set-up) in this sector, which allowed female workers to manifest their hidden potentiality and made them socially and economically independent (Rahman and Siddiqui 2015; Atkiny 2009). Increasing engagement of women in income-generating activities ensures more freedom of decision-making both inside and outside the household and increases their social status both within and outside the family (Atkiny 2009). Empowering women through a job also reduces their vulnerability, and therefore domestic violence is also reduced. Female counterparts have a higher spending propensity toward education, house rent, schooling of family members, and so on than their male counterparts who earn more than them (Zohir 2001). Paul-Majumder and Begum (2000) find that intra-household work distribution has changed among families where female members work in the RMG industry. More than half of female RMG industry workers are helped by their husband in domestic work and spousal involvement in household work increased with the growing participation of women in the RMG industry.

This is revealing with regard to more micro-level impacts, and Raihan (2010) concludes that remarkable success in RMG exports significantly contributed to the achievement in the areas of child and maternal mortality, life expectancy, net primary enrolment rate, women's economic participation, gender parity in primary and secondary education, and so on. An interesting finding by HM is that in places where factories have been operating for 6.4 years, girls have a 0.3 percent lower probability of getting married in those years relative to girls living in control villages in the same district. Another of HM's findings is that women with 6.4 years of factory exposure are 0.23 percentage points less likely to have given birth in those years. It is a great concern that Bangladesh is still fighting with the maternal mortality rate. One of the core reasons for maternal mortality is the tender age of the mother (Khosla 2013). Consequently, Field and Ambrus (2008) found that delay in marriage is associated with an increase in the use of preventive health services. Qian (2008) estimated that an increase in women's income has an immediate and positive effect on the survival rate of girls. Women and adolescent girls now have better access to nutrition than before (Ahmed et al. 1997), which results in the improvement of their health and that of their children, through intergenerational effects.

The HM study further revealed that garment workers have 2.8 years more education on average than residents of non-garment-making villages, and education has a statistically significant positive effect on wage and productivity. As such, higher education is expected to yield a higher income stream in the long run. From this perspective, Atkiny (2009) revealed that remuneration from the job increases the earnings of women and makes it more affordable for them to send their children to primary school. In addition to this, Qian (2008) found that an incremental increase in women's income can increase the educational attainment of children of both sexes. All of this evidence shows that more families are now investing in girls' education to engage them in the RMG industry (Amin 1998; Rashid 2006). Field and Ambrus (2008) found a strong relationship among delay in marriage, years of schooling, and literacy rate, that is, delay in marriage for an additional year would increase 0.22 additional years of schooling and would increase the literacy rate by 5.6 percent.

Challenges and Avenues to Overcome

While we have tended to analyze the sectoral contribution of RMG, we also need to look at the challenges this sector faced from the very outset of its journey since the 1980s. Some of these challenges were internal such as child labor and building collapse, whereas others were external such as phasing out of MFA. We now turn to detailing these challenges.

Challenges to RMG

Child Labor

Bangladesh has been relatively successful in eliminating child labor in the RMG manufacturing sector. However, it remains a significant concern in the formal and informal sectors that produce for the domestic market or feed into the supply chain of international brands through unauthorized subcontracting. Child labor remains a particularly acute problem in home-based activities and informal, unregistered workshops that support large RMG manufacturers. Typical activities carried out by children related to the RMG industry can include embroidery, cutting/trimming, and button stitching, among many others that are subcontracted by the RMG exporters to small local firms which do not follow any code of conduct from the international buyers.

The large RMG exporters have already taken steps in eliminating child labor in their factories. Now the non-compliant small and medium manufacturing firms need to take the initiative toward eradicating child labor. While giving subcontracts to small or medium firms, large and compliant factories need to have a periodic audit to influence smaller firms to follow global compliance policies. Moreover, poverty due to low wages for RMG workers can incentivize them to allow their children to drop out of school and contribute to the family income through child labor practices. The increase of worker salaries to an acceptable range will allow workers to send their children to school, as they will not need the children to contribute to the family income.

MFA Phase-Out

MFA was phased out in January 2005. But before 2005, the global RMG sector experts and researchers widely speculated on the effects of its abolition on the RMG industry of Bangladesh as MFA had positively influenced the growth of this industry in the country. Islam (2001), Yang et al. (1997), and Mlachila and Yang (2004) specified that the phase-out of MFA would not hurt the RMG industry of Bangladesh. Instead, it would create more opportunities for the RMG sector because of the reliable quality image and supply chain relationship. And their prediction proved to be right.

The MFA phase-out did not bring any drastic change to the export performance, market share, or product composition for export but created benefits for the RMG industry of Bangladesh. This was because there was no performance drop in the case of the Bangladesh RMG industry in the post-MFA period but instead quite similar growth performance in the global RMG supply chain (Adhikari and Weeratunge 2007; Joarder et al. 2010). Table 9.8 shows a comparison of the performance of the Bangladesh RMG industry in the MFA era and the post-MFA era.

Industrial Accidents

On April 24, 2013, Bangladesh experienced the most tragic structural failure when a nine-story commercial building called Rana Plaza caved in. The accident claimed 1135 lives and maimed around 2500, mostly females. Inferior construction materials and violation of building code were the

Table 9.8 Major clothing exporters in the world market (values in billion USD)

Countries	*1990*		*2008*		*During MFA (1995–2004)*		*After MFA (2005–08)*	
	Value	*Share (%)*	*Value*	*Share (%)*	*Growth (%)*	*Change in share (%)*	*Growth (%)*	*Change in share (%)*
China	9.7	9	120.0	33	11	9	17	9
Hong Kong	15.4	14	27.9	8	2	−4	1	−2
Italy	11.8	11	25.1	7	3	−2	10	0
Germany	7.9	7	18.1	5	5	0	13	0
Turkey	3.3	3	13.6	4	7	0	5	−1
France	4.7	4	11.5	3	4	−1	11	0
Bangladesh	0.6	1	10.9	3	14	1	17	1
India	2.5	2	10.9	3	6	0	8	0
Belgium	2.0	2	9.7	3	9	1	13	0
Vietnam	NA	NA	9.0	2	NA	2	24	1
World	108.1	100	361.9	100	6	–	9	–

Source: Joarder et al. (2010: 138)

main reasons for this tragic incident, accompanied by owners' negligence and inspectors' inability to identify the risk.

Ensuring Living Wage
The RMG sector directly or indirectly allowed employment for a large number of people and created an opportunity for people to earn an income, but the adequacy of the income of the workers of this industry has always been a talking point. Labor cost being cheap has always been viewed as a competitive advantage for RMG suppliers of Bangladesh while they tried to influence the international buyers. On the other hand, the mismatch of the workload of workers and salary they earned has been responsible for labor unrest, worker strikes, and vandalism by workers over the years. Inadequate income affected the lives of the workers and their families, and this has been focused on by the local and international media since the late 1990s. Upon receiving criticism over the workers' wages and working conditions, especially after the Rana Plaza collapse, the wage board of Bangladesh set a monthly minimum wage of a garment worker at 5300 BDT, which is equivalent to USD 63, in place of the previous monthly minimum wage of 3000 BDT, which is equivalent to USD 36. Even with the new increases, however, these wages fall far short of the

level that is considered a living wage, that is, enough to allow a worker to provide her family with basic human necessities such as food, shelter, clothing, water, health, education, and transport. In September 2018, the government of Bangladesh revised the monthly minimum wage of a garment worker to 8000 BDT or about USD 96, effective January 2019 (BGMEA 2018).

Avenues to Overcome Challenges

Overcoming challenges was not easy for local entrepreneurs and the government. Perhaps this is because the nature of the RMG business (buyer-driven production process, which is often very fragmented) is prone to various challenges. However, often both internal and external governance mechanisms originated to overcome them.

Induction to New Labor Law 2006

The Bangladesh Labor Act (BLA) 2006 has specified provisions with regard to conditions for service and employment for workers, wages and payments, maternity benefits for female workers, health and hygiene and safety of workers at the workplace, welfare for workers, working hours and leave for workers, trade unions, and worker compensation due to accident at work. As many national and international rights organizations and foreign buyers expressed their serious concern over workers' rights and safety, especially after the Rana Plaza and Tazreen Fashions tragedies, the government took steps to amend the BLA 2006 to ensure adequate rights for workers. The proposed Bangladesh Labor (Amendment) Act 2018 is considered more workers' rights-friendly as the workers' participation required to form trade unions at factories would be reduced to 20 percent from the existing 30 percent.

Shift in Governance

The Bangladesh government, EU, International Labour Organization (ILO), and apparel retailers have been working to improve working conditions in the RMG sector by establishing monitoring initiatives and ensuring better building practices and safety codes. Three major monitoring bodies, namely Alliance (US-led), Accord (EU led), and the NTPA, have been formed. As part of the ILO project "Better Work Bangladesh", initiatives were taken in 2014 to help the NTPA in improving the working condition in the RMG sector to a globally acceptable standard (Table 9.9).

Table 9.9 Factory inspection by Accord, Alliance, and NTPA

	Number of factories inspected	*Number of factories terminated/suspended*	*Number of factories closed*	*Number of factories on corrective action plan (CAP)*	*Number of factories completed CAP*
Accord	1631	96	188	1247	127
Alliance	785	162	127	424	234
NTPA	1549		513	780	

Source: Accord, Alliance Fourth Annual Report 2017 and DIFE

Many factories are still under observation for the compliance of their own corrective action plan (CAP). According to Accord and Alliance, 361 factories have completed CAP and in another 2451 factories CAP is ongoing (Rahman and Rahman 2016).

A Change in Mindset

The Rana Plaza incident has drastically changed the outlook of both factory owners and governance bodies. The result of the initiatives taken by RMG sector entrepreneurs during the last 5 years is astonishing. Now Bangladesh has more Leadership in Energy and Environmental Design (LEED)-certified RMG manufacturing factories than any other country in the world (BGMEA 2018). Bangladesh currently hosts seven of the top ten platinum-ranked LEED-certified factories in the world. Moreover, the country has the world's top three platinum-rated garment factories, according to BGMEA. A LEED-certified factory building ensures 25–30 percent less water and energy consumption, and fewer industrial accidents, such as fires, causing fewer casualties with special architectural design. This green factory establishment initiative is an important indicator of sustainable industrial development around the world. The green initiatives taken by various factories are helping Bangladesh to brighten the image of the clothing sector.

Changes in Management Outlook and Creation of Own Brands

The management outlook can have a significant effect on the sustainability of the RMG industry in Bangladesh. Since the late 1970s, the RMG manufacturers of Bangladesh have been manufacturing top-quality apparel for most of the globally renowned apparel brands. However, there has to be a paradigm shift in the management outlook of the RMG entrepreneurs of

Bangladesh from being a supplier of the famous brands to creating their own global brands. The forward linkage initiatives of RMG manufacturers to launch and position their brand among global consumers can introduce a new sphere to the RMG industry of Bangladesh from being "Made in Bangladesh" to "Brand of Bangladesh".

Integration of Compliance within the Stakeholders' Mindset

The RMG manufacturers need to establish their code of conduct and take measures so that the code of conduct is woven into their operation. The policies and strategies for becoming a responsible manufacturer have to be grounded in the compliance standards that ensure the integration of the stakeholders' value and create a global image and reputation for the RMG industry of Bangladesh.

Technological Transformation

Technology transformation and innovation can help an industry toward excellence. Bangladeshi clothing makers are using cutting-edge technology to upgrade production processes and reduce fabric waste by improving measurement accuracy. According to industry insiders and technical experts, around 70 percent of the total manufacturing cost of an apparel product is fabric. This single cost can be reduced by about 10 percent, however, with the introduction of new cutting technology. "It saves fabric, time and money, and improves quality by ensuring accuracy in measurements during the cutting".[13]

Technological transformation has resulted in a change in management practices in the RMG sector, which is providing customer satisfaction, organizational effectiveness, and productivity. By maintaining a transparent flow of information throughout the system, it is creating complete visibility across the supply chain. In this technological era, the value stream map is an extremely effective tool to reduce cycle time, reduce waste, visualize the entire production process, and represent material and information flow. Another concept is enterprise resource planning solutions that can help to establish a smooth material flow from yarn to finished good. Moreover, it also helps to track down the inventory at every stage. Technological tools and techniques are used in the garment industry to improve the overall production and management performance. In short, technology is defining the future of the RMG sector of Bangladesh. In recent years, this sector has dramatically altered the country's export composition through technological upgrades.

Backward Integration

The RMG industry has already proven itself to be resilient and can be a catalyst for further industrialization of Bangladesh. However, this vital industry that has been driving the economic growth of Bangladesh during the last 30 years still depends heavily on imported fabrics. After the liberalization of the quota regime, some of the major textile manufacturing countries such as Thailand, India, China, Hong Kong, Indonesia, and Taiwan increased their own RMG exports. If Bangladesh wants to enjoy increased market access created by the global open market economy, it has no alternative but to produce more textile items competitively at home through the establishment of backward linkage with the RMG industry.

Workforce Training

The RMG industry needs skilled workers to meet the required demand for the workforce. Adequate skills among workers and managers can be a factor to increase productivity and improve the image of the industry. There are many institutions in Bangladesh to teach and prepare the youth for this sector. They are also providing the sector with a dynamic workforce with concept, technique, and knowledge of apparel and textiles. Moreover, technically competent human resources have made significant changes in the apparel, textile, and allied sectors. Highly paid jobs including fashion designing, product development, sourcing and marketing, apparel buying, garment production planning, industrial engineering, retailing, and merchandising are also available in the garment industry for the well-educated and trained workforce. A good number of textile graduates are entering the RMG sector every year. They are contributing to improving efficiency in this sector. Presently, there are 28 textile universities, six government textile diploma institutions, and more than 100 private diploma institutions offering textile-related education. Well-trained graduates from these institutions can ensure sustainable business management practices for the firms in the RMG industry.

Conclusion

Four actors or drivers have steered the fate of RMG in Bangladesh. They are Nurul Quader and his vision to set up Bangladesh's first fully export-oriented garment factory; agreements on textiles and clothing which eventually allowed Bangladesh's export to increase dramatically, even though it was assumed that the country would suffer the most; and revision of the EU's requirement on allowing imported yarn for knitwear and origin requirements further helped Bangladesh's export to grow and became the second highest garment-exporting nation.

Along the way, Bangladesh seems to have overcome negative predictions on the future of the RMG sector after the Rana Plaza incident that raised questions regarding the sectoral efficiency and failure of governance, as well as casting doubt on the export growth performance the country was enjoying beforehand. The size of the global textile and apparel market is projected to increase from USD 1.1 trillion in 2015 to USD 2.1 trillion by 2025 with a compound annual growth rate (CAGR) of 5 percent with forecasted CAGRs for Indian, Chinese, and Russian demand. For Bangladesh, realizing and exercising these opportunities requires sustainable growth of the industry, as well as addressing major problems such as a lack of compliance, competitiveness, capacity utilization and extension, inadequate infrastructure, and a shortage of power.

Moreover, the sector needs to handle four specific issues. Firstly, the trade union. Issues with trade union resulted in buyers' hesitation for placing orders and they keep pressing the manufacturers to come in terms with a particular local federation. However, recent development in setting up Workers Participatory Committees in individual factories and workers' participation to some extent fill the gaps in the absence of a true trade union. The second issue is remediation. Most of the structural flaws in the factories of Bangladesh found by Alliance and Accord are remediable. Funding required for remediation stretches from $250,000 to $500,000. Sources of funds along with the continuation of remediation is now an important issue. However, the process will be time-consuming to be effective. The third issue is product efficiency. It is now essential for factories to invest in techniques and tools. Since there is pressure for efficient costing, smart production and quick turnaround time and automation are inevitable. The last issue is product upgradation. Along with consistency in a supplier's product range, they also seek multiple capabilities. This would enable the customers to place other orders, and factories can maximize products by adjusting and adding machines according to their products' needs. Bangladesh also needs to target better price ranges with complete R&D solutions.

Despite these issues, there are four dreams that Bangladesh can still achieve soon. First, the country aims to reach $50 billion of exports by 2021. To achieve this, Bangladesh must increase its output to 8 percent from 5 percent of the total apparel requirement of the world. This goal is achievable if the government can set up a steady infrastructure and good governance. Bangladesh can become a middle-income nation by 2021 and the country is already getting closer because of the growth of income per capita (12.90 percent achieved this fiscal year). Moreover, the Planning Commission projected that it would cross $2000 by 2021. The income of labor has improved, and unskilled workers now have a salary range of Bangladeshi Taka 8000. The "Made with Pride" tagline and "Happy Workers" tag proposed by Nobel Laureate Professor Muhammad Yunus have created more understanding and compassion.

Despite many challenges, the RMG sector of Bangladesh has continued to exhibit robust performance, competitive strength, and, most importantly, social commitment; hence, its contribution to the economy deserves appreciation and respect. With the resultant effects of this sector, the support that it seeks from the government is justifiable. However, due to Bangladesh's elevation from the LDC Club, some existing policy flexibilities and trade preferences will either be lost or be significantly reduced. Thus, the incentive or push still needed to make the most of these facilities and insufficient supply-response mean that many of the available trade preference schemes are underutilized. Furthermore, after gaining graduation from LDCs, export support measures like cash assistance schemes are unlikely to continue, given the rules and provisions of the World Trade Organization. Therefore, before it loses its LDC preferences and privileges, it is high time for Bangladesh to consider reinvigorated and profound policy support to expand its export base rapidly.

Notes

1. Academics such as Mobarak and Heath (2014) and Rehman Sobhan (1990) and institutions such as Overseas Development Institute (ODI), UK, Commonwealth Secretariat, CPD, Dhaka, and PRI, Dhaka.
2. See Sobhan, R. (1990). *From aid dependence to self-reliance: Development options for Bangladesh.* Dhaka: University Press Limited.
3. Jeffrey Sachs conceives of "sweatshops" (and he explicitly refers to Bangladesh as a positive case example) as the route to progress: "sweatshops are the first rung on the ladder out of the extreme poverty" (Sachs 2005: 11).

4. See Kaushik Basu's Op-ed in Brookings titled "Why is Bangladesh booming?", May 1, 2018. Source: https://www.brookings.edu/opinions/why-is-bangladesh-booming/.
5. Henry Kissinger once labeled Bangladesh a "bottomless basket" during the 1970s.
6. This status was achieved when Bangladesh joined the lower-middle-income country category on July 1, 2015. Conversely, graduation from the LDC group is almost inevitable, but not until 2024, if the country meets all the technical requirements in the coming years. See Debapriya Bhattacharya and Sarah Sabin Khan's Op-ed in the *Daily Star*, "Bangladesh's Graduation from the LDC Group: Pitfalls and Promises Clarifying the MIC-LDC confusion". Source: https://www.thedailystar.net/opinion/economics/clarifying-the-mic-ldc-confusion-1550980.
7. In 2015, the female to male workers' participation ratio was 64:36, but in 2018 it declined to 60.8: 39.2 (CPD 2018).
8. Deussom and Adams (2012), Rossi and Robertson (2011), Barrett and Carter (2010), and Asuyama et al. (2013).
9. There are several incidents of order cancellation and subsequently fewer orders from the retailers due to non-compliance (http://mhssn.igc.org/Chowdhury,Tanimpercent20-AJSSMSpercent202016.pdf).
10. The Accord on Fire and Building Safety in Bangladesh (the Accord) is generally seen as a positive development in ensuring that Bangladeshi garment industry workers have access to safe working conditions. See Salminen, J. (2018). The Accord on fire and building safety in Bangladesh: A new paradigm for limiting buyers' liability in global supply chains. *The American Journal of Comparative Law*, *66*(2), 411–451. August 24, 2018, https://doi.org/10.1093/ajcl/avy030.
11. In 2015, Swedish retail giant H&M decided to double its business to USD 3 billion in Bangladesh over the next five years. This move by the global giant, which sources its materials from some 250 factories in Bangladesh, shows the growing confidence, proliferation, and concentration of foreign buyers in the Bangladesh RMG industry. http://www.textiletoday.com.bd/enzyme-assisted-eco-friendly-green-textile-processing-2/.
12. However, this has also generated several controversies, raised by many authors, including McMichael (2005) and Saurin (1999).
13. Quotation by Atiqul Islam, general manager (admin, HR, and compliance) of Metro Knitting and Dyeing Mills Limited derived from the features titled "RMG factories turn to technology to maintain competitive advantage", which appeared in the *Dhaka Tribune* on November 28, 2017. Source: https://www.dhakatribune.com/feature/tech/2017/11/27/rmg-sector-software-cutting-technology.

References

ACD. (2015). *Garment workers in Bangladesh: Social impact of the garment industry*. Dhaka: Asian Center for Development.

Adhikari, R., & Weeratunge, C. (2007). Textiles and clothing in South Asia current status and future potential. *South Asia Economic Journal, 8*(2), 171–203.

Ahmed, N. (2009). Sustaining ready-made garment exports from Bangladesh. *Journal of Contemporary Asia, 39*(4), 597–618.

Ahmed, F., Hasan, N., & Kabir, Y. (1997). Vitamin A deficiency among adolescent female garment factory worker in Bangladesh. *European Journal of Clinical Nutrition, 51*, 698–702.

Amin, S. (1998). Family structure and change in rural Bangladesh. *Population Studies, 52*(2), 201–213.

Asuyama, Y., Chhun, D., Fukunishi, T., Neou, S., & Yamagata, T. (2013). Firm dynamics in the Cambodian garment industry: Firm turnover, productivity growth and wage profile under trade liberalization. *Journal of the Asia Pacific Economy, 18*(1), 51–70.

Atkiny, D. (2009). *Working for the future: Female factory work and child health in Mexico*. Department of Economics, Princeton University, Princeton, NJ 08544. Retrieved 21 August 2018 from https://www.semanticscholar.org/paper/Working-for-the-Future-%3A-Female-Factory-Work-and-in-Atkin/df98f16ed7b93e199372039517833f639b59ec6f.

Barrett, C. B., & Carter, M. R. (2010). The power and pitfalls of experiments in development economics: Some non-random reflections. *Applied Economic Perspectives and Policy, 32*(4), 515–548.

BER. (2015). *Bangladesh economic review 2015*. Dhaka: Ministry of Finance.

BGMEA. (2018). *Trade information*. Bangladesh Garment and Exporters Association. Retrieved October 21, 2018, from www.bgmea.com.bd/home/pages/tradeInformation.

BGMEA. (2019). *Trade information*. Bangladesh Garment and Exporters Association. Retrieved January 13, 2019, from www.bgmea.com.bd/home/pages/tradeInformation.

Bhattacharya, D., & Rahman, M. (2000). *Experience with implementation of WTOATC and implications for Bangladesh*. CPD Occasional Paper Series, Paper 7, pp. 1–65.

Bhattacharya, D., Rahman, M., & Raihan, A. (2002). *Contribution of the RMG sector to the Bangladesh economy*. CPD Occasional Paper Series, Paper 50, pp. 1–26.

CPD. (2018). *State of the Bangladesh economy in FY 2017–18*. Dhaka: Centre for Policy Dialogue.

Deussom, R., & Adams, E. (2012). *Ensuring a positive practice environment: Occupational safety and health for health worker productivity*. Retrieved January

16, 2018, from http://www.capacityplus.org/files/resources/ensuring-positive-practice-environmentoccupational-safety-health-worker-productivity.pdf.

EPB. (2017). *Statistical data of exports and imports*. Dhaka: Export Promotion Bureau.

Field, E., & Ambrus, A. (2008). Age of menarche and female schooling attainment in Bangladesh. *Journal of Political Economy, 116*(5), 881–930.

Green, D. (1998). *Fashion victims: Together we can clean up the clothes trade: The Asian garment industry and globalisation*. London: CAFOD.

Heath, R., & Mobarak, A. M. (2015). Manufacturing growth and the lives of Bangladeshi women. *Journal of Development Economics, 115*, 1–15.

Inkpen, A., & Choudhury, N. (1995). The seeking of strategy where it is not: Towards a theory of strategy absence. *Strategic Management Journal, 16*(4), 313–323. Wiley Blackwell.

Islam, S. (2001). *The textile and clothing industry of Bangladesh in a changing world economy*. Dhaka: Centre for Policy Dialogue and University Press Limited.

ITC. (2018). Trade map database. Retrieved November 15, 2018, from https://www.trademap.org/Index.aspx.

Joarder, M. A. M., Hossain, A. K. M. N., & Hakim, M. M. (2010). Post-MFA performance of Bangladesh apparel sector. *International Review of Business Research Papers, 6*(4), 134–144.

Khosla, N. (2013). The ready-made garments industry in Bangladesh: A means to reducing gender-based social exclusion of women? *Journal of International Women's Studies, 11*(1), 289–303.

McMichael, P. (2005). The end of poverty: Economic possibilities for our time [Book review]. *International Journal of Comparative Sociology, 46*, 347–355.

Mlachila, M., & Yang, Y. (2004). *The end of textiles quotas: A case study of the impact on Bangladesh*. IMF Working Paper (WP/04/108).

Mobarak, M. A., & Heath, R. (2014). Manufacturing growth and the lives of Bangladeshi women. *Journal of Development Economics, 115*, 1–15.

Mottaleb, K. A., & Sonobe, T. (2011). An inquiry into the rapid growth of the garment industry in Bangladesh. *Economic Development and Cultural Change, 60*(1), 67–89.

Paul-Majumder, P. (1994). Dynamics of wage employment: A case of employment in the garment industry. In S. Amin (Ed.), [A special issue on women, development and change. The Bangladesh Development Studies (BDS)], *Quarterly Journal of the Bangladesh Institute of Development Studies (BIDS), 22*(2–3), 179–216.

Paul-Majumder, P., & Begum, A. (2000). *The gender imbalances in the export garment industry in Bangladesh: Policy research report on gender and development*. Washington, DC: World Bank.

Qian, R. (2008). Missing women and the price of tea in China: The effect of sex-specific earnings on sex imbalance. *The Quarterly Journal of Economics, 123*(3), 1251–1285.

Quddus, M. (1993). Entrepreneurship in the apparel export industry of Bangladesh. *Journal of Asian Business, 9*(4), 24–46.

Quddus, M., & Rashid, S. (2000). *Entrepreneurship and economic development: The remarkable story of garment exports from Bangladesh*. Dhaka: The University Press Limited.

Rahman, K. M., & Rahman, S. (2016). *International political economy and ready-made garments industry: The case of Bangladesh*. GSCG Project Working Paper. Retrieved from www.garmentgov.de.

Rahman, M., Bhattacharya, D., & Moazzem, K. G. (2008). *Bangladesh apparel sector in post MFA era: A study on the ongoing restructuring process*. Dhaka: Centre for Policy Dialogue.

Rahman, M. H., & Siddiqui, S. A. (2015). Female RMG worker: Economic contribution in Bangladesh. *International Journal of Scientific and Research Publications, 9*(5), 1–9.

Raihan, M. A. (2010). Handloom: An option to fight rural poverty in Bangladesh. *Asia-pacific Journal of Rural Development, 20*(1), 112–130.

Rashid, M. A. (2006). *Rise of readymade garments industry in Bangladesh: Entrepreneurial ingenuity or public policy*. Paper presented at the Workshop on Governance and Development, Dhaka.

Rock, M. (2001). Globalisation and Bangladesh: The case of export-oriented garment manufacture. *South Asia: Journal of South Asian Studies, 24*(1), 201–225.

Rossi, A., & Robertson, R. (2011). Better factories Cambodia: An instrument for improving industrial relations in a transnational context. Forthcoming in K. Papadakis (Ed.), *Practices and outcomes of an emerging global industrial relations framework*. International Labour Organization/Palgrave Macmillan.

Sachs, J. (2005). *The end of poverty: How we can make it happen in our lifetime*. London: Penguin Books.

Saurin, J. (1999). The global production of trade and social movements. In A. Taylor & C. Thomas (Eds.), *Global trade and global social issues* (pp. 217–236). London: Routledge.

Shadat, W., Rahman, T., Rahman, K. M., & Hawlader, A. (2017). Cost benefit analysis of RMG compliance to increasing presence of Ready Made Garment (RMG) and new specialized RMG industry zone (Garments Palli). *Bangladesh Priorities Working Paper*. Copenhagen Consensus Centre.

Siddiqi, H. G. A. (2005). *The ready-made garment industry of Bangladesh* (2nd ed.). Dhaka: The University Press Limited.

Smith, A. (2003). Power relations, industrial clusters, and regional transformations: Pan-European integration and outward processing in the Slovak clothing industry. *Economic Geography, 79*(1), 17–40.

Sobhan, R. (1990). *From aid dependence to self-reliance: Development options for Bangladesh*. Dhaka: University Press Limited (UPL).

Vixathep, S., & Matsunaga, N. (2015). Does human and social capital enhance entrepreneurship? A case study of the garments industry in Bangladesh. *The International Journal of Economic Policy Studies, 10*, 29–50.

Yang, Y., Martin, W., & Yanagishima, K. (1997). Evaluating the benefits of abolishing the MFA in the Uruguay round package. In T. Hertel (Ed.), *Global trade analysis: Using the GTAP model* (pp. 253–279). New York: Cambridge University Press.

Yunus, M., & Yamagata, T. (2012). The garment industry in Bangladesh. In T. Fukunishi (Ed.), *Dynamics of the garment industry in low income countries: Experience of Asia and Africa, interim report* (pp. 1–28). Chousaken Kyu, Huokokusho, IDE-JETRO, Chapter 6.

Zohir, S. C. (2001). Social impact of the growth of garment industry in Bangladesh. *The Bangladesh Development Studies, 27*(4), 41–80.

CHAPTER 10

Pace and Prospects of Light Engineering Sector in the Economic Development of Bangladesh

Mohammad Akhtaruzzaman, Mohammad Monirul Islam Sarker, and Md. Masudur Rahman

Introduction

In recent decades, many role models of spectacular growth and development in the Asian region such as China, South Korea, Taiwan, Thailand, Vietnam, and even Japan have proved that uplifting the light engineering sector (LES) is one of the most effective strategies of rapid growth and

The authors are Executive Director (Research), Deputy General Manager (Research) and Assistant Director (Research) of Bangladesh Bank respectively.
The views expressed in this chapter are the authors' own and do not necessarily reflect institutional views.

M. Akhtaruzzaman (✉) · M. M. I. Sarker · M. M. Rahman
Bangladesh Bank, Dhaka, Bangladesh
e-mail: drmd.akhtaruzzaman@bb.org.bd; mohammad.sarker@bb.org.bd; masud.rahman@bb.org.bd

M. K. Barai (ed.), *Bangladesh's Economic and Social Progress*,
https://doi.org/10.1007/978-981-15-1683-2_10

employment generation. Bangladesh's progress in LES activities is somehow less visible though the country's industrial sector as a whole has been playing an increasingly prominent role in the gross domestic product (GDP). The contribution of the overall industrial sector to the GDP of Bangladesh has significantly increased over the years and its share has reached 32.3 percent in FY18, from 10.3 percent in FY73. As a result, the country's annual GDP growth has registered above 7 percent during FY16-FY18. Although the readymade garment (RMG) is the most significant contributing item to the industrial sector of Bangladesh, there are some newly emerged industrial units/products, particularly the light engineering sector (LES) units/products that have been contributing to the industrial sector in a sustained manner. This LES has slowly but steadily emerged over the last few decades and the contribution of this labor-intensive sector to employment generation is also very important in recent years.

The light engineering sector refers to as a mother industry that supports all other primary industries, such as agriculture and service sector based industries by supplying various types of machinery and spare parts, and by providing repairing services (Ahmed and Bakht 2010). Talukder and Jahan (2016) elaborately defined LES as small firms employing engineering or technological process that produce small machinery, equipment, tool, metallic household appliance, or sanitary ware, and electrical, electronic, and electromechanical products mainly by metals; produce spare parts for different types of industrial, agricultural, automobile, and small machinery; and provide repair services.

Basically, the light engineering sector is an import-substituting industry in Bangladesh that has gradually replaced at least 50 percent of imported engineering items used in industrial, agriculture, and construction sectors (LEPBPC 2018b) during the last two to three decades.[1] In addition, the export of light engineering products has increased strikingly over the years and its share in total exports stood at around 0.97 percent in FY18, against 0.02 percent in FY02 percent. In the context of employment generation, around 600,000 people are involved in 50,000 micro and 10,000 small and medium enterprises of the light engineering sector.[2]

Despite huge potential, particularly as a cost-cutting and intensively capital supplying sector for other industries, the policymakers are relatively less attentive regarding the development of the light engineering sector. In this circumstance, it is vital to analyze the pace and prospects of the light engineering sector that will be very helpful for the policymakers to support this sector for further development.

In this backdrop, the broad objectives of this study are to assess the current pace and future prospects of the light engineering sector in Bangladesh economy, while the specific objectives are as below.

- To discuss the evolution and expansion of the light engineering sector in Bangladesh's economy.
- To analyze the contribution of the light engineering sector to Bangladesh's economy.
- To project the future prospects of the light engineering sector in the economy of Bangladesh.
- To identify the major challenges and remedial measures for the development of the light engineering sector in Bangladesh.

To fulfill these objectives, this chapter follows both qualitative and quantitative analyses and uses descriptive research techniques. Different tables and charts are used to analyze the quantitative part of this chapter. Regarding data sources, the existing literature, including journal articles, working papers, magazine and newspaper articles, website articles, and reports are the primary sources of inputs of this chapter, particularly for qualitative data. Regarding quantitative data, we heavily rely on the Bangladesh Bureau of Statistics, Bangladesh Bank, Export Promotion Bureau, and the Ministry of Planning.

Regarding the structure of this chapter, section "Review of Existing Literature" reviews the existing literature, after introducing the background, objectives, methodology, and data sources in section "Introduction". Section "Evolution of Light Engineering Sector in Bangladesh" discusses the evolution of the light engineering sector in Bangladesh. The contribution of the light engineering sector to the Bangladesh economy is analyzed in section "Contribution of Light Engineering Sector to Bangladesh Economy". Section "Prospects of Light Engineering Sector" projects the prospects of the light engineering sector in Bangladesh. Section "Impediments in the Light Engineering Sector" tries to identify the major challenges for the development of the light engineering sector. Finally, the concluding remarks, along with policy recommendations are outlined in section "Concluding Remarks and Recommendations".

Review of Existing Literature

The existing literature directly related to the topic of this study is relatively scarce. However, there are some recent studies related to the light engineering sector of Bangladesh that are reviewed here briefly. Ahmed and Bakht (2010) found that the local market of the light engineering sector in Bangladesh is very big, along with strong forward and backward linkages. There is sufficient demand for light engineering products within the various manufacturing units such as textile mills, readymade garments, railways, jute mills, shoe manufacturers, sugar mills, pharmaceuticals, washing plants, and so on. It has the potential for producing import-substituting goods if proper support is given. The export potential of LES products has also edged up due to the low cost of production, resulted mainly from low labor costs based on extensive use of family labor.

Haque (2013) opined that the light engineering sector has emerged in Bangladesh as import substitution option and been providing vital support to industrial, agricultural, and construction sectors by manufacturing a wide range of spare parts, castings, molds and dices, oil and gas pipeline fittings, and light machinery as well as repairing those. The electrical goods like the bulb, switch, socket, light shed, channel, cables, electrical fans, and generator that are manufactured by LES, are now meeting 48–52 percent of domestic demand, earlier met through import. The LES also provides backup support to cement, paper, jute, rice, textile, sugar, food processing, railway, shipping, and garments industries by repairing and maintaining the capital machinery used in those industries. Thus in many ways, this sector contributes significantly to save hard-earned foreign currency as well as to employment generation.

Hoque (2016) assessed the current upgrading conditions and factors of the light engineering sector of Bangladesh and found a disappointing result. To discover the reasons for such a disappointing result, they collected data from three light engineering clusters of Bangladesh and identified the lack of government's fiscal, financial, and other forms of support in this context.

Talukder and Jahan (2016) emphasized on the development of the light engineering sector that supports the development of the manufacturing sector, needed for sustainable and inclusive economic growth. In this regard, they emphasized the preparedness of institutions that supports the development of the light engineering sector. They thought that the institutions should understand the requirements of the small-scale manufacturing sector, particularly the light engineering sector.

Talukder and Jahan (2017) observed that the indigenous light engineering talents of *Dholaikhal* and *Jinjira* had long been a lifeline for the related and allied manufacturing industries and the automobile sector of Bangladesh. But they were passing hard times, and the government institutions were not supporting them to face the challenges and capture the opportunities of their competitiveness and growth. The researchers attempted to assess the major hindrances of achieving competitiveness and growth for the light engineering sector through a qualitative study that conducted depth interview of the micro, small, and medium-sized enterprise (MSME) owners and validation workshop and found that the major hindrance for the competitiveness and growth were cultural factors such as less preference of consumers to use locally made products, rather than popular view of resource scarcity.

Ahmad and Jahan (2017) observed that the demand for light engineering products is dominated by imported goods, though the workers of the light engineering sector in Bangladesh are highly efficient and their products are not very far behind in comparison with imported ones. They found that relatively wrong perceptions and attitudes of buyers toward local products related to the quality and durability of the local products are the main reason for the dominance of imported light engineering goods.

Banik and Swarna (2018) tried to assess the sector-based need of the light engineering sector of Bangladesh using both qualitative and quantitative methods. They showed that the non-existence of common facilities like lack of metal and heat treatment facilities, constraints related to finance, old and manual technology, unfair competition in the domestic market, accreditation of certification of standards, and so on are the major issues for the light engineering sector.

The existing literature reviewed so far discussed the importance of the light engineering sector in Bangladesh's economy emphasizing its domestic demand. They also discussed the major hindrances of this sector for further development. In this backdrop, this study attempts to analyze the evolution, expansion, contribution, and the prospects of the light engineering sector in Bangladesh with special emphasis on its external demand.

Evolution of Light Engineering Sector in Bangladesh

The light engineering sector (LES) is a sub-sector of small and medium enterprises (SMEs). The development of LES was not so remarkable at the initial period of Independent Bangladesh, mainly due to a lack of government support. The policymakers in Bangladesh always emphasize the large industries, an extravagant popular spree inherited from the Pakistan period. However, some supportive policy measures were implemented during the 1980s through Bangladesh Small and Cottage Industries Corporation (BSCIC) that created a boom in the small industries, including the light engineering sector. But the impact of such policy measures dwindled over the years. Also, the government adopted some wrong policy measures during the 1990s, possibly influenced by vested interest groups that favored imports over the local production, and produced mainly in the small and medium enterprises (Rabbani 2005). Nonetheless, the small and medium enterprises, particularly the light engineering sector (including auto-parts and bicycles) has expanded strikingly in recent years, and thus the government declared it as one of the high priority sectors since 2009 (Government of Bangladesh 2009). The light engineering sector comprises so many sub-sectors, which are summarized in Table 10.1. These sub-sectors of LES are currently producing a total of 3815 types of quality machinery, accessories, and spare parts (LEPBPC 2018a).

Table 10.1 Sub-sectors of the light engineering sector in Bangladesh

1. Automobiles spare parts	15. Metal furniture
2. Railway engine and rail line spare parts	16. Paper and pulp machinery and spare parts
3. Bicycle and cycle rickshaw	17. Mold and dies
4. Machine tools	18. Components and spare parts of gas transmission and distribution
5. Chemical industries machines and spare parts	19. Printing and packaging machinery and spare parts
6. Sugar and food industries machines and spare parts	20. Poultry machinery and spare parts
7. Engineering and metal industries spare parts	21. Kitchenware and bathroom fittings
8. Agriculture machinery and spare parts	22. Metal product and hardware
9. Motor launch and marine transport spare parts	23. LP GAS cylinder and fire extinguisher
10. Textile machinery and spare parts	24. Pharmaceutical machinery and spare parts
11. Jute machinery and spare parts	25. Ship industries spare parts
12. Tea plant machinery and spare parts	
13. Construction machinery and spare parts	
14. Bread, biscuit, and food processing machinery and spare parts	

Source: Ahmad and Jahan (2017) and LEPBPC (2018a)

There are some estimates regarding the expansion of the light engineering sector in Bangladesh. About 1200 light engineering industrial enterprises currently enlisted in BSCIC which are supplying various types of products under the *subcontracting scheme* (LEPBPC 2018a). The light engineering enterprises are scattered throughout the country. However, most of the LES enterprises are located mainly at Dhaka, Chattogram, Narayanganj, Bogura, Gazipur, Rangpur, Sylhet, and Khulna, and in each region/district they are concentrated with specific products (Table 10.2).

Contribution of Light Engineering Sector to Bangladesh Economy

The light engineering sector has emerged as the cornerstone of development, providing the platform for industrial growth, enhancement of trade, and economic prosperity. It has the potency to play a significant role in

Table 10.2 Regional product concentration of light engineering sector in Bangladesh

Region	*Product concentration*
Rangpur	Spare parts of automobiles, railway, mills, maintenance works, and so on.
Sylhet	Spare parts of factories, mills, maintenance work, and so on.
Dhaka/ Gazipur/ Narayanganj	Capital machinery, bicycle, construction equipment and spare parts of automobiles, electrical accessories (fan, switch, circuit breaker, etc.), factory mills, maintenance works, and so on.
Barishal/ Khulna	Spare parts of mills, factories and industries, maintenance works, and so on.
Bogura	Foundry, agro machinery, spare parts of mills factories, LPG cylinder and maintenance works, and so on.
Chattogram	Spare parts of shipbuilding, shipbreaking industry, automobiles, factory mills and maintenance work, and so on.
Khulna	Spare parts and complete machinery of processing mills (rice, flour, jute, etc.), tube well, water pump, and spare parts of brick manufacturing machine.

Source: Government of Bangladesh (2011)

technological and economic development along with a vast scope of employment generation. This section has investigated the contribution of the light engineering sector to the Bangladesh economy, particularly about domestic demand, external demand, employment generation, and industrial sector development are outlined separately.

Contribution to Domestic Demand

The demand for light engineering products has significantly increased in Bangladesh due to the expansion of both industry and service sectors, and *the use of modern technology in the agricultural sector*. The domestic demand for light engineering products was mostly met by imported goods in the earlier, but the scenario has changed over the years. At present, about 50 percent of local demand for light engineering products is met by local productions (LEPBPC 2018b). In another way, about 90 percent of local light engineering enterprises are engaged in meeting the local demand for light engineering products (LEPBPC 2018a).

Contribution to External Demand

The exports of Bangladesh light engineering products significantly increased over the years (Fig. 10.1 and Table 10.3). During FY11-FY17, the trend growth of LES export was 11.4 percent, while that of total export was 7.4 percent. As a result, the trend of the ratio of LES exports in total exports of Bangladesh was increasing, particularly from FY14. But the increasing trend of the exports of LES products drastically declined in FY18 mainly due to low domestic production as well as weak domestic and external demand.

In FY18, the growth of Bangladesh LES production stood at only 1.0 percent, while it was 23.9 percent in FY17 (Source: BBS). The slow growth of LES production in FY18 resulted from low demand in the agricultural sector, reinforced by flood-related damage to a vast area. In the case of external demand, the decreasing trend of the world demand for LES products (HS71-HS88) was important in this regard. Thus the world imports for LES products stood at USD7552 billion in 2017, while it was USD8097 billion in 2014 (Source: UN Comtrade). However, the growth of both production and exports of LES items has been increasing in the current fiscal year (FY19). Thus the growth of LES production stood at

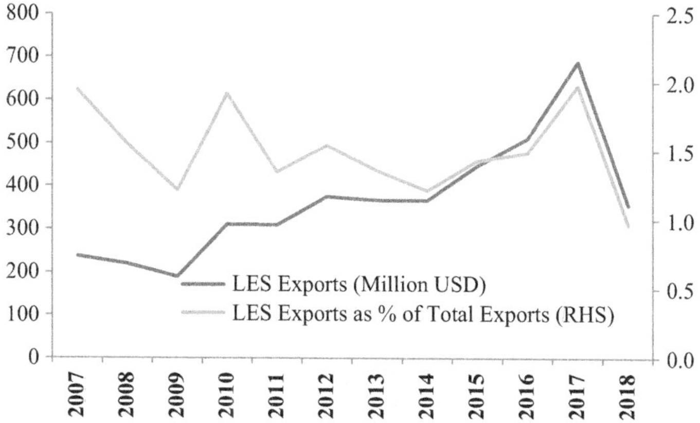

Fig. 10.1 Export performance of LES in Bangladesh. (Source: Export Promotion Bureau)

Table 10.3 Exports of the light engineering sector in Bangladesh (million USD)

Products (HS Code)	*FY10*	*FY11*	*FY12*	*FY13*	*FY14*	*FY15*	*FY16*	*FY17*	*FY18*
Iron and steel (72, 73)	60.42	69.79	59.73	56.81	54.33	57.90	48.56	58.83	48.55
Copper wire (74)	110.86	99.83	50.93	66.38	49.17	27.88	24.47	36.09	53.18
Stainless steel ware (82)	26.11	36.03	3.20	1.58	5.36	3.89	9.22	7.82	4.37
Engineering equipment (84)	23.20	26.07	49.54	48.73	63.06	83.03	174.80	271.09	41.38
Electric products (85)	49.23	65.04	88.53	63.09	54.63	90.11	65.00	68.94	61.96
Bicycle (8712)	2.67	2.43	105.59	105.08	112.89	126.06	99.15	82.46	85.73
Others	38.60	10.36	17.97	25.80	27.19	58.17	88.88	163.61	60.79
Total	311.09	309.55	375.49	367.47	366.63	447.04	510.08	688.84	355.96

Source: Export Promotion Bureau

6.8 percent in July–August 2018 (calculated over the production in July–August 2017), and that of LES exports stood at 7.9 percent for July–December 2018 (calculated over the exports in July–December 2018). Therefore, the overall trend of the exports of Bangladesh LES products is generally increasing in recent years, except for the year 2018. Among the sub-sectors of LES, the largest amount of export earnings comes from bicycle followed by electrical products, copper wire, iron and steel, engineering equipment, and stainless steel ware (Table 10.3).

Contribution to Employment Generation

Although light engineering is a capital intensive sector, it is slightly different in the case of Bangladesh due to lack of capital availability and thus the limited use of modern technology. Therefore, light engineering has remained a labor-intensive sector yet in Bangladesh. In addition, the people who work in this sector are mostly low educated and unskilled, and they work based on their human measurements and judgments instead of any computer-aided designs (Ahmad and Jahan 2017). They apply simple indigenous technology which is available and easy to learn. However, they become skilled after a certain period. In this way, the light engineering sector has been keeping a vital role in generating employment in Bangladesh. According to the estimate of the Planning Commission, around 700,000 people were engaged in the light engineering sector of Bangladesh in 2010 (Government of Bangladesh 2011). A recent study conducted by International Finance Corporation (IFC) in partnership with UK Department for International Development and Norwegian government showed that the light engineering sector in Bangladesh has employed around 600,000 people in its 50,000 micro-enterprises and 10,000 small and medium enterprises (Ahmad and Jahan 2017). Another study conducted by Bangladesh University of Engineering and Technology (BUET), however, estimated that the light engineering sector in Bangladesh comprises around 40,000 enterprises employing around 800,000 people (LEPBPC 2018b). In addition to such employment, there are so many people who are engaged in both forward and backward linkage industries of the light engineering sector.

Contribution to Industrial Sector Development

As mentioned earlier, the light engineering sector is a mother industry that supports all other primary industries including agriculture and service sector based industries by supplying various types of machinery and spare parts, and by providing repair services. In this way, the industrial sector of Bangladesh has been using about 90 percent of products of the light engineering sector that have been substituting about 50 percent of imported light engineering products used in both industries and household consumption. Thus the role of the light engineering sector in the development of the manufacturing industry in Bangladesh is very important.

Prospects of Light Engineering Sector

The prospect of the light engineering sector in Bangladesh's economy is highly positive due to both demand and supply-side factors. As mentioned earlier, the demand for light engineering products in the domestic market has been increasing because of the expansion of industry and service sectors and the use of modern technology in the agriculture sector.

Besides, the reliance on domestic LES products has been increasing due to their increasingly better quality as well as low prices, resulted from low labor wages. The existence oflow wages is a great advantage for Bangladeshi products, including light engineering, to compete in the international market.

As shown in Fig. 10.2, Bangladesh is the fourth country in Asia in the context of monthly minimum wage after Nepal, Sri Lanka, and Myanmar.

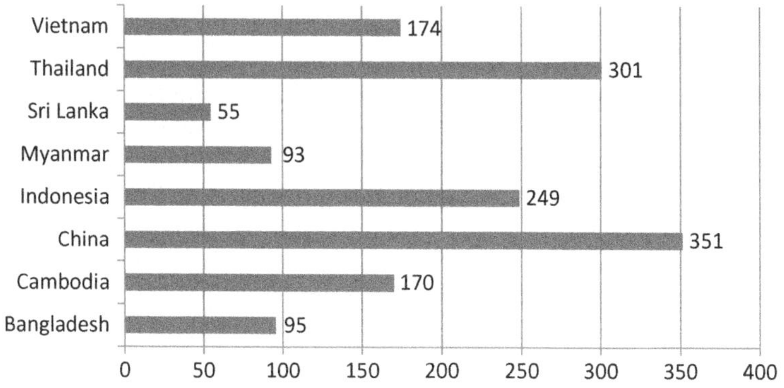

Fig. 10.2 Cross countries' minimum wage in December 2018 (USD/Month). (Source: https://tradingeconomics.com/country-list/minimum-wages?continent=asia)

Fig. 10.3 Share of destination countries of Bangladesh's Exports of LES Products, 2015. (Source: UN Comtrade)

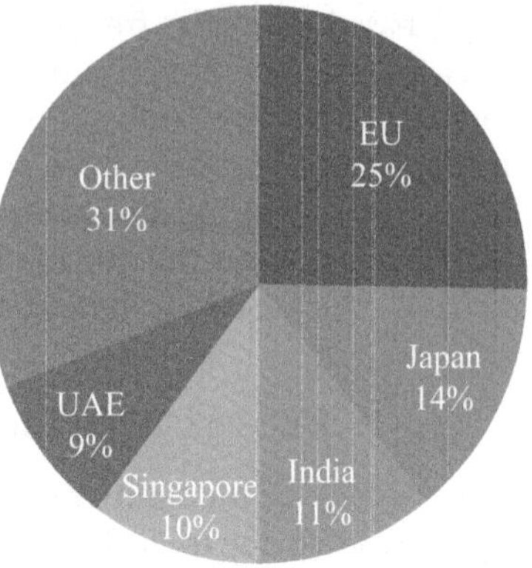

The existence of surplus labor is the main reason behind the low wage in Bangladesh. This excess labor is also the strength of the Bangladesh economy if it can employ to produce more products, including the engineering sector, to meet both domestic and external demand.

Regarding external demand, the EU is the largest destination of Bangladeshi light engineering products followed by Japan, India, Singapore, and the UAE (Fig. 10.3). Among them, Bangladesh, as Least Developed Country (LDC), has been enjoying duty-free access, that is, the generalized system of preferences, from the EU and Japan, the first two largest destinations.[3] The GSP facility will be existed up to 2027, though Bangladesh is going to overcome the LDC status in 2024.[4] As shown in Fig. 10.3, the export of light engineering products is diversified compared to other major export items of Bangladesh, particularly the readymade garments that go mostly to the EU and the USA, around 80 percent. Besides, the share of Asian countries in total exports of light engineering products is significantly high (60.3 percent) compared to the other major export items. Therefore, the diversified structure of the light engineering sector gives a good message for its rapid expansion in the near future. Also, the government initiatives, adopted in the *current 7th Five Year Plan (FY16-FY20)* are also very helpful for the development of this sector. Among them, the cash incentive on the production as well as export earnings of light engineering products is especially mentionable here. At present, the government has been providing 15 percent cash incentives on the exports of light engineering products, starting from July 1, 2018, which will play a critical role in enjoying the fastest growth of LES production as well as exports in the coming years. In addition, the government is also going to provide duty-free imports of raw material for light engineering products under the 7th Five Year Plan (GOB 2016) which will play another vital role to boost the LES production and exports.

The expansion of the light engineering sector is good news for the economic development of the country, but bad for employment, particularly in the agricultural sector as the use of machinery in the agricultural sector enhances the volume of labor surplus. However, the development of the industrial sector, induced mainly by the expansion of LES, can absorb surplus labor, as suggested by Lewis (1954). In this way, the light engineering sector can offer alternative employment opportunities to surplus labor, particularly by developing labor-intensive industries like readymade garments. In this regard, the example of China is well fitted here. China's real GDP per capita grew at a rate of 8.16 percent between 1978 and 2004 mainly for a large-scale reallocation of labor from agriculture to the manufacturing and service sector. Thus, the share of the agricultural sector in total employment declined from 69 percent in 1978 to 32 percent in 2004 (Brandt et al. 2008). In the case of Vietnam, Kien (2014) revealed that the manufacturing sector of Vietnam improved enough to attract massive amounts of unskilled workers from agriculture. Maddison (1991) estimated changing the share of employment in agriculture, industries, and services sectors of sixteen leading industrial countries.[5] In his estimate, between the years 1870 and 1987, agriculture's share of employment fell steadily, while the share of industries and services increased gradually.

In the case of Bangladesh, a healthy expansion of employment-intensive manufacturing especially garments and knitwear have already increased the share of employment in the manufacturing sector by 35 percent between 1991 and 2010 (Khan 2015). Using micro-level survey data, Hossain and Bayes (2007) reported that the proportion of rural workers employed in the household farms fell from 45 percent in 1988 to 41 percent in 2004, and the ratio of workers employed in non-agricultural work increased from 30 percent in 1988 to 47 percent in 2004, which represents an important changes in the occupational distribution of workers from agriculture to industry in Bangladesh.[6] The growing automation in agriculture will further contribute to the decline of employment in this sector, where the light engineering sector can play a significant role in providing alternative job opportunities for them.

Impediments in the Light Engineering Sector

The light engineering sector in Bangladesh started its journey at *Dholaikhal* and *Jinjira* in Dhaka based on indigenous talents who were mostly illiterate and untrained. Although the sector has remarkably spread out all over the country over the years, the workers are still low educated and untrained. Thus, the workers are low skilled compared to other countries that use educated, trained people in this sector. Another impediment in the light engineering sector of Bangladesh is the use of conventional technologies and indigenous machinery instead of modern technology and hi-tech machinery (Hoque 2016). As a result, labor productivity in the light engineering sector of Bangladesh is very low compared to that of the competitive countries, particularly China and India.

There are some other noticeable impediments in the light engineering sector of Bangladesh, which are mentioned in Haque (2013). These are: (i) the absence of cluster development projects including common facility center, (ii) absence of basic steel industry, (iii) absence of international standard laboratory for testing the quality of light engineering products, (iv) insufficient marketing ability for export promotion, and (v) little care taken to address environmental hazards and human safety aspect, especially in shipbreaking yards from where raw materials are being procured.

The light engineering sector in Bangladesh mostly consists of micro, small, and medium enterprises (MSMEs), though there is scope for large industries to come up with strong brands in the sector. Also, as an import substitution sector, more innovative and technologically advanced enterprises have a huge scope for success in the light engineering sector. The shortage of capital is one of the important reasons behind the establishment of large industry and the low use of modern technology in the light engineering sector in Bangladesh. Besides, the reluctance of domestic buyers for local products is another reason for the advancement of the light engineering sector in Bangladesh (Ahmad and Jahan 2017). Also, the undeveloped infrastructure, particularly the low supply of gas and electricity, and undeveloped transportation are significant obstacles for the development of the industrial sector, including light engineering.

Concluding Remarks and Recommendations

Though the industrial sector of Bangladesh has significantly expanded over the years, it is concentrated in some specific industries, particularly to readymade garments. Thus the share of readymade garments in GDP (around 10 percent), exports (around 83 percent) and employment (around 10 percent) is very high compared to other industries. This scenario warrants diversification in the industrial sector for sustainable development. In this context, the expansion of the light engineering sector as an integral component of SMEs' development can help rapid growth of the industrial sector and the overall economy in three ways. First, it can gear up the economic activities by providing necessary engineering equipment to other sectors of the economy, as a mother industry. Second, it can improve the country's trade balance by providing with products as import substitutions as well as for export. Third, it can directly enhance the country's GDP and employment level.

From the analysis of this study, it is observed that the light engineering sector in Bangladesh has strikingly expanded during the last couple of years and contributed to GDP, exports, and employment generations. But it has been facing lots of impediments particularly from the domestic segments that need to mitigate for further development of this sector. In this regard, we suggest the following policy measures.

- The light engineering sector in Bangladesh is unorganized and scattered all over the country. No specific rules and regulations are followed in this sector about production and marketing at home and abroad. So, the government should initiate to organize this sector by formulating specific rules and regulations.
- As mentioned earlier, the productivity in LES is low due to unskilled labor, resulted from low education and training of the workers. So, the governments should emphasize on the vocational training for the workers and establish more training institutions in both public and private level. In this regard, the government should build more technical colleges and vocational institutions to create mid-level as well as elementary level skilled manpower for the light engineering sector.
- Technological upgradation is a critical issue for the development of the light engineering sector. The government should emphasize this issue and creates a fund for research on it.
- As mentioned earlier, domestic buyers are very reluctant to buy local products. Besides, international buyers are less attracted to the Bangladeshi light engineering product due to the absence of international standard brands. Therefore, the initiatives should be taken from both the public and private levels to make the products visible in the domestic and international markets. The creation of an international standard brand is very important here.

- As the light engineering sector stands on small and medium enterprises, they face a financial crisis in many times. Therefore, ensuring the bank finance with a low-interest rate is very significant for the development of this sector. Besides, the government should initiate to create large-scale enterprises by providing necessary supports, including bank financing and interest rate subsidies.
- The government should emphasis infrastructure development particularly the smooth supply of gas and electricity, traffic-free transportation for the development of the industrial sector including LES.
- To boost up both the quality and quantity of light engineering products, the government can establish a light engineering industrial zone along with the establishment of metal and quality testing facilities.
- To boost up the exports of light engineering products, the facilities like the cash incentive on export earnings and the tax waiver on the imported raw materials, used in the production of LES, should be continued, expanded, and enhanced gradually. The Export Promotion Bureau should send business missions to advertise regarding light engineering products abroad. Besides, the Bangladeshi LES product should introduce in the international trade fair.
- Finally, the government should emphasize the research for the development of the light engineering sector and ensure the necessary fund, market facilitation services, and the availability of required data on this industry.

Notes

1. LEPBPC stands for Light Engineering Product Business Promotion Council.
2. According to a recent study conducted by the International Finance Corporation in partnership with the UK Department for International Development and the Norwegian government.
3. Bangladesh has the GSP facility from 38 countries, including the 28 members of the EU. The other GSP providing countries are Australia, Belarus, Canada, Japan, New Zealand, Norway, the Russian Federation, Switzerland, Liechtenstein, and Turkey.
4. After graduation in 2024, there will be a grace period of another 3 years when Bangladesh can enjoy all LDC-specific benefits (Khatun 2018).
5. The countries are Australia, Austria, Belgium, Canada, Denmark, Finland, France, Germany, Italy, Japan, Netherlands, Norway, Sweden, Switzerland, the United Kingdom, and the United States.

6. According to the latest Labor Force Survey 2016–17, published by Bangladesh Bureau of Statistics, 40.6 percent of the employed population are working in agriculture, followed by 39.0 percent in services and 20.4 percent in the industry sector of Bangladesh. Therefore, further development of LES in terms of both productivity and quality will also contribute to this overall industrial employment.

References

Ahmad, F. U., & Jahan, S. M. (2017). Demand dynamics of light engineering sector of Bangladesh and recommendations for local enterprises. *IOSR Journal of Business and Management (IOSR-JBM), 19*(1), 1–7.

Ahmed, N., & Bakht, Z. (2010). *Light engineering industry in Bangladesh: A case study.* Dhaka: Bangladesh Institute of Development Studies.

Banik, T. C., & Swarna, N. R. (2018). A study on sector-based need assessment of light engineering sector of Bangladesh. *American Journal of Economics, 8*(6), 244–253.

Brandt, L., Hsieh, C., & Zhu, X. (2008). Growth and structural transformation in China. In L. Brandt (Ed.), *China's great economic transformation.* Cambridge University Press.

Government of Bangladesh (GOB). (2009). *Export Policy, 2009–12.* Ministry of Commerce, Government of Bangladesh.

Government of Bangladesh. (2011). *Sixth Five Year Plan: FY11–FY15.* Ministry of Planning, Government of Bangladesh.

Government of Bangladesh. (2016). *Seventh Five Year Plan: FY16–FY20.* Ministry of Planning, Government of Bangladesh.

Haque, S. A. (2013, November). Light engineering sector of Bangladesh: An import substitution option. *IDLC Monthly Business Review.*

Hoque, I. (2016). Upgrading status of light engineering clusters in Bangladesh: An analysis. *D. U. Journal of Marketing, 16*(2), 1–16.

Hossain, M., & Bayes, A. (2007). Progress in rural economy in Bangladesh: Insights from repeat sample survey. In *Development prospects of Bangladesh: Emerging challenges.* Dhaka: NFPCSP.

Khan, A. R. (2015). *The economy of Bangladesh: A quarter century of development.* New York: Palgrave Macmillan.

Khatun, F. (2018, March 20). LDC graduation: What it means for Bangladesh. *The Daily Star.* Dhaka.

Kien, N. T. (2014). Employment transformation in the Vietnamese economy in light of the Lewis-Fei-Ranis growth model of a labor-abundant economy. *Journal of Economics and Development, 16*(3), 49–67.

LEPBPC. (2018a). An abridged overview of Bangladesh light engineering product. Retrieved January 2, 2019, from http://www.bpc.org.bd/lepbpc_bridge_overview.php.

LEPBPC. (2018b). Current status of light engineering sector in Bangladesh. Retrieved December 29, 2018, from http://www.bpc.org.bd/lepbpc_current_sector_profile.php.

Lewis, W. A. (1954). Economic development with unlimited supplies of labor. *The Manchester School of Economic and Social Studies, 22*(2), 139–191.

Maddison, A. (1991). *Dynamic forces in capitalist development: A long-run comparative view*. New York: Oxford University Press.

Rabbani, K. S. (2005). Economic Policy Paper on Light Engineering and Electronics Enterprise in Bangladesh. Dhaka: The Dhaka Chamber of Commerce and Industry (DCCI) & The Center for International Private Enterprise (CIPE).

Talukder, M. A., & Jahan, S. M. (2016). Light engineering business ecosystem in Bangladesh: A study on institutional preparedness. *IOSR Journal of Business and Management (IOSR-JBM), 18*(12), 16–26.

Talukder, M. A., & Jahan, S. M. (2017). Competitiveness and growth hindrances of light engineering industry of Bangladesh: A study on Micro, Small and Medium-Sized Enterprise (MSME) owners. *Developing Countries Studies, 7*(2), 30–41.

PART V

Role of Government and NGOs for Development

CHAPTER 11

Explaining Bangladesh's Development Puzzle: Government's Approaches and Civil Servants' Accountability

Swapan Kumar Bala

Introduction

In November 2012, *The Economist* noted that 'basket case' was the dismissive term for Bangladesh used in 1971, by Henry Kissinger, the then US President's adviser for national security affairs.[1] In their book *Bangladesh: The Test Case for Development*, Faaland and Parkinson (1976: 194) concluded: "If development can be made to succeed in Bangladesh, there can

Swapan Kumar Bala, PhD, FCMA, is a Commissioner of Bangladesh Securities and Exchange Commission (BSEC), and a Professor (on deputation) at Department of Accounting & Information Systems, University of Dhaka, Dhaka. The views expressed here are of his own and not linked with his institutional capacities.

S. K. Bala (✉)
Bangladesh Securities and Exchange Commission (BSEC), Dhaka, Bangladesh

Department of Accounting & Information Systems, University of Dhaka, Dhaka, Bangladesh
e-mail: skbala@du.ac.bd

M. K. Barai (ed.), *Bangladesh's Economic and Social Progress*,
https://doi.org/10.1007/978-981-15-1683-2_11

be little doubt that it can be made to succeed anywhere else. It is in this sense that Bangladesh is the test case for development." However, after about 31 years in a revisionist article (initially presented in December 2007 and published in 2009),[2] they have revised their assessment of Bangladesh from 'a uniquely difficult case of development' in early 1970s to 'a successful case of development' at the later stage of the first decade of the twenty-first century with the following note:

> Bangladesh, in its early years, seemed to us to have the characteristics of a real country test case of development. At this point, with three decades and more of experience of limited and chequered progress, sustained development in Bangladesh appears to us within reach, though far from assured. (Faaland and Parkinson 2009: 36)

As a war-ravaged country, in the first year of its independent beginning, Bangladesh lost the gross domestic product (GDP) by around 14 percent. It took more than three decades for its transition from the 'darkness of despair' to 'sunlight of hope' (Khan 2010: 132). The country achieved 6 percent-plus growth for the first time in 2003–04. Then it broke the 6 percent growth rate trap in 2015–16. The pace of growth rate has been continuing to surpass the preceding year since then (7.28 percent in 2016–17 and 7.86 percent in 2017–18). Table 11.1 summarizes the GDP growth picture of Bangladesh from FY 1971–72 to FY 2018–19.

But the economic and social progress in Bangladesh has not ensured good governance, an essential element to run a society toward a cherished path of development. As per the Worldwide Governance Indicators, 2018, the rank of Bangladesh's governance position is not at all satisfactory (see Table 11.2). Even in comparison to last year, the most recent year's situation has slightly deteriorated in cases of 'Voice and Accountability,' 'Political Stability and Absence of Violence/Terrorism,' and 'Regulatory Quality.' However, in the case of 'Rule of Law,' the situation is stable, and the condition of 'Control of Corruption' has improved slightly.

In the backdrop of the poor state of governance, the steady economic and social progress of Bangladesh seems to be a 'development puzzle.' The main objective of this chapter is to explain this puzzle in the contexts of government policy initiatives toward this growth paradox and also from the viewpoint of the delivery of services by the civil servants or government executives of Bangladesh within a new framework of accountability.

Table 11.1 Growth of GDP in Bangladesh (%)

Financial year (FY)/plan period	*Annual average target*	*Actual*
FY 1971–72[a]	–	−14.0
FY 1972–73[a]	–	7.6
First Five Year Plan (FY74–FY78)[b]	5.5	4.0
Two Year Plan (FY79–FY80)[b]	5.6	3.5
Second Five Year Plan (FY81–FY85)[b]	5.4	3.8
Third Five Year Plan (FY86–FY90)[b]	5.4	3.8
Fourth Five Year Plan (FY91–FY95)[b]	5.0	4.2
FY 1995–96[c]	6.0[e]	4.6
FY 1996–97[c]	5.5[e]	5.4
Fifth Five Year Plan (FY98–FY02)[b]	7.1	5.1
FY03–FY06[b]	5.9[e]	5.5
FY07–FY10[b]	6.5[e]	6.3
FY 2010–11[d]	6.7[e]	6.5
Sixth Five Year Plan (FY11–FY15)[f]	7.3	6.3
Seventh Five Year Plan (FY16–FY20)[f]	7.4	–
FY 2015–16[d]	7.0[e]	7.1
FY 2016–17[d]	7.2[e]	7.3
FY 2017–18[d]	7.4[e]	7.9
FY 2018–19[d]	7.8[e]	8.13[g]

Sources: [a]Khan (2010), p. 134; [b]Both target and actual figures from Government of Bangladesh (GOB) (2011), *Sixth Five Year Plan–FY2011–FY2015: Accelerating Growth and Reducing Poverty*, p. 12; [c]Actual figures from GOB (2005), *Bangladesh Economic Review 2005*, p. 252; [d]Actual figures from GOB (2018a), *Bangladesh Economic Review 2018*, p. 252; [e]Target figures (which are averages in cases of multiple years) taken from the corresponding FY's Budget Speech; [f]Both target and actual figures from GOB (2015b), *Seventh Five Year Plan FY2016–FY2020: Accelerating Growth, Empowering Citizens*, pp. xlviii-2; [g]*Budget Speech 2019–20* (dated 13 June 2019) (see Kamal, 2019), p. 17

Note: FY74 = FY 1973–74; FY91 = FY 1990–91; and FY02 = FY 2001–02

Prior Studies

Khan (2010) has seen the success of Bangladesh in three decades after its birth as a denial of 'the last laugh to Kissingers and Cassandras.' Apart from robust increase in per capita income, Khan (2010) identifies five significant achievements: (i) increase in life expectancy; (ii) arresting population growth; (iii) increase in food production; (iv) reduction in poverty; and (v) reduction of aid-dependence (Khan 2010: 132–136). In Bangladesh, life expectancy was 42 years in 1960, 47 years in 1977, 64 years in 2001, and 72 years in 2017; average annual population growth rate was 2.31 percent in 1981, 2.04 percent in 1991, 1.41 percent in 2001, and 1.34 percent in 2017; average yearly food production during

Table 11.2 Governance indicators of Bangladesh (1996–2017)

Year	*V&A*	PS&AV/T	*GE*	*RQ*	*RL*	*CC*
1996	50.00	26.60	27.32	17.93	20.10	17.74
1998	47.26	33.51	38.86	19.69	21.00	30.93
2000	44.78	24.87	30.77	18.46	22.28	10.66
2002	37.31	19.05	28.06	17.86	21.29	2.02
2003	31.84	16.58	24.49	18.37	15.84	2.02
2004	27.88	10.19	20.20	12.32	15.79	1.46
2005	30.29	4.37	19.12	15.69	17.70	3.41
2006	32.21	8.70	22.93	16.67	20.57	3.41
2007	31.25	9.18	27.67	17.48	22.97	13.59
2008	33.17	9.62	25.24	17.48	25.00	15.05
2009	38.39	9.00	24.40	21.53	24.17	13.88
2010	36.97	9.95	26.32	22.01	25.59	14.76
2011	36.15	9.00	24.64	22.75	27.70	14.22
2012	34.74	9.00	24.17	18.96	18.31	21.33
2013	34.74	7.58	23.70	21.33	21.13	20.85
2014	32.02	16.67	22.60	17.79	23.56	19.23
2015	30.54	10.00	24.04	18.27	25.96	22.12
2016	30.54	10.95	25.48	22.12	28.37	18.75
2017	30.05	10.48	22.12	20.67	28.37	19.23

Source: info.worldbank.org/governance/wgi/index.aspx?fileName=wgidataset.xlsx (accessed January 12, 2019)

Notes: V&A = Voice and Accountability; PS&AV/T = Political Stability and Absence of Violence/Terrorism; GE = Government Effectiveness; RQ = Regulatory Quality; RL = Rule of Law; and CC = Control of Corruption. Figures indicate the percentile rank among all countries (ranges from 0 (lowest) to 100 (highest) rank)

1994–95 was 18.1 million metric tons (MMT), 26.5 MMT in 2004–05, and 41.3 MMT in 2017–18; percentage of population below the poverty line has declined from 70 percent in 1970 to 40 percent in 2005, to 31.5 percent in 2010 and to 24.3 percent in 2017; and in 2007 per capita aid to Bangladesh was only $9 against the average per capita aid to low income countries of $31 and the weighted average per capita aid to all low and middle-income countries of $16; although per capita external aid in Bangladesh was $132 in 1993–94, which was increased to $177 in 2016–17) (Khan 2010: 132–136; GOB 2018a).

Also, Khan (2010) has advanced *six hypotheses* in an attempt to explain the puzzle of Bangladesh's 'impressive record of economic growth' within its deteriorating performance in governance during 1996–2008 being fallen within the lowest quartile of poorly governed states. These hypotheses are: (1) Bangladesh's economic growth in the last three decades was accidental and is not likely to last; (2) Though governance in Bangladesh continues to be disappointing in many sectors, growth process in Bangladesh was triggered by critical reforms, such as state's creation of space for vibrant private sector, government encouragement of the migration of workers, creation of space and partnerships with non-governmental organizations (NGOs), pro-poor public expenditure, and improved capacity of disaster management; (3) Bangladesh's growth without good governance attributed to vitality and creativity of her unique and non-replicable civil society particularly of NGOs; (4) Though in short-run governance deficit is not a binding constraint, Bangladesh's growth will be increasingly stifled as Bangladesh approaches the status of a middle-income country; (5) Governance data of World Bank are deficient, and consequently, no meaningful conclusion could be reached from the available data; and (6) Though poor governance does put an outright end to growth, it reduces both the quantity and quality of growth (Khan 2010: 138–141).

However, Mahmud (2008) identifies a number of factors behind the 'development surprise' of Bangladesh in social areas (such as per capita GDP more than doubled since 1975; life expectancy has risen from 50 to 63 years, population growth rates of 3 percent a year halved, child mortality rates of 240 per 1000 births cut by 70 percent, literacy more than doubled, and remarkable progress made in providing universal primary education), that include: a noteworthy process of social transformation involving changes in social norms and attitudes such as toward female schooling or contraceptive adoption; increased public awareness created by effective social mobilization campaigns and from the adoption of low-cost solutions, as child immunization and oral saline treatment for diarrhea, leading to a decline in child mortality; a strong presence of non-governmental organizations (NGOs) and public support in the form of many innovative interventions (e.g., through microcredit programs creating the social environment for other development interventions for rural women to work better; relatively inexpensive interventions such as child immunization and oral saline treatment for diarrhea; reducing the prevailing high child malnutrition rates in Bangladesh through food-healthcare educational interventions) (Mahmud 2008: 79–86).

Ahluwalia and Hussain (2004) identify Bangladesh as a 'feisty fighter' in improving its status along the many dimensions of social development over the three decades from 1971 to 2001. They argue that policy reorientation by "agricultural breakthroughs and external market developments" and the institutional innovations related to NGOs, community-based organizations (CBOs) and public–private partnerships (PPPs), are significant contributors in this regard.

Islam (2015) also enumerated a number of remarkable accomplishments of the country including notable increase in investment as a proportion of GDP with a sea change in the distribution of investment as between the public and the private sector; substantial reduction of dependence on foreign aid; and much higher integration of Bangladesh with the global economy evidenced by phenomenal increase in the contribution of exports and remittances to GDP. He also identifies the key challenges in the face of the country's aspiration to become a middle-income country by 2021 that include the challenge of enhancing investment in both public and private sectors, strengthening the governance-related institutions, meeting infrastructure deficit, ensuring food security, dealing with the impact of climate change, developing human resources, and diversification of production (Islam 2015: 34–41).

Similarly, Riaz (2015: 118–125) also acknowledges the currency of the term 'Bangladesh paradox' due to the continued economic growth of the country by virtue of the pivotal roles of two sectors—readymade garments and remittances from short-term migrant workers, and successes in various social indicators despite lack of political stability and absence of good governance.

Recently, Sawada et al. (2018: xxi–xxvi) argue that given the several unfavorable conditions, including weak governance and political instability, inequalities within the country, the downsides of rapid urbanization, and exposure to several natural disasters, Bangladesh's remarkable economic and social success, which may be called a *miracle*, has been facilitated by several structural transformations (from a farm-based to non-farm-based economy, and from domestic informal sectors-based industries to formal export-oriented manufacturing sectors-based industries). 'Industrialization success,' 'microfinance,' and 'female empowerment,' are the key drivers for those structural transformations and pro-poor development.

However, there remains a conspicuous absence in the existing literature of any meaningful discussion on the role of the government for the economic and social progress in Bangladesh. Indeed, with limited abilities and resources, various governments of Bangladesh have played different roles to affect, aid, and influence the development process by following and implementing various policies and strategies. This chapter will be devoted to filling the existing gap to highlight the role played by the government revolving around the variables identified by Mahmud (2008). Moreover, it aims to focus on the accountability issue of the public servants in the development process, which has so far remained untouched in any study. The originality and contribution of the chapter should be felt in these areas.

Methodology

The study is based on secondary data published by national and international bodies and a number of online sources. As a movement started in 2009 for a digital Bangladesh by 2021, the government regulatory and policy documents are mostly available in multiple websites of various ministries or divisions, autonomous bodies, government-controlled commercial entities or non-profit organizations (NPOs), or international development partners of Bangladesh. The archival electronic depository of resources and publications has been used for both qualitative and quantitative data. The assessment reports of various national policies by development partners or other think tanks have also been used. However, in case of assessing the civil servants' accountability, primary sources of information were the Uniform Resource Locator (URL) of the Cabinet Division of the Government of Bangladesh. Moreover, published sources of the Bangladesh Bureau of Statistics (BBS), various plan documents (Five Year Plans, Perspective Plans, Delta Plan, etc.), strategy papers, action plans, national budget documents and medium-term budgetary frameworks (MTBFs), Bangladesh Economic Reviews, and so on have also been used in the study.

Discussions and Analysis

As commented by Islam (2009: 24),

> In the ultimate analysis, the structure, functions, strength, and weakness of economic policymaking institutions depend on whether the political elite and leadership have the necessary conviction, motivation, and interest to ensure an efficient policymaking process and to achieve an accountable government.

The decade long development may be attributed to the political stability of the country for successive tenures of the government formed by the same political alliances and particularly under the leadership of Prime Minister Sheikh Hasina.

Key Development Initiatives of the Government

As indicated earlier, this section has broadly followed the factors identified by Mahmud (2008) that various governments initiated and executed on the development path. Though the discussion tries to cover most important of them, they do not, however, from an exclusive list.

Government Plans for Development
The 'Vision 2021,' developed on the Election Manifesto of 2008 of Bangladesh Awami League, has envisioned Bangladesh to be a middle-income and also a digital country in 2021.[3] Targets set in the Vision 2021 and the associated Perspective Plan 2010–21, if achieved, will transform the socio-economic environment to the first stages of a middle-income economy (GOB 2012a: 2). Under the Vision 2041, Bangladesh has set the goal to transform itself into a developed country by 2041.[4] On the track, according to the World Bank's classification, Bangladesh was elevated from a low income to a lower-middle-income country (LMIC) status in July 2015 (GOB 2015b: iv). Bangladesh is also set to leave the Least Developed Country (LDC) category by 2024 (UN 2018) (Fig. 11.1).

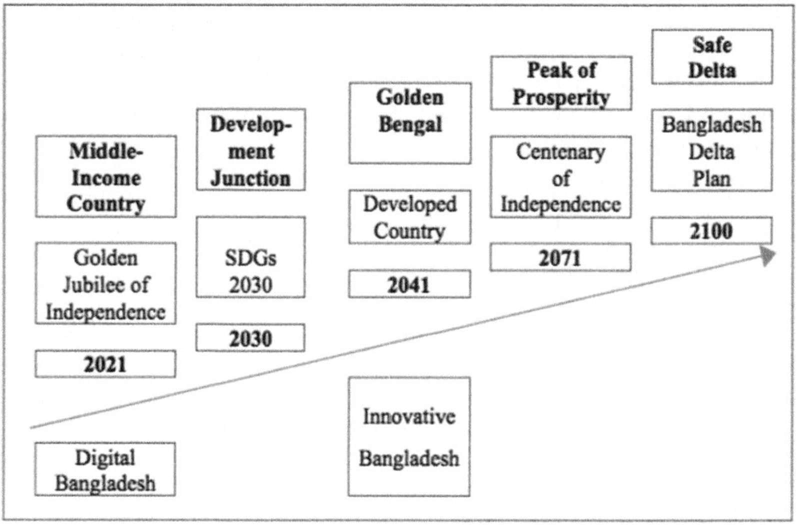

Fig. 11.1 Targets for Bangladesh in long-term plans. (Sources: Various Plan Documents of Bangladesh; Bangladesh Awami League 2018)

In September 2018, the Government, on its part, approved the long-awaited mega strategy 'Bangladesh Delta Plan (BDP) 2100' in a bid to tap the maximum potentials of Bangladesh as a deltaic region through managing water resources, ensuring food and water security and tackling disasters. This strategy is expected to boost the GDP growth by another 1.5 percent by 2030 through, the implementation of the 100-year plan. The short-term plan will be implemented by 2030, the mid-term by 2050 while the long run by 2100 (*The Financial Express* 2018: 1, 7).

Bangladesh is a participant in the Millennium Development Goals (MDGs) whereby eight international development goals had been established following the United Nations Millennium Declaration (General Assembly resolution 55/2). The landmark commitment of the Millennium Declaration was to "spare no effort to free our fellow men, women, and children from the abject and dehumanizing conditions of extreme poverty" (UN 2000: 4). In Bangladesh, 66 indicators were used against 21 targets under 8 MDGs. As per the Government evaluation on the achievement of MDGs in Bangladesh (September 2016), the degree of success was praiseworthy (see Table 11.3).

Table 11.3 Achievement of MDG indicators used by Bangladesh (September 2016)

MDGs	*Indicator*	*Target met*	*Impressive progress*	*On track*	*No end target/no status mentioned*	*Low*	*Need attention*	*Lacks update data/data not available*
Goal 1	12	3	–	–	4	–	2	3
Goal 2	4	–	–	1	–	–	3	–
Goal 3	5	2	–	–	–	–	3	–
Goal 4	3	2	–	–	–	–	1	–
Goal 5	7	–	–	–	1	–	6	–
Goal 6	13	4	–	1	2	1	5	–
Goal 7	11	1	–	1	5	–	3	1
Goal 8	11	1	1	1	2	1	4	1
8 Goals	66 (100.0)	13 (19.7)	1 (1.5)	4 (6.1)	14 (21.2)	2 (3.0)	27 (40.9)	5 (7.6)

Source: Government of Bangladesh. (2016). *Millennium Development Goals: End-period Stocktaking and Final Evaluation Report (2000–2015)*, 108–112

Bangladesh is often mentioned as the landmark achiever of MDGs and received a number of international recognitions for MDG-1 (Eradicate extreme poverty and hunger), MDG-3 (Promote gender equality and empower women), MDG-4 (Reduce child mortality), MDG-5 (Improve maternal health) and MDG-7 (Ensure environmental sustainability). These recognitions include: 'UN MDG Awards 2010' (2010) for reducing under-five child mortality rate (MDG-4), the South-South Award 'Digital Health For Digital Development' (2011) for success on attainment of MDG-4, and MDG-5, and 'Diploma Award' (2013) from Food and Agriculture Organization (FAO) for achieving the MDG-1 ahead of schedule. The award list has been enriched over the years as Bangladesh received a number of other awards, including 'special recognition' (2013) for outstanding progress in fighting hunger and poverty (MDG-1), 'South-South Cooperation Visionary' Award of United Nations (2014) for success in poverty alleviation (MDG-1), 'Women in Parliaments Global Forum Award' (2015), as Bangladesh ranked 10th out of 142 countries in the political sphere and a 'pioneering country in reducing gender discrimination' (MDG-3), FAO's 'Achievement Award' (2015) for the target of 1.C ('Halved between 1990 and 2015, the proportion of people who suffer from hunger') of the MDG-1 to reduce country's population sufferings from undernourishment by at least 50 percent or to bring it below 5 percent, between 1990 and 2015.[5]

These awards are indicative of the success Bangladesh has achieved in the areas mentioned for the awards. The distinctive role of the government cannot be underestimated in any way for the implementation and execution of various plans and projects.

Pro-Poor Public Expenditure Policies

The *National Social Security Strategy Paper 2015* has been formulated for reducing poverty and discrimination. The government has been increasing the allocation for the social safety net sector every year to enhance the condition of the poor. By May 2019, nearly a quarter of the families in the country has been covered under the social safety net programs. As per the Government's Election Manifesto, 2018, budget allocation in this sector will be doubled in the next 5 years (Kamal 2019). This is evident in Table 11.4. Every year from FY2008–09 to FY2018–19, social safety net expenditures, which range from 12.2 to 16.1 percent of total budgeted expenditures, and from 2.0 to 2.6 percent of GDP, have increased by

Table 11.4 Annual Social Safety Net (SSN) expenditures of the government (figures in billion BDT)

FY	*SP(ND)*	*SE(ND)*	*SE(Dev.)*	*SE(Total)*	*SSNE*	*Increase (%)*	*% of TE*	*% of GDP*
2008–09	1136	57	191	248	1385	20.7	14.7	2.3
2009–10	1344	68	258	326	1671	20.7	15.1	2.4
2010–11	1676	52	361	413	2089	25.1	16.1	2.6
2011–12	1724	53	421	474	2198	5.2	13.6	2.4
2012–13	1748	49	513	562	2310	5.1	12.2	2.2
2013–14	1898	57	710	767	2665	15.4	12.3	2.3
2014–15	2153	59	852	911	3064	14.9	12.8	2.0
2015–16	2526	53	1019	1071	3598	17.4	13.6	2.1
2016–17	3058	78	949	1027	4086	13.6	12.9	2.1
2017–18	2880	143	1830	1973	4852	18.8	13.1	2.2
2018–19	4421	197	1800	1997	6418	32.3	13.8	2.5
Av. (08–15)	1669	529	56	472	2197	–	13.5	2.3
Av. (15–19)	3221	1517	118	1399	4738	–	13.4	2.2
Increase in Av. (percent)	93.1	187.0	108.3	196.4	115.6	–	–	–

Sources: Compiled. Data from the Ministry of Finance's ***Budgets for Social Safety Net Programs***; Available at https://mof.portal.gov.bd/site/page/32220b73-846f-4a33-b4c0-a6650c918e25/Safety-Net

Note: Figures from 2008–09 to 2017–18 are from revised budgets and figures of 2018–19 are from original budget. FY = Financial Year; SP = Social Protection; SE = Social Empowerment; ND = Non-development; Dev. = Development; SSNE = Social Safety Net Expenditure in total; percent increase = percent increase over preceding year; percent of TE = SSNE as a percent of Total Expenditure in Revised Budgets from 2008–09 to 2017–18 and Total Expenditure in Budget for 2018–19; percent of GDP = SSNE as a percent of Gross domestic product; Av. (08–15) = Average of 2008–09 to 2014–15; Av. (15–19) = Average of 2015–16 to 2018–19; Increase in Av. (percent) = percent increase in "Av. (15–19)" over "Av. (15–19)"

5.1–32.3 percent. In comparison to average figures over FYs 2008–09 to 2014–15 with that over FYs 2015–16 to 2018–19, expenditures under social protection categories are enhanced by 93.1 percent, but expenditures under social empowerment categories increased by 196.4 percent.

Though the number of programs under social protection declined by 3.9 percent, the number of programs under social empowerment categories, however, increased by 49.2 percent. However, in comparison to average figures over FYs 2008–09 to 2014–15 with that over FYs 2015–16 to 2018–19, beneficiaries under social protection categories declined by 24.1 percent, but beneficiaries under social empowerment categories increased by 408.9 percent (MoF 2019).

Human Resource Development Policies

The importance of human resource development (HRD) has acquired a new dimension in order to face the challenges of globalization. For this reason, the government has included HRD as one of the main goals of its development agenda along with economic growth. The budgetary allocation for HRD has been increased over the years to show this commitment of the government (Table 11.5).

To achieve the HRD goal, the government of Bangladesh has allocated 22.09 percent of the budget to the HRD related sectors, such as—Education and Technology, Health and Family Welfare, Women and Children, Social Welfare, Youth Sports development, Culture, Labor and Employment, and so on. Various programs, including the adoption of the 'National Education Policy 2010' have been undertaken to create skilled and competent. In order to ensure the desired development of women and to ensure their participation in the national development activities, the government has legislated the 'National Women Development Policy 2011' (March 2011). Moreover, two national action plans have been prepared to implement the National Women Development Policy and to

Table 11.5 Government allocation for Human Resource (HR): Annual Development Program (ADP) and total (Crore Taka)

Allocation for Human Resource (HR)	*Budget 2019–20*	*Revised 2018–19*	*Budget 2018–19*	*Actual 2017–18*	*Actual 2016–17*	*Actual 2015–16*	*Actual 2014–15*
ADP Allocation for HR	55,615	42,173	46,452	23,446	22,187	17,009	16,220
(percent of total ADP)	(27.4)	(25.3)	(26.9)	(19.6)	(24.6)	(20.8)	(25.0)
Total Allocation for HR	129,056	109,776	113,208	80,415	75,999	64,824	50,365
(percent of total allocation)	(24.67)	(24.81)	(24.37)	(24.98)	(27.41)	(26.92)	(24.11)
(percent of GDP)	(4.47)	(4.33)	(4.46)	(3.57)	(3.89)	(3.75)	(3.32)

Source: *Budget Speech 2019–20* (Kamal 2019: 105–107)

protect violence against women and children. As a result of the implementation of various development programs, Bangladesh is gradually improving in the Human Development Index (HDI). According to the 'Human Development Report 2018,' the position of Bangladesh has been improved to 136 (GOB 2019b: 195–217).

Private Sector Development Policies

It is essential to increase production, investment, and export in the private sector for making economic development sustainable. For that purpose, a level playing field is also necessary to make the private sector vibrant and effective. Now, the government is implementing different development projects under the PPP model along with individual projects under the government and private initiative. However, the government's share of investment as a percentage of GDP is increasing at a faster pace than the share of the private sector in overall investments in Bangladesh (see Table 11.6).

To facilitate investment barriers in private sectors, one of the major steps taken by the government of Bangladesh is the formation of the Private Sector Development Policy Coordination Committee (PSDPCC) in September 2011 with the membership of all government secretaries involved in trade and business. The objectives of PSDPCC include improving and enabling policy environment for private sector development; helping to create an investment-friendly environment to attract more foreign direct investment (FDI); coordinating both public and private sectors for better business; and reviewing the progress of implantation of private sector development reforms to identify roadblocks to execution and devise strategies to overcome those roadblocks. In an assessment report of PSDPCC (2011–17), it has been mentioned that 35 reform policy papers have been placed through 9 PSDPCC meetings (between February 2012

Table 11.6 Investment in Bangladesh (as % of GDP)

Sector	*FY11*	*F12*	*FY13*	*FY14*	*FY15*	*FY16*	*FY17*	*FY18*	*FY19*	*FY20*
Public	5.26	5.76	6.64	6.55	6.82	6.66	7.41	8.0	8.2	8.6
Private	22.16	22.50	21.75	22.03	22.07	22.99	23.10	23.26	23.4	24.2
Total	27.42	28.26	28.39	28.58	28.89	29.65	39.51	31.23	31.6	32.8

Source: *Budget Speech 2019–20* (Kamal 2019: 102)

Notes: FY11 is Financial Year 2010–11, and FY20 is similarly Financial Year 2019–20

and August 2017) and 498 reform recommendations have been proposed, among which 256 have been approved, 148 implemented, 99 under implementation, and 222 under further review (BUILD 2017). PSDPCC's active agility paves the way to foster public–private collaboration and economic progress through enhanced private sector participation. The private sector is now playing an important role in education, health, infrastructure development, along with the traditional areas of manufacturing, and trade to the advancement of the country.

Third Sector Engagement Policies

Bangladesh is regarded as a land of non-government organizations (NGOs), endowed with a dense and neatly designed network. Usually, NGOs need to receive registration/license from more than one agency to start/continue their activities as a charitable organization. All the microcredit or microfinance NGOs require to obtain license from the Microcredit Regulatory Authority (MRA) since 2006 under the Microcredit Regulatory Authority Act, 2006, while foreign-funded NGOs receive registration from the NGO Affairs Bureau (NGOAB) under the Foreign Donations (Voluntary Activities) Regulation Act 2016, NGOs may get registration from the Registrar of Joint Stock Companies & Firms under the Societies Registration Act, 1860 or the Companies Act, 1994 or some other existing Acts. For different NGOs registration bodies and overlapping of affiliations, the exact estimate of NGOs working in Bangladesh is not computable (BFIU 2015). As of 30 June 2019, there were 2476 foreign-funded NGOs registered with NGOAB (local 2223 and foreign 253) (www.ngaob.gov.bd) and the number of microfinance institutions (MFIs) licensed with the MRA was 724 (www.mra.gov.bd).

In an assessment report, the Bangladesh Financial Intelligence Unit (BFIU 2015) gives an evolutionary role of NGOs in Bangladesh. According to it, there was an emergence of NGOs with expanding the focus on post-independence humanitarian aid, rehabilitation, and reconstruction with an increasing flow of foreign funds to NGOs during 1972–80. The milestone events like the establishment of the Association of Development Agencies of Bangladesh (ADAB) in 1974, the innovation of microcredit, poverty reduction, and advocacy programs took place this time. The NGOAB came into being in 1990. However, 1991–2000 period is termed as the golden age of Government-NGOs Partnership with the expanded role of NGOs in rural development and credit delivery programs, election monitoring, political advocacies, public interest litigation, and voter education, even the beginning of commercial ventures of NGOs. From FY2001 to FY2014–15, though the NGOs community got divided locally, a large number of Bangladeshi NGOs got international orientation as they expanded their programs in different countries all over the world. It is now estimated that the overall contribution of this third sector is around 3–4 percent of the country's GDP (Mir and Bala 2014).

For ensuring transparency and accountability of the NGOs, the establishment of adequate legal structures, a transparent recruitment system for them, enhancement of Government's oversight capacity, and avoidance of bureaucratic intricacies are critically important. In the past decade, the Government on its part is proactively trying to bring a level of transparency and control on the functioning of NGOs through NGOAB, MRA, Bangladesh Bank, and other regulatory bodies.

Foreign Employment Policies

It was a historic decision by the Government to send workforce/labor in the Middle East in 1976. Since then, private agencies have also been allowed to get involved in sending workers abroad. The Ministry of Expatriates' Welfare and Overseas Employment (MoEWOE) was created in December 2001 to look after the issues related to labor migration. The external integration of the labor market has also made Bangladesh sensitive to the external economic shock. In the last 5 years (2014–18), annual average expatriate workers in number increased by 42.1 percent than the preceding 5 years' (2009–13) annual average expatriate workers in number. In the case of male workers, the growth is around 30.0 percent, and the number of female workers grew by 199.3 percent (https://probashi.gov.bd; accessed 15.07.2019).

The Foreign Employment and Immigrant Act, 2013 was enacted by repealing the Emigration Ordinance, 1982 to create the opportunity for foreign employment of workers, and to ensure safe and just migration governance system and welfare of the expatriates. A memorandum of understanding (MoU) was signed with the International Manpower Development Organization, Japan (IM Japan) in 2017 for sending technical intern at zero migration cost. The Probashi Kallyan Bank (bank for expatriates' welfare), established in April 2011, has been approved as a scheduled bank by which service provision is widened, and 100 percent credit facilities are being provided to the migrants. The Wage Earners Welfare Board Act 2018 was also enacted to establish a Wage Earners Welfare Board for giving protection and welfare to the expatriate workers and their dependents. The Bureau of Manpower, Employment and Training (BMET), established in 1976 by the Government as an attached department of the then Ministry of Manpower Development and Social Welfare (now under MoEWOE from December 2001) has been working for the export of manpower by organizing technical training course and expanded training facilities that include language training courses for root level people. Bangladesh Overseas Employment Services Limited (BOESL), established in 1984 as the manpower exporting government company, has been sending skilled and unskilled workers in different countries.

The use of various digital tools in the case of migrant workers has contributed to reducing hassle and corruption significantly through the service process simplification (SPS). Mobile Apps have been introduced for online visa verification purposes. As mentioned by Chowdhury and Zaman (2013: 25), the Union Information and Service Centres (UISCs), now Union Digital Centres (UDCs), made the first-ever hassle-free online registration for Bangladeshi migrant workers to Malaysia (1.4 million job-seekers from all the divisions completed the registration by January 2013). The researchers claim that this is the first digital migration in the world and the role of the UISCs cuts across both the horizontal (G2G or government-to-government) and vertical (G2C or government-to-citizen) dimensions of e-governance (see also Access to Information Programme, 2018).

Disaster Management Policies

Bangladesh is a disaster-prone country. In the *Global Climate Risk Index 2019*, Bangladesh is included in the list of the 10 most affected countries in terms of annual Climate Risk Index (CRI) as well as in the list of the 10 countries most affected from 1998 to 2017 (annual averages) in term of long-term CRI. Bangladesh ranked 9th in 2017 (13th in 2016) in terms of annual CRI and 7th in terms of an annual average of CRI from 1998 to 2017 (6th in terms of an annual average of CRI from 1997 to 2016) (Eckstein et al. 2018). As reported in the World Economic Forum's *The Global Risks Report 2019*, in Bangladesh, a sea-level rise of 0.5 meters would result in a loss of about 11 percent of the country's land, displacing approximately 15 million people. The World Bank estimates salination could cause a 15.6 percent decline in rice yield in Bangladesh (World Economic Forum 2019: 57–58). Disaster management in Bangladesh is under the purview of the Ministry of Disaster Management, and Relief (MoDMR) set up in January 1972. The MoDMR is mainly in charge of the formulation and implementation of laws, policies, and action plans for disaster risk reduction, emergency response and disaster management; humanitarian assistance to ensure food security through the implementation of Rural Infrastructure Development, Test Relief (TR), Vulnerable Group Feeding (VGF), Gratuitous Relief (GR), Food for Work/Kabikha (FFW), and other programs; reduction of disaster risk through construction and repair of small, bridges/culverts, multipurpose cyclone/flood shelters, *Mujib Killas* (rampart made in the name of Bangabandhu Sheikh Mujibur Rahman) or information center-cum-Relief go-down, Herring bone bond roads, and so on. In the last 3 years (FY2016–17 to FY2018–19), 1.1 million forcibly displaced Myanmar citizens have been provided with humanitarian assistance, including food, shelter, medical, and other facilities. Through interactive voice response (IVR) technology, dialing the toll-free number in mobile phone forecasting and weather messages on disasters are now accessible. In three financial years from FY2016–17 to FY2018–19, 2.71 million poor and unemployed people of which one third are women have been employed through Employment Generation Program for the Poorest (EGPP) that ensures employment of rural workers for up to 80 days in two phases. During the same period, the Department of Disaster Management has implemented 1,89,814 projects under the Kabikha program, 4,84,835 projects under TR program, food grains were distributed among 62,42,545 poor families under GR program, house building grants among 1,59,983 families, and dry foods among 24,23,530 families were distributed under VGF program. Similarly, 579 projects have been implemented under the construction of flood shelters (GOB 2019: 673–682).

Bangladesh has shown resilience in the efficient handling of disaster management. Both the government and NGOs played a role here. Eckstein et al. (2018: 16–17) mention that in Bangladesh, a dense network of small cyclone shelters, in vulnerable areas, that can also serve as everyday public buildings, such as schools, has proven much more efficient than large scale cyclone centers.

Financial Inclusion

Since 2009, Bangladesh has been a leading and active member of the Alliance for Financial Inclusion (AFI) and it committed internationally in 2014 to develop its National Financial Inclusion Strategy (NFIS), being one of the signatories of the Maya Declaration.[6] As a follow-up step, the central bank (Bangladesh Bank) and the Ministry of Finance (MoF) of

Bangladesh jointly took the initiative to develop a complete draft of NFIS-Bangladesh (NFIS-B) in 2016. MoF is to prepare a completed version of NFIS-B for 2020–24 (Source: FID, MoF, GOB). The central theme of NFIS-B encompasses two mutually reinforcing aspects: (i) finance for growth and development; and (ii) access to finance for all. Under the NFIS-B, six types of financial services (savings, credit, payments, insurance, capital market instruments, and government-issued instruments) are targeted to be provided by nine types of providers (scheduled banks, non-bank financial institutions, microfinance institutions, cooperatives, insurance companies, Bangladesh Post Office, specialized financial service providers, capital market intermediaries and investment banks, and government instrument intermediaries) with a view to ensuring access of individuals and businesses to those financial services facilitated with technology provided at affordable cost with quality, ease of access and full scope of risk mitigation. Thus a comprehensive financial inclusion framework will be created: (i) to include within the formal financial system the excluded or vulnerable groups and sectors, who are often exposed to income, wealth and climate change shocks; (ii) to minimize marginalization and vulnerabilities amid Bangladesh's transitions; and (iii) to leverage on technology for the reach and sustainability of inclusion initiatives.

Although Bangladesh has introduced a good number of innovative financial products to promote savings and credit for the segments of population who cannot access banking services in any way (e.g., encouraging banks to open No-Frill (BDT 10) accounts for farmers and various unbanked-unserved segment of population; providing banking services for physically challenged persons, students, street children, and third gender); diversified service delivery channels; and introduced massive digital financial services and FinTech, the level of financial inclusion is yet to be satisfactory. In 2017, out of population of 15 years plus age bracket, only 50.0 percent had bank account, 41.1 percent had financial institution account, 21.2 percent had mobile money account, 34.1 percent made or received digital payments, 9.9 percent saved at a financial institution, and 9.2 percent borrowed from a financial institution or used a credit card (Demirgüç-Kunt et al. 2018).

Other Policy Regimes

The Right to Information Act, 2009 was enacted in April 2009, repealing the Right to Information Ordinance, 2009, promulgated in October

2008, with the statutory objective that if the right to information of the people is ensured, the transparency and accountability of all public, autonomous and statutory organizations and of other private institutions constituted or run by government or foreign financing shall increase, corruption of the same shall decrease and good governance of the same shall be established.

The National Integrity Strategy (NIS) of Bangladesh was approved by the government in October 2012 with the vision of "A happy-prosperous Golden Bengal" and the mission of "Establishment of good governance in state institutions and society" (GOB 2012b; GOB 2013). The Whistle Blowers' (Protection) Act, 2011 (or alternatively the Disclosure of Public Interest Information [Providing Protection] Act, 2011 was enacted in June 2011) is yet to get the desired response due to lack of awareness and the Anti-Corruption Commission (ACC) did not file any graft case under the Whistle Blowers' Protection Act up to mid-April 2018. The law ensures the protection of the legal rights of a whistle-blower by concealing their identities if they reveal any corruption taken place inside their offices or elsewhere. The law can play a vital role in checking corruption in both the public and private sectors, because no criminal, civil or departmental proceedings can be initiated against a person for disclosing information in the public interest to the authorities, and his or her identity will not be disclosed without his or her consent. It is expected that the law would help the anti-graft watchdog (ACC) work on the basis of specific information instead of assumptions, and the flow of accurate information on graft to the commission may increase (The *Dhaka Tribune*, 23 April 2018). But things have not been improved much.

Civil Servants' Accountability Frameworks

Khan (2015) argues that the bureaucracy in Bangladesh suffers from Gresham's Law Syndrome, a situation where bad employees dominate the good. This is a major hurdle to efficient government functioning. According to Khan (2015), symptoms like the erosion of confidence in the recruitment process, dilution of merit-based recruitment by a pervasive quota system, politicization of promotion, inability to punish delinquencies and reward the efficient, inappropriate compensation, and the de-professionalization through the inappropriate structure are the manifestation of the Gresham's Law Syndrome.

Nevertheless, a good number of initiatives have been taken recently to break the iceberg of the bureaucratic process and make civil servants more active and accountable to get the government agenda done within the targeted timeframe. Some of these initiatives are as follows.

Medium-Term Budgetary Framework (MTBF)
The Medium-Term Budget Framework (MTBF) is a 3-year estimate of revenue and expenditure, for the budget year and projections for the two forward years. As a pilot basis, MTBF was first prepared for FY2005–06 for five ministries in line with the recommendation of the report of the Public Expenditure Review Commission (December 2003). From FY2009–10, it has been prepared in accordance with the requirements of the Public Money and Budget Management Act 2009. Ministry Budget Frameworks (MBFs) prepared by Ministries, Divisions and other Institutions under the MTBF provide linkages between Government strategic objectives and its policies and resource allocations, and between resource allocations and performance. This rigorous format and sequential monitoring and accountability are enforcing the civil servants to ensure time-bound performance and answerability.

Service Process Simplification (SPS) Through Innovation
First National Information and Communication Technology (ICT) Policy was adopted by the Government of Bangladesh in October 2002, which aimed at building an ICT-driven nation comprising of knowledge-based society by the year 2006. A significant accomplishment was achieved in July 2006 by the establishment of the e-Governance Cell within the Prime Minister's Office (PMO) to implement the "Access to Information (A2I) Programme" within the Cell's organizational mandate (Morshed 2006). The UNDP supported project 'A2I Programme' was started in 2007 in the PMO with a proclaimed goal to leverage ICT in public service delivery and build the necessary capacity of the stakeholders to promote the use of ICTs in development (Access to Information Programme 2009). Through this A2I program, the PMO and the Cabinet Division embarked upon a whole-of-government service process simplification (SPS) work in 2007. SPS is mapped around reducing Time, Cost, and Visit (TCV): (a) *time* to receive a service; (b) *cost* (fees, travel cost, opportunity, and other contingent liabilities); and (c) the number of *visits* to government offices to complete and receive service. TCV helped to provide a standard method to implement SPS reform works across the government. Due to SPS via

UDCs, TCV associated with the traditional face-to-face service delivery model for three public services (birth registration, land record, and migration) was brought down significantly (Zaman 2015). Another impact study (2016) in relation to District e-Service Centres (DESCs), an ICT facilitated one-stop service center in lieu of traditional paper-based manual services at Deputy Commissioner's (DC) office, shows that in comparison to previous service system of DC office, average required time reduced to 8 percent in online service, average cost reduced to 86 percent, and visits reduced by about 33 percent. DESCs e-filing service has made the service delivery process easy by minimizing barriers of culture, class, gender, and distance in the delivery of public services. It also reduces corruption and increases the accountability of government service delivery organizations, teams, officers, and staff. UDCs were in operation across all 4547 union councils by the middle of 2014 (Chowdhury and Zaman 2014: 9).

In the middle of 2008 when the Care Taker Government was in power, through the coordination of the PMO, Cabinet Division (the center of bureaucracy) and Ministry of Public Administration (responsible for human resource management of the government administrative cadre), each of the Secretaries of the Government (a total of 58 as on July 31, 2019) identified one service to be delivered electronically. These initiatives, collectively called the e-Governance 'Quick-Wins,' were meant to quickly showcase the impact of the newly emerged service delivery mechanism to the citizens, receive their feedback and allow the government the necessary preparation time for nationwide implementation (Mahmood and Babool 2009: 385). The success of Quick-Wins paved the way toward setting up a multi-donor Service Innovation Fund (SIF) in March 2013, which institutionalized Quick-Wins through a more formal and financial structure. In addition, drawing lessons learned from the Quick-Wins approach, the Cabinet Division in April 2013 introduced Innovation Teams (iTeams) consisting of Chief Innovation Officer (CIO), Innovation Officer (IO), and team members. CIOs/IOs are being supported by nearly 6000 members, and iTeams can avail of SIF, which is designed to encourage innovative home-grown and localized TCV-based ideas and solutions (Chowdhury and Zaman 2014). The obligatory responsibilities and consequent time-bound monitoring of the CIOs/IOs have transformed the "age-old over-centralization of service delivery, opaqueness in citizens' request processing, and resistance to change by civil services" (Chowdhury and Zaman 2014: 9). There is also a significant step to deliver government services around the clock by using toll-free helplines.

Enactment of the Public Service Act 2018

In November 2018, the Public Service Act 2018 was passed by the Parliament by repealing six statutes: (a) Public Servants (Retirement) Act, 1974; (b) Services (Reorganization and Conditions) Act, 1975; (c) Government Servants (Special Provisions) Ordinance, 1979; (d) Public Employees Discipline (Punctual Attendance) Ordinance, 1982; (e) Public Servants (Dismissal on Conviction) Ordinance, 1985; and (f) Surplus Public Servants Absorption Act, 2016. The purpose of the 2018 Act is to ensure the Constitutional provision of Article 21(2) that every person in the service of the Republic has a duty to serve the people all the time (Ahmed 2019).

Annual Performance Agreement (APA)

The government took the decision to introduce the Government Performance Management System (GPMS) through signing the Annual Performance Agreements (APAs) in February 2014 as an outcome of the recommendation of the Public Administration Reform Commission (PARC) in 2000, as a part of the National Integrity Strategy (NIS). Primary purposes of APA are as follows: (a) moving the focus of the ministries/divisions from process-orientation to result-orientation; and (b) providing an objective and fair basis to evaluate the overall performance of the ministry/division at the end of a financial year (GOB 2014; GOB 2015a; Arafin 2016). The signing of the fifth consecutive APA deal was for infusing dynamism into the implementation of various projects and development programs of the government. The new APA was prepared considering the Vision 2021, Sustainable Development Goal (SDG), Seventh Five Year Plan (FY2016–FY2020), and Ministry Allocation of Business (Work and Regulations Responsibilities). The average achievement of the ministries and divisions according to the agreement in the fiscal year 2017–18 was 91 percent (http://www.bssnews.net/?p=46489&print=print; dated 03.07.2018). Now the ministries, divisions and associated agencies are accustomed to preparing APAs and consequent periodic (quarterly) monitoring on the progress of achieving the performance targets based on scores tagged with specific timelines.

This GPMS through signing APAs is a landmark initiative for improving the performance of the concerned ministry/division and finally, the integrated performance of the country as a whole. Bhuiyan and Jahan (2017) find that the introduction of the GPMS by signing APAs is expected to ensure institutional transparency, accountability, proper utilization of resources, and above all, enhancing institutional efficiency. But they argue that though the government is trying to establish updated GPMS, due to some inherent traditional bureaucratic structural problems and lack of professional knowledge, APA is not performing as effectively as expected. Some measures like a full-fledged participation of the top leaders in the APA activities, introduction of a separate wing in the Cabinet division to deal the APA activities, inclusion of quality measurement indicators along with quantitative indicators, setting up of targets of APA scientifically and logically, and so on can make APA more appropriate (Bhuiyan and Jahan 2017).

Digitization of Office Activities by Using E-Nothi

To make a modern, efficient and service-oriented public administration by using ICT at its highest level, the Government in May 2016 introduced e-file (Nothi) in all government offices up to Upazila levels for an effective and speedy office filing management and maintenance of records. This e-filing was first included in the APA of FY2016–17 of ministries/divisions and directorates/agencies against the strategic objectives relating to functional procedure and improvement of service delivery. In 2018, for implanting the e-Nothi system properly, the following steps were initiated: (i) after prioritizing of sections in an office, e-Nothi system is to be implemented successively for all official files; (ii) not to place again in hard copy of a file already disposed through e-Nothi; (iii) encouraging the use of e-Nothi through mobile apps (applications) based on android and iOS (formerly iPhone OS) operating systems (OS); (iv) giving instructions to compulsorily implement e-Nothi successively to all offices under the concerned ministry/division; (v) discussing the progress on the implementation of e-Nothi system in the monthly coordination meeting and recognizing the best user of the e-Nothi system; and (vi) giving importance to the competency in using e-Nothi system in case of evaluating performance of individual official/employee.

According to the e-Service team of A2I, in February 2019, 69,290 users in 4564 government offices (24 percent of above 19,000 offices) are now using 'e-Nothi' system (www.nothi.gov.bd) to manage their files. The findings of an assessment study, undertaken at the end of 2018 on the 'e-Nothi' system, show that the system has been working very effectively, and the government officials are becoming habituated with the system. On an average 72 percent of the total official activities are performed through 'e-Nothi.' A Facebook Group and two hotline numbers continually provide support to the users (Access to Information Programme 2019).

Virtual Grievance Redress System (GRS)

In accordance with a recommendation made in the 2000 report of the Public Administration Reform Commission (PARC), a cell for receiving complaints was made at a gate of the Secretariat (the central hub of the public administration where citizens' access is allowed only with prior permission). Since September 2007, complaints were sent to a designated 'grievance redress focal point' for disposal thereof. However, at a later stage, an online grievance redress system was introduced to manage the complaints raised properly (GOB 2018: 2). Similarly, an Online Grievance Redress System (GRS) has been introduced in all Ministries and Divisions of the government for improving the quality of service delivery, strengthening good governance, and ensuring accountability of the public administration (Kamal 2019).

Self-Financing to Megaprojects and Their Desired Pace of Advancement

As documented in the *Budget Speech 2018–19*, ten growth-generating large projects, identified as 'Mega Projects,' have been brought under special supervision of the Prime Minister for rapid implementation. These projects are: (1) Padma Multi-purpose Bridge Project; (2) Padma Rail Bridge Project; (3) Ruppur Nuclear Power Project; (4) Rampal Coal Based Power Project; (5) Chattogram-Dohazari to Ramu-Coxes Bazar and Ramu-Gundum Railway Construction Project; (6) Dhaka Mass Rapid Transit Development Project; (7) Construction of Payra Seaport (First Phase) Project; (8) Sonadia Deep Seaport; (9) Matarbari Ultra Super Critical Coal-Fired Power Project; and (10) Construction of Maheshkhali Floating LNG Terminal Project.

Country-Wide Infrastructure Expansion

Two major blank spots in the policy regime were infrastructure sectors and the financial sector. To overcome the severe power shortage of nearly 2000 megawatts (MW), the government's Power System Master Plan 2010 decided to use the quick rental power plants (QRPPs) as its major strategic tool to reduce the shortage in the short run. Under the plan, a total of 20 QRPPs was commissioned by 2012 with a total capacity of more than 1000 MW, although, between the rentals and the quick rentals, the average per-unit cost of gas-based electricity generation is more than 75 percent higher for QRPPs than the rental units. Nevertheless, the additional power supplied to the national grid through the QRPPs has made a significant positive impact in many areas of the economy (Mujeri and Chowdhury 2013). Currently, the power generation capacity of Bangladesh has increased to 21,169 MW, and the government has succeeded to provide access to electricity to approximately 93 percent of population in May 2019 (which was 47 percent in 2008; 62 percent in 2013; 74 percent in 2015; and 90 percent in 2018; see Moazzem and Ali 2019). Besides, projects for the construction of 53 power plants with the capacity to generate 14,202 MW of electricity are underway. It is expected that the plants will begin to function shortly. Moreover, plans have been taken to establish 17 power plants with a capacity to generate 19,650 MW of electricity in the near future. Besides, there are plans to generate extra electricity through 'balancing, modernization, rehabilitation, and expansion' (BMRE) of the existing old power plants. Hence, bearing in mind the Prime Minister's slogan for ensuing electricity in all households, the government has set targets to generate 24,000 MW by 2021, 40,000 MW by 2030, and 60,000 MW by 2041, respectively (Kamal 2019: 36–37).

Telecommunication is another area where Bangladesh is experiencing a boom. By May 2019, the number of internet users has crossed 90 million. Tele-density has crossed 93 percent. Twenty-eight High Tech Parks are being established in the country. Bangladesh became the 57th satellite member country by launching its first satellite Bangabandhu Satellite-1 successfully into space on May 11, 2018. This achievement is a step ahead for Bangladesh to join better global tele-network (Kamal 2019: 7).

Conclusions and Policy Recommendations

This chapter attempts to clarify how various policy initiatives and innovative uses of digital tools for service process simplification have reduced the gap between the ordinary citizens and the government employees by bringing the once inaccessible government services at the citizens' doorsteps. The economic progress in Bangladesh has been linked to reducing the inequality also by direct government interventions through various programs like social safety net expenditures, disaster risk reduction/management projects, and employment generating activities. "The government's enviable capacity to realize this socio-economic vision within the quickest possible time has already been proven. Through the implementation of the planned and inclusive development strategies of the government, the country has achieved a sustained and high rate of growth with unprecedented speed" (Kamal 2019: 99).

Though there are lapses and omissions, the role of the government, sometimes very directive one, in the economic and social progress of Bangladesh cannot be downplayed. Also, a dirigisme government may not be totally unwarranted if Bangladesh wants to become a poverty-free middle-income country by 2021 and a peaceful and developed country by 2041. On her pathway to this progress, a good number of long-term visionary and clearly articulated actions and perspective plans with strategic objectives have to be implemented. They should have measurable targets, key performance indicators, known timeline, periodic and annual accountability monitoring framework, and so on. At the same time, the government should have a responsive bureaucracy with a decentralized structure and virtual service-orientation from routine opaque centralized job-orientation. The discussion has shown that Bangladesh has a definitive formal plan to be a middle-income country by 2021, to reach the development junction by 2030 by achieving SDGs, to be the long-cherished Golden Bengal by 2041 being a developed and innovative nation-state.

Although Bangladesh has initiated or completed many regulatory and policy preparations keeping an upfront developed country agenda, successful instances are still few in cases of taking quick but appropriate and lawful punitive measures against the wrongdoers who are exploiting the benefits for their personal interest. Delayed or no actions even in the e-filing system sometimes frustrate its fundamental purpose, and TCV-led innovation becomes counter-productive. A visible speedy redress process is yet to be obtained. Virtual tools become ineffective if the person to take action is not within reach due to his remote location or poor mobile connectivity. Agencies working with financial and executive independence are not supported in many cases with appropriate human resources and other help where prior approval is needed from the relevant government body. The digital hassle is evident in case of proper maintenance and switching to the latest upper versions of hardware and software and the arrangement of needed training. Transferability of the government executives across the ministries and divisions sometimes causes the problem in taking action or making the individual official accountable for specific prior actions. There are some areas (particularly, in disaster management) where policy-overlapping causes delayed permission or the time-consuming communication with multiple authorities. Hence, there is a need for stocktaking of the government initiatives having unsatisfactory progress, followed by a critical assessment and stakeholder consultation, which will pave the way to smooth functioning of the government service delivery system as a citizen-centric mechanism.

Notes

1. But the fact is that in the meeting of the interdepartmental Washington Special Actions Group (WSAG) held in the White House on December 6, 1971, which was chaired by Kissinger, at one point Ural Alexis Johnson (1908–97), the then US Under Secretary of State, remarked that Bangladesh was likely to be an "international basket case" and Kissinger remarked that it would not necessarily be "our basket case" (Teltsch 1972: 3; Bari 2008).
2. Faaland and Parkinson presented their revisionist article in an international conference organized by the Bangladesh Institute of Development Studies (BIDS) in December 2007 (Shahabuddin and Rahman 2009: xxiii).
3. The Election Manifesto of Bangladesh Awami League in the Ninth National Parliament Election (held on 29 December 2008) was titled as "A Charter for Change" and released in December 2008 (Livsey 2009: 68, 75). See the Election Manifesto of Bangladesh Awami League at the 9th Parliamentary Election 2008, titled "A Charter for Change" for the details of "Vision 2021." In fact, this was translated into a long-term Perspective Plan 2010–21 (GOB 2015b: iii; and http://www.albd.org/articles/news/31125/Election-Manifesto-of-Bangladesh-Awami-League,-9th-Parliamentary-Election,-2008 (accessed 07.09.2018).
4. In the *Seventh Five Year Plan FY2016–FY 2020*, it has been mentioned that Vision 2041 is still being formulated (GOB 2015b: 450). As informed in April 2017 by the Finance Minister A.M.A. Muhith that the 20-year vision document is expected to be ready by 2021, work on which in full swing would begin in 2018. See https://www.dhakatribune.com/bangladesh/2017/04/26/goal-becoming-developed-nation-2041 (accessed 07.09.2018).
5. Personally, Prime Minister Sheikh Hasina was awarded 'UNESCO Peace Tree Award' (2014) for her commitment to women's empowerment and girls" education (MDG-3); "Champions of the Earth" (2015) by United Nations Environment Programme (UNEP) for Policy Leadership (MDG-7); UN-Women recognized her as "Planet 50-50 Champion" (2016) for outstanding contribution in empowering women (MDG-3), and the Global Partnership Forum awarded her "Agent of Change Award" (2016) to recognize her as a champion of gender equality and women's empowerment (MDG-3) (Sen 2018).
6. The Maya Declaration was launched at the 2011 AFI Global Policy Forum in Riviera Maya, Mexico, mainly to promote the making of a country's concrete financial inclusion targets and to implement in-country policy improvements thereon.

References

Access to Information Programme. (2009, November). Digital Bangladesh Concept Note. Dhaka: Prime Minister's Office. Retrieved June 30, 2019, from https://www.apc.org/en/blog/digital-bangladesh-concept-note-access-information-programme-prime-ministers-office-5112009.

Access to Information Programme. (2016). A TCV+ Study on E-filling Service of DESC. Dhaka: Prime Minister's Office. Retrieved June 30, 2019, from https://a2i.gov.bd/wp-content/uploads/2018/01/23-29_E-Filing-Service-of-DESC-A-TCV-study.pdf.

Access to Information Programme. (2018, April). Union Digital Centres. Dhaka: Prime Minister's Office.

Access to Information Programme. (2019, February). *An evaluation of 'e-Nothi' system in government office management*. Dhaka: Prime Minister's Office.

Ahluwalia, I. J., & Hussain, Z. (2004, September 4–10). Development achievements and challenges. *Economic and Political Weekly, 39*(36), 4013–4022.

Ahmed, M. (2019). 54 'helplines' to get services: Most calls come at 999 number. The *Prothom Alo* (a vernacular daily published from Dhaka; dated 4 August 2019), *21*(267), 1–2.

Arafin, K. S. (2016). Concept of Government Performance Management System (GPMS). Retrieved June 30, 2016, from https://rdcd.portal.gov.bd.

Bangladesh Awami League. (2018). *Bangladesh on the march towards prosperity: Election Manifesto 2018*. Dhaka: Bangladesh Awami League; published on December 18, 2018.

Bangladesh Financial Intelligence Unit (BFIU). (2015, October). NGO/NPO Sector Assessment of Bangladesh. Dhaka: Bangladesh Financial Intelligence Unit. Retrieved June 12, 2019, from https://www.bb.org.bd/pub/research/sp_research_work/srw1505.pdf.

Bari, M. R. (2008, March). The basket case. *Forum*, a monthly publication of *The Daily Star*, 3(3). Retrieved December 26, 2018, from https://archive.thedailystar.net/forum/2008/march/basket.htm.

Bhuiyan, A. R., & Jahan, M. (2017). Empirical analysis of critical affairs related to current Annual Performance Agreement in Bangladesh. *IOSR Journal of Humanities and Social Science, 22*(10), 26–30.

Business Initiative Leading Development (BUILD). (2017). *Report on Private Sector Development Policy Coordination Committee (PSDPCC) 2011–2017*. Dhaka: BUILD. Retrieved from www.buildbd.org

Chowdhury, A., & Zaman, H. (2013). Rethinking migration: Role of microenterprises in Bangladesh. *Economic and Political Weekly, 48*(40), 23–25.

Chowdhury, A., & Zaman, H. (2014). Embedding innovation in government's DNA: Lessons from Bangladesh. *Information Technology in Developing Countries, 24*(2), 9–12.

Demirgüç-Kunt, A., Klapper, L., Singer, D., Ansar, S., & Hess, J. (2018). *The Global Findex Database 2017: Measuring financial inclusion and the Fintech revolution*. Washington, DC: World Bank.

Eckstein, D., Hutfils, M.-L., & Winges, M. (2018, December). Global Climate Risk Index 2019: Who suffers most from extreme weather events? Weather-related loss events in 2017 and 1998 to 2017. *Briefing Paper*. Bonn, Germany: Germanwatch e.V. Retrieved June 28, 2019, from https://www.germanwatch.org/sites/germanwatch.org/files/Global%20Climate%20Risk%20Index%202019_2.pdf.

Faaland, J., & Parkinson, J. R. (1976, May). *Bangladesh: The test case for development* (1st ed.). London: C. Hurst & Co. Publishers Ltd.

Faaland, J., & Parkinson, J. R. (2009). Bangladesh: The test case for development revisited. Chap. 3 in Q. Shahabuddin & R. I. Rahman (Eds.), *Development experience and emerging challenges* (pp. 33–39). Dhaka: The University Press Ltd. and Bangladesh Institute of Development Studies.

Government of Bangladesh (GOB). (2005). *Bangladesh Economic Review 2005*. Dhaka: Finance Division, Ministry of Finance Government of the People's Republic of Bangladesh.

Government of Bangladesh (GOB). (2011). *Sixth Five Year Plan—FY2011–FY2015: Accelerating Growth and Reducing Poverty*. Dhaka: General Economics Division, Planning Commission, Government of the People's Republic of Bangladesh.

Government of Bangladesh (GOB). (2012a, April). *Perspective Plan of Bangladesh 2010–2021: Making Vision 2021 a Reality*. Dhaka: General Economics Division, Planning Commission, Government of the People's Republic of Bangladesh.

Government of Bangladesh (GOB). (2012b, October). *National Integrity Strategy of Bangladesh*. Dhaka: Cabinet Division, GOB.

Government of Bangladesh (GOB). (2013, May). *An Independent Review of National Integrity Strategy (NIS)*. Dhaka: Cabinet Division, GOB.

Government of Bangladesh (GOB). (2014). *Guidelines for Annual Performance Agreement (APA) 2014–2015*. Dhaka: Cabinet Division, Government of the People's Republic of Bangladesh.

Government of Bangladesh (GOB). (2015a). *Guidelines for Annual Performance Agreement (APA) 2015–2016*. Dhaka: Cabinet Division, Government of the People's Republic of Bangladesh.

Government of Bangladesh (GOB). (2015b). *Seventh Five Year Plan FY2016–FY 2020: Accelerating Growth, Empowering Citizens*. Dhaka: General Economics Division, Planning Commission, Government of the People's Republic of Bangladesh; December.

Government of Bangladesh (GOB). (2018a). *Bangladesh Economic Review 2018*. Dhaka: Finance Division, Ministry of Finance Government of the People's Republic of Bangladesh.

Government of Bangladesh (GOB). (2018b, December). *Grievance Redress System Guidelines, 2015 (Revised 2018)*. Dhaka: Cabinet Division, Government of the People's Republic of Bangladesh.

Government of Bangladesh (GOB). (2019a, June). *The Medium Term Budget Framework 2019–20*. Dhaka: Finance Division, Ministry of Finance, Government of the People's Republic of Bangladesh.

Government of Bangladesh (GOB). (2019b). *Bangladesh Economic Review 2019*. Dhaka: Finance Division, Ministry of Finance Government of the People's Republic of Bangladesh.

Islam, M. A. (2015, May). *Macro economic management in Bangladesh: Performance, pitfalls and prescriptions*. Dhaka: Gripper Mark Publication.

Islam, N. (2009). Institutions for policymaking for development. Chap. 3 in Q. Shahabuddin & R. I. Rahman (Eds.), *Development experience and emerging challenges* (pp. 3–24). Dhaka: The University Press Ltd. and Bangladesh Institute of Development Studies.

Kamal, A. H. M. M. (2019, June 13). *Bangladesh on a pathway to prosperity—Time is ours, time for Bangladesh: budget speech 2019–20*. Dhaka: Ministry of Finance, Government of Bangladesh.

Khan, A. A. (2010). *Friendly fires, Humpty Dumpty disorder, and other essays: Reflections on economy and governance in Bangladesh*. Dhaka: The University Press Limited.

Khan, A. A. (2015). *Gresham's law syndrome and beyond: An analysis of the Bangladesh bureaucracy*. Dhaka: The University Press Limited.

Livsey, M. (2009, March). *Bangladesh Ninth National Parliament Election-29 December 2008: Final report of the International Election Observation Mission of the Asian Network for Free Elections (ANFREL)*. Bangkok: ANFREL. Retrieved September 6, 2018, from http://aceproject.org.

Mahmood, I., & Babool, A. I. (2009). eGovernance for development: Bangladesh perspectives. *eGOV sharE*, 383–406. Retrieved June 30, 2019, from https://www.academia.edu/8271110/eGOVERNANCE_FOR_DEVELOPMENT_BANGLADESH_PERSPECTIVES.

Mahmud, W. (2008). Social development in Bangladesh: Pathways, surprises and challenges. *Indian Journal of Human Development, 2*(1), 79–92.

Ministry of Finance (MoF). (2019). *Budgets for Social Safety Net Programs*. Retrieved August 20, 2019, from https://mof.portal.gov.bd/site/page/32220b73-846f-4a33-b4c0-a6650c918e25/Safety-Net.

Mir, M., & Bala, S. K. (2014). NGO accountability in Bangladesh: Two contrasting cases. *VOLUNTAS: International Journal of Voluntary and Nonprofit Organizations, 26*(5), 1831–1851.

Moazzem, K. G., & Ali, M. (2019, March). *The power and energy sector of Bangladesh: Challenges of moving beyond the transition stage*. Dhaka: Centre for Policy Dialogue.

Morshed, K. A. M. (2006). Programme Initiation Document: Access to Information (A2I) Programme. Submitted to United Nations Development Programme, Bangladesh Country Office by e-Government Cell, Prime Minister's Office, Government of the People's Republic of Bangladesh. Retrieved June 30, 2019, from https://a2i.gov.bd/wp-content/uploads/2017/11/2-Strategy_a2i_Phase1-2007.pdf.

Mujeri, M. K., & Chowdhury, T. T. (2013). *Quick rental power plants in Bangladesh: An economic appraisal*. Dhaka: Bangladesh Institute of Development Studies.

Riaz, A. (2015, January). *How did we arrive here?* Dhaka: Prothoma Prokashan.

Sawada, Y., Mahmud, M., & Kitano, N. (2018). Introduction. In Y. Sawada, M. Mahmud, & N. Kitano (Eds.), *Economic and social development of Bangladesh: Miracle and challenges* (pp. xxi–xxxix). London and New York: Palgrave Macmillan.

Sen, S. (2018). Achievement of MDGs and adaptation of SDGs: Bangladesh context. Presentation dated 15 February 2018. Retrieved December 20, 2018, from http://brri.portal.gov.bd/sites/default/files/files/brri.portal.gov.bd/page/637ff401_77bd_4246_a17a_589f890b050b/SDGs%20presentation%20for%20BINA%2012.02.18_f.pdf.

Shahabuddin, Q., & Rahman, R. I. (2009). Editor's introduction. In Q. Shahabuddin & R. I. Rahman (Eds.), *Development experience and emerging challenges* (pp. xxiii–xxxxv). Dhaka: The University Press Ltd. and Bangladesh Institute of Development Studies.

Teltsch, K. (1972, January 7). Nations cautious on Bangladesh. *The New York Times*, 3. Retrieved December 28, 2018, from https://www.nytimes.com/1972/01/07/archives/nations-cautious-on-bangladesh.html?smid=pl-share.

The Economist. (2012, November 2). Bangladesh: Out of the basket–Lessons from Bangladesh. Retrieved December 20, 2018, from https://www.economist.com/feast-and-famine/2012/11/02/out-of-the-basket.

The Financial Express. (2018). Govt endorses Delta Plan. Published on September 5, 2018: 1 & 7.

United Nations (UN). (2000). *United Nations millennium declaration*. Retrieved December 20, 2018 from https://www.un.org/en/development/desa/population/migration/generalassembly/docs/globalcompact/A_RES_55_2.pdf.

United Nations. (2018, April 10). Leaving the LDC category: Booming Bangladesh prepares to graduate. Retrieved August 19, 2019, from https://www.un.org/development/desa/capacity-development/2018/04/10/leaving-theldc-category-booming-bangladesh-prepares-to-graduate/.

World Economic Forum. (2019). *The Global Risks Report 2019* (14th ed.). Geneva: World Economic Forum.

Zaman, H. (2015). Service delivery process innovation: Insights from Digital Bangladesh. *Innovation and Development*, 5(1), 165–168.

CHAPTER 12

NGOs for Development: Experience of Bangladesh

Tamgid Ahmed Chowdhury, Ashit Baran Das, Liton Chakraborty, and Munim Kumar Barai

Introduction

Bangladesh became independent in 1971 through a nine-month-long war of liberation. Considered as a 'Basket Case' (refer to Bari 2008 for detail) by prominent leaders and a 'Test Case for Development' by intellectuals (Faaland and Parkinson 1976), Bangladesh successfully took several giant steps over time in achieving most of the Millennium Development Goals

The views expressed here are the authors' own, and in no way reflect the same of the respective institutions they belong to.

T. A. Chowdhury (✉)
School of Business and Economics, North South University, Dhaka, Bangladesh
e-mail: tamgid.ahmed@northsouth.edu

A. B. Das
Financial Planning and Management, BRAC, Dhaka, Bangladesh
e-mail: ashit.das@brac.net

L. Chakraborty
University of Waterloo, Waterloo, ON, Canada

M. K. Barai (ed.), *Bangladesh's Economic and Social Progress*,
https://doi.org/10.1007/978-981-15-1683-2_12

(MDGs) (Planning Commission of GoB 2015). For instance, it was reported that the proportion of people living below the national poverty line (2122 kcal) was 56.7 percent in 1992 and the rate reduced to 31.5 percent whereas the target was to achieve 29 percent within 2015. As per the Household Income and Expenditure Survey 2016–17, the poverty rate is now 24.3 percent only (BBS 2017). Again, the net enrolment rate in primary education found to be 97.7 percent compared to the targeted rate of 100 percent. The under-five mortality rate became 46/1000 even though the target was 48/1000. Similarly, the infant mortality rate per 1000 was targeted to 31; however, achieved to 32 (BBS 2015; Planning Commission of GoB 2015). The Bangladesh economy, unlike many other less-developed countries, has maintained a robust economic growth rate of around six percent for the last decade despite the global financial crisis. In recognition of the excellent performances of the country, the United Nations Department of Economic and Social Affairs (2018) categorized Bangladesh as a country in the league of 'developing nations' and acknowledged Bangladesh as a more stable and balanced economy than any other country in South Asia.

Sen (1984), in his capability approach, argued that the central role of government and other development organizations is to endow people with necessary conditions to actualize necessary capacities. In addition to the support of the government, the ongoing development and balanced economic trend in Bangladesh has mainly been contributed by the non-government organizations (NGOs). Especially in the past two decades, their role is noteworthy (Islam 2016; Jakia 2010). One of the motives for this revived gusto about NGO derives from the fact that this particular sector has contributed to the transformation of the country from a wretchedly poor 'Basket Case' of the 1970s to a harbinger in novelties in social services (particularly for the poor mass) in the 1990s (Chowdhury and Mukhopadhaya 2012). For example, the number of NGOs has grown in maximum by 1160 in the 1990s (known as the golden age of GO-NGO partnership) and 340 in the 2000s (Bangladesh Bank 2015) and on those mentioned periods, the poverty reduction rates were 4.8 percent and 3.5 percent, respectively, which are reported to be highest in the history of Bangladesh (Hossain 2014). Moreover, studies indicated that the percentage of total aid to Bangladesh that was channeled through NGOs increased

M. K. Barai
Graduate School of Management, Ritsumeikan Asia Pacific University, Beppu, Japan
e-mail: baraimk@apu.ac.jp

to 32 percent in 2000 from 10 percent in 1990 (Bangladesh Bank 2015). In 2015, this rate increased to 49 percent of the total aid. All these stated facts approve the credibility as well as the contribution made by the NGO sector in the development of Bangladesh. As NGOs' contributions are well recognized, the question of interest in this chapter is how and in what form the NGO sector aided economic, social, and political development in Bangladesh?

Noticeably, the focus of NGOs has been shifted and expanded over time from rehabilitation in the 1970s to credit delivery, poverty alleviation, and other development services in recent times. This expansion activity was officially recognized by the Government of Bangladesh (GoB) in their fourth Five-Year Plan (1990–95). In the relevant literature, NGO and micro-finance institutions (MFI) are used interchangeably even though there are differences between them. According to the World Bank (1995), NGOs are to relieve suffering, promote the interest of the poor, protect the environment, and provide essential social services. On the other hand, MFIs are entitled to deliver credit to the poor as this segment of the population does not have access to formal financial institutions (FIs). However, as mentioned before, NGOs in Bangladesh have expanded their operation to credit delivery as well, which made MFIs '*credit-only*' and NGOs '*credit-plus*' institutions. Considering the revised scopes of activities, Bangladesh Bank (2015: 31) broadly categorized NGOs as Microcredit NGOs (NGO-MFI) and Development NGOs (NGO-Development). According to the NGO Affair Bureau (NGOAB 2019), currently, 2472 registered NGOs are working in Bangladesh, out of which 2224 are local, and 248 are foreign NGOs. In addition to credit delivery, Bangladeshi NGO-MFIs are working tirelessly on the overall social capacity development for rural population through relief and rehabilitation (such as *Swanirvor Bangladesh* and *Terre Des Hommes*), education (Bangladesh Rural Advancement Committee [BRAC]), health and family planning (*Gono Shastho Kendra*), microcredit (BRAC, ASA), empowerment and legal support Bangladesh Environmental Lawyers Association (BELA), infrastructure development Danish International Development Agency (DANIDA), sanitation and water supply Cooperative for Assistance and Relief Everywhere (CARE), sustainable development programs Oxford Committee for Famine Relief (OXFAM), and research and communication (BRAC) (Bangladesh Bank 2015).

The NGO sector is not free from criticism for reaching less number (only 20 percent) of rural marginal poor (ADB 2010), weaker administrative setup (Islam 2016), involvement in corruption and political patronage (Brinkerhoff et al. 2007), and charging high effective interest rate (MRA 2011). However, in 2015, more than 120,000 people got employment in NGOs, 26 million poor are served by NGOs out of which 20.35 million are credit borrowers (97 percent of that are women) with a loan recovery rate of 95.64 percent, and amount saved by the NGO members is 132.02 billion BDT. To validate the successes of NGOs in Bangladesh a case study on the Bangladesh Rural Advancement Committee (BRAC)—a top-ranked global NGO originated from Bangladesh—is used in this chapter to exemplify how a holistic and philanthropic approach of social development has turned into a role model of self-sustainable organization.

The rest of this chapter is formed as follows: Section "Defining NGO-MFI: A Review of the Growth of NGOs and Their Changing Role in Bangladesh" summarizes the historical evolution of the NGO sector with the theoretical justification of their growth. Section "Appraisal of Evolutionary Changes of NGOs to Address Development" explains the evolutionary changes of NGO operations in Bangladesh. Section "NGO'S Contributions to the Development of Bangladesh" discusses the noticeable contributions of NGOs, which got less attention in the available literature. These are the contributions that seem to have evolved in parallel to the development needs of the country. Section "BRAC's Contribution to the Development of Bangladesh" takes up the case of BRAC as a role model to substantiate the contributions of NGOs in the development of Bangladesh. Section "Concluding Remarks" concludes the chapter with some significant debates on NGO operations and possible remedies to the pitfalls.

A Review of the Growth of NGOs and Their Changing Role in Bangladesh

Even though there are several definitions of NGO are available in the literature (refer to Bebbington and Farrigon 1992), a more operational definition would be:

> NGOs are non-profit and not politically attached organizations that work for social welfare in the public interest. Hence the concept of NGO is generally restricted to social, cultural, environmental, and legal advocacy having a non-commercial vision in public works.

However, as NGOs are heavily engaged in poverty alleviation through the delivery of microcredit, the above definition now includes the 'economic' aspect too and therefore most NGOs are termed as NGO-MFIs (Bangladesh Bank 2015).

The Emergence of NGO-MFIs as a Response to Market Failure

Before 1971 and the 1970s: Relief and Rehabilitation

NGOs have a long history of operations even in the colonial period when Christian Missionaries and Hindu and Muslim community-based organizations established orphanages and schools. During 1947–71 (East Pakistan regime), NGOs mostly performed community services and disaster relief works. Before the war of independence, in the absence of Bangladeshi NGOs, few international voluntary organizations like Catholic Relief Services (CRS), the Society of Friends (Quakers) and CARE were working here with limited activities like relief work and emergency help (Huda 1987). There were very few NGOs who actively served during the liberation war. For example, *Gono Shahstho Kendra* and *Terre Des Hommes* offered medical assistance to freedom fighters and rehabilitation to unwanted war children, respectively.

Soon after the independence, the scenario drastically changed as there was colossal destruction of economic base and infrastructure during the liberation war. Millions of people became homeless and about ten million people went to India for shelter as refugees. After independence, they returned to Bangladesh and lacked food, medicine, shelter, and other fundamental rights and needs. Hence, to support the relief and rehabilitation activities, the first generation of NGOs in Bangladesh emerged. Bangladesh Rural Advancement Committee (BRAC) was founded immediately after the liberation war and played a vital role in the relief and rehabilitation activities. In addition to disbursing humanitarian aid, rehabilitation, and reconstruction, NGOs began contributing to informal education and health care at a small scale (DFID 2005). Also, NGOs helped the government in flood control programs, immunization, and family planning programs. At that time, NGOs were preferred due to their close association with the people, flexibility, and quality assurance. Also, donors started liking NGOs as these non-profit organizations could design a well-suited and appropriate mix of public goods by engaging the poor in the process. The stated reasons for NGO proliferation theoretically support the 'Entrepreneurship theory' of the non-profit, which argues that social entrepreneurs, instead of generating monetary value create social values for the community (Ackerman 1996).

Very soon, it had been realized that the distinctive welfare and charity orientation would not be enough for sustainable development, especially for those who needed more than emergency sustenance. Hence, transformation in NGO activities, especially in their vision and mission, took place in several phases up to the 1980s. In the mid-1970s, it was found that poverty and inflation rates in the country were around 71 percent and 40 percent, respectively (Hossain 2014), and thus there was an immense need to offer finance to those (especially in rural areas) who were living at the bottom of the social ladder in terms of income. These marginal poor neither qualified for a loan from the formal financial institutions because they could not fulfill the requirements (such as collateral or higher cost per customer), nor could they absorb the higher interest rate charged by rural informal moneylenders called *Mohajon* (Yunus 2008). A study by Thomas (1992) reported that in the 1970s, interest on loan charged by Mohajon was as high as 28 percent. So, at that period (1975–80), the emergence of NGO-MFIs is rooted in the failure of formal and informal financial institutions to serve this market. Theoretically, this reason of NGO-MFI proliferation supports 'the Public Goods Theory' offered by Weisbrod (1975) who argued that formal entities (especially government) tend to provide that level of public goods which satisfy the median voter and NGOs emerge to fulfill the demand of unsatisfied individuals whose demand is higher than the median. Failure of the formal and informal financial institutions (FIs) to meet the credit needs helped develop the idea of NGO-MFIs pioneered by the Grameen Bank. Later on, public and private banks also joined this newer market with more flexible financial products "targeted to micro and small enterprises and economically disadvantageous borrowers (Rashid et al. 2010). Figure 12.1 depicts the failure of the formal market to meet the demand for financial support of the marginalized people.

As soon as the number of NGOs increased with the plethora of services, they felt the need for a common platform where they can collaborate their activities and relationship with stakeholders like government, donors, and other NGOs. To meet up this requirement, the Association of Development Agencies in Bangladesh (ADAB) was established in 1974 where they could exchange their experiences and views and work collaboratively (Huda 1987). From 1976 to 1980, institutional building for the poor became a major focus of NGOs as they realized that removing structural impediments by building institutions for the poor was a must for not only providing the elementary facilities but also mitigating mass poverty. Hence, from the beginning of 1976, some NGOs modified their strategies and administered their programs and services to benefit the poor through what they called 'the target group approach' where the poor with similar economic interests were grouped together.

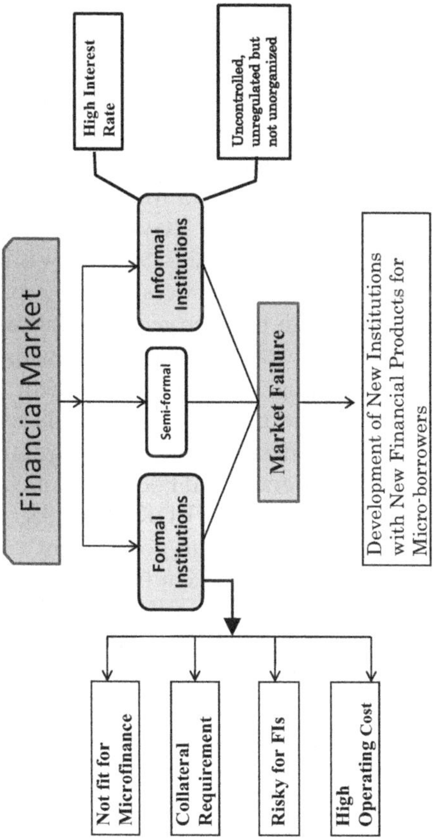

Fig. 12.1 Failure of Financial Market in Bangladesh in the 1970s (Source: Modified. Rashid et al. 2010)

The 1980s: Expansion of NGOs' Activities

During this period, NGOs in Bangladesh flourished significantly by making themselves self-reliant organizations for the impoverished mass and by providing basic facilities in health, family planning, and education. As per NGOAB (2015), 296 new NGOs started their operations during the 1980s. The innovation of collateral-free microcredit facility by Dr. Muhammad Yunus encouraged many NGO-MFIs to contribute to the development of the country. The development of the microcredit industry "has been closely associated with the experiences of NGOs and largely remains within their domain, government has always participated—to a relatively limited extent as providers and regulators, but more crucially in terms of creating an enabling environment for microfinance institutions, or at least not hindering them" (Hulme and Moore 2006). To regulate the rapidly rising microcredit operations by NGO-MFIs, the government established the NGOAB in 1990. In the mid-1980s, it was realized that NGOs' limited operation and small-scale services need to expand in larger segments of the population through broader geographical coverage. As a result, NGOs took the initiative to work in collaboration with the government, donors, and other relevant agencies and complement each other's efforts in rendering benefits to the needy population. Therefore, many collaborative initiatives like immunization and oral rehydration therapy (ORT) with BRAC, agriculture programs and Food for Works with CARE, and agriculture research and extension with RDRS took place. The aim of these collaborations was to complement the government's and donors' programs to a large extent and show a different type of orientation by the NGOs. These successful collaborations reflect the government's recognition and donors' reliance on NGO operations. Gradually, these initial collaborations were further extended to other sectors like health, population, environment, education, livestock and fisheries, women empowerment, youth development, disaster management, and emergency response. By this time, donors were reasonably convinced that NGOs in many aspects are more effective and acceptable than government agencies and other for-profits to the mass poor. More reliance of donors on NGOs approves that the flourishing of NGOs in the 1980s is theoretically supported by 'the Contract Failure Theory' (Hansmann 1980), which says that it is hard for the beneficiaries to police for-profit producers by ordinary contractual devices and therefore creates market failure. Non-profit firms (like NGOs) by contrast offer beneficiaries the advantage by owning the non-distributional constraint and have no chance to take advantage of the beneficiaries. As an example, NGOs could build their credibility due to their significant contribution to disaster management in the aftermath of terrible floods in 1987 and 1988. Also, the government in recognition involved the NGOs in legal aid works, human rights activities, and advocacies (Islam 2016).

The 1990s: Era of Government-NGO Collaboration
In the 1990s, NGO-MFIs engaged in numerous activities with government and other external parties, and some of those projects gained momentum because of GO-NGO collaboration. The Fourth Population and Health Project (World Bank 1996), The General Education Project (GEP), and Integrated Non-formal Education Project (IFEP) are some remarkable examples. Also, the government involved NGOs in election monitoring, political advocacies, public interest litigation, and educating voters (Bangladesh Bank 2016). In the 1990s, NGOs were running their activities almost independently without any interference from the government just by registering under the Societies Registration Act and Social Welfare Registration and Control Ordinance 1961. Bangladesh government offered a 10 percent tax rebate for the NGO-MFIs working in development programs.

Due to the success of microcredit operations and other humanitarian and development works, the NGO sector of Bangladesh received significant attention from the overseas governments and donors. For example, the amount of foreign aid and grants to NGOs has also amplified significantly from US$ 106.6 million in 1990–91 to US$ 310 in 2003–04 (190 percent increase). Also, NGOs' share of total aid to Bangladesh increased from US$ 180.0 million to 379.4 million (World Bank 2006). As the professionalism and credibility of the NGOs were well established among donors, a significant number of local and international NGOs started their operations during this timeframe. According to NGOAB (2015) report, 1160 new foreign-funded NGO-MFIs were registered in the 1990s (also refer to Fig. 12.2). To support the NGO-MFIs in expanding microcredit operations, the government established the *Palli Karma Shahayak Foundation* (PKSF), which served as a credit whole seller to NGO-MFIs. PKSF started working as the apex microcredit funding organization to the poor through partner organizations (POs). Considering the support of the government to the NGOs, it can be argued that the significant growth of this sector supports 'Subsidy Theory' (Fama and Jensen 1983) of

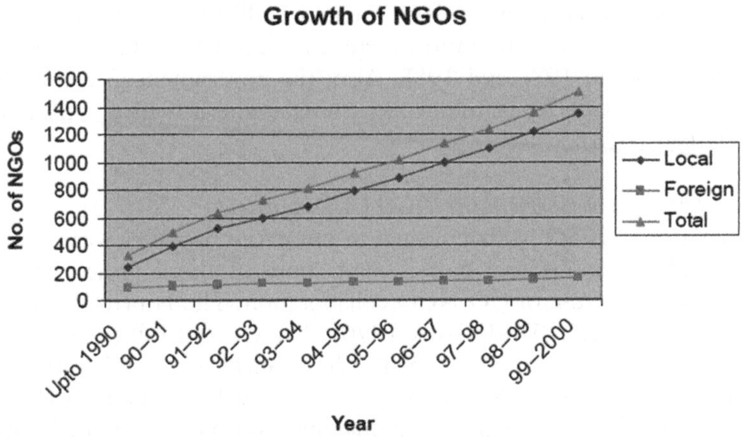

Fig. 12.2 Growth of NGOs in the 1990s. (Source: NGOAB 2015)

non-profits which argues that large scale expansion of non-profits is due to the subsidies provided by the state.

So far, NGOs gained more credibility and strengthened their position by demonstrating the potentiality to work with the government. But then again, before the 1990s, there was an absence of regulation from the government in the operations of NGOs. In a sense, NGOs were running their activities almost independently without any interference from the government. Hence, for making NGO activities accountable, government started applying rules such as (a) Societies Registration Act of 1860 (SRA), (b) Social Welfare Registration and Control Ordinance 1961 (SWR), (c) Foreign Donation (Voluntary Activity) Regulation Ordinance, 1978 (FDR), and (d) Foreign Contribution (Regulation) Ordinance, 1982 (FCO).

Post-2000 Role of NGO-MFIs

During the 2000s, focus and operation areas of NGO-MFIs have not changed by that much. Therefore, income-generating activities of NGOs were the most pronounced program in the development discourse in the 2000s. Besides, NGOs like BRAC started their international operations during this decade. As the living standard and financial condition of the population of Bangladesh, especially the clients of NGOs, improved, NGOs shifted their activities from Benevolent Model to Community

Contribution Model. Also, NGOs' contribution to attaining foreign grants and aid continued. For instance, fund released through NGO-MFIs was US$ 516 million in 2009, which increased to US$ 827 million at the end of 2018 (MRA 2018). This injection of foreign grants and aid contributed significantly to the Annual Development Program (ADP) of Bangladesh. In this period, Bangladeshi NGOs have started organizing international workshops and conferences for human resource development and expansion of their operations.

During the 2000s, there were significant controversies about NGO-MFIs' direct engagement to politics and disagreement within the sector. The split of ADAB and the establishment of the Federation of NGOs justify the mentioned argument. As a result, the government has moved away from the lenient approach and has created the Microcredit Regulatory Authority (MRA) in 2006 as the regulatory and supervising body of MFIs. Section 2(22) of the MRA Act 2006 states: "Microcredit means loan facilities offered by microcredit organization certified under the Act for poverty alleviation, employment generation and facilitate a small entrepreneur—" (MRA 2018: 6). Getting a license from the MRA is now mandatory for any microcredit operations in Bangladesh, and MRA reserves the right to cancel the license of MFIs. Recently, 118 NGO-MFIs lost their licenses due to non-compliance with the regulations of MRA.

Appraisal of Evolutionary Changes of NGOs to Address Development

As a developing country, Bangladesh has several socio-economic complications. Still, 24.3 percent of the total population lives in poverty due to a lack of access to resources and basic education. In recent years, due to significant migration from rural to urban areas, it was found that poverty fell faster in rural areas than the urban counterpart. For instance, between 2010 and 2016, rural poverty reduced from 35.2 to 26.4 percent, whereas for the urban area, the rates were 21.3 and 18.9 percent, respectively (HIES 2017). Observing the socio-economic barriers and infrastructural challenges, many NGOs have started helping the vulnerable urban dwellers of the country. The role of the NGO-MFI sector in the progress of macroeconomic indicators, including recent graduation to the rank of the middle-income country and achievement of food self-sufficiency is vital. For example, rural households have gradually experienced structural shifts in the level and composition of their household income. Per capita income of a rural household rose to US$ 580 in 2015 from US$ 157 in 1988 (PPRC 2016). Moreover, NGOs made a remarkable contribution to creating new income-generating opportunities for the grassroots rather than agriculture. Hence, remittances, business, technical labor, services, and so on became the most promising non-agricultural income. For example, 26 percent of rural people were engaged in businesses in 2015, whereas this rate was around 5–6 percent in the early 1990s (PPRC 2016).

Changes in Microcredit Operations

Over the years, micro-credit operations of NGO-MFIs evolved into three distinguished patterns (refer to Fig. 12.3). These are as follows: (a) *Credit Alone*: Under this minimalist approach, microcredit is seen as the core and critical element to addressing liquidity problems and hence, poverty of the marginalized poor. Many NGOs are still offering credit of this sort and they tend to evaluate successes of their operations in terms of their financial outreach indicators, reaching to women, and repayment rate. (b) *Credit Plus*: This approach considers poverty as a multidimensional issue than merely a liquidity problem and involves other services in addition to

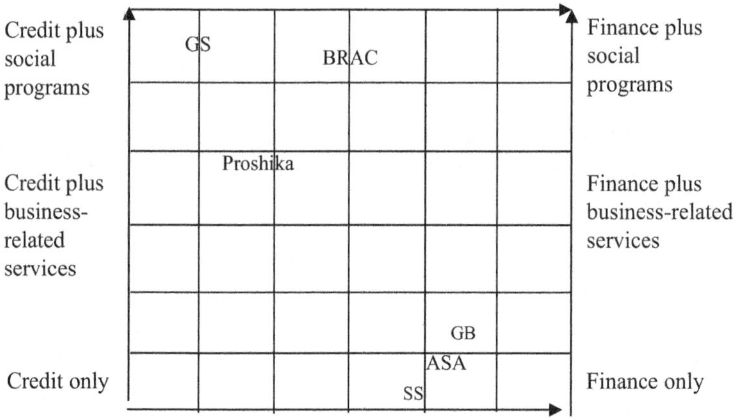

Fig. 12.3 Matrix of microfinance (and related) institutions in Bangladesh (Note: GS—Grameen Shikka, SS—Safe Save, ASA—Association for Social Advancement, BRAC—Bangladesh Rural Advancement Committee, GB—Grameen Bank. Source: Adapted from Hulme and Moore 2006)

credit. The members, for receiving microcredit and services, have to make compulsory and voluntary deposits. (c) *Credit with Social Development*: This approach blends income-generating microcredit with a host of other programs that contribute to the borrowers' skill development, healthcare, basic education, and awareness creation on various social and human rights issues.

Figure 12.3 contains the placement matrix of some of the biggest MFIs like ASA, BRAC, Grameen Bank, Grameen Shikka, Proshika, and Safe Save operating in Bangladesh in the grids to represent the diversity of their existing programs. For identification, the continuum between pure credit provision and broader financial service provision is on the horizontal axis, while the continuum between only credit or finance, credit or finance plus business-related services, and credit or finance plus social programs are shown on the vertical axis.

A quick look at the evolution in credit operation can find that theoretically, the changes are in line with the evolving concepts of poverty which changed over time from a physiological approach to a participatory and human rights approach. This means when poverty was mainly measured with physiological and basic needs approaches, the 'credit alone' method was implemented. However, when poverty was viewed broadly as participatory and human rights approaches, 'credit with social development' method was executed. The evolution has also followed the route of successive amalgamation of different newer and innovative intervention measures with microcredit to create sustainability of the borrowers (Barai and Moral 2002). The sustainability of the borrowers is where the long-term operational viability of microcredit lies. Interestingly, the additional interventions, delivered to the poor through their existing network mostly developed for channeling the microcredit, are intended to increase the effectiveness of the credit schemes as well. However, similar to the microcredit practice in other countries, providing credit has remained at the core of most of the programs of the microcredit practitioners in Bangladesh.

Changes in the Sources of Funds

NGO-MFIs in Bangladesh rely on a variety of sources of funds to finance their clients and dependency on those sources changed over time. In the 1980s to mid-1990s, external resources played an essential role in the experimentation, development, expansion, and subsequent growth in the outreach of microcredit. Not only that, the institutional strengthening of the NGO-MFIs through a management information system and human resource development was benefited by the external funds. Donors had incentives and desire to see that their fund was utilized to create a positive impact. Therefore, larger NGOs with a proven track record and demonstrated success in implementing projects got preference over the smaller ones in the selection and funding process of donors.

Zaman (2004) points out that the large NGOs had been reasonably successful in "managing donors". MFIs with a strategic sustainability plan required investment in the capital base for their expansion. They had to convince donors of the soundness of their strategy to use their funds. Donors with a long-term vision, also in their part, crucially required NGOs who were able to deliver. NGO-MFIs in other countries lacked to provide this sort of strategic view on the best use of donor resources as the resources had often been used to either subsidize final on-lending rates or support MCIs without a solid strategic plan.

The dependency on the external fund, nonetheless, got reduced through progressive internal resource generation by the NGO-MFIs (refer to Table 12.1). Funding share of donors was as high as 60 percent of the total in 1996 and that came down to 1.05 percent only in 2016 (MRA 2018), reducing the importance of the external source to an insignificant level in the process. The emergence of PKSF made a qualitative change in the sourcing of funds by MFIs in Bangladesh. Of late, commercial banks have also started playing an important role in funding the microcredit sector and supplied about one-fifth of the total fund for microcredit lending in 2016.

Table 12.1 Sources of funds for microcredit lending

Year	*Clients savings*	*PKSF loan*	*Banks' loan*	*Donors' fund*
1996 (percent)	25.2	11.9	3.0	60.0
1997 (percent)	17.9	18.0	15.2	33.1
2000 (percent)	27.5	24.8	10.6	20.0
2009 (percent)	30.6	15.6	18.9*	3.1
2011 (percent of total)	34.46	17.3	12.84	3.82
2015 (percent of total)	33.94	9.47	17.19	1.29
June 2016 (BDT mill.)	170,460	40,762	95,014	5108
2016 (percent of total)	34.92	8.35	19.46	1.05

Source: Compiled from MRA (2011, 2016, 2018), Annual Reports and CDF Statistics

Changes in the Outreach of Credit Operations

The outreach of microcredit has continually expanded since its inception to include more and more people in Bangladesh (refer to Table 12.2). The early 1990s, in particular, saw the rapid growth in coverage of microcredit, mainly due to the establishment of a wholesale financing institution, the PKSF (Hulme and Moore 2006). According to Zohir (2010), the annual average growth rate of the number of borrowers had been around 10 percent for major NGOs for more than a decade.

Till June 2016, the MRA has approved licenses in favor of 748 NGOs, while a total of 27.8 million people were the clients of around 16,284 branches of NGO-MFIs all over the country (MRA 2018) (refer to Table 12.2). Out of the total clients, 23.3 million were microcredit borrowers, constituting 14.6 percent of the total population of 160 million. In terms of the number of borrowers, the size grew by 2.2 times between 2003 and 2016. Though factoring out of the overlapping number of clients, whereby one person could be the member of multiple NGOs, could bring down the actual figure of borrowers, this number shows the outreach level of microcredit among the poor in Bangladesh. Looking from the disbursement of the fund point of view, the outstanding loan of the sector stood at BDT 460 billion while they collected BDT 171 billion as micro-savings at the end of June 2016. Again, this growth was maintained with a 96 percent recovery rate by MFIs. It is worthy of mentioning that since the beginning of the microcredit operation, around 97 percent of the borrowers are women (Akhter et al. 2018).

Table 12.2 Outreach of microfinance sector in Bangladesh

Particulars	*2003*	*2010*	*2013*	*2014*	*2015*	*2016*
No. of licensed NGO-MFI	720	516	649	742	753	758
Total clients (million)	14.63	25.28	24.60	25.11	26.0	27.79
Total borrowers (million)	10.65	19.21	19.27	19.42	20.35	23.28
Loan disbursed (billion Tk.)	NA	306.72	432.28	462.00	634.00	787.00
Loan outstanding (billion. TK)	36.49	145.02	257.01	282.20	352.41	459.37
Total savings (billion TK)	15.56	51.36	93.99	106.99	135.41	171.19
Loan recovery rate (percent)		97.35	97.69	95.64	96.02	96.8

Source: MRA Annual Report, various issues

Future of NGO-MFIs: Benevolent Model to Community Contribution Model

Funding has always remained the major challenge in NGOs' operation, and this will pose a much bigger threat as Bangladesh will lose getting grants/aids from donors after the country graduates to developing country status by 2024. For this reason, NGOs are reshaping their programs by introducing community contribution so that they can function appropriately, aligned with MDGs and social development goals. For instance, the currently unsolved challenges in Bangladesh are rapid unplanned urbanization, ensuring quality education for the twenty-first century, youth development, environmental and climate change management, and changes in the lifestyle and psychographic conditions of people. As mentioned before, the urban poverty reduction rate is much lower than that of rural Bangladesh—an important issue yet to be addressed. To tackle the above-mentioned challenges, NGOs can play a significant role due to their proven efficiency in service delivery and project management. As maintaining financial sustainability will become the main challenge to the NGOs shortly, several options are open to them. First, NGOs can serve as part of the government's annual development plan implementation. This will help the government to become a country of upper-middle-income by 2030. Current GO-NGO collaborations are of the best examples of NGOs' contribution as partners to government in the development of the country. To become a country with an annual per capita income of US$4136 (to be upper-middle category), the government needs to ensure development in each corner of the country. In doing so, NGOs' ability of innovation, connection to the grass-root level, and efficacy in project governance can be useful for the government to ensure equity-based development. It has to be ensured that NGOs are operating as per mandate to be coordinated with the national and local governments. Also, funding and expenditure policy has to be transparent and accountable to the concerned government agencies. Second, NGOs can initiate social enterprises to generate funds to run pilot programs subject to government approvals. In return, the part of their surplus that is spent for the welfare of people will be exempted from taxes as provided in taxation laws. For instance, Aarong, BRAC's social enterprise, has created hundreds of jobs and involved over 65,000 artisans across the country in the development process. It is, therefore, expected that the government's policy agenda will focus on incentives to encourage investment by the NGOs and improve security during this term.

But the surfing of various MRA reports (2018) highlights a highly skewed institutional concentration ratio of large MFIs as they are controlling the largest number of market clients, borrowers, and savings collected from the members. This may not augur well to the future of small scale microcredit players in Bangladesh because of severe competition in the microcredit operations and competitive edge of the bigger NGOs.

NGO'S CONTRIBUTIONS TO THE DEVELOPMENT OF BANGLADESH

Financial Inclusion and Employment

Financial inclusion (FI) means "individuals and businesses have access to useful and affordable financial products and services that meet their needs—transactions, payments, savings, credit and insurance—and are delivered in a responsible and sustainable way" (The World Bank 2018). In broader terms, these useful and affordable financial products and services could be from financial institutions, government, or NGOs. For developing countries like Bangladesh, FI is considered to be very crucial as many people have no or limited access to financial services to improve their living standards. FI helps those people (refer to Table 12.3) to make longer-term consumption and investment decisions, participate in productive activities, and cope with unexpected short-term shocks (Park and Mercado 2015).

The recent numbers (Table 12.3) show that a total of 27.79 million or 17.4 percent of the total population were financially included through NGOs. As a single component of finance and underprivileged characteristics of the clients, this has more socioeconomic impacts on the down the line people of the country.

The employment impact of NGOs has to be seen from two positions: the total number of employees engaged in running the microcredit operations of the NGOs as well as the credit-induced employment generated among the borrowers. Table 12.3 shows that as of 2016, there were a total of 127,820 employees working with 758 MFIs in Bangladesh. Taking into consideration of the unregistered NGOs with microcredit operations in remote parts of the country, the internal employment figure should add up further.

Studies (see for instance Chowdhury and Mukhopadhaya 2012), however, indicate mixed results of impacts of microcredit on employment and

Table 12.3 Access to finance and direct employment of NGOs in Bangladesh

Particulars	*2012*	*2013*	*2014*	*2015*	*2016*
No. of licensed NGO-MFIs	590	649	742	753	758
No. of employees	108,654	110,734	109,628	110,728	127,820
Total clients (million)	24.64	24.60	25.11	26.0	27.79
Total borrowers (million)	19.31	19.27	19.42	20.35	23.28
Loan disbursed (billion Tk.)	456.02	432.28	462.00	634.00	787.00
Agricultural loan disbursement (billion Tk.)	110.84	131.98	155.73	266.25	353.00
Agricultural loan as percentage of total disbursement	24.31	30.53	33.71	42.00	44.85

Source: Compiled from MRA (2016)

productivity in Bangladesh. For example, self-employment activities had more than 50 percent contribution to total income for the participants as against 43 percent in the case of non-participants (Ahmed 2004). Also, the average returns of the members are higher from non-agriculture activities compared with those engaged in livestock and agriculture.

Khandker et al. (2016) point out that microcredit could reduce the supply of wage laborers by increasing opportunities for self-employment, possibly leading to a rise in the wage rate. Moreover, microcredit programs significantly impacted total production as average household production increased by 56 percent for Grameen Bank and 57 percent for BRAC in program villages (Khandker et al. 2016). The report also found that a 10 percent rise in men's borrowing raises men's and women's labor supply by 0.5 percent and 0.4 percent, respectively. However, a similar increase in women's loans increases those outcomes by 0.4 percent and 0.6 percent, respectively. While loans for both genders raise non-land household assets by about the same percentage (0.4), men's loans have a comparatively higher impact on net worth.

Another noticeable contribution of NGO-MFIs is the employment generation for the educated labor force as well as the forgotten women, where the rate of unemployment is a burning concern for the government. The World Bank (2016) seems very satisfied at the performance of NGOs in providing microcredit in Bangladesh and thinks of NGO-based institutions as efficient and effective delivery vehicles for overcoming the failure of the formal financial sector to provide financial services to the poor by creating employment opportunity, reducing poverty, and correcting gender inequality.

Table 12.4 Loan Portfolios and Beneficiaries of Top NGOs/MFIs in Bangladesh (2016–17)

NGO-MFI	*Loan portfolio (BDT billion)*	*Loan disbursed (BDT billion)*	*Savings (BDT billion)*	*Borrowers (million)*
BRAC	155.5	269.6	53.4	5.55
ASA	154.7	266.6	66.6	6.79
Buro Bangladesh	32.8	54.4	10.3	0.99
TMSS	18.7	33.1	5.9	0.74
SSS	15.1	27.6	5.8	0.49

Source: MRA (2017), Annual Report 2017

Indeed, the employment impact of microcredit has to be seen from two positions: the total number of employees engaged in running the micro-credit operations of the MFIs as well as the credit-induced employment generated among the borrowers. Table 12.3 shows that as of June 2016, there were a total of 127,820 employees working with 758 MFIs in Bangladesh. Taking into consideration the unregistered informal NOGs which have microcredit operations in remote parts of the country, the internal employment figure should add up further (Barai 2019). The working days for the female labor force also went up over time as the participation of the female labor force in non-agricultural activities has also increased. As the continuation of initiatives, NGOs have arranged many income-generating activities like apiculture, silk production embroidery, fishnet matching, livestock, and poultry to increase the socio-economic condition of women. BRAC, as the biggest microcredit institution, has created a sole opportunity for females in its every branch for the post of the cashier, where local underprivileged women and widows are preferred to join. Table 12.4 shows the contributions of leading NGOs in terms of memberships, loan portfolio, loan disbursement, as well as savings encouragement in the economy for the year 2016–17.

NGO-MFIs and Allocation of Foreign Aid

NGOs in Bangladesh receive aid/grants from foreign sources channeled through multilateral aid agencies via international NGOs, foreign private donors, embassies, and so on. Even though donors provide funds to NGOs in different ways, the most common one is funding for a specific project. In some cases, donors found to have funded the whole range of activities of the NGOs. In recent times, as funding small NGOs has become costlier for donors, they prefer to channel it through larger vehicles.

Table 12.5 Foreign aid flows through NGOs in Bangladesh

Year	*Grants to NGO-MFIs (in Million US$)*	*Share of NGOs to total aid (percent)*
1990–91	106.6	11.4
2000–01	250.9	33.2
2009–10	516.03	44.7
2013–14	719.01	51.37
2014–15	749.8	NA

Source: ERD, Ministry of Finance (2015)

The share of foreign aid going to NGOs had increased sharply and especially in the 2000s (refer to Table 12.5). As could be seen, the total paid to the NGO sector increased from 11.4 percent (US$106.6 million) in 1990–91 to 51.37 percent (US$719.01 million) in 2013–14 (ERD 2015). Notably, the figures reported in Table 12.5 do not include the share of credit funds disbursed by lending agencies channeling through NGOs due to lack of record in the NGOAB. Sector-wise foreign fund allocation through NGOs revealed that in 2015, the health sector got the highest funding of US$15898.68 million, followed by US$9507.62 million in education. Foreign funds to NGOs for environmental protection are rising too, and in 2015, US$314.99 million was disbursed. Figure 12.4 shows the trend of the percentage of foreign aid flow through NGOs in Bangladesh since 1990.

Nevertheless, the size of the ADP has continued to grow at a steady pace and reflects the ambition of a country that has clocked successive years of 6 percent-plus growth rates and is widely celebrated globally as a development miracle. Besides, dependence on aid has decreased over time, as demonstrated by the fact that government spending has increased at a far higher pace than aid where NGO's role is inevitable. NGO's Microcredit Program enabled the poor mass to improve their lifestyle and loan repayable capability. Hence, it is to be noted that by attracting foreign aids and grants and injecting these to the national economy, NGOs of Bangladesh have played a prominent role in this "Rehabilitation to Development" journey.

Humanitarian Response to Rohingya Refugee Crisis

In 2017, nearly a million Rohingya, among whom 60 percent are children with high rates of malnutrition, were forced to flee their homes and seek refuge in Bangladesh. This Rohingya issue has become a significant chal-

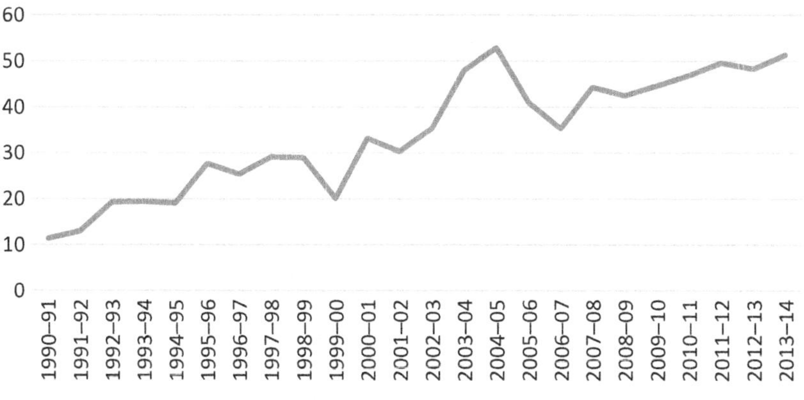

Fig. 12.4 Trend of foreign aid flow through NGOs against total flows to Bangladesh, 1991–2014 (%). (Source: ERD, Ministry of Finance 2015)

lenge to the GoB concerning service delivery and ensuring the supply of basic needs. Therefore, over one hundred local, national, and international NGOs were allowed to respond to the crisis along with the Government and UN agencies. In 2018, US$ 655 million were received by NGOs and Partners from donors to support Rohingya refugees in 10 essential needs. Also, in 2018, the World Bank announced a grant of US$ 480 million. Due to the collaborative effort of government and NGOs, the prevalence of Global Acute Malnutrition among Rohingyas dropped from 19 percent to 12 percent (below the emergency threshold level), food security has significantly improved, immunization coverage increased to 89 percent, and women health facilities rose from 22 percent to 40 percent (UNHCR 2019).

BRAC's Contribution to the Development of Bangladesh

We should not lose sight of working for those who need our hands the most.
—Sir Fazle Hasan Abed KCMG, Founder and Chairperson, BRAC

With a slogan of "Small is beautiful, scale is necessary" BRAC (initially known as Bangladesh Rehabilitation Assistance Committee) was founded in 1972 by Sir Fazle Hasan Abed within a small subdistrict of Bangladesh, Shalla, to help the return of war victims. After the completion of initial relief centric work, BRAC, with a new acronym of the 'Bangladesh Rural Advancement Committee' and then as 'Building Resources Across Communities', realized the need for long-term development activities rather than implementing rehabilitation activities only. As the problems such as poverty, malnutrition, lack of education, empowerment, and so on were structural and chronic, BRAC started their new mission aligned with its vision of creating 'a world free from all sort of exploitation and discrimination where everyone should have an opportunity to realize their potential'. To empower people and communities in the situation of poverty, diseases, illiteracy, social prejudice, and injustice, BRAC's interventions aim at achieving large scale, positive changes through an economic and social program that enabled men and women to realize their potential. BRAC has developed a holistic approach for social development and consequently, turned into a self-sustainable model from the philanthropic model—which is now acknowledged as the number-1 NGO of the world (NGO Advisor 2018). This recognition inspired us to incorporate the contributions of BRAC as a case in the overall development of Bangladesh.

BRAC's Unique Approaches

It is argued that BRAC has several noticeable unique approaches that contributed to the success of the organization. A few of them are discussed here:

1. BRAC's fundamental idea is to start any project on a pilot basis or small scale, and then learn from it, adjust or re-adjust it. When the pilot project starts benefitting the cause, take it to a larger scale. BRAC believes that innovation is the key to their growth and success, and they focus more on social than technical innovation. This pilot-based learning attitude helped BRAC to expand its operations both locally and internationally.
2. BRAC wants to make a significant difference in the lives of poor people. And gradually, BRAC wants to change its free-service recipient beneficiaries to respectful customers. BRAC is identifying the poor's ability to pay as the economic conditions of those people have improved over time. However, in doing so, for a long period, BRAC helped the marginalized people to fight against poverty from multiple fronts. BRAC views poverty as multi-dimensional and BRAC has, therefore, developed support services in the areas of human rights and social empowerment, education and health, economic empowerment and enterprise development, livelihood training, environmental sustainability, and disaster preparedness.

3. BRAC has started moving from donor-dependency to a cost recovery model to gain financial sustainability as the flow of foreign aid is shirking. As an example, BRAC is running 35,000 non-formal schools across Bangladesh found that to run the schools they require 300 Taka per child. They subsidized 200 Taka and taking 100 Taka from the parents to recover some part of the cost. As per BRAC's Annual Report (2017), the organization is no longer depending on donors for health, education, and skill development programs for youth.
4. BRAC's cost recovery model is heavily supported by its strategy of establishing 'social enterprises' which generate a surplus. BRAC operates social enterprises that are strategically connected to its development programs and form crucial value chain linkages which increase the productivity of its members' assets and labor and reduce risks of their enterprises. These enterprises, ranging from agriculture to handicrafts, also help to make them increasingly self-reliant. As an example, BRAC opened an eye healthcare center and set the fees in a way that people can pay it and the fees are higher than the cost of operations.
5. BRAC implemented a special project called 'Ultra-poor Graduation Program' where women who are not only economically extreme poor but are also socially isolated would be served. To help them, BRAC runs a two-year program with the delivery of seven essential services required to break extreme poverty. In the last 10 years, BRAC helped 1.7 million households to graduate out of extreme poverty.

BRAC's Noticeable Contributions in the Service Delivery to Bangladesh

BRAC's socio-economic development activities for rural poor are administered through its development program such as; economic development this is a 'credit-plus' program with savings and credit supported by a range of poultry, livestock, fisheries, agriculture, forestry and sericulture and so on. Social development covers health, primary education, community empowerment, human rights, and legal aid services, water, sanitation, and hygiene. (Jakia 2010: 15)

BRAC's annual expenditure increased to US$1049 million in 2017 from US$728 million in 2013 (BRAC Annual Report 2017) and these investments were made in diversified areas, including: (i) disaster, environment, and climate change; (ii) health, nutrition, and population; (iii) water, sanitation, and hygiene; (iv) education; (v) migration; (vi) agriculture and food security; (vii) integrated development; (viii) skill development program; (ix) microfinance; (x) enterprises and investments; (xi) targeting the ultra-poor; (xii) community empowerment; (xiii) gender justice and diversity; (xiv) human rights and legal aid service; and (xv) urban development (Hossain 2012; Jakia 2010). Few commendable contributions of BRAC are portrayed here:

- *Human development initiatives*: BRAC with the help of a group-based microcredit program, rural development package, and ultra-poor graduation program, contributed to different aspects of poverty reduction. In 2017 alone, BRAC disbursed US$3.62 billion (14 percent more than 2016) among the poor people, and as a result, more than 75,000 households came out of extreme poverty (BRAC Annual Report 2017). By 2017, BRAC reached 5.7 million borrowers with a repayment rate of around 97 percent. The report also said that BRAC helped 1.3 million people in the gender integration process, 49,000 women to participate in the local power structure, and conducted more than 90,000 classes on human rights and legal education.
- *Healthcare initiatives*: Healthcare has always been the primary activity of BRAC. As per their report, in 2017, BRAC reached 90 percent of hard-to-reach regions in Bangladesh, diagnosed and treated 162,219 and 19,145 cases of TB and malaria, respectively, and ensured access to safe water to more than 43,000 families. In 1980, BRAC introduced a nation-wide oral rehydration therapy program, which got significant attention among donors. In the early 1990s, BRAC also started offering reproductive healthcare and nutrition services to women in Bangladesh.
- *Primary education programs*: BRAC initiated a non-formal primary education (NFPE) program in 1985, and till now they established a total of 43,793 schools and centers in Bangladesh where 3.8 million children (60 percent are girls) are enrolled. Also, around 400,000 children between the age of 3 and 5 years have got access to pre-primary programs.

- *Support and training services*: BRAC is well known for its diversified support services including agricultural services, equipment training, safe migration services, support to women after man-made disasters, house building services, and so on. According to the report (Annual Report 2017) 110 million people received services from BRAC out of which 450,000 received agricultural supports, 65,000 received migration services, and more than 110,000 women received services who are the victims of domestic violence. BRAC has set a separate training division for skill development and training of youth.
- *Humanitarian crisis management (Rohingya issue)*: BRAC helped more than 170,000 people in humanitarian responses due to climate change out of which 117,000 were women and children. The organization trained 1855 staff to deliver effective humanitarian services. In response to the Rohingya crisis, BRAC is pursuing an adaptive and phase-wise strategy with a presence in over 30 camps in Ukhiya and Teknaf. So far, 21,000 Rohingya children received basic education, 13,340 people received family planning support, and more than 15,000 and 21,500 refugees got their TB and malaria tested and treated by BRAC (Annual Report 2017). It was also reported that BRAC constructed 15,500 latrines and set 1500 tube wells in the refugee camps.

Concluding Remarks

Bangladesh can certainly take pride in the status of "Development Puzzle" for maintaining sustained economic growth as well as advancement in social indicators such as accelerated economic growth of 7.86 percent in 2018, reduced population growth (from 3.0 to 1.2 percent per year), maintaining food security through increased production of rice (from 10 to 33 million tons of milled rice), reducing crude death rate (5.1 per thousand children from 53 in 2011) and infant mortality rate (24 per thousand in 2018), improving literacy rate (from 24 percent to over 72.3 percent), increasing the attendance rate of children in primary schools (from less than 40 percent to over 95 percent), and eliminating gender disparity in secondary schools. In improving those socio-economic development factors over the last four decades, NGOs have played a pivotal role in supporting government initiatives as well as complementing the government, corporate sector, civil society, and development partners and look ahead for the challenges that need to be addressed for the long-term development. Despite dwindling land base, falling land fertility, existence of rural poverty cycle, and population growth pressure, Bangladesh has also achieved most of the MDGs. The local and global achievements of Bangladesh can be labeled as a success story of social development which other least developed countries can follow. Undoubtedly, these impressive achievements have resulted from a coordinated and cooperative approach among the government, NGOs, and private organizations.

Even though the NGO sector has contributed significantly to achieving MDGs and reducing poverty, these contributions should be investigated by taking into view the potential failures of the sector. From a theoretical perspective, NGO failures in Bangladesh can be rationalized by the theory offered by Salamon (1987), who argued that NGOs may fail due to: philanthropic insufficiency (lack of social services), philanthropic particularism (profit-oriented business venture), philanthropic paternalism (donor-centered policies), and philanthropic amateurism (lack of experience). For instance, the following are a few significant weaknesses/failures of NGOs in Bangladesh, which are in line with Salamon's (1987) theory:

1. NGOs could not reach to the people living in extreme poverty. This means the microcredit program will never be able to truly eradicate poverty until NGOs lack philanthropic sufficiency. In such respect, relatively smaller and grass-root level NGOs might be used in the process, and they may follow the cost recovery and financial sustainability principles of BRAC.
2. According to recent practice, microcredit operations mostly cover women. To broaden the coverage, microcredit should be offered to the needy poor irrespective of the gender of the person.
3. NGO-MFIs sometimes duplicate the services of government which creates confusion among the beneficiaries. For instance, BRAC used to run the Vulnerable Group Feeding program in collaboration with the government. However, later on, they implemented a similar type of program called Ultra-poor gradation program. Sometimes this confuses donors too.
4. The interest rate of microcredit is still high, and for many poor this is unbearable (philanthropic paternalism failure). More research is required to identify the appropriate level of interest rate that can help the poor to generate surplus after paying the interest burden.
5. According to many studies (Chen and Heuser 2013), the NGO sector acts like a 'parallel government' even though they are regulated

by the government. This argument came up as typically NGOs do not elect their decision-makers in a democratic way. More accountability of the operations of NGOs is deserved, especially when it is visible that NGOs are opening profit-motivated businesses in the name of social enterprise (failure due to philanthropic particularism).

6. NGOs need to address two controversies immediately: first, their involvement in politics, and secondly, their reluctance to involve their beneficiaries in the decision-making process of the organizations, even though NGOs work for their empowerment.

References

Ackerman, R. S. (1996). Altruism, non-profits and economic theory. *Journal of Economic Literature, 34*(2), 701–728.

Ahmed, M. U. (2004, July). Socio-demographic correlates of rural poverty in Bangladesh: A case study of Gaibandha Sadar and Tanore Upazillas. *Bangladesh e-Journal of Sociology, 1*(2), 50–66.

Akhter, J., Kun, C., & Chukwononso, O. (2018). The impacts of microcredit on women's empowerment—A case study. *International Journal of Business, Social and Scientific Research, 6*(4), 18–23.

Asian Development Bank (ADB). (2010). Overview of NGOs and civil society in Bangladesh. A civil society brief. NGO and Civil Society Center. Retrieved from https://www.adb.org/sites/default/files/publication/28964/csb-ban.pdf.

Bangladesh Bank. (2015). NGO and NPO sector assessment of Bangladesh. Bangladesh Financial Intelligence Unit of Bangladesh Bank. Retrieved from https://www.bb.org.bd/pub/research/sp_research_work/srw1505.pdf.

Bangladesh Bank. (2016). *NGO/NPO Sector Assessment of Bangladesh*. A report jointly prepared by NGO/NPO sector regulatory authorities.

Bangladesh Bureau of Statistics. *Report of Several Years*, 2015, 2018, 2019.

Bangladesh Bureau of Statistics (BBS). (2017). The Household Income and Expenditure Survey 2016–17. BBS, Dhaka.

Barai, M. K. (2019). The Microcredit Model in Bangladesh: Evidence of Evolutionary Changes and Socioeconomic Impacts. In Rabi Narayan Kar and Kusha Tiwari (eds), *Towards a Sustainable Future: Cross-Cultural Strategies, Practices and Advancements* (pp. 112–128). New Delhi: Bloomsbury India.

Barai, M. K., & Moral, L. H. (2002). Poverty alleviation effort in Bangladesh: Involvement of some selected banks and NGOs. *Bangladesh Journal of Political Economy, 17*(2), 303–324.

Bari, R. (2008). The basket case. Published in Forum—A Monthly Publication of the *Daily Star*, 3(3). Retrieved from https://archive.thedailystar.net/forum/2008/march/basket.htm.

Bebbington, A., & Farrington, J. (1992). *Private voluntary initiatives and governments, NGOs and agricultural development*. London: ODI.

BRAC Annual Report. (2017). Retrieved from http://www.brac.net/annual-reports-and-publications.

Brinkerhoff, J. M., Smith, S. C., & Teegen, H. (2007). *NGOs and the millennium development goals: Citizen action to reduce poverty*. New York: Palgrave Macmillan.

Chen, Y., & Heuser, B. L. (2013). *Microfinance program in BRAC—The largest NGO in the world*. A report published by International Organizations and Economic Development, New York, USA.

Chowdhury, T., & Mukhopadhaya, P. (2012). Assessment of multidimensional poverty and effectiveness of microfinance-driven government and NGO projects in the rural Bangladesh. *The Journal of Socio-Economics, 41*(5), 500–512.

DFID. (2005). Reducing poverty by tackling social exclusion. DFID Publication, September.

ERD (External Resources Division). (2015). Annual report of ERD. Ministry of Finance, GOB.

Faaland, J., & Parkinson, J. R. (1976). *Bangladesh—The test case for development*. London: C. Hurst Publication.

Fama, E., & Jensen, M. (1983). Agency problem and residual claims. *Journal of Law and Economics, 26*, 327–350.

Hansmann, H. B. (1980). The role of non-profit enterprise. *Yale Law Journal, 89*, 835–901.

Hossain, B. (2014). Poverty reduction during 1971–2013 periods: Success and its recent trends in Bangladesh. *Global Journal of Human-Social Science, 14*(5), 11–23.

Hossain, M. K. (2012). Measuring the impact of BRAC microfinance operations: A case study of a village. *International Business Research, 5*(4), 112–123.

Huda, K. S. (1987). The development of NGOs in Bangladesh. *ADAB News, 14*(3pp), 1–10.

Hulme, D., & Moore, K. (2006). Why has microfinance been a policy success in Bangladesh (and beyond)? Global Poverty Research Group. Retrieved fom https://sarpn.org/documents/d0002368/index.php.

Islam, M. S. (2016). The NGOs sector in Bangladesh: Emergence, contribution and current debate. *Advances in Asian Social Science, 7*(2), 1182–1188.

Jakia, U. (2010). *Role of NGO in socio-economic development of rural poor: BRAC as a case*. Dhaka University Institutional Repository.

Khandker, S. R., Samad, H. A., & Khalily, B. M. (2016). *Beyond ending poverty: The dynamics of microfinance in Bangladesh*. Directions in development. Washington, DC: World Bank Group. Retrieved from http://documents.

worldbank.org/curated/en/366431468508832455/Beyond-ending-poverty-the-dynamics-of-microfinance-in-Bangladesh.

Microcredit Regulatory Authority (MRA). (2011). NGO-MFIs in Bangladesh and different annual reports. Published by Microcredit Regulatory Authority (MRA), Dhaka, Bangladesh.

Microcredit Regulatory Authority. (2016). NGO-MFIs in Bangladesh and different annual reports. Published by Microcredit Regulatory Authority, Dhaka, Bangladesh.

Microcredit Regulatory Authority. (2017). *Annual Report 2017*. Dhaka.

Microcredit Regulatory Authority. (2018). NGO-MFIs in Bangladesh and different annual reports. Published by Microcredit Regulatory Authority, Dhaka, Bangladesh.

NGO Adviser. (2018). Annual report on NGO ranking. Retrieved from https://www.ngoadvisor.net/ngoadvisornews/the-2018-edition-of-the-top-500-ngos-world-is-live.

NGO Affair Bureau (NGOAB). (2015). Annual reports. Retrieved from http://www.ngoab.gov.bd/site/page/092eab90-ba5f-4cba-933f-d9f28863d170/NGO-Bureau-at-a-glance.

NGO Affair Bureau (NGOAB). (2019). Annual reports. Retrieved from http://www.ngoab.gov.bd/site/page/092eab90-ba5f-4cba-933f-d9f28863d170/NGO-Bureau-at-a-glance.

Park, C., & Mercado, R. V., Jr. (2015) *Financial inclusion, poverty, and income inequality in developing Asia*. ADB Economics Working Paper Series, No. 426. Manila.

Planning Commission of GOB. (2015). *Millennium development goals, Bangladesh progress report*. General Economics Division (GED), Planning Commission Government of the People's Republic of Bangladesh. With the assistance from Support to Sustainable and Inclusive Planning (SSIP) Project, UNDP Bangladesh.

Power and Participation Research Centre (PPRC). (2016). *Politics, governance and middle income aspirations: Realities and challenges*. Published with the support of UNDP, Dhaka.

Rashid, M., Hassan, M. K., & Ahmad, A. U. F. (2010). Quality perception of the customers towards domestic Islamic Banks in Bangladesh. *Journal of Islamic Economics, Banking and Finance, 5*(1), 109–131.

Salamon, L. M. (1987). Partners in public service: The scope and theory of government-non profit relations. In W. Powell (Ed.), *The nonprofit sector: A research handbook* (pp. 99–117). New Haven: Yale University Press.

Sen, A. K. (1984). Rights and capabilities. In A. K. Sen (Ed.), *Resources, values and development*. Cambridge, MA: Harvard University Press.

World Bank. (1995). Working with NGOs: A practical guide to operational collaboration between the World Bank and non-governmental organizations. Operations Policy Department, World Bank.

World Bank. (2016). *World Development Report 2016: Digital dividends.* Washington, DC: World Bank. Retrieved from https://openknowledge.worldbank.org/handle/10986/23347

Thomas, J. J. (1992). Whatever happened to the urban informal sector? The regressive effect of double dualism on the financial analysis of developing countries. *Bulletin of Latin America Research, 11*(3), 279–294.

United Nations Department of Economic and Social Affairs. (2018). *Leaving the LDC category: Booming Bangladesh prepares to graduate.* Retrieved from https://www.un.org/development/desa/en/news/policy/leaving-the-ldcs-category-booming-bangladesh-prepares-to-graduate.html.

UN High Commissioner for Refugees (UNHCR). (2019). *Joint Response Plan for Rohingya Humanitarian Crisis.* Retrieved from https://reliefweb.int/report/bangladesh/2019-joint-response-plan-rohingya-humanitarian-crisis-january-december-0.

Weisbrod, B. A. (1975). Toward a theory of the voluntary non-profit sector in a three-sector economy. In E. Phelps (Ed.), *Altruism, morality, and economic theory.* New York: Sage Publication.

World Bank. (1996). *Pursuing common goals: Strengthening relations between government and development NGOs in Bangladesh.* Dhaka: University Press Ltd.

World Bank. (2006, April). *Economics and governance of nongovernmental organizations in Bangladesh.* Report No. 35861-BD.

World Bank. (2018). *Financial inclusion.* Retrieved from https://www.worldbank.org/en/topic/financialinclusion/overview.

Yunus, M. (2008). *Creating a world without poverty.* New York: Public Affairs. ISBN-13:978-1-58648-493-4.

Zaman, H. (2004). Microfinance in Bangladesh: Growth, achievements, and lessons. Paper presented in *Scaling Up Poverty Reduction: A Global Learning Process and Conference*, Shanghai, May 25–27.

Zohir, S. (2010). NGO sector in Bangladesh: An overview. *Economic and Political Weekly, 39*(36), 4109–4113.

PART VI

Conclusion

CHAPTER 13

Conclusion: Bangladesh's Development—Challenges to Sustainability and the Way Forward

Munim Kumar Barai

Introduction

The economic and social progress that Bangladesh has achieved should not puzzle pundits as this has not happened organically in a void. The present transformation has become real because of the working of both positive internal and external factors. In the discussion throughout this book, we have included a number of internal beneficial factors like robust economic growth for an extended period of time, the developmental role of the central bank for pushing inclusive and sustainable finance, mass access to finance from microfinance institutions, poverty reduction through inclusive growth policy and climate-resilient development, the impressive growth in the agricultural sector, the increase in the export of ready-made garments, the labor migration led growth in foreign remittances, the broad participation of non-governmental organizations (NGOs) in economic and social activities, public and private investment in

M. K. Barai (✉)
Graduate School of Management, Ritsumeikan Asia Pacific University, Beppu, Japan
e-mail: baraimk@apu.ac.jp

M. K. Barai (ed.), *Bangladesh's Economic and Social Progress*,
https://doi.org/10.1007/978-981-15-1683-2_13

human development initiatives, and the economic and social empowerment of the underprivileged (particularly of women). In these, the evolving roles of NGOs, from the minimalist approach of offering microcredit to larger credit and social development with a host of programs that contribute to reductions in borrowers' poverty levels, skill development, healthcare, basic education, and awareness creation on various social and human rights issues, have been highlighted with due weight. The agriculture sector has responded to these with productivity growth supported by policy reforms, irrigation expansion, widespread mechanization, and technological advances in the harvesting process. At the same time, Bangladesh's development run has been very well supported by a relatively long-term stable macro-economy and a reasonable level of political stability.

But development programs and intervention measures of various governments in Bangladesh have remained necessary. They include a constant attack on poverty through various financial and non-financial interventions, giving access to finance to the people who are at the bottom of the pyramid in a benign and supportive way, creating social safety nets, providing education privilege to the poor and girls in particular, ensuring the economic and social empowerment of the underprivileged, giving conducive working space to NGOs and the private sector with various initiatives, offering a favorable industrial policy for the development of labor-intensive garments and the textile sector, and so on. In all of these areas, interestingly, Bangladesh has seen the use of the state apparatus to direct development activities and the retention of the government's power to constrain, undermine, or facilitate broader development objectives. This has been done in a loose setting, though, as the state has not become omnipotent or omnipresent in every development direction. In this context, the Chinese (state-led) development model (CDM) could be an interesting reference. As Spence (2019) puts it, "Without question, the state has been integral to China's development, not only by investing in areas like infrastructure and technology but also by serving as a backstop as nascent markets and private-sector institutions developed. State involvement is also needed to help manage inequality and ensure that growth patterns are inclusive, which markets alone cannot be counted on to do." Even advocates of the decisive role of markets and the private sector in the economy admit the state's role in Chinese development and its effectiveness. But they also emphasize the role of the private sector in innovation, productivity growth, and overall growth in the Chinese development model (Spence 2019).

Arguably, the role of the state in Bangladesh, in contrast to that in China, has been more of wavering between the neoliberal pressures to open up markets and privatizing state functions versus that of retaining its hold over the private sphere. So, the state seems to have developed two kinds of identities, 'a swing state' and 'a *dirigiste*,' at the same time. Its swing state identity is reflected by its ideologies and how they are manifested in policies, interventions, and their execution. On the other hand, it has the character to be *dirigiste* with its power and influence over the private sphere.

Here, the participation of ordinary people in the inclusive development process of Bangladesh needs to be highlighted with due importance. At the very beginning, a vast majority of poor and needy people participated in all activities, either government-initiated or privately promoted, for their survival and living. Development initiatives by the government, NGOs, or private bodies faced little organized public opposition for long, except for some projects like the Rampal Power Station and the Phulbari Coal Project that we mentioned earlier. Maybe, we can use Maslow's Hierarchy of Needs Theory (1943) to argue that they, being bottom of the ladder, had both first- and second-order needs that needed to be fulfilled before anything else. Indeed, it is natural for every individual to do something good for improving their own life, the households they live in, and the periphery they are surrounded by. This realization might have ensured their participation at the initial stage. But, at the same time, the social, cultural, and linguistic homogeneity of the people is recognized to have played a critical role in their overall participation in various activities.

All these factors in the end, as we have argued in the first chapter, have helped Bangladesh develop a 'Solidary Economic Development Model' where the government, private sector, NGOs and households participate simultaneously in activities that are bringing progress in economic and social arenas. We have also acknowledged the role of external stakeholders but argued that this has been internalized and reflected by the intentions and activities of one or more entities presented in the flow chart of Fig. 1.7.

Nevertheless, following the model, Bangladesh seems to have closed the relative development gap with some of its neighbors in some economic and social fields. Not only that, in some areas, it has excelled and bettered its position. Table 13.1 shows that during 2013–16, Bangladesh's compound annual growth rate (CAGR) has accelerated to go to the highest among the listed countries of India, Pakistan, and China along with itself. Its per capita income has also been growing at a faster rate, life expectancy at birth has

Table 13.1 Bangladesh—closing the gap

Economic				*Social*
Historical trends in GDP growth (CAGR Growth in %, current prices in USD)				Life expectancy at birth (years)
	1970–2010	2010–16	2013–16	2016
Bangladesh	7.6	11.6	12.9	72.5
India	8.7	5.4	5.6	68.6
Pakistan	6.7	8.4	8.6	66.5
China	11.1	10.8	5.2	76.3
Trends in per capita income (US$)				HD indicators (Infant mortality rate, per 1000 live births)
	2012	2014	2016	2016
Bangladesh	828	1086	1355	28.2
India	1473	1576	1706	34.6
Pakistan	1206	1342	1462	64.2
China				8.5

Source: Kant (2018, May 28). Data from UNCTAD, UN Stat and World Bank, for 2016

passed the 70-year mark, and the infant mortality rate per 1000 live births is much better than that of India and Pakistan.

This progress is also reflected by the supplementary indicators about perceptions of well-being, shown in Table 13.2 for three countries. Interestingly, most of the people in Bangladesh are satisfied with healthcare, education quality, and social security provisions, and have trust in the national government. In contrast, perceptions of the Pakistani population on their well-being look to be low in all the areas.

Moreover, the feeling of well-being of the people of Bangladesh on technology adoption appears to be quite surprising. In fact, the adoption and penetration of technology in Bangladesh can be seen in the areas that have more interface with the public; information and communication, agriculture, and transportation. Indeed, the feel-good perception of well-being has shown a clear-cut jump, and people now have faith in the future of the country.

Nonetheless, is all going well for Bangladesh on its path of development? Though not an inclusive list, the people's perceptions in Table 13.2 should also lead us to realize that there may be some troubling issues in the context of the development debate. Not only that, the sustainability of economic and social progress in Bangladesh may depend on how well and

Table 13.2 People's perception of well-being

	Quality of education	*Quality of healthcare*	*Standard of living*	*Feeling safe*	*Trust in the national government*	*Confidence in the judiciary*
Bangladesh	87	59	80	81	72	72
India	69	58	58	52	73	67
Pakistan	53	39	57	50	43	57

Bangladesh—Feelings about progress

Good progress	Areas	*Need to progress*
Life expectancy		Increase in per capita income
Child and maternal mortality		Employment generation
Adoption of new technology		Reducing income inequality

Source: *The Daily Star* (2015, December 21). Based on the 2015 Human Development Report (HDR) released by the United Nations Development Programme

diligently these are being addressed. So, what are the challenges Bangladesh must overcome to make development more sustainable and genuinely inclusive? What is the way forward for it to take the development to the next stage—the efficiency-driven stage—and then to the innovation-driven stage so that its dream of transforming into a developed nation is fulfilled? In the context of Bangladesh's development, this discussion is critical and we have devoted this concluding chapter to addressing some vital issues in this area.

Challenges to the Sustainability of Development

Indeed, there are a number of concerns that may pose a threat to the sustainability of development that Bangladesh has achieved so far. As a prelude, let us have a look at a scenario put forward by the economists of the Public Choice Approach (PCA), otherwise known as the new political economy approach (NPEA). The NPEA, in fact, finds fault with the government for doing nothing right. These theorists have advanced four points to support their claim: (1) politicians utilize public resources to strengthen and sustain themselves in power; (2) top government representatives take advantage of their positions to extract bribes (10 percent contract commission) from citizens and run protected own businesses on the side; (3) the state uses the means at its disposal to track and intimidate potential detractors (critics, opponents) and in extreme cases deprive them of their properties and jail them; (4) citizens use the political influence of friends or relatives to obtain special benefits from government policies (import licenses) (Oumar and Sama 2015: 124). Thus, as Stigler (1971) argued, "Government is always captured by special interest groups. To be sure, there are incentives for producer special interest groups to try to capture, for instance, the regulatory process" (Hoff and Stiglitz 2000: 415).

Like many developing countries, Bangladesh seems to resemble this description to a large extent at the present time. Indeed, this situation may be one of the dimensions of the various challenges Bangladesh is facing in going forward with its economic and social progress. Let us discuss some of them.

Governance, Corruption, and Fragility of the State

In the development discourse, effective governance occupies the central stage and is considered a crucial component of any development strategy (Hye 2000). The World Bank (1992: 1) defines governance as the "use of power in the management of a country's economic and social resources for development." According to the United Nations Development Programme (UNDP) (1997), governance "encompasses the state, but it transcends the state by including the private sector and civil society organizations" (UNDP 1997). As per the UNDP, there are three domains of governance—the state, the private sector, and civil society, and each must play its unique role in achieving sustainable human development (UNDP 1997). Public corruption, on the other hand, is a phenomenon broadly defined as the use of government officials' authority for private gain in designing and implementing public policies (Tanzi 1997). To be sure, corruption is also a governance issue and all the governance issues together from key obstacles to sustainable and equitable development.

Unfortunately, governance and corruption have been a continuing problem in Bangladesh for quite a long time. It routinely finds itself among the not well-governed and most corrupt countries in the world in the rankings of the major rating institutions. Column 2 of Table 13.3 includes Governance Indicators for Bangladesh for 1996–2017. Evidently, between 1996 and 2017, among the six indicators, Bangladesh only registered reasonable improvement in two of them, namely 'Voice and Accountability' and 'Political Stability and Absence of Violence/ Terrorism.' Improvement in 'Political Stability and Absence of Violence/ Terrorism' happened after a massive deterioration in 2014 because of the

Table 13.3 Governance indicators and fragility index of Bangladesh

Year	*Governance indicators, 1996–2017*						*Fragile States Index 2017*	
	V&A	*PS&AV/T*	*GE*	*RQ*	*RL*	*CC*	*BD Rank*	*Total countries*
1996	50.00	26.60	27.32	17.93	20.10	17.74	–	–
2000	44.78	24.87	30.77	18.46	22.28	10.66	–	–
2005	30.29	4.37	19.12	15.69	17.70	3.41	–	–
2010	36.97	9.95	26.32	22.01	25.59	14.76	24	177
2011	36.15	9.00	24.64	22.75	27.70	14.22	25	177
2012	34.74	9.00	24.17	18.96	18.31	21.33	29	177
2013	34.74	7.58	23.70	21.33	21.13	20.85	29	178
2014	32.02	16.67	22.60	17.79	23.56	19.23	29	178
2015	30.54	10.00	24.04	18.27	25.96	22.12	32	178
2016	30.54	10.95	25.48	22.12	28.37	18.75	36	178
2017	30.05	10.48	22.12	20.67	28.37	19.23	39	178

Sources: World Bank (2019b) and Fund for Peace (2019)

Notes: V&A = Voice and Accountability; PS&AV/T = Political Stability and Absence of Violence/Terrorism; GE = Government Effectiveness; RQ = Regulatory Quality; RL = Rule of Law; and CC = Control of Corruption. Figures indicate the percentile rank among all countries (ranges from 0 (lowest) to 100 (highest) rank).

pre- and post-election violence in that year. 'Government Effectiveness' is another area where only marginal improvement has been recorded. Unfortunately for Bangladesh, its scores on the indicators of 'Regulatory Quality,' 'Rule of Law' and 'Control of Corruption,' have rather declined from 1996. Going further with corruption, we find that Transparency International's 2017 Corruption Perception Index ranks Bangladesh 143rd out of 180 countries (TI 2017). Most of the corrupted sectors of the country are public sectors under government control. Interestingly, results for all the indicators in 2005 showed a much-improved position in governance that the immediately preceding and succeeding years for some unexplained reasons.

Similarly, we have included the Fragile States Index that shows Bangladesh ranked 32nd in 178 countries in 2015 but had gone further down to the 39th position in 2017, marking a worsening of the situation (Fund for Peace 2019).

While in all these crucial indicators Bangladesh has found itself in the lower rank of nations, its high economic growth rate vis-à-vis weak governance has remained a development puzzle. In fact, poor governance, corruption, and a fragile state apparatus have not been able to bar the path of growth and development. In previous chapters, we have seen an explanation for this. But we should not and cannot be oblivious to the fact that for long-term sustainable development, the governance and corruption level problems of the state must be tackled. The scale of the challenge that weak governance poses to gains in development can be understood from the findings of a firm-level survey of common sectors in Bangladesh, the People's Republic of China (PRC), Ethiopia, and Pakistan. This study found that if Bangladesh could have matched the investment climate of the PRC then, on average, its total factor productivity (TFP) would be 110 percent higher, its return to capital 80 percent higher and its output growth 3.7 percent more (Roy 2006: 4). A more recent study by Rahman (2018) found that reducing corruption to the level of Scandinavian countries could add 2.1–2.9 percent to Bangladesh's annual per capita GDP growth.

Infrastructure Development

Bangladesh is still a hugely infrastructure-deficit country. Andrés et al. (2013) showed that infrastructure bottlenecks are among the largest inhibitors of economic growth in Bangladesh. Back in 2013, their study estimated that the country would need to spend \$7.4–\$10 billion (7.4–10.0 percent in GDP terms) a year until 2020 to bring its power grids, roads, and water supplies up to the standard needed to serve its growing population. During this period, the transportation sector alone would require between \$36 and \$45 billion to be invested. Water supply and sanitation, solid waste management, and telecommunications were the priority areas (Andrés et al. 2013: 12–13).

The infrastructural development need has been underscored by the poor performance Bangladesh has shown in several annual Global Competitiveness Reports (GCR) by the World Economic Forum (WEF). The GCR 2013 ranked the overall infrastructure quality in Bangladesh at 134th out of 142 countries. The resulting problems, such as electricity shortages, were seen as significant across the nation. Only 47 percent of the population had access to electricity. This report also showed that the various modes of transport within Bangladesh lack integration, creating an overdependence on road transport. Though Bangladesh has improved significantly in respect of electrification, roads have emerged to be the major bottleneck. In terms of both connectivity and quality values, roads have remained very low. While Bangladesh has emerged to be the 39th biggest economy in the world (International Monetary Fund 2019), a 121 ranking on the road connectivity index gives a poor picture of this critical infrastructure, which happens to be the primary component of transportation in Bangladesh. As a reference, from 1975 to 2005, road transport's modal share rose from 54 percent to 88 percent for passenger traffic and from 35 percent to 80 percent for freight in Bangladesh (Asian Development Bank 2019). Table 13.4 shows that Bangladesh is ranked 109 among 140 countries in 2018 overall in terms of available infrastructural facilities.

Noticeably, in recent years, public investment in infrastructure development has increased, including 10 mega projects to address these issues. Improving the investment climate for private investment in infrastructure is necessary to keep up with the current growth trend. As we know, growth is one of the results of infrastructural investment while the sustainability of growth and development is dependent on the state of the infrastructure of a country.

Human Capital Development and Job Creation

Creating quality human capital and generating jobs for them have continued to be two areas of concern for Bangladesh. In the organizational context, human resource development means a process by which employees

Table 13.4 Infrastructure standing of Bangladesh, 2018

	Index component	*Value*	*Score*	*Rank/140*
	Infrastructure 0–100 (best)	–	53.4	109
1	Road connectivity index 0–100 (best)	34.3	34.3	121
2	Quality of roads 1–7 (best)	3.1	35.2	111
3	Railroad density km of roads/square km	19.2	48.0	40
4	Efficiency of train services 1–7 (best)	3.2	36.3	68
5	Airport connectivity score	48,504.1	51.4	63
6	Efficiency of air transport services 1–7 (best)	3.7	45.5	109
7	Liner Shipping Connectivity Index 0–157.1 (best)	10.8	10.8	81
8	Efficiency of seaport services 1–7 (best)	3.5	40.9	93
9	Electrification rate % pop	75.0	75.0	108
10	Electric power transmission and distribution losses % output	11.0	92.7	71
11	Exposure to unsafe drinking water % pop	41.0	60.2	126
12	Reliability of water supply 1–7 (best)	3.9	48.0	106

Source: WEF (2018)

Table 13.5 Health and skills standing of Bangladesh, 2018

	Index component	*Value*	*Score*	*Rank/140*
Pillar	Health 0–100 (best)		71.2	96
1	Healthy life expectancy years	62.8	71.2	95
Pillar	Skills 0–100 (best)		44.0	116
1	Mean years of schooling years	5.2	34.7	119
2	Extent of staff training 1–7 (best)	3.3	38.2	126
3	Quality of vocational training 1–7 (best)	3.4	39.5	122
4	Skillset of graduates 1–7 (best)	3.4	40.1	121
5	Digital skills among population 1–7 (best)	3.3	38.9	120
6	Ease of finding skilled employees 1–7 (best)	3.7	44.4	105
7	School life expectancy years	11.7	65.0	105
8	Critical thinking in teaching 1–7 (best)	2.9	31.9	107
9	Pupil-to-teacher ratio in primary education ratio	33.9	40.2	114

Source: WEF (2018)

of an organization are continuously facilitated to acquire the capabilities (skills, knowledge, perspective, attitude, and values) necessary to perform various tasks or functions associated with their present or future expected roles (Lakshmi 2005).

Though Bangladesh has consistently improved its score in the UNDP's human development index and its HDI score of 0.608 in 2017 (UNDP 2018) puts it in the middle-ranking countries; from the quality perspective soul searching may be needed. As we know, health and skills are considered to be the pillars of human resource development. Table 13.5 gives the value, score, and rankings of various components of the health and skills of the Bangladeshi population according to the 2018 Global Competitiveness Report of the WEF. Though Bangladesh has risen to a relatively better position in terms of healthy life expectancy, its population has to cover a lot of ground in various skill sets. When it comes to the questions of critical thinking in teaching, quality of vocational training, the skillset of graduates, and digital skills among the population, the respective area ranks for Bangladesh have remained below 100 among the 140 listed counties.

Though Bangladesh should have initiated programs to address this issue through the allocation of resources for education and health, in practice that seems to have not been the case. Table 13.6 gives the budgetary allocation for education and health for the five years since 2014–15. It looks like that the education budget has stagnated at around 2.1 percent

Table 13.6 Budgetary allocation for education and health, 2014–15 to 2018–19

Fiscal year	*Education*		*Health*	
	Share of budget	*Share of GDP*	*Share of budget*	*Share of GDP*
2014–15	11.7	1.85	4.35	0.69
2015–16	14.3	2.18	4.76	0.73
2016–17	16.1	2.19	2.46	0.34
2017–18	12.6	2.09	5.39	0.89
2018–19	11.4	2.09	5.03	0.92

Source: Compiled and calculated. Data from Ministry of Finance (MoF) (2019)

of GDP. In fact, the allocation for education as a proportion of the total budget has dropped to 11.4 percent from 12.6 percent in FY2017–18. Bangladesh's budget allocation for education in terms of percentage of GDP has it investing the second-lowest share among countries, according to a survey conducted by ESCAP (2019). In contrast, Bhutan, Maldives, and Nepal, all spend nearly 5 percent of their GDP on education.

Similarly, the share of health allocation in budgets has remained less than 1 percent of GDP. In fact, the share of GDP given to health in Bangladesh fell from 1.1 percent in 2010 to 0.9 percent in 2017 and is now the lowest among the 21 countries of south, southwest and southeast Asia (Economic and Social Commission for Asia and the Pacific 2019). However, Bangladesh signed the Dakar declaration in Senegal in April 2000, committing to spend at least 6 percent of its GDP or 20 percent of the national budget on education. UNESCO's Education 2030 Framework for Action recommends spending at least 4–6 percent of GDP on education (Chaity 2018). This is very much needed for the creation of quality education and training standards and infrastructure to support them.

We came across two areas where the results of the quality of higher education in Bangladesh and its level of vocational training are probably reflected. Be it public or private, technical or general, not a single university from Bangladesh could reach a rank lower than 1000 on any of the lists prepared by various organizations. Likewise, the composition of Bangladeshi migrant workers shows that they massively form the unskilled and semi-skilled groups in their overseas employment, whereas migrants from India, Vietnam, and the Philippines are much better skilled and hold higher-level overseas jobs.

Again, the importance of the creation of quality human capital is felt when it comes to the question of job creation in the country. Currently, 58.7 percent of the total population of Bangladesh is active (MoF 2019). Not only that, 2 million youths are entering the job market every year (World Bank 2018). This has placed job creation as the country's top development priority. As we saw in Chap. 1, the sectorial job structure has developed a sort of anomaly as well. This is to say that the agriculture sector, the smallest among all the sectors in terms of its GDP contribution (13.1 percent in 2018), has the highest level of share of employment in the economy (40.2 percent in 2018). This may have two facets—either most of the employment seeking workforce are not skilled or educated enough to move to the secondary and tertiary sectors of the economy for job seeking, or the upper-level sectors are not getting enough skilled labor for their expansion and growth.

Moreover, the education industry has experienced a slowdown in job creation between 2010 and 2015 (World Bank 2018). Raihan (2018) argued that "The current level and quality of human capital in the country discourages enhanced private investment in high valued and diversified sectors. The country, therefore, needs to emphasize the improvement of the existing low level of human capital by enhancing investment in education, skill development, and health facilities."

Rising Inequality

The impressive progress Bangladesh achieved in poverty reduction, in fact, meant that it was beyond the Millennium Development Goals' (MDG) target of halving poverty well ahead of time. Bangladesh's success in poverty reduction is similar (though not as dynamic) to what some of the East Asian countries were able to achieve during the days of their economic miracles. But a by-product of this success, again similar to the East Asian experience, is that income inequality has been rising in Bangladesh. This rise may pose a serious question about the inclusivity of development it supposedly wants to achieve.

Figure 13.1 shows three trends in the Gini coefficient measuring income inequality for Bangladesh for a period of 43 years. Analysis of the table further indicates that between 1973 and 2016, all the Gini values for all three categories went up by 0.09, 0.05, and 0.12 for rural, urban, and national levels, respectively. In other words, we get an annual average growth rate in inequality of 0.62 percent for rural areas, 0.50 percent for urban areas, and 0.76 percent at the national level.

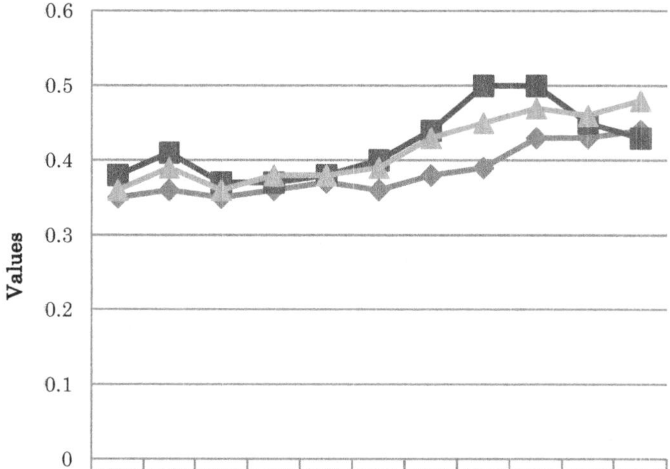

	1973	1981	1983	1985	1988	1991	1995	2000	2005	2010	2016
Rural	0.35	0.36	0.35	0.36	0.37	0.36	0.38	0.39	0.43	0.43	0.44
Urban	0.38	0.41	0.37	0.37	0.38	0.4	0.44	0.5	0.5	0.45	0.43
National	0.36	0.39	0.36	0.38	0.38	0.39	0.43	0.45	0.47	0.46	0.48

Fig. 13.1 Index of income inequality for Bangladesh, 1973–2016. (Source: Constructed. Data from Chowdhury and Hossain, https://arxiv.org/ftp/arxiv/papers/1812/1812.09385.pdf)

The analysis in Chap. 2, for instance, shows that the Gini coefficient rose from 0.458 in 2010 to 0.483 in 2016. Though this seems like a marginal increase, alternate measures indicate that the rise in inequality is far more pronounced. In 2010, the bottom 5 percent of the rural population received 0.88 percent of national income, but this went down to a mere 0.25 percent in 2016 according to the latest round of Household Income and Expenditure Survey (HIES) (BSS 2016). At the other end of the income scale, the top 5 percent of rural households' share of income rose from 22.93 percent in 2010 to 24.25 percent in 2016. Further analysis of the latest HIES shows similar changes in the share of income that are leading to higher inequality. The bottom 40 percent of the population earned only 14.32 percent of total income in 2010.

This situation reflects the overall impact of economic growth and structural change on poverty and the distribution of income within the country. Bangladesh's success lies in the consistency of its track record on poverty and social development. However, evidence suggests that inequality has fluctuated far more. In Bangladesh, the first decade of the 2000s registered a decline in income inequality as measured through the Gini index. Since 2010, however, income inequality is on the rise again.

The policy planners should also be mindful of the fact that corruption can affect income inequality and even poverty "through various channels, including overall growth, biased tax systems, and poor targeting of social programs as well as through its impact on asset ownership, human capital formation, education inequalities, and uncertainty in factor accumulation" (Gupta et al. 1998: 6). Indeed, Bangladesh experienced its highest rate in the increment of wealthy people for the last two decades. This, in a sense, is posing a threat to the inclusive nature of its economic growth. If the benefits of growth become skewed or are channeled mainly to particular segments of the society in a country like Bangladesh, the development of such economic stratification is neither healthy nor desirable. Moreover, this may also sow the seeds of social unrest, an area where Bangladesh has had plenty of previous experience.

The Rise of Religious Extremism

Bangladesh is experiencing the rise of several religious militant groups that are opposed to many of the values, ideas, beliefs, and faiths that constitute the fabric of its social foundation. Those groups are also against the concept of female empowerment, secularism, and multi-religious cohabitation. Obviously, any increase in their presence may pose a serious threat to the development process and prospects of Bangladesh. Pakistan is the best case example in this regard; for it, many hopes for development turned out to be false due to the rise of religious extremism and intolerance.

The question that bothers many is how come Bangladesh has reached a level that these forces can gain a foothold in the country. In this section, we trace a number of developments that might have created the space for their birth and growth. After the assassination of the Father of the Nation in 1975, all military governments or military-backed parties which were in power until the end of 1990 courted far-right parties and religious ideologues in the power structure of the state. Also, a subsequent development that has not been discussed much in the literature is the influence of returnee migrants mainly from the Kingdom of Saudi Arabia (KSA) and other Middle East countries. Social scientists in Bangladesh have missed exploring the correlation between the rise in influence of a brand of Islam called Wahhabi Islam[1] associated with returnee migrants in Bangladesh.

The link of migration and remittances combined with this religious phenomenon is direct and has had a far-reaching social impact with cross border implications. An elaboration may be of help.

The Arabian Gulf countries were flush with petrodollars in the 1970s, and they have been employing a large number of workers from Bangladesh since that time. The KSA has remained the top destination for Bangladeshi laborers for a quite long time and now houses the highest number of Bangladeshi workers outside the country. However, the exodus and subsequent return of these laborers from the gulf countries created a group in Bangladesh that fall into the same class as 'Eid,' a character from the area of Nashawy in Egypt in the famous literary work 'In an Antique Land' by Amitav Ghosh. The writer says, "Eid had been away in Saudi Arabia for some three or four years, and had done very well for himself, working in the construction industry. He had come back with a color television set, a fridge, a washing machine and many other things of that kind. On top of that, he had also saved a lot of money and was soon going to buy his family a tractor: 'Eid is soon to be married. He is going to pay a large sum of money as a marriage-payment'" (Ghosh 2009: 185).

In reality, the first-time expatriates from Bangladesh in that region, particularly in the KSA, were mostly unskilled and illiterate and they came back not only with their fortunes like 'Eid' but were also carrying the influence of the Saudi brand of Wahhabi Islam. During their stay in the KSA, this form of Islam seems to have influenced their religious faith and cultural behavior. Over the years, an amalgamation of political and religious powers based on these people has created a course for Bangladesh opposite to the one for which it fought the independence war in 1971.[2] A favorable international environment due to developments in some Middle East countries and Afghanistan helped their rise as well. The problem is that their growth has ultimately influenced the shrinkage of the public sphere for democratic rights and societal tolerance to religious and cultural diversity in Bangladesh. A thorough study should be devoted to examining the depth and true nature of the socio-political changes due to increasing Islamization of the society and the role of remittances, inter alia, in this regard.

Nonetheless, in development theory, Rostow and others suggested that the attitudes of the members of the society or citizens of the state toward life are an important determinant of that society's and state's development (Gow and Mallick 2005; Rostow 1959, 1960). Drawing the rise of religious fanaticism in Pakistan as an analogy, Basu (2018) warns that

Bangladesh faces a risk to its development. According to him: "there is an even deeper threat posed by orthodox groups and religious fundamentalists who oppose Bangladesh's early investments in progressive social reforms. A reversal of those investments would cause a severe and prolonged economic setback. This is not merely a passing concern: vibrant economies have been derailed by zealotry many times throughout history" (Basu 2018).

The Way Forward

We have just identified some of the critical challenges to the sustainability of economic and social development in Bangladesh, and many more could be added to that. The government of Bangladesh needs to face and address them appropriately to sustain the progress it has achieved so far. However, for the future orientation of the economy toward a developed nation, Bangladesh needs to chalk out a broader strategy to handle some other important issues that are expected to have a profound impact on the future development path and destiny of the nation. These issues are vital for its graduation from the first stage to the second stage and then to the final stage of development, a fully developed country. We will now try to identify some of the issues Bangladesh should adhere to so that it can progress on the path to reach this destination by 2041.

Creating Human Capital for the Future to Encash the Demographic Dividend

For a population-rich developing country, human capital is expected to become the most powerful resource in this century. This assumption is gaining ground as all the northern hemispheric countries are turning gray and increasingly becoming human deficit zones. The replacement of human workforces with artificially intelligent (AI) devices and robots looks to be a possibility, but it will take time for those elements to become an effective replacement of educated and skilled human assets.

For Bangladesh, its large population has so far remained a burden on the limited national resources and is putting pressure on all infrastructural facilities. Ironically, the population is the best possible asset Bangladesh has for the future. For that, Bangladesh must turn its people into human assets and then encash this demographic dividend fully. The initial change in the age structure of the population may, therefore, have offered Bangladesh a space to reap the benefits.

The concept of demographic dividend is related to "the potential economic benefit offered by changes in the age structure of the population, during the demographic transition, when there is an increase in working-age population and an associated decline in the dependent age population" (Khan 2012). Demographically, Bangladesh is passing through a transition and seems to have been experiencing a demographic dividend whereby the working-age population is increasing while the dependency ratio is declining. All the indicators for Bangladesh support the view that the first demographic dividend started in 1980 and will continue for 60 years up to 2040 (Khan 2012). As a result, there is a possibility of a second dividend in the form of gains in per capita income, rises in productivity, and an increase in the standard of living for generations. However, to materialize the economic benefits of this demographic dividend, Bangladesh must have an adequate investment in education, public health, and physical capital to support building this human capital. Flexibility in labor market policies, incentives for investment and savings, lowering the cost of employment-related overseas migration, and so on, will enhance the volume of this dividend (Khan 2012).

Has Bangladesh already started to derive a dividend in the forms of a growing class of entrepreneurs, an educated workforce, or migrant workers? If so, then to the extent the economic and social impact is due, this dividend needs investigation and estimation. First, external migration is undoubtedly an area where Bangladesh may have been reaping the benefits of the demographic dividend. The benefits here are of two types—employment generation of the surplus labor force and the net wealth added to Bangladesh from their remittances, for which the figure has become substantial (Fig. 13.2).

On the contrary, if appropriate policies are not formulated, the demographic dividend might, in fact, be a cost, leading to unemployment and an unbearable strain on education resources, healthcare systems, and old age security. So, a note of caution should be sounded here as the potential 'demographic dividend' may turn into a national nightmare. Strategic initiatives to improve and transform the current low level of human capital into a futuristic workforce are needed. For that, enhancing investment to an adequate level for education, skill development, health, and infrastructural facilities cannot be avoided.

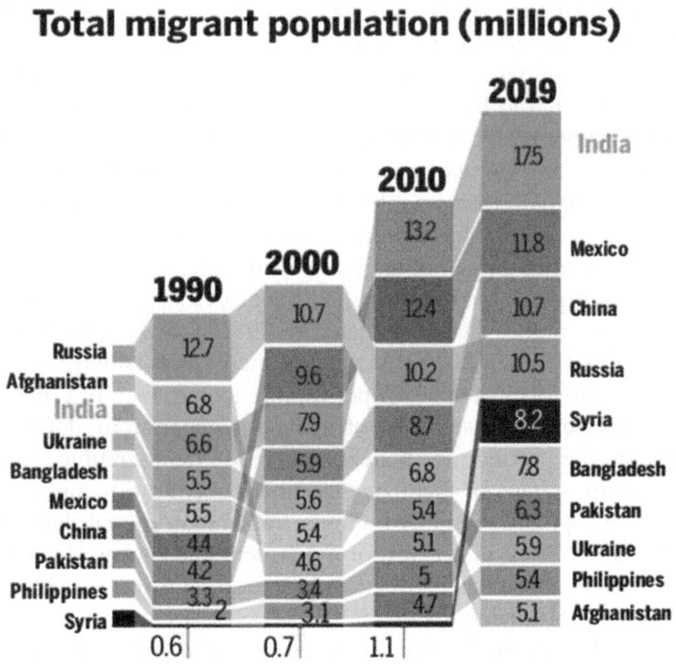

Fig. 13.2 Top migrant originating countries, 2019. (Source: *The Times of India* 2019, September 23. Data adopted from UN Department of Economic and Social Affairs)

Playing Wise with Its Geostrategic Location

Bangladesh is strategically located between a 'flying dragon' China and a running elephant, India. China is now the second-largest economy in the world. They are also rivals. The Indian footsteps are also getting louder in the regional and international areas. So, the physical location of Bangladesh itself is a challenge, as well as an opportunity. At the same time, Bangladesh is also the South Asian gateway to South East Asia. So, playing the location card to its advantage becomes an important challenge too. Thus, Bangladesh should follow such steps that can make it more integrated into the regional economic infrastructure and reap the future benefits of trade and economic expansion out of those arrangements:

- *Regional Connectivity*: Though as a regional organization, the South Asian Association for Regional Cooperation (SAARC) was never a cohesive body, several South Asian regional connectivity initiatives under SAARC have been implemented in the region. Indeed, the 16th Summit in Thimphu, Bhutan, in 2010, member countries[3] declared 2010–20 as the 'Decade of Intra-regional Connectivity' in SAARC. The importance of developing transport infrastructure and transit facilities, especially for landlocked countries, as a means to promote intra-SAARC trade was the force behind this. In cooperation with India, Nepal, and Bhutan, Bangladesh is also implementing several projects under the financial support of ADB and the World Bank;
- *AIIB and the Chinese BRI*: The Asian Infrastructure Investment Bank (AIIB) and the Belt and Road Initiative (BRI) are the two Chinese strategic moves with potentials to change the economic landscape of Asia, Europe, and Africa. Though BRI has become a contentious issue between China and India, the AIIB has been grown to be approved by 100 countries so far. Bangladesh, being a partner in both the initiatives, needs to position itself in a manner to reap the future economic benefits of these moves.
- *Indian Backyard Markets*: Though trade flows from Bangladesh have been mainly moving toward mainland India, the 'seven-sister states'[4] of the Indian North East look to be the natural backyard markets for Bangladeshi products. Reaching a population of over 46 million, which mainland Indian manufacturers have huge logistic problems to reach, could play a positive role in the future economic expansion of Bangladesh.

The World Bank under the 'One South Asia' program, supported by five other trust funds, has been promoting regional connectivity and integration through improving transportation and border infrastructure (World Bank 2019a). This should be utilized to build trade and investment relations with other regional members and benefit economically in the future. A study by Kathuria (2018) estimates that intraregional trade could increase almost threefold, from the present $23 billion to $67 billion, among the South Asian countries. Along with India, Bangladesh is well placed to benefit from this increase.

Technology Adoption and Reducing the Gap in Digital Divide

In Table 13.2, we saw that Bangladeshis are happy with the level of technology adoption in their society. But that should not create any complacency as technology is going to a crucial part of every aspect of life everywhere in the future. Being a developing country, Bangladesh has financial constraints as the major disadvantage on its way to the technologization of the country. But at the same time, Bangladesh has young people who can quickly adopt and adapt newer technology devices. The rapid spread of mobile banking in Bangladesh could be an eye-opener in this regard. Thus, the areas where Bangladesh should be focusing more on a future 'tech-savvy' nation should be to reach people with more education and internet facilities, create further clusters of techno-parks, encourage tech startups, and put more investment into Research and Development. Falling behind in this area may perpetuate Bangladesh's status as a supplier of the unskilled labor force in the international market. Not only that, the relative abundance of the population may then never be turned from a burden into a powerful asset to reap the benefits of the 'demographic dividend.'

Advance 'Growth and Development Facilitators' in the Next Stages of Development

We would like to develop our argument for the future development of Bangladesh here based on the Global Competitive Report 2013–14 of the World Economic Forum on global competitiveness identification for nations. Following this report, we have slightly modified and identified two categories of factors, viz., growth contributors and growth modifiers which influence the economic development of three types of economies—factor-driven (primary), efficiency-driven (secondary), and innovative driven (Fig. 13.3).

Looking at all the elements, we can still align Bangladesh with a factor-driven economy, though in some sectors, like garments and pharmaceuticals, it may have just reached the gate of the efficiency-driven stage. So there is no debate that Bangladesh should now draw a development strategy to move to the second stage of development with more focus on manufacturing sector building. The modifiers of growth at this stage would be higher education and training, product-market efficiency, labor market efficiency, and financial market development. We have vigorously

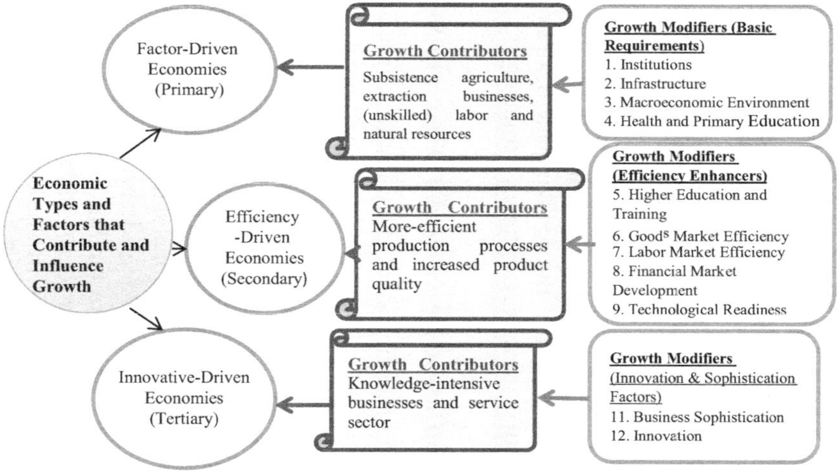

Fig. 13.3 Growth contributors and growth modifiers. (Source: Modified. Adopted from WEF's GCR 2013–14)

argued for human capital development. Hopefully, a simultaneous development may be followed by efficiency and quality improvement of products and production processes to affect economic development ultimately.

Though for Bangladesh, like all other countries aspiring to develop, the ultimate goal of development is to become an innovation-driven economy, it should now try to orient this more to the manufacturing sector to push for its development. Chapter 10 of this book argued that the 'light-engineering sector' growth could open the immense potential for employment and exports for the nation. Looking at the availability of manpower, the potential for the scaling up of ability from the agriculture sector to the manufacturing sector, and their education and skill-wise readiness for employment, a combination of labor-intensive and capital-intensive industries may be the best focus of the development path of Bangladesh.

Developing efficiency and bringing innovation in the production factors and value chain to become more relevant and competitive should be the target goal of development. But for Bangladesh, this may take some time while the manufacturing base becomes stronger.

Build Institutions for a Free and Democratic Society

For an inclusive and sustainable democracy, institutions building and their preservation become imperative for the government and the state. Bangladesh still lacks the full range of institutions, and these have to be created and developed as the nation marches forward. In fact, much of governance deficiency and corruption proliferation in Bangladesh might have been checked had there been a strong institutional base in existence. The *Global Competitiveness Report 2018* ranked Bangladesh at 108th place out of 140 countries for its institutional status (WEF 2018: 91). So, 'institutional deficit' is a state that Bangladesh has to overcome along with other obstacles for the immediate and future development of the country.

In the *Global Competitiveness Report 2018*, Bangladesh seems to have done reasonably well with some institutions like budget transparency, e-participation, conflict of interest regulation, the burden of government regulation, and the future orientation of government performance. But a headache remains with many of them, like the reliability of the police service, freedom of the press, the incidence of corruption, the quality of land administration, the strength of auditing and reporting standards, the efficiency of the legal framework in settling disputes, and low levels of social capital. An independent Election Commission and institutions for establishing democratic rights for opposition parties, minorities, and so on are also not the strength of Bangladesh.

We must keep in mind that the maturity of the market or economy is not the same as the maturity of a nation. The latter is also tested by the exercise and institutional protection of the rights of the residents of a country. Not only that, once a society starts developing and maturing, the urge for better civic life with more freedom may get stronger. Without a proper institutional support base, this development is bound to suffer.

Conclusion

Mankind has always been involved in a search for progress since the very beginning of clustering together to form tribes and communities. There have been ups and downs in this pursuit throughout history, but it has remained a constant process. The emergence of the nation-state has added many components to development, but economic progress has continued to be the essential constituent since time immemorial. However, development cannot be treated as a purely economic phenomenon, it is more than that: "In an ultimate sense, it must encompass more than the material and financial side of people's lives, to expand human freedoms. Development should, therefore, be perceived as a multidimensional process involving the reorganization and reorientation of entire economic and social systems. In addition to improvements in incomes and output, it typically involves radical changes in institutional, social, and administrative structures as well as in popular attitudes and even customs and beliefs" (Todaro and Smith 2015: 118).

However, development has become harder to achieve by developing countries today as there are more obstacles than ever before on the path of their economic growth. For Bangladesh to enter the middle-income bracket, it needs to follow appropriate economic, financial, and social structural policies that would boost potential growth and the living standard of all. Though it has made significant progress in many economic and social areas, in an inclusive growth and development paradigm, Bangladesh needs to increase its potential economic growth further. The World Bank (2018) stresses the need to accelerate physical and human capital growth, remove barriers to female labor participation, and improve institutions to raise potential growth and reduce inequality. In the shorter term, a possibility is there that the already achieved economic and social development might put Bangladesh in a position to push it into a virtuous cycle of further human and social progress which would lead to higher growth. But this circling of beneficial effects is likely to suffer the inertia that occurs when various institutional, physical, human, and social barriers emerge as binding constraints.

Moreover, Bangladesh must position itself on a future growth path where economic expansion possibilities would lie across its borders. So, Bangladesh should also look beyond those borders to get connected with the countries in South and Southeast Asia as well as coping with the issues of internal origin like creating human capital, developing institutions, and changing the production process and structure. A delicate balancing act in its economic and political relationship with India and China could be vital.

To this end, this book has covered the salient factors and features of the development process and model relating to Bangladesh. It has also identified the various challenges Bangladesh is facing to sustain the development pace and suggested some future initiatives to reach its desired destination as a developed country. From this book, policy planners in developing countries will be able to answer the query of whether Bangladesh per se offers a realistic and feasible development model for them to follow instead of the ones already available locally or internationally.

Notes

1. Muhammad ibn Abd al-Wahhab (d. 1792) was an Islamic theologist who propagated the Wahhabi brand of Islam. Wahhab made the central point of his reform movement the principle that absolutely every idea added to Islam after the third century of the Muslim era (about 950 CE) was false and should be eliminated. Muslims, in order to be true Muslims, must adhere solely and strictly to the original beliefs set forth by Muhammad.
2. Bangladesh fought for independence based on four basic ideologies: democracy, socialism, secularism, and nationalism. These were enshrined in the preamble to the constitution 1972. But in the years after 1975, the principles of socialism, secularism, and nationalism were diluted to give a place for an Islamic identity of the state.
3. They are Bangladesh, Bhutan, India, the Maldives, Nepal, Pakistan, and Sri Lanka. Afghanistan has been added as the 8th member nation to SAARC.
4. These Indian states are—Meghalaya, Assam, Arunachal, Mizoram, Manipur, Nagaland, and Tripura.

References

Andrés, L., Biller, D., & Dappe, M. H. (2013, December). Reducing poverty by closing South Asia's infrastructure gap. Washington, DC: The World Bank. Retrieved September 21, 2019, from https://www.worldbank.org/content/dam/Worldbank/document/SAR/Reducing%20Poverty%20by%20Closing%20South%20Asia's%20Infrastructure%20Gap_Web.pdf.

Asian Development Bank (ADB). (2019). Sector assessment (summary): Subregional road transport. Retrieved August 5, 2019, from https://www.adb.org/sites/default/files/linked-documents/40540-014-ban-ssa.pdf.

Bangladesh Bureau of Statistics (BBS). (2016). *Households Income and Expenditure Survey 2016*. Dhaka: Bangladesh Ministry of Planning.

Basu, K. (2018). Why is Bangladesh booming? *Project Syndicate*. Retrieved from https://www.project-syndicate.org/commentary/bangladesh-sources-of-economic-growth-by-kaushik-basu-2018-04.

Chaity, A. J. (2018, June 29). Budget allocations for health, education continue to shrink. *The Dhaka Tribune*. Dhaka.

Economic and Social Commission for Asia and the Pacific (ESCAP). (2019, May). *Economic and Social Survey of Asia and the Pacific 2018*. United Nations.

Fund for Peace. (2019). Fragile State Index. Retrieved from https://fragilestatesindex.org/.

Ghosh, A. (2009). *In an antique land*. New Delhi: Penguin Books.

Gow, J., & Mallick, O. B. (2005). Development theory, Rostow's five stage model of development and its relevance in globalization. Retrieved from https://www.academia.edu/7226928/Development_theory_Rostows_five-stage_model_of_development_and_ist_relevance_in_Globalization.

Gupta, S., Davoodi, H., & Alonso-Terme, R. (1998, May). *Does corruption affect income inequality and poverty?* IMF Working Paper 98/17. Washington, DC: International Monetary Fund.

Hoff, K., & Stiglitz, J. E. (2000). Modern economic theory and development. In G. M. Meier & J. E. Stiglitz (Eds.), *Frontiers of development economics: The future in perspective* (pp. 389–485). Washington, DC: World Bank/Oxford University Press. Retrieved from https://sites.hks.harvard.edu/cid/archive/events/cidneudc/papers/eudcstiglitz.pdf

Hye, H. A. (Ed.). (2000). *Governance: South Asian perspectives*. Dhaka: The University Press Limited.

International Monetary Fund (IMF). (2019, April). World Economic Outlook database. Washington, DC: IMF.

Kant, K. (2018, May 28). At current rates, Bangladesh could top India's per capita income by 2020. *Business Standard*. Retrieved September 1, 2019, from https://www.business-standard.com/article/economy-policy/bangladesh-pips-india-in-economic-growth-and-social-development-indicators-118052700710_1.html.

Kathuria, S. (2018). *A glass half full: The promise of regional trade in South Asia* (South Asia Development Forum). Washington, DC: World Bank.

Khan, A. M. (2012). *The demographic dividend in Bangladesh: An illustrative study*. Paper presented at the 18th Biennial Conference of the Bangladesh Economic Association held on 12–14 July, 2012 in Dhaka, Bangladesh.

Lakshmi, C. S. (2005). *Human recourses development in public enterprises*. New Delhi: Discovery Publishing House.

Maslow, A. H. (1943). A theory of human motivation. *Psychological Review, 50*(4), 370–396.

Ministry of Finance (MoF). 2019. Bangladesh Economic Survey 2019. Government of Bangladesh.

Oumar, S. B., & Sama, C. M. (2015). International dependency and the economic development of less advanced countries. *International Business Research, 8*(6), 117–134.

Rahman, M. A. (2018). Governance matters: Climate change, corruption, and livelihoods in Bangladesh. *Climatic Change, 147*(1–2), 313–326.

Raihan, S. (2018, November 8). Why isn't private investment growing faster? *The Daily Star*. Dhaka.

Rostow, W. W. (1959). The stages of economic growth. *The Economic History Review, 12*(1), 1–16. Retrieved from http://sites.jmu.edu/soci348/files/2012/05/Rostow.pdf

Rostow, W. W. (1960). *The stages of economic growth*. Cambridge: Cambridge University Press.

Roy, D. K. (2006). Governance, competitiveness and growth: The challenges for Bangladesh ADB Institute Discussion Paper No. 53. Tokyo.

Spence, M. (2019, January 21). What next for China's development model? *Project Syndicate*. Retrieved September 12, 2019, from https://www.project-syndicate.org/commentary/china-development-model-tensions-with-west-by-michael-spence-2019-01.

Stigler, G. (1971). The economic theory of regulation. *Bell Journal of Economics, 2*(Spring), 3–21.

Tanzi, V. (1997). *Corruption in the public finance*. Paper presented at the 8th International Anti-Corruption Conference, Lima, Peru, September 7–11. Unpublished; International Monetary Fund, Washington, DC.

The Daily Star. (2015, December 21). Human development index: Steady progress shows hope. Retrieved from http://103.16.74.140/frontpage/steady-progress-shows-hope-190366.

Times of India. (2019, September 24). These Indians are the reasons Trump couldn't ignore 'Howdy Modi. Retrieved from https://timesofindia.indiatimes.com/india/these-indians-are-the-reason-trump-couldnt-ignore-howdy-modi/articleshow/71214670.cms.

Todaro, M. P., & Smith, S. C. (2015). *Economic development* (12th ed.). New York: Pearson.

Transparency International (TI). (2017). Corruption Perceptions Index 2017. Retrieved September 12, 2019, from www.transparency.org.

United Nations Development Programme (UNDP). (1997). Governance for sustainable human development: A UNDP policy document. New York: UNDP.

United Nations Development Programme. (2018). *Human Development Report 2018*. Geneva.

World Bank. (1992). Governance and development. Washington, DC: World Bank.

World Bank. (2018). Bangladesh development update. Retrieved September 20, 2019, from https://www.worldbank.org/en/news/feature/2018/04/09/bangladesh-development-update-building-on-resilience.

World Bank. (2019a). One South Asia. Retrieved from https://www.worldbank.org/en/programs/south-asia-regional-integration.

World Bank. (2019b). Worldwide governance indicator. Retrieved from https://databank.worldbank.org/source/worldwide-governance-indicators.

World Economic Forum (WEF). (2013). *The Global Competitiveness Report 2013–14*. Geneva: GEF.

World Economic Forum. (2018). *The Global Competitiveness Report 2018*. Geneva: GEF.

Index[1]

[1] Note: Page numbers followed by 'n' refer to notes.

M. K. Barai (ed.), *Bangladesh's Economic and Social Progress*,
https://doi.org/10.1007/978-981-15-1683-2

T

U

V

W

The manufacturer's authorised representative in the EU is Springer Nature Customer Service Centre GmbH, Europaplatz 3, 69115 Heidelberg, Germany. If you have any concerns regarding our products, please contact ProductSafety@springernature.com

Printed and bound by CPI Group (UK) Ltd, Croydon, CR0 4YY

30/09/2026

02225461-0020